Ethnic Renewal in
Philadelphia's Chinatown

In the series *Urban Life, Landscape, and Policy*, edited by Zane L. Miller, David Stradling, and Larry Bennett

Also in this series:

Ethnic Renewal in Philadelphia's Chinatown

SPACE, PLACE, AND STRUGGLE

KATHRYN E. WILSON

TEMPLE UNIVERSITY PRESS
Philadelphia • *Rome* • *Tokyo*

TEMPLE UNIVERSITY PRESS
Philadelphia, Pennsylvania 19122
www.temple.edu/tempress

Library of Congress Cataloging-in-Publication Data

Wilson, Kathryn E. (Kathryn Elizabeth), 1963–
  Ethnic renewal in Philadelphia's Chinatown : space, place, and struggle / Kathryn E.
Wilson.
     pages cm. — (Urban life, landscape, and policy)
  Includes bibliographical references and index.
  ISBN 978-1-4399-1214-0 (cloth : alk. paper) — ISBN 978-1-4399-1215-7 (pbk. : alk.
paper) — ISBN 978-1-4399-1216-4 (e-book) 1. Chinatown (Philadelphia, Pa.)—History.
2. Chinatown (Philadelphia, Pa.)—Social conditions. 3. Chinatown (Philadelphia,
Pa.)—Ethnic relations. 4. Chinese Americans—Pennsylvania—Philadelphia—History.
5. Chinese Americans—Pennsylvania—Philadelphia—Social conditions. 6. Philadelphia (Pa.)—History. 7. Philadelphia (Pa.)—Social conditions. 8. Philadelphia (Pa.)—
Ethnic relations. I. Title.
  F158.68.C47.W55 2015
  974.8'11—dc23

                                                                    2014042917

∞ The paper used in this publication meets the requirements of the American
National Standard for Information Sciences—Permanence of Paper for Printed Library
Materials, ANSI Z39.48-1992

Printed in the United States of America

9 8 7 6 5 4 3 2 1

To my family
and the families of Chinatown,
past, present, and future

Contents

List of Figures and Tables

Figures

Tables

M y first experience with Philadelphia's Chinatown was a common one. During graduate school in the late 1980s and early 1990s, my fellow folklore students and I, always in search of interesting yet inexpensive food, often dined in Chinatown. We favored one Vietnamese place in particular for its vegetable crepes and strong sweet coffee. But as often as we went to Chinatown, I do not remember paying much attention to the neighborhood.

Chinatown really emerged as a neighborhood for me when I went to work for the Balch Institute for Ethnic Studies in 1997. The Balch Institute was a Philadelphia library, archive, and museum devoted to the immigrant and ethnic experience in North America. The Balch was active from 1972 to 2000, when it merged into the Historical Society of Pennsylvania (HSP). One of the first projects I was involved with at the Balch was *Building the Gold Mountain*, an exhibit and program series that told the story of Philadelphia's Chinatown through images, artifacts, and oral histories. Shortly before the exhibit was finished and scheduled to open, the institute invited the community advisory committee to review the results. The committee included, among others, Cecilia Moy Yep, George Moy, Mitzie Mackenzie, and Inspector Anthony Wong. At the time, I was unaware that these people were legends in Chinatown, but soon they made quite an impression on me.

We laid out the exhibit materials on the conference table, walking through each section describing the storyline. At the end of the presentation, Cecilia Moy Yep said something to the effect of, "Well, this is fine, but we need more pictures of Chinatown as it is today." She explained that although people tended to see Chinatown as a mere collection of restaurants, it was a "living community" that needed to be depicted as such in the exhibit. Her comment revealed that for ethnic and immigrant communities like Chinatown, a public history representation must be a usable past, one that not only portrays historic struggles but also links them to present concerns. This usable past is not some simplistic presentism. Rather, it is a living legacy for a community addressing issues that are both historic and ongoing. In response to this request, I took on the task of using the time that remained to create a final section of the exhibit to represent that living community as best we could. I got my camera and spent a day walking around Chinatown, taking pictures. With Cecilia Moy Yep's words echoing in my head, I focused on capturing images of sites that represented a range of community businesses and spaces, such as a Vietnamese beauty salon, a driving school, doctors' offices, and a wonderful mural illustrating the community's history. And as I contacted community organizations, such as Asian Americans United (AAU), to request images and artifacts, I learned about a variety of community issues.

In the process of developing a program series to accompany the exhibit, I met such residents as Dun Mark and Joseph Eng, old-timers who led a senior tai-chi group in the neighborhood. I observed Philadelphia Chinatown Development Corporation (PCDC) activists sharing their memories and telling their stories. I screened the video *Save Chinatown*, which portrayed young people perched atop bulldozed rubble and a diminutive but strident young Mary Yee galvanizing a protesting crowd. Later, a stint as an oral-history consultant for the Asian Arts Initiative's (AAI's) "Chinatown Lives" project further deepened my sense of the neighborhood's diversity. I attended AAI's programs on Chinatown and participated in a rally against the proposed baseball stadium in 2000. My connection to the community over the years was never more than casual, but I never forgot the inspiring story of the Chinatown activists and their mandate to look, in their words, "beyond the restaurants."

From 1997 to 2007, I worked with a number of ethnic and immigrant communities in Philadelphia—South Asian, Arab, African, and Latino—to produce public programs, exhibits, educational materials, and publications. Powerful narratives emerged from these projects—stories about what it was like to be a young Indian doctor in the late 1960s, to be resettled as an Ethiopian refugee in the early 1980s, to live as an Arab American after the Oklahoma City bombing in the 1990s, and to live under the radar as an undocumented worker from Honduras in the early 2000s. As we negotiated these projects with our community partners, several issues surfaced again and again, including the challenges immigrant communities faced that culture could address (such as self-representation, image, advocacy, and education) and those it could not (such as poverty, disenfranchisement, and crime). Always there was the imperative to create a usable past that spoke to the needs of the present, address acute anxieties about representation vis-à-vis stereotypes and other forms of misrepresentation, and account for the inherent diversity of even the most seemingly homogeneous community. These projects taught me to listen and look for contradiction, tension, and diversity; to negotiate the meanings of history, culture, and identity through dialogue; and to understand that when communities of color enter into public space and culture, the expression of their identities and experiences is fraught with underlying dilemmas.

When I returned to academe to pursue my own research, Chinatown almost immediately came to mind. I remembered how I had been schooled by community leaders in 1997, and I wanted to know more about this special neighborhood, its history of activism, and its urban landscape creation. I wondered how Chinatown developers had addressed some of the dilemmas of ethnic self-representation that I had encountered in other communities, particularly the Latino *barrio*. I knew my research could not be an insider's look at Chinatown—I am not the person for that project, especially because I have no knowledge of Chinese. That is not the focus of this book, nor does this book do full justice to the vitally important role that first-generation immigrants play in creating and sustaining Chinatown.

Rather, I have sought to understand, from various perspectives and my own, how the shape and identity of Chinatown emerged historically, how community members understood their landscape, and how and why they worked to defend, renew, and expand it. Early on, I discovered in the PCDC archives evidence of how the neighborhood had been self-consciously constructed in the late twentieth century and how PCDC had worked systematically with the city of Philadelphia to fulfill that goal. I uncovered differences within the community with respect to generation and political ideology that revealed the sophistication of the community's coalition building in the past few decades. I observed the crucial nature of the work of American-born Chinese, who were often dismissed as *juk sing*, in the survival of the neighborhood and its traditions.[1] And I came to understand that the dilemmas of ethnic urban renewal that I found so interesting had a long history.

My approach to this book has been deeply influenced by theories of ethnicity that see it as a fundamentally interactive and highly strategic phenomenon, the result of both attribution from without and self-representation from within. In this way, I appreciate that ethnic places are made, not just inhabited; that they are intimately connected to larger relationships with other communities; and that, more often than not, people must fight for them. In the same way, they must be renewed—often through new immigration, which perpetually reconfigures the landscape, the local microeconomy, and the community infrastructure. In Philadelphia's Chinatown, as elsewhere, newcomers infuse the neighborhood with a new sense of cultural authenticity, while long-time residents and their leaders work to preserve a sense of place by living the legacies of past struggle. I have tried to look and listen, and I hope that my representation of these efforts does them some degree of justice and encourages others to engage with and explore the many facets of this resilient and unique community.

Acknowledgments

I must first thank all the folks in Chinatown who helped me research this book, in particular the individuals who graciously granted me interviews: Father Tom Betz, Lai Har Cheung, John Chin, the Reverend Peter Chow, Kenneth Eng, Stanley (Stosh) Eng, Helen Gym, Glenn Hing, Esther Ho, Gayle Isa, Ed Kung, Brendan Lee, Harry Leong, the Reverend Leslie Leung, Xu Lin, Joseph Lowe, Rachel Mak, Dun Mark, George Moy, Ellen Somekawa, the Reverend Laurence Tom, Andy Toy, Debbie Wei, Carol Wong, Jacqueline Wong, Juliet Wong, Melody Wong, Mary Yee, and Cecilia Moy Yep. Others outside Chinatown who offered important perspectives were Joe Eastman, Barry Seymour, Sarah McEneaney, and Patricia Washington. I am also grateful for the assistance of Joe Lowe and Jackie Wong in connecting me with the basketball guys of Holy Redeemer.

I offer deepest gratitude to the people and organizations that shared their files and archives with me: in particular, Ellen Somekawa at Asian Americans United (AAU); Harry Leong and the Board at Chinese Christian Church and Center; and John Chin at Philadelphia Chinatown Development Corporation (PCDC), who trusted me and gave me full and unrestricted access to the PCDC archives. Rachel Mak graciously made room for me in the small bustling office space of PCDC. Jackie Wong provided Cantonese translation for several interviews in 2009. I also thank Fon Wang and her Penn Preservation Studio students for sharing their research on 907–909 Race Street and the Chinese Cultural and Community Center.

I am thankful for the able staff at the Historical Society of Pennsylvania (HSP), Temple University Urban Archives, Philadelphia City Archives, and National Archives and Records Administration Mid Atlantic Branch, where I did my archival research. HSP's commitment to Chinatown, I am happy to say, has continued beyond my tenure there. I am grateful for the opportunity to be involved in ongoing programs and publications. I thank Tammy Gaskell for keeping me involved and for helping me secure illustrations.

The Department of History at Georgia State University (GSU) provided crucial summer funding in 2009, 2010, and 2012, which enabled the bulk of the research and fieldwork for this book and additional support for production-related costs. The following colleagues and students listened, read, and offered constructive feedback throughout the process: Robert Baker, Alex Cummings, Denise Davidson, Marni Davis, Ian Fletcher, Katherine Hankins, Daniel Horowitz, Brian Ingrassia, Clifford Kuhn, Matthew Lasner, Sara Patenaude, Michele Reid, Jake Selwood, and Jeffrey Trask. I am grateful to the Association of GSU Historians (AGSUH) for inviting me to speak about my Chinatown research as part of a 2013 "Bodies in Space" roundtable, which helped refine my thinking. Graduate research assistants Amy Rocamora, James Herman, and Sarah Edwards provided assistance with interview transcription. Amber Boll patiently worked with me to create wonderful maps.

I am deeply indebted to Zane Miller for reading and meticulously editing multiple drafts and for (mostly) gently nudging me away from academic jargon. His interest in this project came at a critical time in its development; his gracious generosity of time and spirit was formative. I am also grateful for the thoughts and support of Larry Bennett. I thank past and present Temple University Press editors Mick Gusinde-Duffy, who offered early encouragement, and Aaron Javsicas, who handled the review process and shepherded the project to completion. I also thank the anonymous reviewers for Temple University Press, who provided thoughtful and honest feedback that strengthened the work. Domenic Vitiello helped me see lacunae in my approach. Bob St. George introduced me to the work of Christopher Yip. Mary Yee, Ellen Somekawa, Debbie Wei, Cecilia Moy Yep, and John Chin all read portions (or, in Mary's case, all) of the manuscript and provided important revisions and insights from a community perspective.

Philadelphia's public-history community gave birth to this project and helped it reach maturity. Eric Pumroy, who hired me for my first real job at the Balch Institute, brought me into the *Building the Gold Mountain* project and the story of Chinatown's struggle. I relied, in part, on interviews conducted by Jianshe Wang, a former intern at the Balch Institute, and interviews conducted by the Asian Arts Initiative (AAI) under the direction of Lena Sze. Howard Gillette, Mickey Herr, and Randall Miller all saw to it that I did not want for news about Chinatown after I moved to Georgia. Maria Möller showed me around her East Passyunk neighborhood and shared information on current arts and heritage funding. Joan Decker provided generous help with City Archives' rights and reproduction. Asian Americans United (AAU) and PCDC generously provided illustrations.

Laura Sauer Palmer and her family—Dave, Vivian, Henry, and the late Buddy Palmer—welcomed me into their fold and fed and housed me during my stays in Philadelphia. This book could not have been completed without their love, support, and generosity.

To my sweet Alain, whose arrival made this book more difficult to complete but gave writing about families and community so much more meaning, and to Lionel Laratte, who endured my mental preoccupation and long summer absences with humor and patience and also "took the baby" on innumerable occasions, I offer my deepest love and gratitude.

Ethnic Renewal in
Philadelphia's Chinatown

Introduction
Imagining Chinatown

It is a little before 9:00 A.M. on a summer morning in July 2009, and Chinatown is just waking up. As I walk up Ninth Street toward Vine, I see men unloading a large whole pig from a nondescript white delivery truck through the front door of a small storefront. Looking ahead, I see a busy highway and, farther off, a massive rusting industrial structure. Ninth Street does not continue over Vine Street, so I move over to Tenth Street via Spring, a quiet side street populated by antebellum row houses and a blond brick church with a red tile roof, the Chinese Christian Church and Center (CCC&C). Over on Tenth Street, storeowners are setting up umbrellas and crates of fruits and vegetables on the sidewalk. Elderly men and women walk slowly down the street, carrying bags of groceries, their backs bowed from a lifetime of labor. Many stop every five minutes or so to greet and talk animatedly with others they know. Unceasing traffic clatters down Tenth Street, dodging potholes and construction cones. I see one little boy, about six years old, supporting the arm of his elderly grandfather. Most of the shops and restaurants are closed, the neon lights dimmed until lunchtime. In one vacant storefront hangs a poster depicting five Chinese boys in baseball uniforms, standing in front of a bulldozer. "Looking Back," its text asserts. In the window of the On Lok Social Service Center, a yellow photocopied flyer declares, "Bad for our City, Bad for Chinatown. No Casino."

Philadelphia's Chinatown is a neighborhood where elderly men gather in cafés every morning and afternoon to drink tea and share news and stories; where teenagers play basketball on the church playground after school or congregate in bakeries to drink bubble tea and huddle over each other's cellphone screens; where senior residents can walk down any street and point to the second-story rooms where they were born; and where second- and third-generation Chinese Americans who live in the suburbs commute in on weekends to maintain their grandparents' shops, attend church, visit the family association, or take their children to kung-fu class. This is the Chinatown of families, children, elders, churches, and kinship associations, and it is a Chinatown that almost ceased to exist. That it still does exist is the story of this book.

Philadelphia's Chinatown has a lot in common with other Chinatowns around the United States. It is a marginalized community born historically of intense segregation that was viewed for more than a century by outsiders through alternate lenses of exotic spectacle and impure danger. It is a transnational community that has incorporated successive waves of increasingly diverse new immigrants. Philadelphia's Chinatown is much smaller than the well-known Chinatowns of New York, San Francisco, and Los Angeles; it is even smaller than Chicago's or Boston's. But at a time when many smaller Chinatowns disappeared or became attenuated into touristy shopping districts, Philadelphia's Chinatown survived and remained a community where families live, raise children, go to church, care for the elderly, play basketball, and, of course, do business.

In 1945, this community was on the brink of major change. Five years earlier, a new Chinese Catholic mission church—Holy Redeemer Chinese Catholic Church and School—had been dedicated at the corner of Tenth and Vine Streets. It was not the first mission to be located in this neighborhood, but it was the first Catholic Church for Chinese in the Western Hemisphere, and the first school in Chinatown. As World War II ended and immigration restrictions were lifted, servicemen and others brought wives from China, and more families settled in Philadelphia's Chinatown. This church and the CCC&C, founded in 1941 on the other side of Vine Street, at Tenth and Race Streets, became central sites of activity and identity for a new generation of Chinese Americans whose youth was shaped by Chinatown and who in turn would grow to shape the neighborhood's future.

That same year, 1945, Philadelphia's city planners studied surveys of traffic patterns and made elaborate models of a newly imagined urban landscape. Discussing theories and plans for the postwar city, they measured travel times across the city, calculated traffic-light timings, and dreamed of a rational metropolis encircled and crosscut by several major expressways that would enable efficient movement in, through, and out of the city. They conjured high rises, shopping malls, and historic districts that would draw visitors to downtown. Two years later, the planners offered their ideas to the public in the Better Philadelphia Exhibition, displayed at Gimbel's department store just a few blocks from Chinatown. Offering a vision of the city in twenty-five years, the exhibit displayed a model of Center City that flipped over to show the city in 1982. Included were many projects that eventually became part of the Planning Commission's 1960 master plan for the city: an expressway loop around the city, a national park surrounding Independence Hall, a retail project joined to an underground train station (Market East), and the development of the Far Northeast.[1] The first three of these four projects would directly affect Chinatown in the coming decades. One of the proposed expressways, along Vine Street, would entail the destruction or relocation of the recently erected Catholic Church in Chinatown—Holy Redeemer—a fact that escaped notice for several decades, or if it was noticed, was not deemed important. After all, the church was located right next to Skid Row, and no one really lived there—except the Chinese.

Chinatown's inconvenient location in Philadelphia's Center City was typical. Most Chinatowns in North America were located near the old downtowns of cities, often near the docks (as so many Chinese were early on involved in shipping) or on the outskirts of central commercial districts. In Philadelphia, this area was northwest of the warehouse district abutting Market and Chestnut Streets, an area dominated by working people's boardinghouses and some small-scale manufacturing, the backstage of Philadelphia's bustling commercial downtown. The earliest Chinese presence in the United States was the result of trade networks with China, supported by the demand for "fancy" Oriental and Chinese goods throughout the eighteenth and nineteenth centuries.

Eastern Chinatowns had their genesis in the displacement of Chinese Americans from the American West. The first Chinatowns in North America appeared in the nineteenth century in major cities along the west coast: San Francisco, Sacramento, Stockton, and Seattle. San Francisco and Seattle boasted the largest Chinese populations, in part because they were major points of entry for Chinese immigrants. Most nineteenth-century Chinese immigrants came from the province of Guangdong, particularly Canton (Guangzhou) in South China. Canton was a cosmopolitan port city heavily involved in trade with North America, including Philadelphia. Later, the discovery of gold in California led Chinese to try their luck in the minefields of "Gold Mountain" or take up business to provide support services in mining camps, such as domestic service, food service, and laundry—services traditionally provided by women, who were in short supply. By the 1860s, railroad work beckoned, and the Union Pacific Railroad actively recruited Chinese labor. Most were sojourners who never intended to permanently settle in the United States but rather make their fortune on "Gold Mountain" and then return to China.[2]

After the completion of the Transcontinental Railroad in 1869, Chinese immigrants in western states experienced a violent backlash, known as the "Great Driving Out." Throughout the 1870s, violence and intimidation against Chinese laborers were commonplace in California, Washington, Oregon, Colorado, and other western states. A labor-based movement emerged from the sandlots of San Francisco, led by rabble-rouser Dennis Kearney and rallied around the anti-Chinese cry, "The Chinese Must Go!"[3] This persecution sent many Chinese laborers deeper into established western Chinatowns and east to such cities as New York, Chicago, Saint Louis, Boston, and Philadelphia, where they formed new Chinatowns.[4] As sojourners, most Chinese had left their families in China, seeking their fortune as single men, although many were married in China. Settling in Chinatowns, they found employment and cultural refuge, often living in extended-kin arrangements and socially supported by many traditional associations.

The passage of the Chinese Exclusion Act in 1882 further isolated the Chinese and their Chinatown communities. With travel to and from China effectively ended except for merchants and others of substantial property, most Chinese men in America could not marry or rarely, if ever, see their wives and families in China. Chinatowns remained largely "bachelor" enclaves, and a hierarchy between merchants and laboring men solidified.[5] The prevalence of men living as single in Chinatowns—although the product of American law—also contributed to the public perception of the Chinese as essentially and unrelentingly foreign. Unlike other immigrants of the period from Europe and the Middle East, the Chinese could never "become white," and unlike African Americans, who were also segregated and viewed as racially inferior, they could never become American, since naturalization was denied them until 1943.[6] Large-scale immigration from China and Asia would not be possible until after the passage of new immigration legislation in 1965. While second- and third-generation Chinese Americans took advantage of new opportunities in mainstream American society, Chinatown remained an important entry point and stepping-stone for new immigrants from China, Hong Kong, and Southeast Asia.

Space

From its beginnings, Philadelphia's Chinatown was both segregated space and immigrant sanctuary. Like other Chinatowns, it was formed from both necessity and desire, as Chinese men sought the safety of segregated space and the cultural and social comfort of their own people. At a time when a great wave of European immigrants found work in burgeoning manufacturing and other industries—when Philadelphia boasted of being "the Workshop of the World"—Chinese immigrants and migrants were restricted to domestic service, laundry work, and small commercial ventures, such as import/export gift shops, groceries, and later restaurants.[7] Likewise, they were largely restricted from living anywhere but their own shops (many laundrymen ate and slept in the backrooms of their laundries) or the boardinghouses of what became known as Chinatown.[8]

This kind of ethnic segregation was not uncommon in postbellum Philadelphia, which underwent dramatic economic and demographic change during this period, engendering an increasingly segmented and segregated urban landscape. During the last decades of the nineteenth century, white middle-class families flocked to new streetcar suburbs, escaping the disorder of the city center. New immigrant neighborhoods emerged in areas just outside Center City. In South Philadelphia, long home to concentrations of African Americans and Irish immigrants, Italians and Eastern European Jews established enclaves along South Ninth and Fourth Streets, respectively. Eastern Europeans and other immigrants who clustered around opportunities for factory work in a variety of industries settled neighborhoods to the immediate northeast, such as Kensington, Bridesburg, and Fishtown. But in the case of the Chinese, boundaries were even less fluid; violence and harassment kept them in their segregated place.[9]

Situated within a larger urban landscape of power, Chinatowns are often as much about the attitudes and behaviors of non-Chinese as they are about Chinese cultural or social needs. The very idea of Chinatown is a predominantly white idea, a projection of the Western imaginary that produces larger relationships between place, race, and power, in which space embodies a larger racial ideology.[10] Chinatown is Chinatown not only because Chinese, whether by desire or under duress, live there; Chinatown is also Chinatown because of discriminatory racial attitudes toward the Chinese and the need to distance Chinese Americans as exotic and essentially non-American. This distancing shaped not only the need for Chinatowns as separate spaces but also outsiders' perceptions of the ways Chinese Americans created and inhabited those spaces. Seeing the space of Chinatown as exotic, sinful, and mysterious was an articulation of Orientalism. In Orientalist discourse, the "East" exists for and in relation to the West as an inferior mirror image that is separate, backward, sensual, passive, deviant, often coded feminine, and invariably mute. It is constituted in part by the production of knowledge about the East, what are really the "ideological suppositions, images, and fantasies" about a "region of the world called the Orient," an "imaginative geography." Categories of social, cultural, and scientific knowledge, implemented through the state, gave this imaginative geography a cognitive and material reality through the production of space. To this extent, Chinatowns were and are a racial category embodied by landscape.[11] Chinatowns were also perceived in the early twentieth century as mysterious and dangerous spaces where non-Chinese could consume inexpensive cuisine or exotic cultural displays while thrilling to the presumed presence of white slavery, tong violence, gambling, and drug use. In this way, Chinatowns have something in common with Harlem of the same period, as a space for the consumption of transgressive jazz culture and the display of black bodies. So too did non-Chinese consumers enter Chinatowns with the expectation of license and exotic spectacle.[12] Embodied in its name, Chinatown was constructed as a separate entity within the city, where one would travel to experience the customs of a distant land.

Chinatowns are sometimes referred to as "gilded ghettos," ethnic neighborhoods that sport the colorful flavor of a Little Italy yet are tightly bounded by the larger spatial control of an African American ghetto.[13] While all immigrant and ethnic neighborhoods manifest this dynamic of vibrancy and constraint to some extent, it is much more insidious for communities of color, which historically have been both contained and consumed by the larger society that marginalizes them. Like other ethnic neighborhoods, Chinatowns function as immigrant enclaves, offering culturally specific businesses and institutions that serve the immediate community, particularly new immigrants, and constitute local microeconomies. And while Chinatowns historically were economically relatively self-sufficient, many of their residents have been poor, and the neighborhoods neglected by city services.[14] These neighborhoods, vibrant but marginalized, were often vulnerable and consistently threatened by displacement or encroachment by other urban priorities.

Beyond the racial constructions, Chinatowns have served different functions over time and been characterized by scholars of Asian immigration in a variety of ways. Chinatowns have been conceptualized as bachelor societies marked by a hierarchy between merchants and workers, as urban villages, gilded ghettos, ethnic enclaves, and even festival marketplaces.[15] Originally places of safety and cultural specificity, Chinatowns were segregated enclaves that commercially connected to a wider society but remained socially and culturally apart. After World War II, with changing immigration and urban redevelopment (as well as suburbanization), Chinatowns became less central to Asian immigrant life but remained important cultural and community centers. During this period, many Chinatowns were also threatened by twentieth-century urban-renewal plans; some disappeared, were relocated, or became attenuated.

More recently, changing trends in Asian immigration have complicated spatial expressions of Chinatowns, and the functions and identities of Chinatowns have changed again. While historically most Chinatown residents originated from Guangzhou in South China, subsequent second and third waves of immigration have arrived from Hong Kong, Taiwan, Southeast Asia, and more recently Fujian province in China. Increasingly Mandarin, not Cantonese, is the language of Chinatowns. In addition, Chinatowns have become increasingly pan-Asian, due in part to the resettlement of Southeast Asian refugees from Vietnam and Cambodia in the 1980s (many of them ethnic Chinese), groups that formed their own enclaves as well as diversified Chinatowns' geographies, primarily through commercial ventures. In addition to Vietnamese, Philadelphia's Chinatown also includes Malaysian, Indonesian, Burmese, Japanese, and Korean businesses.[16] Most new Chinese and Asian immigrants live or work outside Chinatown; since 1965, a significant percentage of these immigrants have been professionals who settle directly in the suburbs, where housing and jobs are more accessible. Philadelphia's Chinatown also has important ties to New York City.

Increasingly, most Chinatowns are linked across a larger geographic region to "satellite Chinatowns," or suburban concentrations of immigrant settlement.

In New York, Flushing, Queens, and Sunset Park, Brooklyn, have emerged as secondary Chinatowns, as has Monterey Park in California.[17] Today the touristic function of Chinatowns is heightened, and their roles as symbolic centers are increasingly significant. Chinatown is one node in a larger cultural diaspora, located within larger transnational economic resources and social networks, an organizing point for immigrant labor, a delivery site for cultural heritage, an asset for the globalized city.[18] More common are Chinese or Asian clusters in suburban areas "ethnoburbs" that coexist with traditional inner-city enclaves. Such spaces exist as part of larger "ethno-spectrums" linking historic Chinatowns to a larger network of Asian settlement and commerce. In Philadelphia, potential ethnoburbs have emerged in Northeast Philadelphia and Montgomery County, where Asian immigrants have created small, enclave-type spaces in shopping centers and established local houses of worship and other spaces, while other community institutions, such as family and regional associations, have remained in Chinatown. None of these outlying areas in the Philadelphia area currently rival Chinatown, and many residents of these areas still maintain strong connections to Chinatown. Likewise, Philadelphia's Chinatown retains the residential aspect of the residential/commercial mixed use that characterizes Chinatowns historically, remaining a living community despite its increased role as a symbolic cultural center.[19] As sites within larger "ethno-spectrums," historic Chinatowns are specific kinds of space and place. Some Chinatowns, such as London's and or those in other European cities, have recently been developed or augmented to serve as global emblems and may or may not contain historic structures or be located in original areas of Chinese settlement. The older Chinatowns of North America are based in spatial templates and senses of place deeply conditioned by history. They are a specific kind of ethnoscape within the larger spatial spectrum of the Asian diaspora and remain salient as historic points of origin and symbols of Asian American struggle and survivance.[20]

Place

Many historic Chinatowns today are hybrid spaces that balance multiple functions and remain relevant spaces for local and regional Chinese and Asian populations. In Philadelphia, Chinatown still functions as an immigrant entry point where new arrivals can secure a foothold through language access and employment opportunities, even if they live elsewhere in the city or region (and some new immigrants still live in Chinatown). Chinatown also functions within a larger regional geography as an important site of historical and cultural point of origin. Many family and other traditional associations are located in Chinatown, as are ethnic-specific cultural resources, such as traditional-medicine practitioners, martial-arts schools, language classes, senior centers, and banquet facilities. Festivals and other cultural events are held in Chinatown, which is a

spatial repository of memory, both individual and collective. Across the generations, Chinatown is a historical point of origin, a place of cultural expression,
and a "cultural home space" where many claim actual or fictive roots. This home
space is characterized by a specific sense of place; a site of ethnic self-expression
in living arrangements, social space, cultural events, and spiritual life; a distinct
cultural, economic, and social environment, where "a sense of ethnic attachment to place based on historical, actual and/or perceived experience" drives
claims to urban space and racial justice.[21]

The creation of this place, like Chinese American identity and ethnicity, was not a monolithic process, but rather the result of a dynamic inter-
play between attribution from without and self-representation from within,
an entity interactively co-constituted by Chinese and non-Chinese Philadelphians. Its boundaries were both physical/spatial as well as cultural/social,
dual and overlapping, creating and defending an ethnic urban territory.[22] Such
territory could be called an "ethnoscape," a term describing neighborhood
landscapes that emerge in globalized cities as a dimension of global cultural
flows.[23] Ethnoscapes represent the ways in which diasporic communities free
themselves from localizations, from place-bounded restraints in commercial
and cultural activities. Yet ethnoscapes remain localized in the city of resettlement and are still highly significant as "focal points of economy, culture, and
heritage."[24] As such they are sites of spectacle, objectified by visitors in search of
the exotic or the "authentic," as well sites of identity and meaning for resident
ethnic groups.[25]

Chinatown's sense of place, embodied in part by the ethnoscape, was historically conditioned by prior spatial use and earlier constructions of Chinese
culture and identity, often within a discourse of Orientalism. Chinese in early-
twentieth-century Philadelphia inscribed a sense of identity on the existing
urban landscape, with specialized shops, services, and sites (such as houses
of worship and family association halls); foreign-language signage; ancient
decorative elements; and other material markers of culture.[26] Its residents
also altered that landscape architecturally, imbuing the built environment
with Asian architectural features, particularly along façades, upper stories,
and rooflines of turn-of-the century buildings. Many of these architectural
features represented or marked the unique ways in which Chinese immigrants
used space, devoting the upper stories of commercial buildings to residential
and community purposes, a mixed-use strategy that characterizes Chinatown
to this day. Most of these new architectural features also referenced, at least
nominally, the stylistic template established by San Francisco's Chinatown,
particularly after the 1906 earthquake, when Chinatown merchants commissioned a renewed landscape and aesthetic for Chinatown that Orientalized
the urban environment through color schemes, eaved pagoda-style lines, tiled
roofs, lanterns, and other imagined markers of Chinese identity. These Oriental features celebrated traditional Chinese art and culture on the one hand but

also replicated the terms of a larger cultural discourse of Chinese racial and cultural divergence, embodied by and in space.[27]

This transformation of the landscape also embodied a sense of place in the sense of the contemporary or historic rights of persons to own a piece of land or occupy a social world, the creation of a territory through culturally and socially meaningful interventions in the urban landscape.[28] This sense of place as territory took on new meaning in Chinatown in the second half of the twentieth century, as new waves of immigration transformed a blighted area of the city into a community made meaningful by the presence of churches and family businesses alongside traditional Chinese institutions, and subsequent immigration dispersed into suburban clusters and satellite Chinatowns. Despite the challenges of life in this neighborhood, families made lives and memories in Chinatown. For the Chinese American youth who grew up there during the 1940s–1970s, the neighborhood was and is a powerful site of attachment and place of memory.[29]

Writ large, these attachments constitute a memoryscape, in which collective or individual associations shape and are shaped by the landscape and constitute place as the embodiment of memory. Such memoryscapes function to locate the self in a sense of identity tied to where one comes from, of a history somewhere, promoting a sense of belonging and thus a key component of community building and of history.[30] They are also spaces in which one can be recognized, as Debbie Wei's son reflects; he likes to buy candy in Chinatown at a particular shop, because the shopkeeper there "knows my Chinese name."[31] As a product of history, memoryscapes also provide powerful counternarratives of the past or resources for resistance and contestation over the use and meaning of space.[32] Ethnic or minority memoryscapes may become zones of conflict or construct and maintain "counterspaces" of cultural autonomy or empowerment. They are also often vulnerable to erasure or truncation, particularly in ever-changing urban environments.[33] They may constitute "place-based collective-action frames," catalyzing activism based on an idea of a neighborhood and the material experiences of that place.[34] All these senses of place—attachment, memoryscape, territory, action frame— catalyzed the movement to "Save Chinatown" in the 1960s and 1970s, when urban-renewal projects threatened Philadelphia's Chinatown's survival.

Ethnoscapes and their creators have played an important role in revitalizing urban spaces as well as resisting displacement by larger urban-renewal entities. Yet immigrant and ethnic communities are largely missing from existing historical narratives of urban renewal in the United States, which tend to focus on larger structural changes within cities and their effects across a black/white racial binary. Thus while we know a good deal about ethnoscapes and the ways in which immigrants transform urban spaces in their neighborhoods, this transformation is rarely situated within larger changes in or discourses about the urban landscape.[35] The revitalizing efforts of immigrant and ethnic populations in blighted neighborhoods are likewise largely unexplored. Ethnic and immigrant communities were also vulnerable as communities of color, often displaced or left as vestiges of themselves after suburbanization. Asians in particular are left out of this history, even though most Chinatowns and other Asian enclaves across the country felt the negative impacts of urban renewal, and many resisted through activism and protest. Their histories of activism and community rebuilding provide an important counternarrative to larger stories of urban progress or decline.[36]

Struggle

Activism in the "Save Chinatown" movement in Philadelphia emerged specifically from the struggle against urban redevelopment, which led to mass demolitions on the eastern, southern, and northern boundaries of Chinatown at a time when the area was in the midst of a growth period. This struggle against urban redevelopment played out in other cities as well, born of larger efforts to contend with a postwar "urban crisis" characterized by a decline in industry and manufacturing, disinvestment, white flight, and failed urban-renewal and public-housing initiatives. In other areas of the country, minority neighborhoods were razed and their resident populations warehoused in public housing, fueling gentrification and further urban problems.[37] In Philadelphia, neighborhoods in North Philadelphia that had been manufacturing centers declined as factories closed. Decaying housing stock, abandoned factory buildings, and vacant warehouses came to characterize this neighborhood landscape. As former immigrant residents relocated to suburban areas and the Greater Northeast, the inner ring of neighborhoods around Center City became almost entirely black and Latino. Local industries collapsed, making these residents "displaced labor migrants" who occupied areas now stigmatized as blighted.[38] Some of these areas, referred to as "gray areas" by the city, were the focus of initial renewal efforts by the Philadelphia City Planning Commission and Philadelphia Redevelopment Authority in the 1950s, before the redevelopment of downtown took center stage. Many others were and remain neglected. This struggle was similar to those of other neighborhoods that resisted urban-renewal projects during this period, fighting back against slum clearance, expressways, housing, gentrification, and displacement due to the development of downtown attractions.[39] Most resistance in Philadelphia, however, was conducted by middle-class whites, sometimes in alliance with African Americans. In this respect, both Chinatown's central location and its ethnic composition were unique, as was its history and economic life.[40]

Lacking any industrial base in a local microeconomy that was largely based in service and retail (with the exception of small-scale garment manufacturing in the 1980s–1990s and current wholesale provision to the restaurant industry), Chinatown escaped the direct experience of deindustrialization and economic dislocation that reshaped so many other neighborhoods in the city in the 1950s–1980s. At a time when urban neighborhoods in Philadelphia experienced rapid racial and ethnic change, and the city an overall population loss, Chinatown remained stable and expanded through new waves of immigration, initially from Hong Kong, later from Vietnam and other parts of China and Asia. Unable to secure sufficient housing in Chinatown and enjoying a new period of opportunity after World War II, more Chinese and other Asians settled in the suburbs, a trend that diluted Chinatown's resident population but ultimately strengthened its position as a symbolic center for Asians in the region.

As redevelopment efforts in Philadelphia turned to Center City, Chinatown's location adjacent to this central business district became a liability. Numerous renewal projects (Independence Mall, a commuter rail station and tunnel, a downtown mall, and a crosstown expressway) threatened Chinatown's housing and community institutions with demolition or relocation. These projects were part of a postindustrial move to make over the spaces of the city to improve Philadelphia's "symbolic economy," remaking the urban landscape into a "marketable commodity destination for tourism, consumerism, and resettlement."[41] The campaign to "Save Chinatown," rooted in a second generation's attachment to the neighborhood and the radicalism of a new Asian American movement, worked in coalition with the first-generation leaders of traditional family and other associations to challenge these projects, force the city's hand on the redevelopment of Chinatown, and create a new, more inclusive community leadership structure. The community's efforts to save and renew itself through urban planning, territorial claims, and culturally specific rebuilding led to Chinatown's growth and its continued ability to serve as a reception point for subsequent waves of new immigration.

The story of the "Save Chinatown" movement's struggle to defend and preserve the neighborhood remains a central narrative in the collective memory of this community. It is commemorated on local murals, invoked when new threats to the community emerge, referenced at community events, and featured on local tours of the neighborhood. And the struggle goes on, as Chinatown in the contemporary era continues its vigilance regarding the retention of cultural specificity, room to grow and expand on its own terms, and the preservation of its past. More than anything, it still struggles for recognition of its existence as a "living community," a neighborhood for families and new immigrants "beyond the restaurants."

Spatial Justice for Chinatown: Enduring Legacies and Dilemmas

Chinatown's ability to remain a living community is still precarious, even though Chinatowns in general retain an important place within globalized city landscapes. As recent studies of transnational Chinatowns have pointed out, Chinatowns are increasingly global emblems, urban markers in an age of interplace competition between cities, part of the "standard inventory" of urban attractions. Chinatown, as a themed space, is a sign of Philadelphia's globalized identity, a marker of its status as a destination city and a player in global trade and communications networks. Chinatown functions here as an emblem, a recognizable landscape of "Chinatown-ness," a "projection surface" for cultural performances aimed at outside consumption.[42] This function perpetuates an old story of strategic self-commodification and self-Orientalization that dates back to Chinatown's origins.

Chinatowns are important because they were the first "ethnic neighborhoods" in American culture—that is, the first urban landscapes to be identified and commodified as ethnic—and a prototype for later ethnic enclaves and today's destination neighborhoods. Histories of Chinatowns allow us to chart the emergence of such areas and their place within larger histories of urban development. Like other Chinatowns across North America, Philadelphia's Chinatown was settled and created by a demonized immigrant group who occupied undesirable urban space in the commercial margins of the inner city. Like other Chinatowns, Philadelphia's consistently experienced stigmatization and encroachment. Like some Chinatowns and other Asian ethnic enclaves, Philadelphia's resisted renewal and survived to reclaim space and place within the city. Others did not survive. Philadelphia's Chinatown highlights the role of urban space as land in all its manifestations. It is commodified as real estate, its value subject to the demands of local, regional, and even global markets. It is territory, a space for expression, identity, and cultural inheritance. As a shared community resource, urban space is a foundation for collective place making and claims to justice. The struggles of Philadelphia's Chinatown to remain a living space remind us that place making, a popular idea today in public arts and urban renewal, is only partially about themed space and landscape; that it is deeply shaped by time, social interaction, identity, experience, and power; that it is the embodiment of historical legacies and personal/collective memories; and that not all places are made or created equal.[43] Thus we might be as fruitfully concerned with "place keeping" as "place making." Place keeping acknowledges the necessity of struggle for place as a "consequential geography" shaped by historical legacies, and that the "right to the city" is complemented by a "right to difference." Both "rights" are a foundation for larger spatial justice.[44]

On today's cultural landscape of multiculturalism and consumption-driven urban development, we might take for granted the presence of ethnically identifiable areas to go and eat, shop, and experience "difference." The creation of these areas is now part of established neoliberal strategies for neighborhood renewal (often attended by gentrification), such as branding, heritage tourism, or historic preservation.[45] These strategies, inflected by multiculturalism, necessitate the commodification of Chinatown as a product for outside consumption. For communities of color like Chinatown, this commodification is located within a much deeper history of objectification and risks solidifying, not undoing, racial preconceptions as well as effacing real socioeconomic inequalities.[46] The community's visible, racialized difference can perpetuate a marginalization that works against the aims of community developers and activists to claim rights and resources for Chinatown as just another Philly neighborhood. What spatial justice looks like in this context is complicated and fraught with dilemmas.

Geospatial racialization made Philadelphia's Chinatown vulnerable to displacement in the 1960s and 1970s. Yet packaged as an ethnic image, it was also the means of Chinatown's renewal and redevelopment in the 1980s and beyond. Being an entry point for new immigrants renews its cultural connections to China and Asia and allows the neighborhood to continue as a center for a larger, geographically dispersed cultural community as well as an even larger transnational Chinese diaspora.[47] At the same time, Chinatown's position locally as an immigrant neighborhood, underserved and underrepresented within the larger power dynamics of the city and serving working people's needs, makes creating the resources needed for the non-destination aspects of the neighborhood challenging. Low- or mixed-income housing for working immigrants, for example, is often challenged as fiscally unfeasible and at odds with image making, place marketing, and transnational commerce. In Philadelphia's Chinatown, place making, and community development have gone hand in hand with activism for a significant part of its history. Chinatown is thus consistently under threat, its everyday living space and authentic sense of place in need of vigilant protection in a quest for spatial justice.

Chinatown's development was shaped from the beginning by the needs of its largely working-class residents and by the expectations of outside consumers in productive, sometimes contested, dialogue with one another. Born of segregation and continually reliant on ethnic spectacle and struggle for its survival, since the early twentieth century, this place has emerged from a series of tensions between neighborhood life/ethnic representation, inside/outside, past/present, and themed space/lived reality, tensions that embody the neighborhood's multiple existences as an intergenerational family community, immigrant entry point, cultural center, historic touchstone, globalized urban marker, and tourist destination. They also embody the instability of the larger racial categories that define Chinatown, revealing the hybrid and strategic ways in which Chinatown's denizens negotiate their identities, represent their history, and create their community. Like other immigrant and ethnic communities, Chinatowns are agents of urban renewal, historically occupying and rejuvenating urban spaces, infusing capital into blighted areas, and serving as destinations within an urban-heritage tourism market. Their histories and contemporary realities yield insights into the precarious and multifaceted effects of neoliberal urban development, the now-ubiquitous practices of spatial theming and branding, place marketing, and other consumption-driven development strategies that constitute many urban-renewal movements today.

Tracing the beginnings of Philadelphia's Chinatown in the late nineteenth century as a refuge for Chinese laborers and merchants, through the organizing activities of the community during the postwar period, to Chinatown's relationship to urban renewal today, this book outlines the varied spatial inscriptions of identity, memory, struggle, and transformation in Chinatown. Chapters 1 and 2 describe how immigrants claimed space and created a place called Chinatown that was home to successive generations of Chinese Americans. Chapters 3 and 4 explore the ways community members, driven by a sense of attachment to place and sense of social justice, mounted challenges to urban renewal in the 1960s and 1970s. These challenges were balanced with the strategic redevelopment of the neighborhood along clear ethnic lines, creating a key component of the contemporary Chinatown landscape. Chapters 5 and 6 examine the legacies of the community's resistance to and engagement with urban renewal, outlining continuing struggles and the ways in which the American-born and immigrant Chinese, other Asians, and others who live in, work in, or advocate for Philadelphia's Chinatown understand and work to preserve a sense of place that is part ethnic expression, part Western imaginary, part memoryscape, and, above all, lived space.

Claiming Space, Creating Chinatown, 1870–1940

I n 1876, the Philadelphia press matter-of-factly noted a new influx of Chinese immigrants into the city: "We do not know the actual facts respecting
the movements of Chinese emigrants from the Pacific coast to the Atlantic
States," reported the business-minded *North American*, "but if we may judge by
what we see every day in the streets of Philadelphia, it must have been considerable. These Chinese are so common a sight that no notice is taken of them":

> They all appear to be working at something. Their laundry enterprises
> have been quite successful, and they follow up that line of business so
> pertinaciously that it would not be at all surprising to see them get
> control of it. As they have not thus far engaged in any large industrial
> establishment in a body as operatives, there has been no trouble about
> them on the labor question. Nor can we discover that there is any dis-
> tinct Chinese quarter. They seem to scatter, and all are neat and clean
> in attire and person.[1]

Small in number, geographically dispersed, politically passive, Chinese
migrants posed little threat to the emerging order of the postbellum industrial
city. And although the paper could not discern a "distinct Chinese quarter"
in 1876, Philadelphians soon took notice of the presence and growing size of
a new Chinatown in their midst.

This Chinatown took shape within a matter of years, as Chinese migrants
to Philadelphia transformed a small area around the 900 block of Race Street
into a small but thriving ethnic enclave (see Figures 1.1 and 1.2). Unassuming-
ly tucked away behind the warehouses of Market and Arch Streets, just north
of the main commercial district, this area grew into a safe haven for Chinese

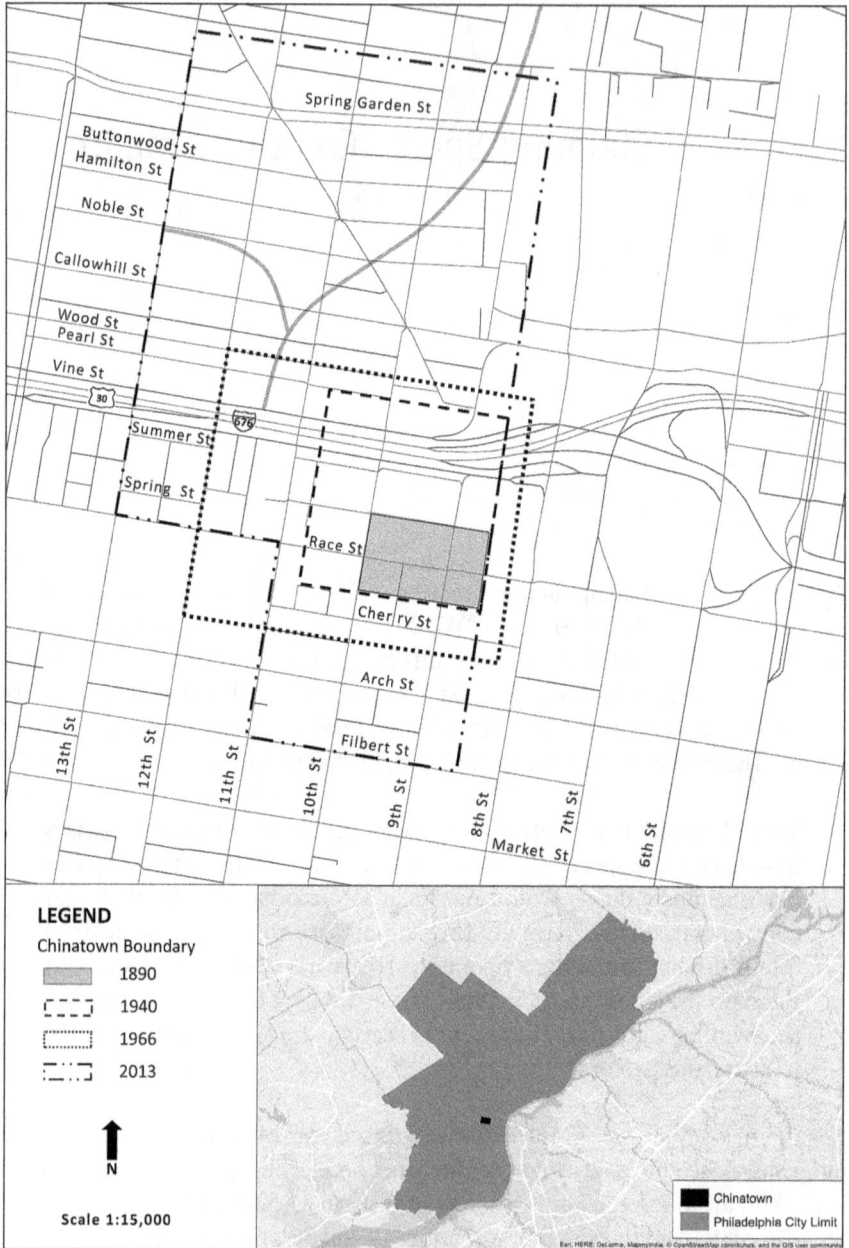

Figure 1.1. Chinatown boundaries, 1890–2013. (Illustration by Amber J. Boll and Damien E. Hesse.)

Figure 1.2. Chinatown core landmarks. (Illustration by Amber J. Boll and Damien E. Hesse.)

1. Holy Redeemer Church
2. Grand View condominiums
3. 6th District Police station
4. Mei Wah Yuen
5. Tuck Hing Grocery
6. History of Chinatown mural
7. Chinese Christian Church and Center
8. On Lok House
9. On Leong Association
10. Lee Fong's first laundry and restaurant
11. Former Far East Restaurant
12. Franklin Square
13. Philadelphia Convention Center
14. Ten Ten Condominiums
15. Former Chinese Christian Church Center
16. Hip Sing Association
17. Chinese Benevolent Association
18. AT&T
19. Gim San Plaza
20. Fo Shou Temple
21. "House of Dragons" Phila. Fire Dept, Engine 20/Ladder 23
22. Cheung's Hung Gar King Fu Academy
23. Fujian Association
24. Chinese Cultural and Community Center
25. Pearl condominiums
26. Asian Bank
27. Friendship Gate
28. Market East/Gallery
29. Independence National Park

immigrants, who in turn created a distinct ethnoscape, appropriating existing building stock and refashioning it into a landscape that embodied their
commitments to family and kinship, mutual assistance, and cultural survival.
This landscape established a spatial template for the future and engendered a
sense of place from which the Chinese community could launch the self-con-
scious performance of Chinese identity for the larger public of Philadelphia.
By claiming space, the Chinese created Chinatown.

But Chinatown was also a rigidly circumscribed space of racial Otherness, and the perceived boundaries of early Chinatown worked to contain
the presence of Chinese bodies in the city. The area was viewed as an exotic,
picturesque urban quarter on the one hand, and a site of racial pollution that
had to be policed and surveilled on the other. These multiple conceptions of
Chinatown—as a site of sin and sanctuary, as slum and stage—all shaped the
area's meaning in the late nineteenth century and beyond and informed the
strategies of Chinese American identity and self-representation. The Asian
features of the landscape celebrated traditional Chinese art and culture even
as they replicated the terms of a larger cultural discourse of Chinese racial and
cultural divergence, embodied by and in space.

Claiming Space: Chinatown's Settlement

The specific origins of Philadelphia's Chinatown are somewhat obscure. Evidence suggests the presence of Chinese men in Philadelphia before the western
Gold Rush; Saint Andrew's Church established a Sunday school for Chinese
laundrymen in 1850 and the first Chinese Christian in Philadelphia was bap-
tized at Saint Andrew's in 1856. A second Sunday school for Chinese men
opened in 1859 at the First Reformed Presbyterian Church on the 300 block
of Broad Street between Spruce and Pine Streets.[2] But these early migrants
seemingly did not establish a concentrated area of settlement. Like many Chinatowns in the eastern and midwestern United States, Philadelphia's had its
roots in the "great driving out" of Chinese from western states that followed
the completion of the transcontinental railroad in 1869 and culminated in the
Exclusion Act of 1882, when violence, harassment, and disenfranchisement
sent Chinese men east.[3]

Over the course of the 1880s and 1890s, Chinese migrants—most of them
young men in their early twenties—came from San Francisco and Seattle and
set up laundries around the city.[4] According to Stewart Culin, a Penn anthropologist who studied the Chinese community in Philadelphia during the
1880s and 1890s, a Mr. Thomas of Belleville, New Jersey, brought fifty Chinese
laundrymen from San Francisco to work in laundries in the area around 1869.
In another account, a group of Chinese men from California were recruited
by a Captain James Hervey to work in his North Arlington, New Jersey, steam
laundry as strikebreakers. Chinese strikebreakers were also brought to Beaver

Falls, Pennsylvania, in 1872 to work in a cutlery factory. Some of these men undoubtedly made their way to Philadelphia to seek their fortunes.[5] By 1870, 13 Chinese men lived in Philadelphia; by 1900, that number had grown to 1,177, of whom 235 lived in Chinatown.[6]

Chinese opened laundries around the city in the 1870s and 1880s, and by the 1890s, the 900 block of Race Street had taken shape as a center of Chinese life in the city. According to Culin, the first laundry in Chinatown was established in 1870 by Lee Fong, also known as Ah Lee, described as "an angular hollow-cheeked man . . . more like the portrait of a corpse than of a human being," "doleful," but "very kind-hearted," who also acted as a distributor of opium, Chinese tea, and incense. Ten years later, a restaurant, Mei Hsiang Low, was opened on the second floor above the laundry, "where the vender of tea and incense divided his time between his scales and his flat-iron." This place soon became the Chinese center in Philadelphia: "On Sundays and Mondays it would be packed with Chinamen, and the strains of the Chinese fiddle could be heard over the never-ending click of the dominoes, from midday to midnight."[7] Ninth and Race provided refuge in part due to its adjacency to the warehouse and central commercial district of Philadelphia—it was both a location convenient for Chinese merchants as well as a part of the city that few wanted to live in.[8] It also occupied a central position vis-à-vis a dispersed geography of Chinese laundries. Mapping the existing Chinese laundries in 1880, for example, reveals that although Chinese laundrymen were located all over the city (as far west as Sixteenth Street), most clustered to the north and south of Market from Christian to Spring Garden, and more than one-third of these were located within five blocks of Ninth and Race.[9] In the immediate vicinity of 913, Chinese operated laundries at 205 North Tenth Street, 836 Race, and 159 North Ninth Street, the latter two concerns managed by members of the Lee family, suggesting an emerging central cluster of Chinese laundries in that one-block radius.

At the time Chinese settled in the area around Ninth and Race Streets, Philadelphia was becoming the "Workshop of the World," drawing new and old immigrants to its burgeoning manufacturing economy. Primary industries included textile and clothing manufacture, machine-shop and hardware manufacture (saws, locomotives, electrical machinery, tools, and locks, for example), printing and publishing, and leather production as well as railroad and construction work. These industries employed skilled European immigrants (Jews, Italians, and some Poles and Eastern Europeans), older ethnic populations (Irish, German) and African Americans, each occupying specific niches and residential neighborhoods north and south of the city center. Although a few Chinese from Cuba may have worked in cigar manufacturing, others were restricted to domestic service, laundry work, and small commercial ventures, such as import/export gift shops, groceries, and later restaurants.[10] In an era when immigrants' lives were often geographically structured around the proximity of home and work, Chinese segregation followed a slightly different pattern; laundrymen lived and worked in locations across the city but were not integrated into those neighborhoods. Viewed as fundamentally foreign, their real home was in Chinatown, a place apart.

The neighborhood that the Chinese chose to inhabit was an in-between urban zone on the northern fringes of the central business district. In the 1870s, the area around 900 Race was home to miscellaneous small-scale manufacturing concerns: safe and brush factories on Eighth Street, an iron foundry at 814–818 Race, and an iron-railing factory at 197 North Tenth, among others. Workers' housing predominated, with small alleyways carved into the blocks of Spring and Winter (then Sergeant and Morgan) Streets. A public school (present since at least the 1850s until the early 1900s) was located on the 900 block of Spring Street, and a district police station sat at Eleventh and Winter Streets. Arch Street was home to the Arch Street Opera House at Tenth (later the burlesque Trocadero Theater) and Wood's Dime Museum at Ninth. The row houses and boardinghouses on Tenth, Ninth, Winter, and Spring Streets were home to diverse populations of working people. Skilled and unskilled laborers of various ethnic backgrounds, many Irish and German, often second generation, were the primary residents of the area in the 1870s and 1880s, some in family homes on the smaller side streets (Winter, Spring, Cherry), and many others in boardinghouses on Tenth and Ninth Streets. These residents took up various occupations: day labor, factory work, shoemaking and other skilled crafts, domestic service, and saloon keeping. A number were clerks who presumably worked in nearby businesses.[11] During the early twentieth century, the neighborhood briefly saw an influx of small numbers of immigrant families from Lithuania, Russia, Albania, and Greece living in boardinghouses on North Tenth and pursuing such occupations as dressmaking, baking, waitressing, and electrical work.[12] This occupational diversity contrasted with the almost-uniform occupations of the Chinese: laundryman, cook, or merchant. Nevertheless, Chinese merchants and their laboring tenants undoubtedly found a haven in this ethnic miscellany.

As time passed, businesses left, and other immigrants found new housing opportunities outside the central business district, this neighborhood became considerably more Chinese in character. It also became more stigmatized.[13] By the early 1900s, many of the manufacturing businesses, save a chair factory at 1010 Race, were gone, and the area was characterized by a "diversity of marginal uses including warehouses, skid rows, cheap rooming houses and slum dwellings" as well as a "wide variety of vice and entertainment."[14] Four theaters now occupied Eighth Street above Race in addition to the one on Arch.[15] The area of Philadelphia north of Market and east of Broad was now home to "Skid Row" (in the eastern part of the area near the river to Eighth Street) and the "Tenderloin" district (Market to Callowhill from Ninth to Eleventh). Skid

Row was characterized by flophouses, cheap restaurants, saloons, missions, and other facilities that constituted the "hobohemia" of the city, inhabited by a mixed group of homeless men and other displaced persons. Burlesque theaters, cabarets, dancehalls, brothels, and gambling dens dominated the Tenderloin. A 1913 Philadelphia vice commission estimated that more than one hundred houses of prostitution operated in this small area in addition to streetwalkers.[16] At Ninth and Race, Chinatown sat right in the center between the two districts.

By 1900, the 900 block of Race was almost exclusively Chinese. Despite the environment, Chinese stayed in this area in part due to violence and harassment well into the twentieth century, illustrated by the experience of Joseph Eng. Born in Philadelphia in 1920 to a laundryman, Eng was accustomed to harassment and discrimination as a Chinese American: "For the Chinese it was the worst. I caught it at that time. The Chinese were so dead, we can't walk anywhere. We cannot walk to Arch Street. We cannot go to Eleventh Street, because that is not our territory. We stop right here, thank you, between Ninth and Tenth and that's it."[17] Such spatial regulation was typical of other Chinatowns during this period (one might say central to their definition), with social boundaries policed and managed through harassment, stigmatization, and surveillance.[18]

Shop, *Fong*, Street, Mission: The Spaces of Chinatown

Within segregated Chinatown, a distinct pattern of spatial use emerged that characterized the area as a cultural landscape. Chinese adapted the existing building stock, composed primarily of antebellum row houses and late-nineteenth-century commercial buildings, to meet the various needs of the immigrant community. Space, like life, was organized tightly around commercial imperatives and communal values, particularly those related to kinship. The landscape of Chinatown was (and still is) mixed, accommodating residential and commercial uses. Many buildings on 900 Race were modified to embody these multiple uses, establishing a spatial template that characterizes much of the main streets of Chinatown today (see Figure 1.3). While the first floors of buildings were occupied by shops, laundries, and eventually restaurants, the second, third, and attic floors of these commercial ventures were devoted to living quarters as well as a variety of social functions.[19] Representative spaces within this landscape included the shop; *fong*, or common room (usually linked to associations); the street; and the Christian mission.

First-floor shops—laundries, groceries or other businesses, and eventually restaurants—anchored each building in Chinatown, providing livelihoods and a focus of public commercial activity. Culin describes these shops in 1887 as being the cornerstone of Chinatown life:

Figure 1.3. The 900 block of Race Street, 1933. (*Philadelphia Record* Photograph Morgue, Historical Society of Pennsylvania.)

As soon as several men have collected in a town or city, one of them will send to the nearest place of supply and purchase such Chinese groceries and other wares as may be needed by the colony. These he will sell to his comrades, without at first discontinuing his usual avocation. If the colony increases in numbers he may rent a small store and with the assistance of some of his friends form a store company. Several men are usually associated in such enterprises, one of whom will be placed in charge as manager. A general assortment of Chinese merchandise is obtained, either from New York or San Francisco or direct from China itself, and an auspicious name is selected for the company and prominently displayed without the store door.[20]

Many of the firms located on 900 Race were general stores, such as Kwong Hop and Company at 937 Race, which in 1913 sold Chinese general merchandise and drugs and also manufactured noodles. Kwong Hop and Company supplied all the Chinese restaurants in Philadelphia and the vicinity and rented its second floor to Lee Moy to use for a restaurant; some of the firm's partners were also employed in that enterprise.[21] Stores acted as gathering places and banks as well as grocers and druggists. Kwong Hop and Company, inspected in 1913 by the Immigration and Naturalization Service (INS), did not use a bank but kept its funds in the café.[22] Mark Woo, laborer, lived over the Lee Yick Teung store at 938 Race, which "kept his money for him."[23] Chinatown's merchants, although restricted to doing business in this quarter, were not solely devoted to a Chinese clientele; most routinely dealt with non-Chinese merchants and dealers, sometimes as tenants and customers, other times as suppliers.[24]

If the first floors of Chinatown buildings were devoted to commercial businesses, the second and third floors fulfilled a variety of functions, serving as boardingrooms or family living spaces as well as common gathering spaces for the community. The configuration of the store Yee Wah at 915 Race Street, one of the primary concerns of early Chinatown, was typical, emphasizing the communal nature of the mercantile enterprise and the intermingling of living and commerce. Yee Wah dealt in Chinese merchandise, drugs, and Chinese and Japanese art goods on the first floor and stored stock on the second floor of the building. The first floor was divided into three areas: the front store, a middle dining room, and a rear kitchen.[25] Some of the partners lived in quarters on the third floor and rented the fourth-floor attic, a large open room, to "Chinamen for sleeping quarters." Tom Leing, a teacher and former laundryman who came to Philadelphia in 1881, taught Sunday School classes over Yee Wah in the early 1900s. Business was transacted in common rooms or temporary sleeping rooms; in many cases, the resident store also acted as a bank. When Lim Quen, laundryman, lent money to Lum Ping and Dun Chatt in 1908, the loans were negotiated in the front room of the second floor of 906 Race and in the "back room of Tuck Wah's store." Quen then deposited his money with Wah.[26] In another case, Moy Sam, laundryman, sold his laundry at 934 Race Street in February 1908 to Charley Lee for $500 (the usual amount) and subsequently loaned money to Long Gee so that Gee could buy a laundry at 764 South Fifth Street. Both transactions took place in the back room of the Kwon Wo Lung store at 934 Race Street, where Sam temporarily lodged.[27]

Residential quarters were small and densely occupied. Most Chinese men lived in tightly shared rooms on Race, averaging fourteen to fifteen persons per address in 1910.[28] These living arrangements were often arranged with extended kin who also shared interest in a common commercial concern or occupation. The nature of Asian exclusion, with exemptions for merchants, engendered the prevalence of chain migration within small-scale commercial enterprises. The creation of a *woi/hui*, or traditional guild partnership (literally meaning "get together" or "put together") associated with an extended clan, provided a collective loan fund as well as a way of establishing partnerships in a commercial enterprise to claim eligibility for immigration and travel.[29] For instance, in 1900, Long Lee, a grocer and titular "head" of the household, and nine "roomers" occupied 915 Race Street. Seven of these men—Ban Lee, Yong Lee, Lon Lee, Ming Lee, Hong Lee, Hy Bing Lee, and Kee Bing La—were grocery clerks, presumably in the same shop. They came to the United States between the 1876 and 1883 and ranged in age from twenty-nine to fifty. Living arrangements were structured along extended family lines, fictive or otherwise. Ming Lee, a grocer aged twenty-six, lived at 925 Race in 1900 with Jung Lee, fifty-nine, a cook; Tin Luck Lee, twenty-six, a grocery clerk; Duong Lee, thirty-seven, a grocery clerk; and Ding Lee, thirty, a grocery clerk. The young men all came to the United States between 1888 and 1890.[30]

Other residents of Chinatown were short-term lodgers; for those out of work or coming from or going to China, the neighborhood was an important way station. Laundrymen routinely sold their laundries before departing for China, and the association's common rooms provided temporary living quarters and served as an official address while their paperwork was being processed. Departing laundrymen Mark Sing and Lee Sing used the addresses of 938 Race and 925 Race Street, respectively, when they applied to leave for China in 1907. Mark Sun testified that he previously owned a laundry in Jenkintown but "stopped" at 933 Race Street after he sold his laundry and was recuperating from a hospitalization.[31]

The most common use of second and third floors in Chinatown was as *fongs*, or "common rooms." *Fongs* were one of the centers of social life in Chinatown; these rooms were important gathering spaces that served as not only club rooms or recreational spaces but also sleeping quarters for visitors or the unemployed and even isolation hospitals or sick rooms for those who were ill. *Fongs* were rented by small groups of Chinese immigrants as meeting spaces for a multitude of associations tied to various kin, regional, and trade relationships. Many were devoted to those sharing the same surname, often an extended kin group. They might be known as *Kung-so* or "Public Place," *Wei-kun*, or "Association House," and *T'ung-yip-kung-wei*, or "Same Occupation Public Association." *Kung-so* were tribal and regional organizations based on the same surname. In the 1890s, Culin identifies seven *kung-so* in Philadelphia that also correspond to the familiar family names of many long-term community residents, such as Lee, Moy, Mark, and Wong.[32]

In addition, Chinatown was home to mutual beneficial associations that worked to maintain order, protest abuse of Chinese "treaty rights," arbitrate disputes, certify documents and deeds, do charitable work, maintain a cemetery, and serve as a reception committee for foreign dignitaries.[33] According to Penn sociologist David Cheng, who volunteered as a teacher in the community in the 1940s, these "tongs" were "like chop suey, another American concoction devised to meet certain needs." Tongs were secret societies tied to family-clan affiliations or economic business interests. The I Hing Tong occupied two rooms on the second floor of a house on Race Street. In 1889, the Hip Sing Tong was formed with recruits from the I Hing to become one of the two most powerful societies in Chinatown in the early twentieth century. The other tong, On Leong, was associated with the merchant class. Tong rivalry mapped onto the geography of Race Street; residents' reports claim the division was north/south, occupied by On Leong and Hip Sing, respectively.[34]

Sundays animated the *fongs* of Chinatown, as men from around the region gathered on their one day off for various recreational activities. Chinatown was where the laundryman felt "more at home, where he shops for daily necessities and attends to business matters, and above all, where he is recognized as a person, enjoying a life of primary relations where sentiments and attitudes are warm, intimate and spontaneous."[35] Men traded gossip, dominated by news from China. Communal drinking of tea and spirits and games of chance, such as *mah-jongg* and *fan tan*, usually for money, were common pastimes. Family and extended-kin associations also supported the practice of ancestor worship, and many meeting rooms accommodated altars for this purpose.[36] Helen Louie recalled that her father, Henry Jung's, gift shop at 230 North Tenth Street was a hub of activity on Sundays, as men would gather on the second floor to play *mah-jongg* while her mother cooked fried noodles and other dishes in the first-floor kitchen. "All the Jungs from all over Philadelphia would come to our house," Louie remembered. "They all had laundries. In those days, every Jung was a cousin."[37]

The architectural features of Chinatown signaled many of these spatial functions as well as the identity of Chinese American life in Philadelphia. The built environment of Chinatown was invariably hybrid, based in early- and mid-nineteenth-century buildings with Chinese architectural features mapped onto their façades and culturally specific spatial uses hidden within. Many buildings of early Chinatown resembled other small-scale commercial buildings of the period, with a large plate-glass window on the first floor featuring the business name, sheltered by an awning that extended over the sidewalk. By the turn of the twentieth century, many businesses, especially restaurants, invested in larger-scale signage in English and Chinese characters. One of the most distinctive additions to the early Chinatown landscape was the modification of many second-floor façades to create recessed or projecting balconies, often elaborately decorated with upwardly curved eaves and tiled roofs. In the 1900s, on the north side of Race Street, 931, 917, 915, and 913 Race all featured projecting wrought-iron balconies; the façade of 907–909 was dominated by a bi-level balcony, with the lower level protruding and topped by a smaller recessed balcony. Upper-story balconies were common in southern Chinese cities, such as Canton, where they helped regulate the internal temperature of buildings in winter or summer. In the context of Chinatown, balconies were culturally recognizable architectural features that also highlighted the communal, social, and political functions of buildings' upper floors, giving them a public community face, as these balconies were most common on buildings that housed association headquarters or meeting rooms. The balconies not only signaled the important public function of the spaces but also allowed access to the street, as people could witness parades, processions, or other public events from these balconies.[38]

Many of the activities of the Chinatown community itself were private in character, hidden from the larger public's notice in second-floor rooms, attics, basements, and back rooms. But Chinese Americans also increasingly claimed the public street as a space for Chinese-themed activities, such as processions and marches that displayed aspects of Chinese history or culture. These events, although largely internally driven, consistently drew the attention of non-Chinese Philadelphians and the local media fascinated with exotic culture. Funerals were a prominently observed activity before 1930, often reported in the larger press. Although in 1888 Philadelphia's Chinese were granted land for a burial ground in Lower Merion Township outside the city (Merion Memorial Park; they later purchased land for a national cemetery in Wynnewood), funeral processions still took place in Chinatown and were important public affairs.[39] Funerals celebrated elite merchants or other wealthy men in elaborate street processions that embodied the deceased's status, wealth, and honor. In 1910, Jung Jo, the local head of On Leong, was mourned by Chinese and "many Americans" in a procession of one Chinese and two American bands and fifty taxicabs that passed from the Chinese Christian League at 918 Race Street and circled Chinatown (Tenth to Spring to Race).[40] When Wong Sing Yow, a local merchant, died in March 1921, he was honored by a "procession of mourners, dressed in Oriental garb"; the group paraded through Chinatown to the accompaniment of strains from "two native bands, and an American band."[41] These funerals displayed the already-hybrid nature of Chinatown cultural practices, even as they were constructed as essentially Oriental in the larger culture.[42]

Political demonstrations were another important public display in Chinatown. Of particular importance was the National Day of the Chinese Republic on October 10, known as "Ten Ten." In 1921, Chinatown residents marked the occasion with a march down Race Street in celebration of the tenth birthday of the Chinese Republic: "From the joss-house in Chinatown, which stretches along Race Street, between Ninth and Tenth comes the thumping of tom-toms and the shrill note of the flute. In shops and restaurants, myriad lanterns cast multi-colored rays of light, and all members of the Celestial race, irrespective of Tong hatreds, unite in the festival." The parade did not stay contained in Chinatown, however, marching from Tenth and Race to Market Street, rounding City Hall to Broad, Chestnut, and back up Ninth Street to Race. The parade featured floats graced by the presence of Chinese women and children, some in Oriental costume. Marching delegations represented the Kuomintang, the Chinese M. E. Mission, the Chinese Baptist Church, Hip Sing Tong, On Leong Tong, and the Chinese Merchants' Association. In an interesting American twist, Mrs. Thomas D. Wong, wife of the marshal, portrayed the "Goddess of Liberty."[43]

By far the most public expression of Chinese identity was the annual Chinese New Year celebration. Chinese New Year made Chinatown visible within the discourse of the ethnic "urban picturesque," allowing Americans to indulge a fascination with quaint Chinese customs:

> Midnight will usher in the Chinese New Year. The new republic will be four years old, and the music of automatic pianos will mingle with the tom-tom and the Chinese flute, thus bringing the past and present together. Chinatown is in picturesque array for the occasion. Dragon flags, varicolored pennants fly with those of the United States, while thousands of lanterns help to emphasize the spirit. At midnight many of the older Chinese will assemble in the Joss House at North Ninth Street and pay their respect to Confucius. They will eat the food and sing the songs of their native land, while a short distance away, the younger Chinese . . . will listen to the tango music and combine their menu with that of the present time. Bow Fine, the oldest resident of Chinatown, will hold a reception at his home at Ninth and Race streets. . . . There will be fireworks.[44]

"Bringing the past and present together" referred to not only the timeless traditional quality of the festival but also the contrasting pastimes of the older and younger Americanized residents of Chinatown. The following year, the *Ledger* reports again on the celebration, highlighting the role of non-Chinese visitors in the creation of the spectacle:

> The Chinese Merchants' Association had a parade today. Lee Sing, a merchant, headed the parade. A banquet followed. All sorts of strange music were heard today in the Joss houses. Americans lined the street and listened attentively to the strains of the banging of Chinese musical instruments. Joe Sing, for 15 years keeper-in-chief of the Chinese Temple had the interior of the temple washed. He was on duty inviting Americans to visit the place. For hours Chinese packed the temple, where they dropped themselves to the floor and delivered prayers to the bronze figure.[45]

Chinese New Year solidified the role of Chinatown in providing ethnic color to the city and an exotic spectacle for local residents.

Although not created by the Chinese themselves, Christian missions were significant spaces within the Chinatown landscape. Initiated by outsiders with a paternalistic interest in the community, missions provided services and took on social and cultural functions over time. Drawing on traditions of missionary work among Chinese overseas, the first of these organizations was the Chinese American Union, located near the Race Street district at 1024 Walnut

Figure 1.4. First Chinese Baptist Church, 1006 Race Street, circa 1900. This site would later become the Chinese Christian Church and Center. (Yam Tong Hoh Papers [MS 126], Historical Society of Pennsylvania.)

Street. Founded in 1885 by the Reverend Frederick Poole, the Union's mission was to address "the increasing immigration to our State and city of the Mongolian race, and their moral destitution and civil helplessness through ignorance of our language, religion, laws, and customs." The Union also sought to address incidences of "crime and ill-treatment," promote activities employed for their "social and moral elevation," and publish "information and manuals of religious instruction in their own language."[46] The Union established a Chinatown location in 1896, the Christian Mission League, at 929 Race Street.[47] The First Chinese Baptist Church, run by the recently ordained Reverend Lee Hong, was founded at 1006 Race in 1898 (see Figure 1.4).[48] One of the missions' primary functions was to establish Sunday Schools, which were attractive to immigrants because they offered English- and Chinese-language instruction. The Union set up a Department of Instruction in 1872 that offered Sunday School in English and Chinese. In addition to religious instruction, the missions targeted the perceived Chinese ignorance of "Western manners and customs, negligent of the laws of health and of sanitary regulations." The latter spoke to the concerns missionaries had about the environment in which the Chinese lived:

"Without homes or home influences, living often in sellars [sic] and damp and sickly places, frequently the slaves of opium and other debasing habits, their physical and social condition was manifestly undesirable and needed improvement." Later the Union's Department of Health and Social Improvement provided medical assistance to the Chinese population to "rescue this strangely isolated and neglected people from the nurseries of disease and the haunts of vice, and to humanize and purify their social condition."[49]

Missions served as mediators between Chinatown and the larger community. The Union often expressed concern about the economic and cultural vulnerability of the Chinese, who were "frequently subjected to insult, to persecution and even violence, by those of other nationalities prejudiced against them on account of their religion, dress, and habits of life."[50] The terms within which missions articulated these concerns, however, relied on established ideas about the Chinese. The Union often deployed Orientalist tropes to promote its cause, from a discussion of Chinatown's deviance and squalor to the exhibition of exotic Chinese lifeways. In 1890, for example, the Union planned a "Chinese Village" exhibition to raise funds for its efforts, which would "introduce many features of Chinese life hitherto unknown."[51] Presented on February 11, 1890, at Horticultural Hall, the village was "one of the most unique and interesting exhibitions ever presented in this city, being a representation of Chinese customs, dwellings, and industries, with thoroughly Chinese decorations, transforming the interior of the Hall into a veritable Chinese street." Although pleased with the outcome of the display, the Union had to concede that the proceeds were "disappointing," suggesting that by 1890 the imagined Orient of another time and place was less interesting to the Philadelphia public than the local Orient of Chinatown and its perceived vices.[52]

"Philadelphia is clearly getting educated on the Chinese question": Attitudes toward Chinatown

Concerns about Chinatown and these perceived vices emerged as the small quarter grew more concentrated and recognizable in the city landscape. In 1882—the same year the federal government passed legislation effectively barring new immigration from China to the United States—Philadelphians were still sanguine about the Chinese newcomers to the city: "Chinese immigration is represented by a few inoffensive, industrious and efficient laundrymen. . . . [T]he number of Chinamen who come to this country is small and decreasing, and that those who have come have done, upon the whole, much more good than harm, is, we believe, incontestable."[53] A "small and decreasing" number of "inoffensive" Chinese, isolated and dispersed, was no cause for alarm. But as the population began consolidating in one area of the city, greater public ambivalence emerged that was rooted in a variety of factors, shaped by an ongoing preoccupation with Chinese difference as a source of both fascination and discomfort.

Chinatown soon became subject to police surveillance and neighborhood protest. In August 1882, Philadelphia police conducted the first documented raid on Chinatown, entering Lee Fong's establishment and arresting him and his cousin, Lee Wang, for running an illegal gambling house.[54] Five years later, as the colony continued to grow, seventy-seven property owners and residents on both sides of Race Street, from Tenth to Eleventh Street, appealed to Mayor Edwin Fitler to help rid the neighborhood of the "great crowd of Chinese gamblers who have swarmed in upon them within six months," on the grounds that the "restaurants, as they are called by the chinamen," are "nuisances, prejudicial to the health and morals of the community." Neighbors were also concerned about a possible decline in property values with the recent influx: "They make the declaration that the property in a single square where the nuisances exist has depreciated so much in value that $150,000 loss would be a low estimate. They are also determined to find a way to restore not only the value of their property, but also the peace and quiet of the neighborhood, especially on Sunday."[55] Specifically, the petition called attention to the "immoral actions" of the Chinese men: "Unchaste appearance in public, by reason of the style of clothing worn by them, often partially revealing their nude forms"; the "use of vile language" on the street; "opium smoking habits, which are frequently prolonged until morning"; violation of the Sabbath; "congregating in crowds on the sidewalks"; "disorderly and sacrilegious deportment"; "hideous music and noise"; "constant gambling"; and "selling goods on Sunday and consequently bringing to this neighborhood vast crowds of Chinamen from all parts of the city." The petitioners claimed that they were "not fighting or opposing the Chinese as Chinese, or because they were Chinese," but simply protesting the nuisance that they created.[56] That same Sunday, health inspectors visited six houses, which contained thirty-seven rooms housing forty-four residents, stores and restaurants on the ground floors, and extra rooms "ostensibly used for lodging" but believed to be devoted to gambling and opium smoking.[57] "Philadelphia is clearly getting educated on the Chinese question," San Francisco's *Evening Bulletin* smugly concluded.[58]

Two days later, the *Public Ledger* printed a formal protest in response, signed by six Chinese men and "the usual white renegade" (namely, a Mr. C. Pond), disputing the claims of the petition. The protest was based in the community's identity as overseas Chinese and thus was a matter of diplomacy, echoing the Chinese American organizations' implication in larger transnational diplomatic structures and their exclusion from American citizenship. "We will not agree that the Chinese must go," the protestors asserted, emphasizing that they had "rights so long as we behave ourselves."[59] They pointed to the U.S. treaty with China that prohibited "damages to peaceful Chinese."

They threatened to "sue the United States," and "then they will have to suffer for what they do to us."[60] Earlier that year, Philadelphia police officers had been reprimanded after a search and seizure of money at various locations in Chinatown. According to the sympathetic judge who reviewed the seizures, the actions of the police "cannot at all be justified or approved. . . . If it had been our own citizens it would not have been attempted. If the defendants were strangers, and almost helpless and defenceless [sic], they still have their rights, and the officers have no right to trample on their personal rights any more than on the personal rights of natural born citizens."[61] Portraying the Chinese as helpless and defenseless strangers, this judge affirmed human rights while also perpetuating Chinese difference, much as the Chinese themselves had.[62]

Attitudes toward the Chinese ambivalently hinged between fear and disgust and fascination and paternalism. When Chinatown was visible, it was a problem. But the invisible Chinatown was also a problem, housing the back rooms, cellars, and attics where vice presumably flourished unseen by respectable society. Chinatown's savage nature was most often represented in the reportage on the so-called tong wars of the 1910s and 1920s, in which Chinatown was imagined—usually erroneously—as a dark den of Eastern decadence and violent danger, a common Orientalist trope.[63] Between 1890 and 1910, Chinatown was increasingly targeted by the police on various charges ranging from failure to observe the Sabbath to more criminal activities. Chinatown residents were placed on house arrest on July 12, 1898, in response to a double murder the weekend before, linked to a tong war. Police searched houses for guns and ammunition but found little evidence of either. A month later, in August 1898, police cracked down on Chinatown businesses to "enforce the Sunday closing law," rounding up twenty offenders.[64] In 1899, police raided 276 residents of Chinatown in thirty-three dwellings; fifteen groceries; five restaurants, "which do a big 'white' trade"; five variety stores; and one meat shop. According to the North American, "If signs have any portent, Chinatown will continue to revel in its wide assortment of Oriental vices. Efforts have been made in the past to stamp out the flagrant wickedness of the colony, and these efforts are to be repeated, but the outlook for genuine action is anything but promising. To-day Race street is 'wide open'—a triumph for gambling, opium, and low women in the heart of a civilized city." Philadelphians were warned that "under their very feet are being carried out the vilest orgies of the East."[65]

"Chinatown is in picturesque array": Orientalism and Self-Orientalism

Fixation on the "vilest orgies of the East" and "Oriental vices" located Chinatown firmly within a discourse of Orientalism, which objectified the area and its inhabitants within familiar tropes of exoticism, darkness, deviance, backwardness, and sensuality. The unseen Chinatown as secret and threatening—vice-ridden Chinatown as cultural attraction—produced such difference and distance through the picturesque. As a world apart, Chinatown represented an imaginative geography and history that helped "the mind to intensify its own sense of self by dramatizing the difference and distance between what is close to it and what is far away," a common feature of Orientalism.[66]

This "imaginative geography" was shaped in part by preexisting ideas of Chinese people and culture constructed over the prior century through ongoing trade with China and the exhibition of Chinese art and culture, both of which promised consumers and spectators intimacy and privilege vis-à-vis a primitive and ancient foreign culture. As the major American port of the new republic, Philadelphia was a dynamic mercantile destination populated by diverse immigrants and sojourners, including a small population of Chinese seamen involved in the China trade. The connection of elite Philadelphia merchants to China fostered an interest in Chinese cultural artifacts. Merchant and philanthropist Nathan Dunn (1782–1844) amassed a formidable collection of Chinese cultural artifacts in the early nineteenth century that became the basis for the Chinese Museum at Ninth and George (now Sansom) Streets. This museum attracted Philadelphians from 1838 to 1841 with its "ten thousand Chinese things," a variety of objects, art, and life-size figures set in recreated Chinese rooms. An estimated one hundred thousand people visited Dunn's Chinese Museum during its short life, purchasing fifty thousand copies of its catalogue. At Dunn's, visitors found themselves, "as it were, transported to a new world."[67] This imagined transportation was enabled by eleven dioramas or "life groups" inhabited by life-size clay figures dressed in Chinese costumes representing the ranks of Chinese society. Also on display at the museum were "live Chinamen" in the form of two performers who demonstrated Chinese art and music:

> The collection was very attractive for several years and the interest was increased by the presence of a couple of real Chinamen in their native costume, one of whom was a clerkly gentleman who used to write the names of visitors upon a card in Chinese characters at the consideration of a shilling a head. His brother Chinaman was a musician, who was wont to discourse the most abominable strains that were ever produced by a squawking human voice and an instrument, which seemed to be a cross between a hurdy-gurdy and a plantation banjo.[68]

Situated near Chestnut Street, in the heart of the city's commercial spectacle—a spectacle that increasingly relied on ethnic stereotypes in visual culture to stimulate commerce—the Chinese Museum made explicit the link between the flows of commodities, including labor, in the mercantile network and the commodification of all things Chinese, including Chinese people.[69]

Philadelphians' interest in the new Chinese presence may also have been intensified by viewing the Chinese Pavilion at the 1876 Centennial Exhibition, which displayed a variety of Chinese art and artifacts: silk, fans, and figurines placed in pagoda-shaped glass showcases; and a profusion of vases, lacquered boxes, and ornate wood furniture, all framed by large wood and stone gateways.[70] These displays, like Dunn's Museum, married the commercial and the educational, exercising categorical control over things Chinese. As much a bazaar as a museum, the exhibition promoted the commodification of knowledge and consumption of Chinese culture, stimulating desire as many spectators purchased porcelain and other artifacts.[71] The exhibition pavilion was also linked to a wider range of emerging display institutions that developed and circulated new kinds of disciplinary knowledge (history, biology, art history, anthropology) and discursive formations (the past, evolution, aesthetics, man) in new technologies of vision and power.[72] These new technologies were also deployed in the commodification of differences in commercial culture. Wanamaker's great department store on Market Street, for example, offered *chinoiserie* among its wares and illustrated its advertisements and trade cards with exotic Oriental or whimsical Chinese figures.[73] It is difficult to know just how these glimpses into Chinese culture (real or imagined) and material life in particular shaped how Philadelphians perceived and welcomed, or did not welcome, the new foreigners in their midst. But they certainly reinforced an image of exotic Chinese difference and of Chinatown as another world.

The otherworldly quality of Chinese culture and Chinatowns lent itself to exhibition and commodification for tourism. As early as the 1880s and 1890s, San Francisco's white entrepreneurs cultivated touristic interest in that city's Chinatown. Chinese merchants and residents responded with their own vision, rechanneling tourists' interest and harnessing it to a larger sociopolitical agenda. Chinese San Franciscans who sought to capitalize on tourists' fascination with the quarter made more headway in the struggle against anti-Chinese racism, but their success also came at a price. They contested white entrepreneurs' representations of a vice-ridden Chinatown but substituted their own claims that Chinatown's authenticity lay in the exoticism of its architecture, theatrical performances, curios, and cuisine. These claims affirmed perceptions of Chinese Americans as authentic "Others" more systematically and thus more forcefully. Speaking to an antimodern appeal of "authenticity," bohemians recast Chinatown as a vital preserve of authentic, premodern culture, conveniently if curiously located amid the swirl of modernity. Thus, the quarter became an antimodern refuge that offered the possibility of alternative experiences. After the 1906 earthquake in San Francisco, Chinese merchants hired American architects to rebuild the city's Chinatown around imagined Orientalist lines, in part to attract tours and tourists. In this case, the Orientalization of the area was key to the survival of the neighborhood in the face of calls for it to disappear or relocate.[74]

By the 1910s and 1920s, Philadelphia's Chinatown merchants likewise began cultivating a more public image that drew on some of these themes, embodied by exotic spectacle. Chinese merchants and others sought visibility in the larger city landscape and culture through not only their commercial dealings with non-Chinese but also the staging of banquets and other ritual occasions that served as occasions for hosting associates and dignitaries. Initially restaurants were also located on second floors or the back of first floors in commercial concerns, serving as communal eating places for firm members, extended kin, or association members. Over time, restaurants moved to the first floors or to the fronts of many buildings, signaling the emergence of a larger non-Chinese market for Chinese food in Philadelphia. The most visible and well known of these restaurants was the Far East Restaurant, located on the second floor of 907–909 Race Street. Opened in 1908, this "Chinese Café" announced its presence on the block with an elaborate second-floor balcony and flamboyant displays of Chinese lanterns, bells, flags, banners, and, later, neon lights. A front entryway over the sidewalk was emblazoned with a large rising sun that displayed the restaurant's name. The Far East was one of the first Chinatown restaurants to serve both Chinese and non-Chinese customers and contributed greatly to the development of Chinatown business, serving as a public landmark for the neighborhood, particularly for outsiders.[75]

Chinese firms dealing in groceries and other cultural staples likewise pursued a wider marketing of Chinese art goods in the 1910s and 1920s, undoubtedly catering to a non-Chinese clientele. Some drew back the curtain of secrecy and mystery surrounding Chinatown, inviting outsiders into hitherto private spaces; others claimed the public space of the street for enactments of ethnic identity. The Masonic Lodge held banquets in the second-story restaurants at 907 Race Street and 936 Race Street. In 1888, the first of these events celebrated the opening of a new Masonic chapter in Philadelphia, with Grand Master Yung Yim from New York presiding. The Masonic Lodge at 922 Race Street boasted four hundred members at its inception, and its banquets attracted Chinese and non-Chinese, who were awed by the ornate décor:

> The room in the rear was a blaze of gold. A huge arch made of carved wood stood at the back of the room. It was covered with thick gilt and carved in a thousand fantastic designs. Back of the arch in the alcove was a picture of a joss overcoming the devil. The joss had a saintly expression; the devil was very fierce looking and wore a full black beard. In front of the arch were a number of candelabra and a brass pan full on incense in which were stuck hundreds of joss sticks. In two large urns incense was burning. It burns night and day, and is replenished by Wong Pock, who is the Secretary of the Masons in this city.[76]

The move to showcase the exotic food and décor of Chinatown was not exclusive to Philadelphia but was central to the survival of Chinatowns across the country during the past century.

Merchants in particular tied their survival to retaining and using an ethnic sense of place to pursue new clientele for Chinese businesses. There is some evidence that by the 1930s, Chinatown's business community actively catered to a non-Chinese trade through various strategies of "self-Orientalism."[77] In 1936, as a bid to attract visitors to their district during the upcoming National Democratic Convention, local Chinese American businesses worked to revitalize their storefronts. According to the *Philadelphia Record*, "more progressive" merchants were "bringing back the glamour" and "fame of Gay 90s" with Chinese decorations and "lavish interiors with Oriental trimmings" created by painters and stonemasons at the instigation of the Ling Yung Beneficial Association. Some of the "exotic splendors" that would "live again," according to the *Record*, included "sleepy-eyed Celestials," "dimly-lit chophouses," "picturesque shops with *objets d'art* of teakwood and ivory," "eerie music of ethnic bands," "garish dragons of the festivals," and mysterious places that were no more, displaced by warehouses: the "House of a Hundred Rooms"; the Mission of Dr. Pu Shen Sang; the House of Choy Lum Gyan, "the little slave girl"; Gypsy Torrence's; and the "Joss house." After being "pushed into oblivion by Progress," Chinatown would rise again to its "past glory." During the convention week, the community planned to stage specific events to attract visitors to the quarter. A "Water Dragon festival of Lung Ju" (dragon parade down Race Street) was thought to "lure Convention visitors." The businesses also considered hiring actor troupes from New York and "dressing up store and restaurant attendants in picturesque garb" as well as installing street lighting in the "style of the bright-light sections of Hong Kong, Canton and other cities of China."[78] According to the *Record*, some of the older "bland-faced" men were against the measures, claiming that it was "commercializing tradition." Younger entrepreneurs, however, embraced the effort, according to King Thom, secretary of the Ling Yung Beneficial Association, who claimed, "We will have a native section which will rank with the Chinatowns of San Francisco and New York. The city will be proud of its Chinese colony." Here the merchants embodied the paradox of modernizing by evoking a premodern past, embracing progress by commodifying stereotypes of timeless antiquity. "Modernizing past glory" amounted to producing ethnic spectacle as self-representation and heritage.[79]

"A thing of the past"

"Past glory" might have referred as well to the increasing portrayal, in the 1920s and 1930s, of Chinatown as an "endangered enclave" that was on its way out. Ethnic marking was a mixed blessing; it generated income in the quarter but also perpetuated the community's economic and political marginalization, a marginalization that made the neighborhood more vulnerable during hard times. Accounts of Chinatown's impending demise were rife with familiar Orientalist themes, reproducing images of Chinatown as a picturesque premodern enclave that was destined to disappear with the forward march of modern urban progress.[80]

By the 1920s, the threat to Philadelphia's Chinatown came not from law enforcement or anti-vice efforts but from plans to create a new city and reform the urban landscape. These plans did not specifically target Chinatown, but they did indirectly affect the area by reshaping the needs for downtown land use. Like other working-class enclaves, Chinatown was antithetical to the early-twentieth-century designs for a "City Beautiful" that led to the displacement and transformation of some industrial neighborhoods, such as Bush Hill and Spring Garden, to make way for the Ben Franklin Parkway.[81] Nearby Market Street, by now dominated by major department stores, was an important destination for middle-class shoppers, throwing the squalor of neighborhoods to the north into high relief. Perhaps more influential was the increasing dominance of the automobile in urban life. In the 1920s, Philadelphia designated more than two hundred streets, including Race, as major one-way thoroughfares across the city; Race became a major artery to the Delaware Valley Bridge, begun in 1922 and completed in 1926. Increased need for parking lots and garages also claimed downtown real estate, including Chinatown.[82] In 1923, ten parcels on the southeast corner of Ninth and Race (900–922) were purchased by Bell Telephone Co. to be used for a new Bell building and an associated parking lot.

Later that year, the *Evening Bulletin* declared, "City's Chinatown Soon Only Memory: Modern Commerce Clawing at Heart of Area, While Residents Sit Unperturbed." Here "Commerce" was portrayed as a bird of prey whose "talons . . . are tearing the heart out of historic Chinatown."[83] Three years later, the paper pointed to "Dwindling Race Street Chinatown Doomed by Opening of Bridge. House of Hundred Rooms among Those to Vanish as Bland Orientals See Garage Rise on Site Where Pipes and Fan-Tan Flourished." This article concluded, "The Delaware River Bridge has come and Chinatown must go," echoing the anti-immigrant slogan, "The Chinese Must Go," of a previous generation. Chinatown was endangered, according to the *Bulletin*, by the "remorseless edict of commerce," since Race Street was a major artery to the bridge, "with value far above Joss houses and restaurants. And Commerce must be served." "The Chinese, in their slow, imperturbable way, are resisting the dictum with all their power," the paper observed, "but slowly their numbers are diminishing, slowly the foothold of the new force becomes stronger, and with increasing impetus, the inevitability of Chinatown's final disappearance is being borne in upon its inhabitants."[84]

In June 1928, the *Bulletin* once again claimed that Chinatown was now "Just a Memory," reporting that residents were opening their clubrooms to the public, "marking the Passage of Old Days":

> Those days when Chinatown figured violently in police news here and lured nocturnal slumming parties have passed. In the vicinity of Race and Ninth streets no one really marked its passing. It was just a transition. Many persons still visit what remains of Chinatown, a district of small shops with large storerooms adjoining restaurants, a mission and, tucked away out of sight of the stray visitor, a Chinese school. But the old Chinatown of dens for the "beautiful sleep," thrilling raids and flaming tong wars has vanished, pushed out of the picture by two restaurant agencies.

For the *Bulletin*, the "Chinatown" that was disappearing was an imagined place of ethnic vice and color, its demise attributed to "the economic demand for the land on which Chinatown had stood for sixty years," which now constituted the "direct arterial approach to the Delaware River Bridge."[85] This death sentence was predicated on a view of Chinatown as the Orientalist fantasy of the tong-war years.

By contrast, the Chinatown in which "Progress Killed Tradition" was now characterized by increasing Americanization: "Louis M. Yeck, restaurant owner said that among the 1000 Chinese at a recent banquet dozens of the diners, who twenty years ago might have worn queues and the garments of black silk, were attired in dinner jackets or evening clothes." The *Bulletin* claimed, "Two-thirds of the members [of the banquet's sponsoring association] no longer live in the narrow quarters of Chinatown, but reside in outlying sections of the city much in the American fashion." The paper lamented the passing of the old exotic enclave as it gave way to modernity and suburbanization: "What has become of the House of a Hundred Rooms? An auto parking place occupies the site, and where have the Chinese gone who once dwelt in congested Chinatown? Their Occidental neighbors do not know, except in the case of this or that individual. But they may be found in the outlying residential districts, not gathered clannishly as in old days, but living much as Americans of similar means live."[86]

Going along with progress, Chinatown was no longer Chinatown, "Playing Its Swan Song" in 1929.[87] The neighborhood had to be visibly marked and defined in ways that were recognizable to Philadelphians as Chinese. In 1934, the press once again sounded the death knell of Chinatown. In a short feature titled "Phila. Chinatown Soon To Be a Thing of the Past," the *Philadelphia Evening Bulletin* asserted, "Within a few years the paper dragon will not wriggle down Chinatown's part of Race Street on Chinese New Year, and sightseers no longer will be able to goggle into the dusty Chinese shops, seeing dope, dens, and beautiful blonde captives where there is only a grocery store. Philadelphia's Chinatown is almost a thing of the past."[88] Stripped of its savage, exotic Otherness, Chinatown could not exist in the larger public imagination, for it could not be seen. Chinatown did not exist if Chinese lived "much as Americans of similar means live" or started entrepreneurial ventures, such restaurant agencies, instead of sleepily smoking opium.

In the face of the repeated heralds of Chinatown's demise, Race Street remained a commercial district where a non-Chinese public could experience and consume essentialized Chinese difference throughout the 1930s and 1940s. But despite the public's attempts to imagine Chinatown's exoticism and local merchants' efforts to cash in on such longings, modern Chinatown's urban reality as an aging commercial district produced, as in these descriptions of Race Street in 1940, an uneven effect that often belied the exotic. David Cheng, a Penn sociologist who volunteered at the Chinese Christian Church and Center (CCC&C) in the early 1940s, notes the uneven effect:

> Chinatown is the center where the Peking, Golden-Fountain, Long How, Chung-King, South China, Shanghai Garden, and Far East restaurants cluster along the North side of Race Street, while Mei-Hung and Chopstick face them on the South side. These restaurants in Chinatown cater to Chinese customers and to the general American public who enjoys a Chinatown week-end adventure, not only to eat "chop-suey" and "chow mein" but also to watch the yellow "Chinaman" talk and act and to breathe an atmosphere pervaded by Oriental color, sound and symbolism. It is, in fact, these restaurant buildings that give Chinatown its Oriental color with their dragon lanterns and neon lights. Unfortunately much of it is defaced by the ugly fire-escapes which look very much out of place as any New Jersey bus rider would surely notice.[89]

By this time, Chinatown was already considered blighted, its older buildings deteriorating amid the remnants of the Tenderloin and the influences of Skid Row to the east.

Chinese immigrants had claimed a space within the city of Philadelphia. For more than five decades, they had occupied territory on the margins of the commercial district and transformed it into an identifiable home, a space safe from violence, harassment, and discrimination. They shaped the character of this space to their needs and marked the landscape with their celebrations and rituals, language, aesthetics, and commerce. The meaning of this landscape and its relationship to the larger city was fluid, often contested and always negotiated. Framed within an existing discourse of Orientalism, Chinatown's space was subject to surveillance, prescriptive interventions, and ambivalent public fascination. It was challenged by changing urban economic and physical imperatives. To the extent they could, Chinatown merchants relied on ethnic spectacle and "self-Orientalism" as a strategy for survival in changing times, even it if meant perpetuating an image of the enclave as a "thing of the past." During the midst of the Depression and the gradual decline of the surrounding district into blight and disrepair, the future of Chinatown was uncertain to many who lived and worked there. Chinatown was a thing of the past, but it had a future. Chinatown would be renewed, and this renewal would mark the transition of Chinatown to a contemporary urban village, a community that would thrive amid blight and decay, transformed into a home for new generations of Chinese American families.

2
"Chinatown was the safe space"

Community, Memory, and Place, 1940–1980

M ost afternoons in the 1970s, a teenage Brendan Lee and his friends could be found playing basketball or hanging out on the corner of Tenth and Spring Streets in Chinatown, outside Tuck Hing's grocery. "Everybody knew we were on the corner," he recalls. Tuck's provided a safe and central location for Chinatown's young people to gather and socialize because it was one of the few corners in the area in the 1960s and 1970s that was not occupied by a bar ("We didn't hang out on Ninth and Race because of the go-go bar") and because the owner left milk crates outside the storefront that functioned as informal seating:

> It was a neighborhood thing. . . . It was us at Tuck Hing's. We talked about anything and everything. The girls would meet us there too. We were at Tenth and Spring. Whenever we would do anything, we met at Tuck Hing's. . . . We met there; we socialized there; we hung out there. Every different part of the day, it was Tuck Hing's. No matter where we were going. Tuck Hing's was it.[1]

Tuck Hing's location was also strategic—along Tenth Street, the main street of Chinatown, and positioned at the northern entrance to the neighborhood: "We watched Chinatown; we were right outside of Spring, so it was a major corridor for people going back and forth: tourists, people coming from neighborhoods into Chinatown."[2]

Lee, now a retired Philadelphia city police officer, remembers conflict around the neighborhood boundary and harassment from non-Chinese:

Did people try to challenge us as they walked into Chinatown? Absolutely. We were sitting at Tuck Hing's or we were sitting in Chinatown as a group. . . . [W]hite guys and black guys come by and try and get smart with us and not think that we weren't gonna defend ourselves or react to it. . . . [W]e'd go into it—fistfighting. . . . Or they would try to be brave and a block away turn around and start "ching-chonging" us—seriously, that type of thing. And we went back down, and we were chasing them out of the neighborhood. . . . This is our turf and we watched it. We seriously watched it. And we were on the main corridor. . . . We had our interracial fights and stuff like that.[3]

Lee's experience hanging on the corner—a common and quintessential memory of urban life in Philadelphia's "city of neighborhoods"—also embodies the paradoxes of Chinatown as a landscape of danger and safety, blight and vibrancy. Lee's memories, like others', map Chinatown as ethnic territory, remembered space, and lived place.

During the period following World War II, the old "bachelor society" of Chinatown was transformed by new relationships, institutions, and spaces created to ensure that Chinatown was a "safe space" for immigrant workers and their families. Churches, playgrounds, and other spaces like Tuck's provided important antidotes to the bleak environment surrounding Chinatown, an environment that clearly posed other challenges besides the presence of Skid Row. These spaces became important sites in the creation of a sense of place in Chinatown in the second half of the twentieth century, as new immigration renewed a blighted area of the city into a community made meaningful by the presence of young people, families, churches, and new businesses as well as traditional Chinese organizations. For the Chinese American youth who grew up in Chinatown during the 1940s–1980s, the neighborhood became a powerful site of attachment and memory.[4]

"Kind of a derelict alley"

Chinatown was hardly the only Philadelphia neighborhood to undergo change after World War II. In 1940, the city in some ways remained as it had been formed by the nineteenth-century industrial order. Rigid segregation by ethnicity and race was tied to niche occupations and industries, particularly in North and South Philadelphia, areas that were destinations for several generations of immigrants from Southern and Eastern Europe. The boom and growth of the industrial years had waned in Philadelphia after a brief postwar boom, beginning a decades-long decline in the manufacturing base of the economy, accompanied by the transition to a service-based/professional economy that would come to characterize so many cities during the late twentieth century. In Philadelphia, the structure and location of major industries, such as textile manufacturing, shifted to the suburbs, the nonunionized South, and later abroad. The "inner-ring" immigrant neighborhoods, the site of most large- and small-scale manufacturing in the previous century, were most affected by these changes. In many cases, the ethnic identity of these areas disappeared or changed dramatically during this period.[5] Whites of many different ethnicities relocated to the Greater Northeast and suburbs outside the city, as the population of Philadelphia declined between 1960 and 1980 from 2.1 million to 1.7 million. Neighborhoods in North Philadelphia were hit hardest, losing an average of 40 percent of their population.[6] Simultaneously, the nonwhite population of Center City declined as city planners courted reinvestment in the city's downtown and minorities were displaced by redevelopment.

At the same time, the city witnessed an influx of African American and Puerto Rican migrants who changed the racial composition of many older immigrant neighborhoods, particularly in North and West Philadelphia. The economic decline of these neighborhoods was accompanied by an increase in racial strife as blacks moved into predominately white ethnic areas, encountering violence and harassment. Occupying neighborhoods in the midst of economic restructuring, many blacks and Latinos became "displaced labor migrants" as industries left. Now-minority neighborhoods were marked by stigma, subject to systematic disinvestment (through such practices as redlining) that fed a decline in homeownership (and an attendant rise in low-income rentals, absentee landlordism, and abandonment), undermining the economic and social bases of these areas. North Philadelphia bore the brunt of the worst overcrowding, unemployment, and intensive policing, a burden that heightened racial polarization and led to civil disturbances, most notably the Columbia Avenue riots in 1964. Civil-rights struggles for access to wartime jobs were transferred to struggles for resources and investment in newly segregated black ghettos.[7]

Chinatown was also a racially segregated immigrant neighborhood, but it witnessed these changes rather than participated directly in them. Lacking any industrial base in a local microeconomy that was long based in service and retail, Chinatown escaped the direct experience of deindustrialization and economic dislocation that reshaped so many other neighborhoods in the city in the 1960s–1980s. For Chinatown, these decades were an era of resurgence and growth. At a time when urban neighborhoods in Philadelphia experienced rapid racial and ethnic change, and the city an overall population loss, Chinatown remained stable and even expanded its population and physical boundaries. For Chinatown, the postwar flight from the inner city by white ethnics constituted an opportunity for Chinese to purchase property and invest in their own community for the first time. Certainly the physical boundaries of Chinatown expanded dramatically during this period, moving beyond 900 Race Street to adjacent North Tenth and Ninth Streets; north to Spring, Winter, Vine Streets, and beyond; and east and west to the 800 and 1000 blocks of Race Street. At the same time, Chinatown's situation as a disenfranchised immigrant enclave marked by a deteriorating physical environment made it vulnerable when redevelopment energies turned to downtown.

Although city agencies did not directly examine or officially designate Chinatown as such during this period, by all accounts it would have been considered a slum by the 1940s and 1950s. Aging building stock, cramped and deteriorating living conditions, a multitude of bars and brothels, and a large transient population all marked Chinatown as an undesirable urban environment. Many of the buildings in Chinatown dated to the previous century, some as early as the 1820s and 1830s, and they were considerably deteriorated by the 1940s. As described by David Cheng in 1944, the neighborhood was characterized by a "Salvation Army junk station" at Race and Eleventh, cheap hotels on Tenth Street and Race between Eighth and Ninth, a "fairly big burlesque theatre" (the Trocadero) at Arch and Tenth, and bars on the corners of Eleventh, Tenth, and Race Streets. The northern boundary of Chinatown on Vine Street was "surrounded by poor Negro residences with many empty lots," and Eighth and Vine was the "loafing place for idlers and bums," known as Skid Row.[8] The 1940 Census confirms this impression by the presence of many lodging houses and hotels populated by a predominately male (non-Chinese) population. The southeast corner of Spring and Tenth was the site of the Atlanta Hotel; North Ninth Street was peppered with lodging houses and flophouses for middle-aged and elderly men.[9] The area also sat at the intersection of several major thoroughfares through the city—namely, Race Street east to the Ben Franklin Bridge and Ninth Street northbound, where "once every half hour, a string of thundering buses pass through on their way to New Jersey by way of the Delaware Bridge."[10]

Those who lived and worked in Chinatown during the 1940s–1980s all remember blight as a central feature of the neighborhood, and many repeat the refrain of a "bar on every corner," especially at the intersection of Tenth and Race. Joseph Eng recalled the effect that so many bars had on the neighborhood:

You could smell beer joints all over. Eighth is Metropolitan Hospital now, [but] it used to be called the Tenderloin, which had a theater. Ten cents to see two main features, a cartoon, and a coming attraction for a dime. Bars were all over Chinatown. The four corners on Tenth and Race were called merry-go-round; you could smell the beer all around. My church was right next to a saloon, and before you went up the steps on 1006 [1006 Race, the Baptist Church] where I went to learn ABCD, you could always smell it.[11]

George Moy echoes the overpowering presence of the bars in this area:

> At that time, [on] every corner and in the middle of the block were
> bars. On Ninth Street, there was at least three. One in the middle of
> the block on the west side. One on the east side of Ninth Street, [and]
> up toward Vine Street there was a bar with what they call a flophouse.
> In fact, there was another bar at Spring, Ninth and Spring. And on
> Tenth Street, all four corners were bars. A little south of Race Street on
> Tenth on the east side was a bar. On Eleventh Street, there was a bar at
> Winter Street. I forget what existed before they tore it down—on the
> north side of actually Winter Street. But there were at least 10 bars.[12]

Wai Lum (William) Chin, who immigrated from Hong Kong in 1964, described the eastern edge of Chinatown: "The most memorable thing from my
early days was Ninth Street. There were only abandoned houses and a lot of
drunks, bars, and homeless people around."[13]

For Debbie Wei, traveling into Chinatown on the weekends with her
family in the 1970s evoked a sense of cultural familiarity mixed with environmental caution:

> I grew up in Upper Darby, and my earliest memories of Chinatown
> were just going there to shop, because that's where we went every
> week. There was a little grocery store on Ninth Street, and my mom
> used to go there faithfully and get the groceries that she would need
> for the week and stuff like cleavers. . . . I remember my parents not
> wanting me to go out, like I had to hang in the store, and the store
> was crowded. . . . [M]y parents didn't want me to run around outside
> because there were bums. . . . [I]t was kind of a skeezy neighborhood.[14]

Harry Leong, now the director of the Chinese Christian Church and Center
(CCC&C), also remembers the neighborhood as "kind of a derelict alley":

> About the sixties and seventies, I just remember looking down the
> street and often seeing hobos, bums, or whatever you want to call it—
> they used to be all around the community. And very distinctive was
> almost every corner had a bar. There was a bar, like, at Tenth and Race,
> which [was] at one point considered the heart of Chinatown—the four
> corners were all bars, and then slowly they kind of trickled out, to
> where all the bars closed down. We had an open lot across the street
> from my house, and in the lot were tires, so we would spend hours—
> literally hours—playing in the lot with tires. I got hit by a police car
> when I was four or five.[15]

The only public space where Chinatown children could play was neglected Franklin Square, known by all as "Bum's Park." The neighborhood had no city recreation center, public school, or formal park. A 1974 *Inquirer* feature portrayed the neighborhood as menaced by the shadows of Skid Row: "Evening deepens and gradually one's sense of the place changes," highlighting the presence of belligerent drunks accosting tourists and women soliciting Johns outside 150 Bar on Tenth and Race. The feature reported that the Pennsylvania Crime Commission found that of forty-seven "bar girls" found in Central Division (Center City), nearly thirty operated in three bars at Tenth and Race Streets: 150 Bar, Bridge Bar, and Chick's Bar. Prostitutes took their customers to a hotel at 224 North Tenth Street.[16]

But those who grew up in Chinatown remember feeling safe and cared for by their community. "Everybody felt very, very safe growing up as a kid," according to Lee:

Chinatown had a go-go bar. I remember growing up with that. . . . [T]he barber shop that I went to was originally on Ninth Street, right next to all the bars. So, yeah, there were guys in the street passed out, and there was a liquor store on Ninth Street—besides the bars. . . . Yeah, there was guys passed out and sleeping, bottles all over the place. . . . Nothing ever happened. Like, the guys who went there were there to drink—no one did harm to a kid.[17]

Much of this safety was due to the small size and familiarity of community residents and businesspeople who watched out for young people. Leong describes the neighborhood as a "tight-knit" community: "Our neighborhood was fairly small and pretty tight-knit and if you did anything bad, your brothers or sisters would know about it; then you'd be in trouble. . . . [T]he parents were focused on working, and that's prevalent among many families where the parents are really focused on their careers or their professions are cooks, restaurant workers, and sewing operators."[18] John Chin's memories echo common feelings about the neighborhood's being small and familiar:

It felt like a very small neighborhood. We basically knew everybody in the neighborhood at that time; this is during the seventies. And you were literally afraid to misbehave at any point in time; I mean it's true, because at any point in time, a neighbor might catch you doing something, [and] you did not want that neighbor calling your parents up. And all the kids knew each other's parents, and my parents felt comfortable enough that I could go off on my own to my friend's house without them walking me across the street. There was a lot less people, a lot less traffic.[19]

Chinatown was a neighborhood where one grew up "knowing every-body on the block and everybody knowing you, whether you liked it or not," according to Glenn Hing, who now practices law on Ninth Street. He recalls: "I'm not going to say it was a nice neighborhood; it just happened to be down-town Philadelphia, but it was—it had a very small-town feel but in a big-town situation. It was a pretty tight-knit community; it was a very safe community. . . . [L]ife was a lot simpler, like everything else. We never locked our doors, I never had a key to my house, but then again, we didn't need it."[20] Lee also remembers: "We never locked the doors of our home. I lived literally twenty-five yards from Tenth and Spring, so I would just walk up, and my door would be open all twenty-four hours a day, unlocked. That's how it was back then."[21]

Most Chinatown residents understood that the blighted nature of the neighborhood was tied closely to the historic exclusion of Chinese from par-ticipation in the larger society; Chinese, constrained by prejudice and vio-lence, chose to live in an area of the city where few wanted to dwell. As Moy points out: "I guess you kind of accepted it. 'That's the way life was' kind of thing. I'd point out that our people were forced to live in that area because nobody else would invite us in their area. If we tried to establish a Chinatown at that time, say, down in South Philadelphia, there probably would have been a lot of resistance. Or any [other] parts of the city."[22]

Despite the challenges of blight and urban neglect, Chinatown endured as an important spatial and cultural center for Chinese (and later other Asians) in the region, a safe cultural and social space. Kenneth Eng experienced this safety as a new immigrant in the 1970s: "People just knew each other, we played ball together, we hung out together—it was never a major problem, like crime and stealing. I could walk in Chinatown and feel safe; I felt safe even late at night."[23] This role as a safe haven grew as more Chinese and other Asians immigrated to the greater Philadelphia area, settling in other city neighbor-hoods and the surrounding suburbs. According to Wei, "The Asian popula-tion still viewed Chinatown as a place to go to get familiar foods, a place to go where you felt kind of safe. . . . Even back then, there was something that drew Asians across ethnicity together. . . . [T]he fact [is] that Chinatown was the safe space."[24]

World War II: A Turning Point

Chinatown's role as a central safe space for Chinese and other Asian immi-grants was renewed, after several decades of decline, in the period during and after World War II, which was a major turning point for Chinese Americans. The war and its aftermath engendered more sympathetic attitudes toward Chinese Americans, opportunities for citizenship, new immigration, and community growth.[25] As China shifted in its relationship to the United States, so too did Chinese Americans see a small shift in public attitudes about their communities. In the decade before the U.S. entry into World War II, Chinese and Chinatown existed largely under the radar of mainstream Philadelphia, thought of merely as a dying vice district. As China became a site of conflict in East Asia, however, the local media turned to the people who lived in Chinatown for perspective and local color. Chinatown residents watched events abroad with anxiety and organized to help their homeland. The 1937 invasion of China by Japan sent the local media into Chinatown to highlight Chinese Americans' campaign for China War Relief. In January 1938, community leaders canceled the Chinese New Year parade and celebration so that the saved expenses could be sent to the Chinese Defense Fund. Many Chinatown merchants also organized a boycott of Japanese goods.[26]

When the United States later entered World War II, China's position as an ally engendered a more positive image of Chinese Americans and their contribution to the war effort, highlighting for Philadelphians the presence of Chinese Americans in their midst. According to Mitzie Mackenzie, a social worker who kept extensive notes on the community, 108 of Chinatown's men, some nearing age forty, fought in the armed forces during World War II to gain American citizenship.[27] Young residents of Chinatown joined the armed services, including Henry Wong, the twenty-year-old son of Chinatown "Mayor" Wong Wah Ding and a student at the Wharton School at the University of Pennsylvania. The elder Wong noted the contradiction inherent in his son's service in the face of continued Chinese exclusion: "I cannot become a citizen myself because of the law," he said, "but I am happy that my only son is giving his services to the country I love best."[28]

Working as a busboy at a Howard Johnson's in 1942, Joseph Eng experienced the change in attitudes toward Chinese after Pearl Harbor:

One day in the afternoon, about round two o'clock in the afternoon, one of the men speak up. "Hey"—speaking to the waitress—"that boy over there, is he Chinese or Japanese?" The waitress said proudly, "That's our Chinese friend." And you know that man want me to come over to his table, and everybody—the six of them—come in and shook my hand. And I was surprised. He said, "Didn't you hear the news?" He said the Japanese had just bombed Pearl Harbor and declared war on the United States. "You are our friends. You are *my* friend." Everybody shook my hand.[29]

Like many young male residents of Chinatown, Eng served in the armed forces during the war. After the war, Eng married and brought his Chinese wife to the United States. He studied to be an electrician on the GI Bill, eventually landing a job at the Philadelphia Navy Shipyard; he was the first Chinese American ever hired there, and he worked there until his retirement.[30] For Eng and others, Pearl Harbor and the onset of World War II was a "turning point."

This new goodwill engendered by the war did not necessarily translate into new occupational or residential opportunities for all Chinese. For those who encountered occupational and residential barriers, Chinatown was still a refuge from discrimination and an economic fallback.[31] While Eng found opportunity through the GI Bill, he recalls another friend who was less successful: "One guy, Jack Voy . . . he was the one and only Chinese graduate from UP, University of Pennsylvania. But he took the diploma, went over to RCA, GE—all that company—put the application in. None of them called him. He get so mad, he come back to Chinatown and open a gift shop—Fong Chung Company."[32] For others, Chinatown was a landing place for returning Chinese American GIs, like Dun Mark, who came back to Chinatown in 1945 and lived with his brother on Ninth Street while he worked as a waiter at Shanghai Garden and trained to be an electrical engineer.[33]

Opening the Gates

While the war created new attitudes toward and opportunities for Chinese American GIs, even more dramatic changes resulted from revisions to U.S. immigration laws that opened up immigration and allowed new Chinese American citizens to marry and bring families from China. The population of Chinatown had been declining before the war while also changing in character. In 1900, for example, 249 Chinese lived in Chinatown; by 1920, the number had declined to 144. But by war's end, the Chinese population of Philadelphia was estimated at 1,300, about one-fourth of whom lived in Chinatown (325) and about three-fourths of whom were Chinese born. The population likewise changed in composition as more nuclear families became part of the community: nuclear families numbered five in 1910, nine in 1920, seventeen in 1930, and twenty by 1940. New postwar immigration expanded the resident population and continued the trend toward nuclear families.

The formation of families in Chinatown was facilitated by changes in U.S. immigration laws during and after the war. These changes ushered in a new era in Chinatown increasing the presence of families, women, and youth.[34] Passage of the Magnuson Act in 1943 repealed the Chinese Exclusion Act and made citizenship available to Chinese for the first time. Chinese American servicemen were granted citizenship, and a 1945 War Brides Act, which permitted immigration of foreign wives, husbands, fiancés, and children of U.S. Army personnel, made it possible for Chinese American men to marry and bring wives from China. The population of Chinatown burgeoned, and the community increasingly took on the character of a family community. Two decades later, in 1965, the Hart Celler Act removed the old "national origins" quota system and opened immigration from China to the United States in substantial ways for the first time. Emphasizing family reunification and the importation of skilled and technical labor (as well as provisions for refugees), the law fed a new wave of immigration from Asia, including many Chinese from Hong Kong, Taiwan, and, later, Vietnam and Cambodia. New immigrants were laborers and entrepreneurs looking to start a variety of businesses as well as a growing number of students and professionals (entering under the new H1B visa category). Under these changes, the population of Chinese and other Asians in Philadelphia and elsewhere exploded. By 1980, the city of Philadelphia was home to 17,764 Asians (4,987 of whom were Chinese), while the larger metropolitan region was 34,781 (7,964 Chinese).[35] After passage of the Refugee Act of 1980, ethnic Chinese from Vietnam resettled as refugees joined new immigrants in Chinatown. In 1980, 2,038 Vietnamese lived in Philadelphia (but only a fraction—24—lived in Chinatown); that number in Philadelphia would double twice over in the next two decades. This growth came with an even larger increase in Asian immigration overall during this period, including immigrants from China, most of whom settled outside Chinatown.

The rise in immigration during the postwar period renewed Chinese American commitment to the Chinatown area, leading to geographic expansion as well. During the late 1940s and 1950s, Chinatown gradually expanded beyond Race Street to encompass the surrounding blocks of Winter, Spring, Tenth, and Ninth Streets. By the late 1960s and early 1970s, families were living north of Vine Street, according to residents' memories. While Ninth and Tenth Streets retained the mixed-use template that characterized much of Chinatown, Winter and Spring introduced a more residential feeling to the neighborhood, for these streets were occupied primarily by single families in row homes. In 1940, Winter Street was home to widow Ann Lee (1031) and her seven children and another widow, Susie Lee (915), her two children, and an adult male cousin. Merchant William Mark moved from his business address at 935 Race to a single-family home at 911 Spring. There he joined several other Chinese families who had relocated from Race: Bingwah Young and his family (who like Mark moved from 903 Race to 915 Spring) and the Moy family at 919, who had lived there at least since 1930 (the house had been Chinese since 1920, previously home to Mock Lye and his family). Ray Jung's family also relocated from Race Street, to a home on 213 Tenth Street that accommodated eleven lodgers from his extended family.[36] These families illustrate the growing prosperity of Chinese families, who now had means to move from the upper floors of commercial addresses on Race Street to single-family homes on adjacent streets.

Chinese Americans likewise made a significant push to acquire property in the Chinatown area during the 1940s and 1950s. Associations purchased parcels on Race and adjoining streets; in 1947, the On Leong Association bought 911–913 Race Street, and the Tung Oh Association bought 129–131 North Tenth Street. In 1955, the Hip Sing Association obtained 932, 934, and 938 Race Street. A newly organized Chinese Benevolent Association purchased its headquarters at 930 Race in 1957. Individuals and families also bought homes in the area and rehabilitated a number of properties. Moy's mother purchased lots at 832, 834, 836, and 838 Race in the early 1940s. In many cases, the structures on these properties were more than one hundred years old, suffering from deferred maintenance and deterioration. "They needed a lot of work," Moy recalls. "I remember putting a whole new floor in, joist flooring, stairways. Rebuilding, really, because we would add a whole second floor . . . rebuilding the whole house almost. I and my brother worked on the four houses that we owned, put a whole new heating system in, whole new plumbing system in, out to the street and all that." Moy took up residence at 836 Race, and the family ran a hardware store out of 834, renting out the remainder of the building.[37] Dun Mark moved back to Chinatown after serving in the military, going to college, and marrying. He purchased two homes on Spring Street in 1954, renting one and living in the other. For Mark, Chinatown was the only place to settle permanently, since his wife, who had recently arrived from China, did not speak English:

> After I got married, come back, I finish college, got a job with RCA, and I spent I think it was fourteen years with RCA. So I got a good job, and I'm working—why would I move? Where am I going? And Chinatown [was] pretty nice. Close to everything. Lit Brothers, Gimbel's— remember those stores? Snellenberg's. All around the area within walking distance. My wife, she [was] just beginning to learn a little bit of English, but it was good for her, because she could go out buying things she wanted. That's why we stay[ed] on. . . . I could move to New Jersey with a couple friends of mine that I knew for long time back at RCA. They bought houses over there, but I couldn't do it. I would love to go there, but I wouldn't do it because [of] my wife. She wouldn't be happy because she couldn't speak with the neighbor, and it's tough for her. Here she go next door and yak, yak, yak, walk downtown, know everybody, see mostly Chinese people.[38]

The 900 block of Spring Street became a concentrated block of Chinese-owned residences in the 1950s, according to Mark: "The whole street was bought by Chinese people."[39]

New immigration renewed Chinatown's commitment to China and Hong Kong, fostering an exponential growth in businesses—not only restaurants but also grocery stores, gift shops/bookstores, and a variety of services—during the period between 1960 and 1980. Other immigrants sought work in growing numbers of garment factories located in Chinatown by the late 1960s. With new settlement came new family businesses—many of them restaurants and gift shops: Magic Fan, Dragon Gate, China Castle, and Lotus Inn were some of the most popular and well-known establishments that catered to American

tastes. John Chin's parents, like many, opened a restaurant, Happy Garden.
The growth of restaurants, coincident with the decline in the hand-laundry
business, also opened Chinatown to a greater level of consumption by non-
Chinese Philadelphians, who were the primary clientele for such establishments. As early as 1955, the *Inquirer* noted a new image for the neighborhood:
"The restaurants in Chinatown have a different look. Oriental writing, pictures and lanterns are suddenly around. The place is ever so slightly beginning
to look like Chinatown again."[40] In 1951, a chapter of the Chinese Benevolent
Association was created in Philadelphia as an umbrella organization for the
many trade and family associations, to mediate conflicts and assist immigrants with housing and other services. It also organized traditional cultural
events, sponsoring an annual Chinese New Year celebration.

Many Chinese immigrants increasingly settled not in Chinatown—which
had limited housing to accommodate them by the 1960s—but in the suburbs
or other parts of the city, such as South, West, or Northeast Philadelphia. But,
like laundrymen before them, they gravitated to Chinatown on weekends.
Sunday continued to be an important day in Chinatown, as Chinese from
around the area came to shop, worship, dine, and socialize. According to Wai
Man Ip, who now owns three stores in Chinatown, new immigrants could find
familiar ways in Chinatown:

Vietnamese Chinese were used to shopping in the streets. When they
first came here, they didn't know English; so on Saturdays and Sundays, they all rushed to Chinatown to buy rice or flour in bags of all
sizes. I was really happy when I saw this happening. There were so
many Chinese. All of Chinatown started to change. After people had
been here for some time, things became stable.[41]

The transnational sensibilities of new immigrants were bolstered by the
opening of relations between China and the United States during the Nixon
administration in 1972, which enabled greater freedom of movement for
people, ideas, and goods between the two nations. Ip remembers the change:

Chinatown at that time was very barren. The buildings were all
dilapidated, some were just old. There were very few shops. I could
remember only three.... As for restaurants, there were nine or ten....
Chinatown was so small.... Not long after I arrived in the States, in
1979, we started our first bookstore. There wasn't much to sell—mainly
magazines from Hong Kong. We hoped that people who worked in the
restaurants and didn't speak English would buy some.... Later *Sing
Tao* [a New York–based Chinese-language newspaper] learned that
we were selling magazines in Philly. They were interested in doing
business, saw our bookstore, and asked us if we would be interested

in becoming their sole agent. They had papers sent in every day from New York. We were the first to distribute their paper.[42]

This growth, while perpetuating long-held class divides in the community between poorer working families and more prosperous businesspeople, also renewed the Chinatown landscape and connections with China, a trend that would continue into the 1990s and 2000s with new immigration from Fujian.[43] Resettlement of refugees from Vietnam diversified the ethnic landscape of Chinatown, particularly in terms of restaurants, even as the bulk of this settlement occurred in West and South Philadelphia.

"Loyalty to a place can be developed": Spaces of Community, Attachment, and Memory

The new immigrants of the 1960s, 1970s, and 1980s came to a Chinatown that was different in character from that of a previous generation. From the 1940s to the 1960s, new relationships, institutions, and spaces had developed to ensure that Chinatown was a "safe space" for immigrant working families. Churches and cultural organizations started programs to address the needs of community residents, to improve neighborhood life, preserve Chinese culture, and provide services to new immigrants and growing numbers of Chinese American youth. These ventures were created in part to reform and intervene in the perceived deficits of the Chinatown community, deficits shaped historically by the marginalization and essentialized difference of Asian immigrants. Such programs would ensure the Americanization and assimilation of Chinese, particularly youth, and create an environment of "sanitized exoticism" that allowed for tourism and engagement with the larger society. Yet at the same time, these organizations and the relationships they fostered contributed to the perception that many long-time residents and former residents share—that Chinatown of this period was a tightly knit community where everyone knew each other, providing a safe haven for residents despite persistent blight.[44]

Churches played a vital role in providing services to a community largely ignored by the city, as Hing recalls: "We would hang out on the corner, primarily because there was no place to hang out. Chinatown never had the benefit of community centers, rec centers. Our recreational facilities were provided for by the churches."[45] The two churches that became central to the community in the 1940s and 1950s (and remain so today) were Holy Redeemer Chinese Catholic Church and School, at Tenth and Vine, and the Chinese Christian Church and Center (CCC&C) at 1006 Race Street, later Tenth and Spring Streets. Both these churches created spaces that became central in Chinatown residents' sense of place, community, and collective identity.

Figure 2.1. Opening of Holy Redeemer Chinese Catholic Church, 1940. (Holy Redeemer Photographs, Photogroup 120, Historical Society of Pennsylvania.)

Holy Redeemer, or "HR," as it is fondly referred to by community members, had its genesis in a 1939 visit by Bishop Paul Yu Pin, then vicar of Nanking, China. The church formally opened its doors in 1941, the first Chinese Catholic Church in the Western Hemisphere (see Figure 2.1). Holy Redeemer grew to play a large role in the lives of several generations of young Chinese who grew up in Chinatown from the 1940s through the 1970s. It was the only school in the neighborhood and the only gymnasium. Long-time resident Dun Mark recalls the impact of the church's opening:

When they opened up the church in here, all the kids come in, go to school for free. Father Cavanaugh is the one that open[ed] the place. He was a great guy. Oh, very great. All my kids, most [of] my older kids, didn't have to pay tuition . . . [the school] was supported from the church itself. And that's [the] main reason. The second thing is, we keep the church open in the evening, for the kids to come in instead of walking around the street and get[ting] into different kinds of things. They come here, they play basketball at night. They play games. So, lots of Chinese people come here.[46]

The *Philadelphia Inquirer* echoed the openness of the church in providing resources to neighborhood youth in the late 1940s:

> Every afternoon and evening Holy Redeemer center is over-run by neighborhood children and Chinese young people from Philadelphia high schools and universities. Father Sailer makes it a point to provide all facilities possible to the young people in the imposing center, where in addition to a beautiful chapel and class rooms, there are a spacious gym, club rooms, a game room and all other needed facilities.[47]

These facilities addressed a vital need for space in the community, particularly space for youth activities.

Early on, the church hosted a youth group, the Yu Pin Club, which sponsored a variety of activities aimed at Chinese American youth. Weekly activities in the 1940s and 1950s included bowling, skating, flute and singing lessons, and Sunday-evening dances. The club also published a newsletter, the *Chinese Lantern*, which reported on the successes of athletic teams, various club activities, and social gossip. In December 1948, for example, the *Lantern* carried news about a checker tournament, the institution of a weekly Saturday-night dance for "outsiders" with twenty-five-cent admission, and theatricals starring, among others, Herbert Jung and Cecilia Hing (later Cecilia Moy Yep). An annual Chinese New Year dance was held in the Holy Redeemer auditorium (in 1948, music was provided by Bill Hammersley and His Orchestra). Many activities fostered relationships with Chinese clubs in other eastern cities, particularly New York and Washington. In June 1949, members of the Yu Pin Club undertook a bus trip to New York as the guests of the Chinese Community Club for annual field-day exercises, dinner, and a dance. Yu Pin organized men's and women's basketball, football, and baseball teams. The lot adjacent to the church (now the church parking lot) was a baseball field.

Basketball for both boys and girls became a primary sport. According to Joe Lowe, who grew up in the neighborhood in the 1960s, basketball was "the sport of choice—or the sport of survival," and it was played at the only gym in the neighborhood, Holy Redeemer's: "Most of my activity was done at Holy Redeemer. Holy Redeemer for me was where I went to school, where I played constantly during the summer. HR was always open at all hours. The gym was there, that was always open to us. We like to think it was 24/7, [but] I'm sure we were disobeying some kind of rules, [because] we were in there all the time."[48] Brendan Lee remembers spending weekends at Holy Redeemer ("from Friday night to Saturday afternoon, we were at HR") honing his skills. At HR, Lee and others were schooled by older brothers and friends (Brendan's older brother Kevin introduced him to the game) who taught them a form of tough street ball that emphasized fast footwork, intricate passing, and long outside shots (since players who were often shorter of stature found it difficult to get to the net). They played all comers, including a team composed entirely of waiters who would join them on the court on Saturday mornings.[49] The HR Chinatown team played in the city's Catholic league and faced basketball teams from other Chinatowns along the northeast coast: New York, Boston, Baltimore, and Washington, DC. The first annual basketball tournament was held in April 1949, hosting clubs from New York and Washington in the HR gymnasium.[50] Like dances and other church activities, sports drew second-generation youth into a larger network of relationships outside the Chinatown community.

Basketball was also a favorite sport at the CCC&C, where Gilbert Lum, a young American-born Chinese minister from San Francisco, acted as coach in the early 1950s. Founded as a mission center in 1941, the CCC&C was the ecumenical creation of the American Baptist Churches (USA), the Episcopal Church, the Evangelical and Reformed denomination (presently United Church of Christ), the United Methodist Church, and the Presbyterian Church (USA), united in a concerted evangelical effort to form an interdenominational board of directors for the purpose of supporting mission outreach among Chinese. This led to the official incorporation of the CCC&C in July 1946, together with the purchase of the current premises, at Tenth and Spring Streets, for a new church building in 1947.[51] In 1949, Pastor Lum inaugurated a building campaign during his tenure, resulting in the construction of a physical church at that location that opened in 1952.

Prior to 1952, the church operated out of the center at 1006 Race, the site of a former Baptist mission. In many ways, the center remained the heart and soul of the CCC&C's community presence, particularly for youth, under the direction of Maribelle "Mitzie" Mackenzie. Although not a resident of Chinatown, Mackenzie was involved in many aspects of Chinatown life, knew the stories of many of the families in the neighborhood, and was a tireless and beloved advocate for the community until her death in 2009. She fell into the job in the early 1940s: "After graduation, I got a letter saying, 'Would you mind going down to Chinatown and start something?' so I was given the key to 1006 Race Street, which used to be a Chinese mission Sunday School. . . . My mission was to make them Americans. The first thing we did was have a girls' club, where they learned how to cook American dishes to introduce to their parents."[52] Under Mackenzie's leadership, the center adopted an "open-door" policy and sponsored Girl Scout and Boy Scout troops, tutoring, and recreation (the center had billiards and ping-pong tables). It offered a variety of programs for youth and adults, as illustrated by the "Weekly Program of the Church and Center" included in the program for the October 3, 1954, World Wide Communion Service, which details a variety of activities, including English classes for adults, little girls' and boys' clubs, crafts and recreation for children, teenage "Y," young people's night, and a women's association meeting. On the following Sunday, a special worship service "commemorate[d] the founding of the Chinese Republic" with the Ten Ten celebration.[53] The center also offered cooking classes and provided polio shots during the 1950s. Throughout her tenure, Mackenzie offered assistance to community members on immigration matters, helping new war brides adjust and keeping up with resident alien registrations from the 1940s through the 1970s, noting the families' situations in her records.[54]

Like other missionaries before her, Mackenzie drew on the exhibition of Chinese culture and people to promote her community work. The center mounted an annual "China Night," a play, often penned by Mackenzie, which drew on symbols and stories from an imagined ancient China and was performed by the center kids. China Night became an important fund-raiser for the center's programs in the 1950s. In 1951, for example, $1,174.55 was raised by the "Legend of the Willow Plate."[55] China Night also served, through the display of Chinese American youth, as a manifestation of an older exhibitionary impulse: "Being the only Protestant work among the Chinese in Philadelphia we get a great number of calls for our young people or children to 'make an appearance' in the Caucasian churches. In answer to those calls and for many other reasons an annual 'China Night' program has been presented during the past eight years."[56]

Perhaps the most utilized and valued contribution CCC&C made to the community landscape was its "playground ministry," inaugurated in 1954 with the construction of a playground at Tenth and Spring adjacent to the newly constructed church.[57] Pointing to the success of the gymnasium at Holy Redeemer, the Reverend Lum observed, "The lack of recreational facilities in Chinatown is one of the causes for poor physical and personal development. There is a lack of opportunities in various sport activities which should be introduced at the grammar school level. The Roman Catholics have a 10 year jump on us in providing this recreational space. They also have many more times the space that we will hope to have for our children." What was required then was a space connected to the church, a "children's room, back yard and fair size recreation room" to "meet the needs of the children." Because "all our sport activities are held away from the church," Lum concluded, even a "playing pastor" could not compensate for the lack of dedicated space. The goal of the playground was "fellowship in play," through hosted recreational activities, such as badminton, volleyball, and basketball. Being on the court, "fellows 'hand around' the basketball court or in other words are *in* the church." Activities would then also engender a sense of connection not only to the playground but to the church as a meaningful place in Chinatown: "Loyalty to a *place* can be developed and easily identified with the organization (Jr Hi Club) and then transferred to the Church. With more attractive recreational facilities, more individuals of this group will 'drop in,' thus a chance for personal guidance. There will be more dates to be made in 'Meet you at the Church to play.'"[58]

This playground, expanded in the 1960s, provided additional space for recreation "for the people of the 'Chinatown' neighborhood" as well as members of the CCC&C and their families.[59] This small playground was used to capacity in serving the needs of both children and adults in the community. In 1965, for example, the newsletter noted, "The playground was very successful this year. Some of the waiters from Chinatown restaurants made use of the playground as late as 10–12 midnight since they came after work."[60] On several occasions, Spring Street was closed for special recreational programs and neighborhood events. In a neighborhood that had no public community center, park, or recreational facilities, the church playground effectively functioned as public space for Chinatown residents and workers.

Although Mackenzie had no prior interest in or connection to anything Chinese, she made the center an important place in the local geography of the neighborhood, transcending its original, narrower missionary orientation. Generations of young people passed through the center doors, and many remember her kindness and involvement in the neighborhood. Harry Leong, Mackenzie's successor at the center, recalls: "She really cared for our people in this community that no one really cared for. Particularly in the fifties, with just the war brides, and she had to deal with all that, and then this area, where it was Skid Row, basically."[61] Kenneth Eng remembers the center's open-door policy and Mackenzie's assistance with new immigrants: "You could come in, she's there, there's a basement, there's a ping-pong table, pool table—you could do whatever you want and she let you do it, as long as you found a place. And I remember my family had just settled here, [so] if I had a question about school, a question about a job, she always helped."[62] Mackenzie was known to walk around the Chinatown neighborhood in the early-morning hours, looking for "lonely people."[63] Her success was based in her unabashed love of the community residents. She always learned and remembered Chinese names and made a point of getting to know as many people in the neighborhood as possible. Eng recalls:

> I didn't meet her at the center; I met her on the street. Other people introduced me to her; people say, "This is a person you need to know." ... So, who is this lady around town that everybody so respected? This is Chinatown, right? And long, long, long after that, I find out that she'd been there for a while and people really loved her, not just lip service. I mean, I would get to know her every time I walked into Chinatown. It would take hours to walk through Chinatown. We used to walk. She used to stay in [the] Chinatown playground until real late at night; the time was different then. ... [W]e used to walk up to Eighth and Market Train Station; it took a while to walk to the train station because she [was] stopped by people. We would come up to her and say, "How are you?" ... [W]e look back and it's funny, because how many people really take that long to walk?[64]

At Mackenzie's request, when the church building expanded to incorporate the center in 1989, double glass doors were installed to allow visibility from a main office that faced the entrance, so that she could observe what was happening outside, reiterating her commitment to the neighborhood's public street life.[65] Her involvement in the community made her the embodiment of CCC&C for many, an important site of community meaning and nostalgia.

The activities sponsored by Holy Redeemer and CCC&C and other activities were central in the creation of a sense of attachment to Chinatown as a meaningful homeplace. They also actively cultivated a hybrid second-generation identity and experience that was both Chinese and American. Commenting on "Chinatown's American youth," in a 1948 feature on Chinatown, *Philadelphia Magazine* observed, "It is apparent that Chinatown's young blood is striving to Americanize itself. It finds it is no longer limited to a career in a laundry. Some of the young people are in business, some in industry and about 150 are in universities and colleges somewhere in eastern United States."[66] Both Holy Redeemer and CCC&C offered Chinese American youth a chance to participate in mainstream American pastimes. And unlike traditional Chinatown associations and the Chinese Benevolent Association, these new community organizations were gender and age inclusive, catering resources to women and children. CCC&C actively reached out to assist new Chinese war brides during the late 1940s and 1950s, and the bulk of its space, like Holy Redeemer's, was devoted to youth activities. These spaces, and the identities they engendered, embodied an evolution in the power structures of traditional Chinatown toward the inclusion of women, youth, and the second generation.[67]

"A meeting place for the occidental and oriental communities"

If Holy Redeemer, CCC&C, and other sites served and fostered a second-generation Chinese American experience within the community, the Chinese Cultural and Community Center (CC&CC) at 125 North Tenth Street, established in 1955 by T. T. Chang as an outgrowth of the YMCA, focused on cultivating traditional Chinese culture for outsiders. In addition to general recreation, this center cosponsored, with the Chinese Benevolent Association, a Dragon Club that trained youth in the performance of the traditional lion dance.[68] Chang actively portrayed himself, and was seen outside the community, as a Chinese American go-getter and change agent. Morley Cassidy, a columnist at the *Philadelphia Inquirer*, described Chang in 1958 as "a deceptively mild mannered fireball who organized and runs this branch of the Y, [and] had assembled a representative group of Philadelphia's Chinese community who are active in this effort to help Chinese get to know each other and other Philadelphians."[69] Three years earlier, Chang had come to the notice of the *Inquirer* as a "smart cookie" who "spurs fortunes." According to Cassidy, Chang immigrated to the United States in 1952 after serving as director of personnel for Chiang Kai-shek in China. Seeking to establish pro-American bona fides for a recent immigrant during the Cold War, Cassidy took pains to explain that Chang served in the forces against Japan in World War II and fled communism in China after the war. Chang's involvement with the YMCA movement overseas led to an association with the organization stateside.

Chang's stated goal was to promote a positive image of Philadelphia's Chinatown aimed at counteracting older stereotypes and addressing blight in the community, particularly what he described as the presence of "slumlike" conditions. According to Chang, "The Center would promote interracial and international understanding by serving as a meeting place for the occidental and oriental communities in Philadelphia." Chang also claimed the center would spur business activity in Chinatown: "The Cultural Center will not only serve as a tourist attraction, but will stimulate a 'Do it Yourself' type of redevelopment in Chinatown and further the development of Chinatown businesses."[70] In a 1965 report on the Chinatown Y, Chang characterized the neighborhood as a "slum" that "cries out for redevelopment" and a fractured community that "despite its outward appearance of clannish cohesiveness" was "divided and debilitated by language, dialectical and racial differences, lack of recreational facilities, anxiety caused by uncertain legal immigration status and the unhappiness caused by separation from family groups behind the Bamboo Curtain." He noted that although the strength of the Chinese family system and the teaching of Confucian traditions of filial piety and respect for elders "keep the rate of juvenile delinquency low[,] . . . living in slum conditions as they now are with few activities, young people in the area could easily become prey to juvenile delinquency." For Chang, this development would come in the form of outside help catalyzed by a new understanding of Chinese society based on cultural education.[71]

The CC&CC building was outfitted with authentic Chinese architectural features built by artisans Chang imported from China. A "Chinese-style façade" designed by Chinese architect C. C. Yang was constructed in and imported from Taiwan and attached to the front of an 1830s row house. Chang also secured and installed portions of China's exhibit at the Montreal Expo '67 (also designed by Yang) in the interior, reproducing the effect of a Chinese palace or temple:

> Passing through its small well-appointed doors is like entering a small, well-appointed palace. Materials used in the renovation were imported from Formosa. A carpenter was brought over, too, and maintained by the Chinese community for two years while he worked on the inlaid panels, carved ceilings and other fancy woodwork. A colossal wooden Confucius looms over the stairway, a 100-foot dancing dragon snoozes downstairs in the dining room, and dance hall used by neighborhood kids.[72]

This attention to classical detail underscored Chang's intention of display and spectacle for a non-Chinese constituency, particularly manifested by the use of materials from a World's Fair, with its exhibitionary modes of representation.

Chang rooted his promotion of Chinatown, as he did his leadership, in a traditional vision of authentic Chinese heritage, in contrast to the more hybrid Chinese American/Chinatown image engendered by other organizations. Describing his vision for the CC&CC in 1966, Chang declared, "This is the kind of building we want for our cultural center—real Chinese, not pseudo-Chinese imitation, not architectural chop suey. Chop suey is good, but it is not real Chinese food." Chang promoted tourism as the economic basis for Chinatown and its contribution to the larger city: "Can you imagine how curious tourists would become if they were driving across the Benjamin Franklin Bridge and saw a red tile Chinese roof rising above the trees somewhere west of Franklin Square? It would be a natural place for tourists to go after they have visited Independence Hall [and] it might get them to stay longer in Philadelphia."[73]

In June 1965, Chang debuted what would become a standard formula for CC&CC programming: a Chinese banquet meal with cultural program. On Monday through Thursday, the center offered a five-course Chinese meal followed by a tour of Chinatown. The tour promised an unveiled look at the secret, unknown, and hitherto-unseen Chinatown: "Open to outsiders for the first time in Chinatown's eight decades will be the temples of the On Leong and Hip Sing tongs, as well as the meeting room of the Benevolent Association, where the heads of the city's Chinese organizations settle private disputes in Oriental style." This reference to the neighborhood's tong-war past disappointed at least one commentator, who expected something more exotic: "Tong temples, long forbidden to foreigners, are set up much like other lodge rooms except for notably carved chairs and their ornate memorial altars. Incense and punk are burned at these shrines and back in the decorated recesses the face of the bearded warrior Kuan Kang (of Han Dynasty 221 A.D.) glares out fiercely."[74] Cooking classes were added in March 1966, held in the Ardmore Y and Main Branch Y downtown. The cooking course concluded in Chinatown with a tour and a Chinese banquet.

These programs allowed Chang to position himself and the center as a bridge between Chinatown and the larger Philadelphia community: "Civil, social, and religious organizations, in visiting the Chinatown area and learning about the Oriental way of life turn to the Chinatown YMCA for information about the Chinese culture. They often call on us to act as a liaison between themselves and the Chinatown community."[75] Outwardly looking, Chang sought to leverage public interest in Chinese culture into investment in Chinatown. Chang's vision for the marketing of Chinatown was represented as a new vision for the area and a new way of doing business, yet his tactics were far from new. Chang utilized strategies, such as opening temples and lodges for public view and arranging public demonstrations of traditional Chinese culture that had been employed as early as the 1880s. He emphasized an image of Chinatown as ancient, closed, and mysterious, promising to shed a light on its shadows. By focusing specifically on authentic Chinese cultural tradition and stressing his role as cultural broker, Chang worked to produce a continuing vision of Chinese difference, effacing Chinese American activities and transformations of the community as well as sidelining community issues of housing, recreation, and immigrant adjustment addressed by other organizations.[76] Yet his temple-like community center, with its classically Chinese façade, became one of the landmarks of the neighborhood, contributing to but not defining its residents' sense of place.

Located in an undesirable part of the city, Chinatown historically provided Chinese throughout the Delaware Valley with a real and symbolic sanctuary. This sanctuary was a space within which Chinatown's residents across the generations created a new sense of place for Chinese Americans. Following World War II, new immigration and generational changes engendered the emergence of institutions and spaces that were created to serve and cultivate a sense of attachment to Chinatown as the embodiment of Chinese American ethnicity and identity. These spaces engendered a strong sense of origin and urban territory for several generations of Chinatown residents. Remembering this territory, Chinatown community members map environmental challenges and positive attributes of Chinatown life: well-loved "public" spaces, committed community institutions, intergenerational cooperation, and enduring commitments to the neighborhood's well-being. In the 1960s and beyond, these memories and their sense of place would inform the community's response to challenges from the larger city that would forever change the face of Chinatown.

3

"We want homes, not highways"

Urban Renewal and
the "Save Chinatown" Movement

Joe Lowe remembers the morning in 1973 when he stepped onto the rubble:

> I know when they first started to demolish. . . . [M]y sister Nancy called me up. . . . They had already started building their pile of dirt right where Colonial Electric was [Tenth and Winter]. They had half of the building demolished already. There was a family across the alley from Colonial Electric, and they didn't know what was happening; there was this big Hawthorne crane. . . .
>
> Kevin [Lee] and I, it was probably about 7:30 in the morning—they knew there was going to be something, that they couldn't just come in on a regular time schedule and do that. . . .
>
> Kevin and I got out there. . . . We didn't know what to do at first. And then we said, "Let's just go sit up on the pile." And that's what we did. We were the first two up on the pile. And I guess that was our Tiananmen Square.
>
> We were there for the better part of the day, and we had about nine or twelve kids up there. And they came up, and they saw me and Kevin up there, and they said, "What are you guys doing?" and we said, "We're trying to save the church. . . ."
>
> We sat up there. To us, Holy Redeemer was our life. We knew what was going on.[1]

"What was going on" was the demolition of row houses claimed through eminent domain to make way for a new expressway running along Vine Street.

But more broadly, it was the destruction of and threat to spaces that were perceived as critical to Chinatown's life, survival, and future.

By 1973, the Chinatown community had been subject to relocations and demolitions for a decade, and a clear pattern had emerged. From the mid-1960s through the 1980s, urban redevelopment and renewal laid waste to each of Chinatown's borders. Two kinds of projects had the most impact on Chinatown: transportation infrastructure and large-scale destination projects, such as Independence Mall and Gallery/Market East. The construction of Gallery/Market East to the south effectively blocked any future settlement below Arch Street. In the 1960s and 1970s, relocations and demolitions made way for the expansion of Independence Mall to the east of Eighth Street, a commuter rail tunnel along Ninth Street, and a crosstown expressway on Vine Street that also included exit and entrance ramps on Ninth and Tenth Streets. The expressway, ramps, and tunnel led to extensive demolition along the northern and eastern edges of Chinatown, including the threat to Holy Redeemer Church and School. In each instance, Chinatown's leadership struggled to craft resistance to these city and state plans while advocating for the neighborhood's participation in urban renewal. This struggle was a coming-together and coalition-building opportunity for the community that catalyzed an internal generational shift in leadership and significantly redirected the future of community development in the neighborhood. The presence of a movement led by women and young people was also a dramatic new development for Chinatown, one that overturned traditional hierarchies of authority in the community and bridged traditional class divides when older working-class Chinatown residents came out to join the movement.[2] Above all, the moment and the movement drew on and consolidated a sense of place, represented through attachment to and memories of specific spaces as well as ideas of spatial self-determination, to create a larger movement that defined Chinatown's claims to land and resources in the context of citizenship, history, and cultural worth.

For Chinatown residents, the stakes in resisting redevelopment were high; failure meant the demise of their neighborhood as a living community. For the city, the stakes were also high: success ensured the survival of the metropolis as an economically viable entity. The redevelopment schemes that threatened Philadelphia's Chinatown in the 1960s represented, for planners and city government, critical steps toward shoring up the decline of the city in the face of suburbanization and deindustrialization. As a response to decades of corruption, a new generation of reform-minded Democrats, the "Young Turks," came into power in 1950, bringing with them a commitment to planning and redevelopment as a means to realize a more vital and viable city. A new Home Rule Charter was forged in 1951 that created, among other entities, the Human Relations Commission and the Parks and Recreation Department, both aimed at improving urban life, particularly in the city's neighborhoods. The charter also reaffirmed a commitment to the Philadelphia City Planning Commission (PCPC), headed by Edmund Bacon after 1949, a central figure in the movement to harness city planning for urban reform. Bacon's vision was supplemented by William Rafsky, housing coordinator under Mayor Joseph Clark and eventually director of the Philadelphia Redevelopment Authority (PRA) under Mayor Richard Dilworth, who also came to exercise considerable influence on planning in Philadelphia.

Unlike other cities of the period, Philadelphia avoided the wholesale demolition of slum clearance, driven in part by the terms and priorities of federal funding for most urban-renewal plans of the postwar period. Rather, Philadelphia's planners advocated for selective demolition and conservation of historic structures, particularly in neighborhoods, such as Society Hill, that could become residential destinations for gentrifying elites. Early efforts at neighborhood redevelopment in 1957 focused on East Poplar, an urban core African American neighborhood north of downtown, and Eastwick, an integrated, semi-rural area on the city's southwest limits. In East Poplar, the city sought, unsuccessfully, to create racially integrated housing in new and rehabilitated structures, ultimately reinforcing segregation. North Philadelphia would eventually fall within the Model Cities program in the late 1960s.[3] In Eastwick, thousands of residents were displaced, after protests, to make room for major redevelopment.[4] West Philadelphia was redeveloped to make way for expansions of Drexel University and the University of Pennsylvania, displacing large tracts of the former streetcar suburbs there. In Society Hill, a Center City neighborhood considered one of Bacon's greatest successes, blighted eighteenth-century structures were condemned and then rehabilitated to create a neighborhood that would draw suburban elites and developers back into the city. Although the area escaped wholesale demolition, only 726 out of 2,197 buildings were retained, supplemented with new modernist construction by I. M. Pei. Conservation largely applied to buildings however; historic preservation in Society Hill displaced as many existing residents (some six thousand, most of them African American) as if the neighborhood had been razed through slum clearance.[5]

Society Hill's gentrification embodied in part the city's embrace of redevelopment processes in which private-public partnerships between city government, local developers, and financial institutions would drive a movement of capital back into the inner city, specifically downtown.[6] Both Bacon and Rafsky, an ambitious "urban entrepreneur" who later served as head of the Old Philadelphia Development Corporation (OPDC) that actively promoted Society Hill, sought a revitalization of downtown to attract business and capital investment as well as to relieve congestion, promote open space, and create more aesthetically pleasing urban structures.[7] One result of Bacon and Rafsky's planning was the Central Urban Renewal Area (CURA) outlined in 1956, a study that recommended a three-point economic-renewal program focused on Center City redevelopment, assistance to universities, and industrial renewal to counteract the loss of manufacturing jobs.[8] At heart, this plan, like many of the period's urban-renewal schemes, "sought to replace social and geographic history of the city with a mythical future" that was scientific, corporate, and efficient.[9] This efficiency was enabled by expressways that would move residents and visitors in and through the city to retail and tourism sites downtown, a city designed to compete effectively with the increasing draw of suburban housing developments and shopping centers. The recommendations found fruition in a comprehensive plan for Philadelphia unveiled in 1960, followed by a specific plan for Center City in 1963. The plan expressed its hope in the "initiative potential of the private enterprise system," outlining designs for the creation of a pedestrian mall at Independence National Park, a retail/transportation hub along Market Street East, and crosstown expressways along Vine and South Streets. The plans for Center City embodied the shift in many postindustrial cities away from the comprehensive planning of the liberal era toward an emerging "neoliberal" consensus on urban redevelopment that valued urban-entrepreneurialism concepts like Rafsky's, investing in new "symbolic economies" of spectacle and consumerism that would draw suburban elites back into the city.[10]

By erasing existing social geographies, these plans also effectively displaced the historical and contemporary presence of minorities in the urban landscape and their agency in creating it. By focusing exclusively on narrowly defined economic interests, the plans neglected the needs of low-income and minority city residents, focusing neighborhood efforts in areas that were designated as "conservable" "gray areas," "beginning to show the first signs of blight," largely white neighborhoods ringing the central core of the city. Jeremy Alvarez, a city planner with the Planning Commission, expressed the need to sacrifice neighborhoods (most of which were working class and/or African American) in the interest of urban commerce: "I feel that Philadelphia is up against a rock and a hard place. It's absolutely our aorta that we get those middle class people to move into town and if there is a small price to be paid in the old neighborhood, it is almost trivial when compared to the . . . survival of the metropolis."[11]

"We cannot be very helpful on Chinatown"

Philadelphia's Chinatown was not alone in facing issues of encroachment and displacement; the era was challenging for many traditional ethnic enclaves and other urban neighborhoods that faced an uncertain fate amid decades of urban redevelopment. In many North American cities, a similar pattern developed: rising land values, mass demolition, and the use of eminent domain to claim land and remove immigrant or minority residents. Since many Asian enclaves were located in the urban core near central business districts, occupying aging building stock, they were vulnerable to displacement or encroachment by major anti-blight or redevelopment projects. Across the country, Chinatowns, Japantowns, Manilatowns, and Little Tokyos all felt the threat of urban renewal. Communities responded, their efforts centered on the defense and stabilization of ethnic enclaves for working-class, elderly, and low-income residents. Some did not survive these challenges. Chinatown ("Hop Alley") in St. Louis was razed in 1965–1966 as part of an urban-renewal movement and became part of a parking lot near Busch Stadium. Pittsburgh's Chinatown was destroyed by a highway. Seattle's International District, where many Chinese and other Asians lived, was bisected by a freeway in the 1960s and then partially destroyed by the construction of the Kingdome, which began in 1972. Many residents were displaced, and although the district survived and is home to several Asian landmarks (such as the Wing Luke Museum), it is no longer a thriving resident community. San Francisco's Chinatown was threatened by expansion of the financial district, and in its Manilatown, activists fought for the elderly low-income Asian American tenants of the International Hotel. Evictions were also the focus of organizing efforts in Los Angeles's Little Tokyo in the early 1970s, where residents were threatened with displacement. In New York's Chinatown, activists worked to defend tenants' rights to remain in their homes and for the inclusion of Chinatown labor in the construction of Confucius Plaza. Many Chinatowns, including Philadelphia's, were deeply affected by the construction of major highways during this period: both Chicago's and Boston's Chinatowns were truncated or bisected by two expressways in the 1950s, and in both cases the communities did not protest or mitigate the highways' effects. In Canada, Vancouver's Chinatown was slated for slum clearance in the early 1960s, but the community protested, successfully preventing a highway project that would have damaged the neighborhood.[12]

Philadelphia's Chinatown was largely ignored by neighborhood-revitalization activities, rarely appearing in city plans until 1975. In 1950, the neighborhood was a small dark spot in otherwise blank space on a PCPC map illustrating patterns of crowded housing conditions.[13] Ignored by neighborhood initiatives, Chinatown's location in the heart of downtown meant that it was dramatically affected by the other side of urban renewal—the focus on downtown redevelopment. The three projects that had the most impact on Chinatown were the creation of a crosstown expressway along Vine Street to the north, the expansion of Independence Park to the east, and the creation of a large downtown mall (the Gallery) and transportation center (Market East) to the south. Developers of Independence Mall and Market East were concerned about the proximity of Skid Row (concentrated in the 1950s between Vine and Arch Streets, from Seventh to Ninth Streets, right next to Chinatown) to these projects, which were to be designed to attract tourists and suburbanites into the city. A 1952 report from the Health and Welfare Council titled *What about Philadelphia's Skid Row?* specifically mentioned the ugly visibility of the blighted area from an approach into the city along Vine Street from the Ben Franklin Bridge. Chinatown was not named in this report, but it surely suffered from association and proximity.[14]

While the Vine Street Expressway and other major redevelopment projects were conceived as early as 1945, the PCPC or PRA did not specifically consider remodeling Chinatown until the early 1960s. Under Bacon's influence, the PCPC ideally sought to involve community members in the discussion of urban plans. In many cases, however, this approach targeted other professionals, such as architects and designers, as in the Citizens' Council on City Planning, or middle- to upper-middle-class residents already engaged in civic processes. It was not as capable of engaging minority communities or surmounting the challenges that less-enfranchised populations posed (such as language access and education) to create a level playing field for meaningful dialogue.

In the summer of 1963, PCPC considered the question of Chinatown and the Center City plan. In July 1963, R. Damon Childs, a planner with the PCPC, wrote to Bacon:

> On July 29 I had an extensive discussion with Mr. T. T. Chang of the Chinatown YMCA. He feels it is important that the City should state its policy concerning the future of Chinatown. He feels that there are many Chinese businessmen and residents who would be willing to put capital improvements into their properties if they had assurance that they were not going to be acquired. It would be my proposal to prepare a special plan for this area, which would be an amendment to the Center City Redevelopment Area Plan. . . . This plan would also propose the rehabilitation of the existing buildings for single and multifamily residences, with the elimination of rooming houses and hotels. It could also show possible locations for housing the elderly, which Mr. Chang expressed interest in sponsoring.

Childs's memo suggests that the city was already in the process of acquiring properties in the Chinatown area by the early 1960s as well as considering the survival of Chinatown. Significantly, the memo also gestured toward the coming conflict over the expressway: "The YMCA and the Chinese Catholic Church, which is in the path of the Vine Street Expressway, could be relocated into this area."[15] It is unclear whether Chang was informed of the expressway's potential impact on the community at this time; others in Chinatown did not learn of the plan until 1966.

The city agencies involved did not seem to anticipate any resistance to their plans from Chinatown residents, although resistance had emerged in other

Philadelphia neighborhoods affected by renewal. In Society Hill, local African American residents, rallying around a group of women known as the "Octavia Hill Seven," protested their eviction and relocation, arguing that their long, multigenerational presence in the neighborhood entitled them to stay or be relocated nearby. They proposed housing for a vacant lot on the southern edge of the area, at Sixth and Lombard, which was opposed by newer residents as "public housing." One recent arrival questioned their claim to remain, revealing the class and race biases of urban place making, arguing, "By what authority do these people have roots? If you don't own, you don't have roots. What have they planted, their feet on the ground?" The "Octavia Hill Seven" and their neighbors were ultimately relocated to West Philadelphia in defiance of their sense of place.[16] The newer residents of Society Hill fared better. Proposals for an elevated highway along the Delaware Riverfront (I-95) were actively opposed by residents of a newly gentrified Society Hill, galvanized by the leadership of architect Denise Scott Brown, a resident of the now-elite neighborhood. To the south, Queen Village residents, with the help of local preservationists, protested a proposed crosstown expressway along South Street that would eliminate the commercial heart of a historic neighborhood. In both these cases, middle- and upper-middle-class residents held agencies accountable to the ideal of community inclusion and consultation. I-95 became a sunken expressway with pedestrian walkways, and the southern crosstown expressway plan was abandoned altogether. As the Vine Street Expressway plans were publicized as early as 1945, public concern over how the expressway would affect the urban environment centered around the newly created façade of the Free Library, Logan Circle, and other privately held businesses west of Broad Street.[17]

Given these precedents, some officials seemed to make assumptions about the disengagement and passivity of the Chinatown community when they did not plan for inclusion or opposition.[18] These assumptions were rooted in long-standing images of Chinatown's antimodern alterity, expressed by *Center City Philadelphia* magazine in 1963: "It is in the love of the Chinese for their own culture that cause for both hope and despair lie. The standing resistance to assimilation may breathe life into the politically apathetic community by uniting it in the face of outside threats. Yet the tendency to shy away from matters beyond the realm of Chinatown may choke this political awakening until it is too late."[19] Resistance to assimilation and insularity were charges often levied at Chinese Americans, as if the community's marginalization was an essential part of its nature rather than the result of larger patterns of racial segregation and exclusion.

Bacon seems to have been sincere in, if disengaged from, the effort to respond to Chinatown's situation. Even with good intentions, lack of knowledge of the community certainly proved a challenge; PCPC correspondence reveals that the agency had difficulty discerning whom to deal with in the

Chinatown community. A month after Childs submitted his memo, the department was scrambling to craft a follow-up. PCPC staffer R. H. Uhlig expressed this concern to senior planner Graham Finney: "The commission has a request before it from the head of the YMCA in Chinatown for certain planning actions. The question arises as to whether the YMCA is a representative institution of the Chinese community and whether our planning efforts should be geared through them, and, if not, through whom."[20] A couple of days later, Uhlig reported:

> I have asked Bob McMullin to look into our material on the subject. I expect we have little information but we shall see. I did check with Merrill Conover, our recreation consultant, who called Roy Smail, Associate General Secretary, YMCA, about Chang. I thought you would not mind if I went this far. Smail tells Conover that Chang, who works through the Central Y, rates very well with the Chinese community. He is a go-getter, always coming up with new ideas. He apparently knows the area well and is in on virtually everything of importance. I do not know more than this but if you would like to make a survey of the various "tongs" give me a buzz and some money.[21]

He concluded, "We cannot be very helpful on Chinatown. You might glance through the attached and see what it adds up to." Emily Nugent, a PCPC employee whose daily commute took her through Chinatown, pulled together a list of community organizations. Nugent's list included the main churches (Chinese Christian, Chinese Gospel, and Holy Redeemer), Galilee Missions, Sunday Breakfast Association, and district police and fire stations. "Having passed through this area in the streetcar for several weeks on my way to the Neighborhood Guild," she wrote, "I can add that there are numerous Chinese restaurants, stores, and although not Chinese, 'palm reading establishments.'"[22] Another lead pointed Uhlig to Mitzie Mackenzie: "Bob tells me that this McKenzie [sic] woman mentioned in his memo has been in the area for 18 years." It is not clear, however, whether there was much, if any, follow-up to these initial investigations.

Uhlig's confusion about Chinatown is understandable, according to Cecilia Moy Yep:

> Every group had their own people. Beside the family associations, the Christian Church had their group, the people who went to Christian Church; and we as Catholics went to Holy Redeemer, we had our own thing going; and Chinatown politics were going on [where] they [Chinese Benevolent Association] kind of represented the Chinese speaking group, and none of us really intermingled.[23]

Chinatown's existing leadership was likewise ill-equipped to deal with the city and the challenges the neighborhood was facing: "There was a person who had control of CBA [Chinese Benevolent Association] and was worried that he was going to be useless and was worried about losing power. . . . CBA didn't know what he was doing half of the time."[24] In addition, competing visions for the neighborhood complicated efforts to work with city and state agencies that had no knowledge of the community.

T. T. Chang, director of the Chinatown YMCA and a prominent member of the Chinese Benevolent Association (CBA), was proactive in putting himself forward as the community's representative in the 1960s within a traditional model of leadership, as the latest "mayor of Chinatown." Chang sought to leverage the possibility of creating Chinatown as a tourist destination showcasing ancient Chinese culture to secure monies for redevelopment. He struck this note over and over in various communications with the media and city agencies. To Robert Epp, who worked with *Center City Philadelphia* in 1963, he wrote: "The Chinese community is anxious to improve the area and preserve the ancient culture and tradition. They would like to develop Chinatown into an outstanding tourist attraction for our 'City of Brotherly Love.'"[25] Specifically, Chang had extensive plans for a Chinese community center, which would showcase authentic Chinese culture to a broader Philadelphia community. The proposed project would encompass an entire block of Chinatown between Tenth and Eleventh Streets and Spring and Race (the center of the neighborhood adjacent to the historic block and about one-fourth of the neighborhood area at that time; see Figure 3.1). The $2-million-plus project would include a Confucian Hall and Chinese Garden of "authentic Chinese design" to serve as a tourist attraction, with a community center housing an auditorium, classrooms, residential rooms, library, restaurant, gift shops, and office space. Proposed sketches show a templelike structure and garden surrounded by several buildings with curved pagoda eaves, tile roofs, and multiple storefronts. The goal would be to "promote international and intercultural understanding between the Chinese community and the rest of the Greater Philadelphia community."[26] Over the next two years, Chang worked to garner financial support for the project, securing a $15,000 gift from Philadelphia attorney Graham French, who also served as chairman of the Y's finance committee. He discussed the project with Rafsky, now at OPDC, who seems to have assisted Chang in courting "outstanding citizens" for the project. He also dealt with Francis Lammer at the PRA, who outlined a five-year timeline for such a project. With only $85,000 saved and elderly benefactor French balking at the extended timeline, Chang was persuaded in 1967 to undertake a shorter-term project, the renovation of the building at 125 North Tenth Street to temporarily house the Chinatown YMCA as the Chinese Cultural and Community Center (CC&CC), with the plan of selling the building when the larger center was completed.

Expo Lends a Hand to Chinatown

Figure 3.1. T. T. Chang's plan for a Chinese Community Center, 1967. (From the *Philadelphia Inquirer Magazine*, October 15, 1967, Philadelphia City Planning Commission papers. Courtesy of the Philadelphia City Archives and City Planning Commission.)

Chang's leadership style relied on traditional authority structures like CBA and an emphasis on the "mayor of Chinatown" model of leadership based in the hierarchy of the traditional associations, reoriented toward making contacts and wielding influence with powerful bureaucrats in city government. He frequently wrote letters to the mayor and to directors of various city agencies. Chang's ambitions were not matched by the effectiveness of his methods. Typical of his interactions with representatives of city agencies were the indifference and eventual confusion that attended his correspondence with Bacon and the PCPC. Chang met with Bacon in December 1963, after the appearance of an article in *Center City Philadelphia* magazine that declared Chinatown was being squeezed by urban renewal. He invited Bacon to dinner at his recently remodeled "authentically Chinese-style home." Bacon declined, inviting Chang instead to a lunch meeting at Stouffer's Restaurant.[27] Little seems to have resulted from Chang's meeting with Bacon, who reportedly remarked to Chang that the only thing "Chinese" about Chinatown was the "smell of Chinese food."[28] Five years later, after the creation of the Philadelphia Chinatown Development Corporation, which was now working with the Redevelopment Authority and the PCPC on plans to redevelop Chinatown, Chang wrote to Bacon again, explaining the delays in the center project and asking for a meeting. In response, Bacon scrawled a cover memo on a letter to Childs: "Pls discuss with me." Childs responded: "I have not been close to this recently. I do not know what Chang's present status is. The community is proceeding with the housing project west of Tenth Street," a reference to the Redevelopment Authority's work with the fledgling PCDC to build new housing, a project that would eventually become Mei Wah Yuen.[29]

Chang's methods were also questioned by other members of the community. Some viewed him as an "arrogant son of a bitch," questioning his courting of non-Chinese powerbrokers and his governing the CC&CC with an all-white board. They accused him of unfair competition with local restaurateurs, especially through the importation of chefs from China that undercut local labor and sidestepped local restaurant permits and taxes for financial gain. Others resented his attempts to position himself as the spokesperson for the community, another "mayor of Chinatown," which "irked everybody to no end" in part because Chang was not Cantonese and was perceived as an outsider:

> Because he was northern, he was not Cantonese; he didn't speak Cantonese, or if he did, he spoke it with a terrible accent, right? He really didn't fit in. So in Chinatown, wherever, it was the same thing, people from the North tended to be more educated and better off. For instance, the minister of the Chinese Christian Church, when I got there, was a northerner, and so it was almost like they were missionaries to the Cantonese. It was really an unfavorable relationship.[30]

For others, Chang's vision for the community was most at issue. According to Mary Yee, "His view of Chinatown, since he didn't live in Chinatown, was that it was a tourist attraction." George Moy recalls that Chang's approach, either naïve or self-interested, was ineffective for addressing the challenges that the community faced:

> He was an ambitious person who wanted to establish himself as a key leader in Chinatown. Now he spoke the language, he spoke Mandarin—I mean, he had education that initially would give him respect; he was educated, you['ve] got to respect that. But what you don't take in[to] account is what his ambitions were. There was one time where he got about three leaders from CBA to go with him to see the head at the Redevelopment Authority. He has his meeting. He comes back and reports, "Chinatown is not gonna be touched."[31]

Demolitions and the "Chinatown Alamo"

But Chinatown was being touched. Throughout the 1960s, acquisitions and demolitions proceeded apace along Chinatown's northern and eastern boundaries. In 1963, the Independence Mall project removed 25 percent of Chinatown's homes and businesses off east Ninth Street—long before there was a concrete plan to construct a commuter rail tunnel at this site. Arthur Lou, who had run a travel agency at 832 Race since 1946, occupied one of three row-house properties on the southeast corner of Ninth and Race Streets that survived widespread demolition on this block. "Ironically business is good in Chinatown," Lou commented to the *Bulletin* in 1969. "People keep wanting to come here and go into business but there's no room for them. We had 12 people come here from Rangoon last month. They had to find quarters elsewhere in the city."[32] In a community already struggling for space, demolitions had a powerfully negative impact, particularly in the midst of a renewed wave of immigration from Asia in the late 1960s.

The community did not realize the full consequences of these demolitions until later, with the onset of other redevelopment mega-projects, such as the expressway and the commuter rail tunnel. Both George Moy and Cecilia Moy Yep eventually lost their homes. The buildings on the 800 block of Race that Moy's family purchased and renovated in the 1950s were claimed as part of eminent domain. Moy's situation was typical of those who owned homes in Chinatown: as working-class people, they were economically vulnerable, and their informal investment in the neighborhood, primarily in the form of renovation and improvement, was not recognized by developers. This disregard negatively affected the value of Chinatown properties and the compensation paid to those who were displaced, such as Moy:

> Well, they were supposed to give you the value at that time and take it. But they never told us—I don't remember ever seeing a formal—under eminent domain we're going to take your house for blight removal. So if I'm spending hours rebuilding or building, adding on sections to the house, I'm not getting a salary, so how am I going to prove the value of what I put into the house? It's only when they come out and say, "Well this"—whatever standards they use—"this is the value."[33]

Yep echoes Moy's recollection: "They said that they were taking the property under the eminent domain law. And that they [Chinatown residents] had, I think, sixty days to find another residence, and they would be compensated. Not saying how much, because later on they had an appraiser come through and gave 'em peanuts. Everybody got peanuts." Resistance to demolitions and property seizures did not seem possible to most residents, as Yep explains: "You have to understand [that] at that time, we didn't understand urban renewal. . . . [T]he general consensus was that you could not fight City Hall, so from 1960 to 1966, they were tearing down properties, and we were not fighting City Hall for the most part."[34]

According to Moy and Yep, the city systematically acquired properties without indicating what larger plans were involved or what rights residents might have. Yep explains: "[It was] the early 1960s [when] a lot of the properties on the east side of Ninth Street were taken, commercial, residentials. People were relocated without knowing what their rights were. We were just told the city was just taking their property, knocking them down, and we all had to move. We had no relocation rights. . . . [T]hey just said, 'You have to move, and this is what we're giving you for your property. If you don't like it, take us to court.'"[35] In the end, Moy reluctantly decided to sell:

> I was very Chinesey—you know, you listen, you obey, you listen to your elders, and you don't make waves and things like that. . . . We knew nothing about eminent domain. We knew that the city wanted to get rid of Skid Row, blight. What they called blight. But we didn't know to what extent, and in what guise. Well getting rid of the blight, sure, you could be for it. But what remedial steps they would take, there were none. At that time, a father of seven children, having my own contracting business as a handyman, trying to survive, provide for my family, I had my hands full to begin with. And my situation was not very different from those other Chinese families living in Chinatown or having interests in Chinatown.[36]

Yep, unwilling to leave Chinatown, refused to sell: "I refused to move, because basically there was no place to move to. There was no decent affordable housing in Chinatown. Most of the houses were over a hundred years old."[37] Unclear on how to preserve her home, Yep stubbornly stayed put, regardless of the consequences: "And so they kept taking the properties on East Ninth Street. I was the only house standing on the whole block from Race to Filbert. From Ninth to Eighth. My electric bill was unbelievable—300 something every month. My gas bill, to try to heat that place for the kids. So I stayed. . . . The city said, 'We've gotta do something. We gotta get housing for her.' Because they would look pretty good putting out a widow with three little kids."[38] Yep's fervent refusal was grounded in the belief that hers was a last stand for Chinatown: "They knew they had to deal with me. If I move out, they're going to knock this [house] down, and nothing will be left of Chinatown. So I stayed. . . . They called mine the 'Chinatown Alamo' because it was the only house standing on the whole block. And I refused to move out of it.[39] Evoking the "Alamo" in her rhetoric, Yep and others framed her stand in terms of territorial claims and resistance to outside aggression, a theme that would be struck many times over the succeeding decades.

By spring 1966, the implications of the acquisitions and demolition became clearer when the community learned that plans for the Vine Street Expressway would involve the site of Holy Redeemer Chinese Catholic Church and School. Yep recalls the community reaction:

We found out they were taking the church in March 1966 at a meeting at Logan Circle at the Free Library, which advised people of the
community that the state was coming in and taking the church and
school. It was at that meeting that the community was kind of out-
raged, because the church and school was built in 1941, so it's pretty
new in '66. We had our children going to school there, a lot of us went
to church there, and so we felt we couldn't let the state do this.[40]

A "Save Our Church" group, formed by Holy Redeemer congregants (many
of them mothers), began mobilizing the community against the demolition of
the church. This group and the larger organizational entities that followed were
largely constituted by American-born, second-generation Chinese Americans
whose investments were in the neighborhood institutions that held importance
in their childhoods or everyday lives. Unlike T. T. Chang, they lived in the
neighborhood and had personal and familial histories there as well as a dis-
tinctly American sense of their rights. The fight to save the church grew into
a fight to save the neighborhood, creating an intergenerational coalition that
bridged internal community differences, created new community leadership,
and articulated a new image for the neighborhood.

Save Our Church; Save Chinatown

There is no evidence that city planners wished Chinatown gone in the 1960s.
In fact, the PCPC and the PRA seemed to value a small, commercially oriented
Chinatown as part of a revitalized, consumer-oriented downtown landscape,
and the historic core of Chinatown along 900 Race was never in danger from
redevelopment plans. But planners' conceptions of Chinatown and residents'
conceptions of Chinatown were radically different. For residents, the boundaries of Chinatown extended geographically well beyond Ninth, Tenth, and
Race Streets. And for residents, Chinatown was more than the restaurants
and businesses of the core. The prospect of losing the Holy Redeemer Church
and School was seen as a larger threat to the fabric of Chinatown itself,
because, like housing, it was a spatial aspect of the neighborhood that was
central to a sense of place, to what made Chinatown a "living community,"
a home. Yep believed the loss of Holy Redeemer sounded the death knell of
the neighborhood: "A lot of people thought it was a church issue. There was
a group called 'Save Our Church,' which was fine, but we said it's more than
a church issue, it's a community issue, and that's what a few of us thought.
So we got our friends together at my kitchen table and talked about it. They
think it's just church, we think its community, so we'll work on it from a
community level, and we protested. We protested everywhere."[41]

Yep was determined to fight and enlisted the help of the Chinatown community leadership, first approaching Joseph Lowe Sr., the head of the CBA:

I went to Joe Lowe Sr., and I said, "Joe, they're going to take the church, and this is going to break up the whole community; this is the worst thing that could happen to us, to take away a church and a school, because after that. . . . [T]hey already took the businesses; they take the school [and] there's nothing left for us to stay here. So, we have kids; we have to worry about the future." Joe Lowe said, "I don't know what to do. I don't know how to do it. I can't even speak English well."[42]

Lowe Sr.'s reluctance to get involved was typical of the traditional hierarchy and structures of authority in Chinatown, which invested power in the traditional associations and their umbrella organization, the CBA. These associations had historically been focused on resolving internal conflicts between individuals, associations, and businesses; providing mutual assistance; and managing housing, turning outward only when larger "treaty rights" were involved. The CBA was largely composed of older Chinese-born men, many of whom did not speak English (or at least not fluently). Understanding these limitations, Yep decided to begin organizing herself: "So we had this first town meeting, which I organized. I went around and gave out circulars, word of mouth, and I told Joe [to] invite everyone from all the associations, I want everyone to hear what's going on, so everybody can help and work together."[43]

Yep's determination to speak out and take a public leadership role bucked traditional roles for Chinatown's women. For her, leadership seems to have come naturally. Her position as a widow—a woman who had no man to speak for her—perhaps helped create a space for her to be seen and heard in new ways. But the change in leadership was one of not only gender but also generation and cultural style. For Moy, it was a step outside his comfort zone to join the fight. He recalls his reluctance to speak up: "Now when all this came to a crisis, what to do about the highway, I was a different person then. I was very reserved, sort of just stayed in the shadows, the background. . . . Cecilia was very outspoken." When another younger community leader declined to assume leadership of the effort, Moy felt compelled to get more involved: "I couldn't sit back and say, 'Well, that's it, he doesn't want to do anything'—if anything, you might say I'm persistent. I felt that something had to be done, and I just couldn't say it had to be done, [but] you do it. So I joined in."[44] Yep and Moy both served as presidents of what would become the Philadelphia Chinatown Development Corporation (PCDC). As second-generation Chinese Americans, theirs was a new face for Chinatown.

Deference to the CBA was critical to the movement's viability early on, according to Moy, since the organization both represented and challenged traditional Chinatown leadership:

We had to organize. But if you're going to organize as a new group, claiming to represent Chinatown or part of Chinatown, you were dragged head on into the Chinese Benevolent Association. They were an established organization in Chinatown. I don't know just who would recognize them as being but they are, like with the city officials at that time. To have a community fighting amongst themselves as to who's the leader, the city'll just come right in and bowl you over. So we knew that it was our recognition that you respect your elders. So Cecilia was able to get Joe Lowe [Sr.] to support us, because he was a leader in CBA, because what we were trying to do was the right thing to do. Because they weren't able to do it, they didn't speak the language, they didn't know the ins and outs of local government, let alone eminent domain and all of that. So we acknowledged that we would be a committee under them, not threaten their prestige or their claim. We knew we just had to either respect them, or we had to fight them and, on the other hand, fight the government.... [W]e didn't challenge their authority; we acknowledged their superiority.[45]

Deference posed some challenges when the coalition's need for action bumped up against CBA sensibilities and priorities. The expressway fight was not a major priority of the CBA. Internal politics also got in the way, according to Moy: "For a period of time in the early years of PCDC and pre-PCDC, we would go to their [CBA's] monthly meetings that supposedly started at ten o'clock Sunday night to keep them informed.... [S]ometimes they had to send somebody out to get a board member to make a quorum, and we'd [not] get started until maybe eleven o'clock, and they would have their meeting." As the discussion of business proceeded late into the night, Moy recalls, minute details of building management or interpersonal conflicts would overshadow any sense of urgency about the effects of redevelopment: "'Oh so-and-so this in our building or our apartment, our cubicle upstairs didn't pay their rent or are sick, and what do we do?' and so forth. There's a conflict between a Lee and a Jung, because if you're a Lee you're [on] one side of the street and your tong doesn't establish a restaurant on the other. I remember one time one of them said, 'Kill 'em.' 'Okay, your report.' 'Okay, well, PennDOT's [Pennsylvania Department of Transportation] going to take down these houses here and the city's taking down the houses on Ninth Street'—like an adjunct, a little incident—bulldozers coming through tomorrow."[46] In some cases, the need for deference tied activists' hands: "But that took a toll on us, we had to go to work the next day, and you had to react, and what do you do with PennDOT coming at you with a bulldozer or something like that? You had to be more on the ball and not wait until you get a report on what to do."[47]

But by working with the CBA, Moy and Yep were able to secure contingent support for a wider effort:

We went to CBA. We called a town meeting. We had it at the On Leong Association; that's the biggest place outside the church. I didn't want to have it at the church, because at that time I wanted to get neutral ground. . . . I got On Leong Association. I don't know how I had any of these smarts—that's why I say it had to have been an act of God that I did the things I did, because I had no experience at this community organizing or anything else. But out of that meeting came the decision from the CBA that they couldn't handle the situation and that they were going to write a letter to people at the meeting to take care of the situation. That [was] the start of PCDC. It started out as a committee.

Although the CBA had authorized the creation of the committee, its leaders expected to retain control: "I had a hard time convincing them that culturally they were still in charge. . . . I used to have to go and report to them every week; it was maddening for me, because I had three little kids. At the time, [I] was a widow. So we'd go to the meeting, report to them." CBA representatives would insist on inclusion in city meetings—for example, "Even when we went to the mayor, we had people talking Chinese, because, you see, we invited CBA to everything." Moy and Yep addressed this situation by consistently emphasizing the limited role of the committee as a representative of Chinatown only in matters of community development. Within this area, Yep insists, "We [were] in charge."[48]

Despite these internal obstacles, Yep, Moy, and others began mobilizing the community. Initial efforts had an improvisational character as organizers took a crash course in organizing and civic engagement. Various contingents within the "Save Chinatown" movement pursued a variety of strategies, including protests, petitions, letter writing, and political lobbying. The campaign was characterized by improvisation because, according to Yep, "We didn't know what we were doing." Throughout 1973, when the demolition of the church loomed imminent, the coalition organized a series of meetings and demonstrations against the expressway. On February 9, 1973, PCDC staged a protest demonstration involving two hundred schoolchildren, community representatives, and concerned individuals, who marched from Holy Redeemer to PennDOT's local offices. The group spent two hours chanting slogans and passing out leaflets to save Chinatown. Another demonstration in 1973 at the dedication of a statue of Copernicus outside the Saints Peter and Paul Cathedral on Logan Square was focused against the Catholic Archdiocese, which was perceived as capitulating to PennDOT on the issue of Holy Redeemer. Another demonstration was enacted in a blocked-off section of Race between Ninth and Tenth Streets on April 14, 1973, to express concern over the construction of Market East and the expressway. Activists also seized opportunities to address city officials directly. At a community meeting at On Leong Association on May 3, 1973, activists confronted PRA representative Lynne Abraham, demanding answers about various urban renewal projects,

Figure 3.2. Demonstrators holding up signs in support of the Holy Redeemer Chinese Catholic Church and School during City Council hearings in Philadelphia's City Hall, 1973. The Philadelphia Redevelopment Authority's James Martin and Lynne M. Abraham (sitting at the table) testify. (From the *Philadelphia Evening Bulletin*, May 9, 1973. Courtesy of the Special Collections Research Center, Temple University Libraries, Philadelphia, PA.)

and questioning PRA's intentions to provide housing for Chinatown. Activists pointed to the availability of city funds for nearby Gimbel's department store and Reading Terminal, but not for housing in Chinatown. About one hundred Chinatown residents attended another public hearing at City Hall in 1973, where testimony focused on the Ninth Street ramps for the expressway that would entail the destruction of Holy Redeemer (see Figure 3.2).

On another front, activists learned how to work the political system and eventually identified local and state politicians who could help address other lawmakers. In May 1973, activists took a bus trip to Harrisburg to visit Governor Milton Shapp. Moy testified on behalf of the group: "Our community will be destroyed or dispersed as a result of this project if it is continued in its present form without regard for the consequences to the community."[49] For Yep, the visit to Shapp provided important lessons in how to address state government, particularly the importance of involving local political representatives:

And so we did a protest to Governor Shapp, up in Harrisburg. . . . [W]e didn't notify anybody we were coming or anything, and Jim Tayoun [state representative from Philadelphia district] saw me and said, "Ciel, what are you doing here?" I said, "We're coming up here to protest the taking of the church." He said, "Where is your state representative?" I said, "I don't know." How do I know where he is? So he said, "He should be with you." . . . And so he said, "Just a minute, you stay right here." He went and got him and brought him out. And he said, "These people here are protesting the—they're your people; they're your constituents; why aren't you with them?" . . . So the state rep went in to the governor and said, "I have a group of people down there; I didn't know they were coming, but would you give 'em a few minutes of your time?" So the governor came out, and we told him that we did not want him to take the church and school.[50]

Shapp, caught off guard, promised that demolitions would not proceed without PCDC's prior knowledge. Yep reflects, "I learned a lot about community organizing, through practice, through mistakes like not notifying your state representative."

Despite these assurances from the governor, PennDOT began demolition at Tenth and Vine in July 1973. In several instances, groups of local children and teenagers joined activists in occupied lots on this and an adjacent block of Winter Street, confronting bulldozers and climbing onto rubble to oppose further demolition. On July 30, community members organized a picket line and blocked Tenth Street traffic. Picketing continued for three days until demolition of the southwest corner stopped. The bulldozers returned on August 2 at 5:00 A.M. to resume work. By 7:30 A.M., demonstrators had assembled around the site and asked the foreman to cease work, then they climbed onto the rubble to face off the crane, forcing workmen to stop and prompting a meeting with PennDOT representatives that afternoon (see Figure 3.3).[51]

For Harry Leong, now director of the Chinese Christian Church and Center (CCC&C), involvement in the protests was an extension of growing up and having membership in the community:

I was a pretty young child, but I do remember that we used to go to the demonstrations, because it was our community thing; we were such a tight-knit community that we just jumped out—that's just a normal thing, where we go to demonstrations. We would carry signs, and we'd do different things. We did what we could with whatever. We just blocked places.[52]

For many children in Chinatown, the experience of resisting the bulldozers was definitive, an introduction to activism, according to Glenn Hing:

Figure 3.3. Protestors atop a pile of rubble, 1973. Mary Yee is in front, behind the banner. (From the *Philadelphia Inquirer*, August 3, 1973. Photograph by Michael Viola. Used with permission of the *Philadelphia Inquirer*. Copyright © 2014. All rights reserved.)

The start of my community activism was when PCDC was getting formed, because they were formed primarily to fight the expansion of the Vine Street Expressway that was endangering Chinatown and also Holy Redeemer. And I remember when they started demolishing buildings. A whole group of kids, literally kids, ran up on top of the piles. . . . That was at Tenth and Vine, and I was one of those kids.

The sense was that they [the city] were knocking down Chinatown, and they [residents] wanted to stop it. . . . I guess I was a little young to realize what was going on, but it was just that we see a lot of people out there upset about something, with something happening. . . . It was like, stop, stop the bulldozers! At the time it was just something that everybody did. It was very spontaneous, and it was fun.[53]

Hing, Leong, Lowe, and the other youth who protested were a new face of Chinatown: young, American born, and symbols of the family-oriented community that had expanded during the postwar years.

The protests of young people against the cranes and bulldozers turned out to be a defining moment for the "Save Chinatown" movement. Yee recalls their occupation and the media attention it garnered:

Early in the morning, five o'clock in the morning, bulldozers came to knock down some houses on the north side of Winter Street. . . . [P]eople in the community called everybody we knew, all went down to Chinatown, and some of us, I was among about a dozen of people, we climbed on the buildings and we stopped the bulldozers, because they couldn't do anything with people there. We stayed there the whole day. . . . We called the newspapers and we called the TV people, we called everybody, and we said, "This is a violation," so they stopped the demolition.[54]

The incident was reported by television crews and major local newspapers, becoming a symbol of the community's resistance. One television reporter joined the young people, reporting from atop the pile of debris. The *Philadelphia Inquirer* picked up the story, portraying Holy Redeemer as a "symbol of the community itself: dignified, offenseless, and threatened with extinction":

For seven years, the battle over the church raged; then, last August, bulldozers started pushing down houses on the south side of Vine Street. For three days, young people from Chinatown demonstrated and finally stopped demolition by lying down in front of the machines. Some climbed the hills of rubble, and refused to come down. The Chinatown community was aroused, and soon there were old men and shopkeepers sitting down in the rubble with the youthful demonstrators.[55]

The portrayal of Chinatown as dignified and offenseless was a radical change from the ways in which the community had historically been represented. Although the rhetoric of Chinatown's being "threatened with extinction" echoed language from earlier in the century, the face of what was threatened was radically new. Accompanied by a cover photo of five Chinatown boys dressed in baseball uniforms standing in front of a bulldozer, the feature suggested Chinatown had an American identity, embodied by its younger residents. The prominent place of women and children in the movement's representation likewise emphasized the nature of the community as a home for families, a change from its original image as a "bachelor society." Their visibility elevated Chinatown to public status as a neighborhood beyond its historic role as a niche commercial district. Several other news features followed in the next couple of years that solidified this sense of Chinatown as a threatened family enclave.

The rhetoric of the "Save Chinatown" movement struck several notes, claiming natural rights for residents, the long history of Chinatown at this site, and the importance of Chinatown to the larger city. A petition that circulated in 1973–1974, emblazoned with the heading "Help Save Chinatown" and illustrated with an image of a dragon, drew on several strands of this rhetoric:

Chinatown's heritage has been part of the Philadelphia scene for over a hundred years. The community celebrated its centennial in 1972. Its people and businesses contribute to the cultural as well as the social-economic well-being of Philadelphia. The development of the Vine Street Expressway and the Market Street East Development are detrimental to the future of Chinatown, affecting both the residential and commercial stability of the community. As taxpayers, the community has the right and responsibility to determine its future.[56]

"Our Town, Chinatown" declared another flyer. One announcement for an April 1973 Easter Sunday rally urged community members to get involved: "Your involvement, support and understanding is needed. Chinatown belongs to the Philadelphia community. Chinatown belongs to you."[57] A 1974 town meeting announcement also urged residents to consider the movement as a springboard for addressing other issues that the community faced: "The struggle to save Chinatown is only the beginning. There are many issues still unresolved that effect [sic] the community. . . . Your homes and life are involved."[58]

Consistently, Chinatown was portrayed as threatened, attacked, or strangled, with a noose around its neck, as in a December 4, 1979, flyer for a town meeting on construction-induced street closings that would block Chinatown off from Center City: "The noose is tightening!! Chinatown is being strangled by these street closings!! Chinatown is being hurt economically and socially by these street closings. The streets will be closed for five years. Will businesses in and around Chinatown be able to survive?" Activists also claimed that residents' health was "endangered by the dirt and noise pollution" as well as a rat problem caused by digging for the commuter rail tunnel: "It is unsafe for Chinatown residents and customers to leave or to come to Chinatown at night."[59]

In some of its rhetoric, PCDC tackled negative outside images of Chinatown head on. Historically, Chinatown had been portrayed as anti-modern, threatened by progress. PCDC challenged the idea that Chinatown was obstructing change:

Recent events have led people to believe that the Chinese community is against progress—against the City's attempt to promote commerce and revitalize the inner core. That is *untrue*. We believe that these things should happen in the interests of the people. However, when projects are promoted without regard to the rights and livelihood of the people they will affect, we feel that this is neither in the interest of progress nor of the City at large. On the contrary, we feel it is a great injustice to the basic principle of equal individual rights, on which are founded our great American democratic traditions. . . . Chinatown as an ethnic community and an important cultural nucleus is a significant part of the city's social fabric and a worthy contribution to its commercial life.[60]

PCDC attempted to hold city and state agencies accountable to its stated process of community involvement, insisting on their membership in the Philadelphia community. The configuration of the exit/entrance ramp planned for Ninth Street was a particular site of insistent concern. In December 1973, the group led a protest at City Council public, claiming that "the fight to save the Chinatown community isn't over! Market Street East ramps are still threatening to box in Chinatown! Once again the agencies involved are trying to slip another bill by the Chinatown community. We will not have the Market Street East ramps forced down our throats! Let's fill city council chambers with people to show the city that any community has a right to survive and determine its own future!" Another 1975 PCDC flyer declared, "CHINATOWN HAS NOT YET WON ITS FIGHT! CHINATOWN'S STRUGGLE MUST GO ON!"[61]

Also prominent in PCDC's rhetoric was the language of the American civil-rights movement and a radical insistence on self-determination. This language was largely crafted by activist Yee, as in her representative remarks at the On Leong Association on May 1973, shortly before the occupations of demolition sites: "Saving Chinatown is not merely an issue of preserving a number of houses and businesses for some people who happen to be Chinese; more significantly the movement is based on the issue of self-determination—i.e., the right of the Chinese community to take part in making decisions affecting it. We see this as a democratic right long recognized in principle in the tradition of American government." Yee went on to indict the city in its pursuit of progress as narrowly defined by the interests of "big business": "The newspapers continually talk about revitalizing the inner city; they talk about progress and change. City agencies talking about this kind of progress talk about the Bicentennial and Market Street East. They talk about the necessity of Third World communities like Chinatown and communities in South Philadelphia to give way to highways and urban renewal. . . . [I]t means that the city considers greater profits for big business to be synonymous with progress. What happened to the great American principle of government by the people and for the people?"[62] Yee linked the struggle of the Chinatown community against big business to the American Revolution in a critique of development strategies associated with the upcoming 1976 Bicentennial: "In order to meet the commercial demands of the Bicentennial which is projected to bring millions of tourists to Philadelphia, the Vine Street Expressway Extension and I-95 are wrecking the fabric of our communities. It is ironic that preparation for celebrating the American Revolution—a struggle for self-determination on the part of the colonies against Great Britain—should in fact deny that right to the people of Philadelphia."[63] She also emphasized rights within the American system: "The Chinatown Community doesn't want appeasement, we want our rights."[64]

"Same struggle, same fight!": Yellow Seeds

Yee exemplified the new spirit of Asian American activism that helped animate the "Save Chinatown" movement. Yee, who grew up in Boston's Chinatown, came to Philadelphia in 1970 to study urban planning and quickly
identified the dangers facing the community:

> I was interested in community development. Because in Boston, major
> highways had taken half of the housing in Chinatown. A lot of them
> [residents] had to leave there. I noticed a big difference, because that
> has caused a lot of Chinese population to disperse to the suburbs and
> surrounding area. So the neighborhood was no longer cohesive. A lot
> of social relationships were difficult to maintain. It was really sad for
> a while. . . . At the same time, I was aware of the black communities,
> the same kind of thing was going on. Major projects were destroying
> the neighborhood. And I was interested in how to help the neighbor-
> hoods to survive. . . . [I]n Boston I had seen what had happened and I
> also felt strongly about social justice. So when I came to Philadelphia
> and started to get to know Chinatown, it was clear that they had these
> problems on the horizon. . . . It was clear that it wasn't going to be one
> project in Chinatown. There were going to be three or four projects in
> Chinatown.[65]

Yee's concern for the area and her involvement in the "Save Chinatown" movement had been catalyzed by her participation in an Asian American Movement organization called Yellow Seeds. Yee formed Yellow Seeds with other
Philadelphians, including Howard Chin, a student of noted architect Louis
Kahn, and other students from around the area: Tony To, an urban studies
major; Jaime Kawano, a high school student in the city's progressive Parkway
High School program; Ti Hua Chang, an antiwar activist; and David Toy, an
engineer.

Like Yee, many Yellow Seeds founders came from working-class families
and had connections to and familiarity with the social and cultural dynamics
common to diverse Chinatowns. This allowed them to relate to Philadelphia's
Chinatown's workers and "regular folks":

> We had a lot of personal ties—I mean, between Tony, David, and
> myself especially, because we were Chinese speakers. So we realized
> what a big difference that made, and also because David and I came
> from the same background. Our parents were garment workers, were
> restaurant workers. Tony came from a more middle-class family, but
> his Cantonese was better than ours [laughs]. So, yeah, so we really
> were able to relate to the regular folks in Chinatown.[66]

Yellow Seeds attempted to bridge the generational and class divides within the community through its newspaper: "We would go deliver our papers in the restaurants and we'd sit and chat with people or meet them on the street and chat with them about stuff, or they'd ask us questions about the articles. . . . [P]eople wouldn't overtly say they agreed, but it certainly started discussions."[67] Yellow Seeds activists used their histories as members of working-class immigrant families to connect with a broad base of residents:

> The important thing about Yellow Seeds was that half of us spoke Cantonese or Toisanese. . . . [W]e were able to communicate and we were able to coalesce people so that the older generation of single males, a lot of them, worked to support us. They got us donations, they bought us a film projector, they paid our heating bill, they got our boiler fixed, they paid for folding chairs, and then we had programs. We had films from China; we had magazines; we had fund-raisers. At that time, Nixon still hadn't gone to China. And we were able to basically organize sentiment against the Vine Street Expressway.[68]

Like Asian American activists in other cities, Yellow Seeds' concern for social justice also led it to offer services to the community, sponsoring English lessons (many of the participating students were female garment workers and teenagers) and a drop-in center out of its offices on Winter Street that offered immigration assistance, translation services and tutoring, and health care information and referrals. The organization also sponsored cultural activities, such as screenings of movies from China, holiday celebrations (such as an October 1 commemoration of the founding of the People's Republic of China "at HR of all places"), a choral group, and dance performances.[69]

For PCDC and the "Save Our Church" coalition, opposition to the expressway was a claim to spatial ownership, and Chinatown was a homeplace that required defending. For many in Yellow Seeds, working in and with the local Chinatown "homeplace" was an important part of their activist philosophy that drew them to the "Save Chinatown" fight. Yellow Seeds' strategies and rhetoric echoed and participated in a growing Asian American Movement that focused on a variety of issues from cultural imperialism and war in Asia, to the establishment of Asian studies programs in universities, to the needs and threatened status of Asian American communities. These student-led organizations supported community protests and development under the umbrella of promoting racial justice more broadly, characterized by coalitional politics with other organizations in their ethnic urban communities. Many were interracial in nature and borrowed rhetoric and sought alliances with other Asian, African American, and Latino activist organizations. Like those in the Basement Workshop in New York City, Yellow Seeds members followed the exhortation of C. T. Wu of Hunter College, a mentor to the New

York student movement, to develop Chinatown as site for the amelioration of social problems and a power base for Asian American activism.[70] Chinatown was more than just a neighborhood—it was a space of racialized identity, a place for self-determination, and a zone of potential empowerment. Given the historic segregation and marginalization of Chinese and other Asians, defense of Chinatown was a radical claim that entailed a larger questioning of various authorities, including those within Chinatown, as well as a positive assertion of ethnic and racial identity. Against an image of the proposed expressway's tangle of ramps, a coalition flyer declared, "Save Chinatown!! Stop the Cultural Genocide!!"[71] By using such terms as "cultural genocide," Yellow Seeds made the fight about race and social/spatial justice.

Like PCDC, Yellow Seeds focused on housing as a primary issue facing the community. The *Yellow Seeds* magazine ran exposés on the conditions for elderly Chinese men, including housing owned and managed by CBA. For all its radicalism, Yellow Seeds was also consistently focused on concerns that might be considered traditionally Chinese, especially a concern for community elders. Like other Asian American student activists, they allied themselves with older workers and community residents, many of whom were most negatively affected by exploitive working conditions and substandard living arrangements. As activists in West Coast cities fought the eviction of elderly residents from such buildings as the International Hotel in San Francisco, Yellow Seeds drew attention to the squalid living conditions of CBA boardinghouses in Philadelphia.[72] In "The Neglected Chinatown Elderly," *Yellow Seeds* chastised the Chinatown leadership for its "neglect and selfishness" shown to the "retired men of this community, one-time waiters, cooks, and laundrymen, who are without families or friends to take care of them":

> They live in upstairs rooms, above stores, restaurants and association buildings. These apartments are substandard, and unfit. They are without hot water, safe drinking water, heating and toilets. Bare wood floors, falling ceilings, broken windows and dangerous electrical wiring exist everywhere. The alternatives to these conditions are flop house rooms, hospital beds and the isolation of a nursing home, the socially accepted form of neglect. Living in these unfit rooms and apartments is not free. A two room fire trap with an open flame gas heater can cost from $30 to $50 a month and the eviction of tenants of any age is not uncommon in Chinatown. The problems are basic: hunger, disease, and fear. . . . Bad health and disease are the results of infested living conditions, bad diets, and the inaccessibility of medical services. The neglect and isolation that is a part of old age in this community makes the Chinatown elderly more vulnerable to theft and robbery. There is little concern within the community about the safety and security of those who are retired and no longer an asset to business.[73]

The paper drew attention to violations of housing codes: "Plumbing, heating and cooking facilities are lacking or broken. Some people are stuck in fourth-floor attic apartments which are illegal because of the fire hazard and lack of elevator. More often there are leaky ceilings, holes in the floors or walls, peeling paint and wallpaper, jammed windows and broken stairs and railings."[74] Another feature, "This Is Where Mr. Lao Lives," described in detail the squalor of the rooming houses:

> It is dark; it is cold; and it smells like human feces, urine, and vomit. It is dark because there are no lights. It is cold because there is only an open flame heater. It smells because Mr. Lao is over 80 and too sick to walk down the two flights of stairs to the bathroom. He is too weak to walk one hour down the four flights of stairs to eat his only meal of the day. After 50 years of working in San Francisco, New York, and Phila as a water, cook, and laundryman; he has finally reached retirement. He has no relatives and no friends. He can barely walk when healthy, and when we found him he was on the sidewalk, unable to move in freezing weather.[75]

Not only was existing housing physically inadequate; there was not enough of it:

> Presently the housing in Chinatown is very inadequate. Not only is there much overcrowding, i.e., families with not enough bedrooms, but much housing is also below standard. . . . [I]t is structurally unsafe or violates the requirements of the City's housing code—a legal document. . . . Solving the problem of bad housing is not, however, as simple as forcing the landlords to fix up their properties. If the landlords are presently forced to conform to the City's law many families and old men will have to move out. There are hardly any vacancies in Chinatown into which they can move.[76]

By focusing on housing, *Yellow Seeds* was not only supporting an older generation of workers; it was highlighting the living nature of the Chinatown community, the spaces where families lived and worked. As one *Yellow Seeds* editorial observed, "Housing is a basic necessity of life. It is, however, more than just shelter. It is the heart of a community; for without housing there is no community. . . . [T]he community includes stores, schools, churches, playgrounds, and other facilities. But it is housing that gives the community its source of life."

With its emphasis on living conditions for the elderly and the less enfranchised of Chinatown's residents, Yellow Seeds members entered into direct conflict with some of Chinatown's traditional movers and shakers. One particular target of the organization's wrath was T. T. Chang. Chang's vision of Chinatown as a tourist destination was very much at odds with Yellow Seeds' vision of Chinatown as a space of empowerment for workers, youth, and families. "Let us all watch out for the people in the community who try to sell us out," a *Yellow Seeds* article warned. In 1975, *Yellow Seeds* ran an editorial attacking Chang—"T. T. Chang: Who Is He Really Helping?"—illustrated with a picture of Chang as an octopus grabbing at money. Chang was also portrayed by *Yellow Seeds* cartoonist Howard Chin as a puppet master controlling CBA and as a snake in the grass, his tail waving a clutch of dollar bills. *Yellow Seeds* consistently questioned Chang's use of funds and attacked Chang for putting the needs of his center and outside interests above the needs of the community, particularly when it came to youth services and housing: "T. T. Chang doesn't think Chinatown should be a residential community for Chinese families, but only a tourist center with some apartments for transients. He envisions a 10 story office building as epitomizing Chinatown's goals for its people—no houses, no community facilities, nothing for the people—just money for those in the tourist business." *Yellow Seeds* accused Chang of undermining the "Save Chinatown" movement from within by portraying himself as the "mayor of Chinatown," helping "urban renewal tear Chinatown down by making what this community wants seem divided." "He does not represent the sentiments of the majority of Chinatown people," the article continued, offering a "self-proclaimed service that no one requested and caused disruption and misunderstanding." "Why has he never made a public statement in meetings with public officials or never made a public statement in support to save the community and his opposition to the ramps?" queried *Yellow Seeds* in fall 1974.[77]

Chang's focus on the CC&CC building was a particular object of scorn, a symbol of Chang's neglect of internal community needs:

> If we look at the Chinatown YMCA, also known as the Chinese Cultural Center, today there is very little that resembles what most people would expect. There are private offices, museum exhibits, and gift counters. Ceilings and walls are decorated with wood and stone carvings, and everywhere artifacts abound. It certainly is a wealth of cultural material for one community, but we have to remember that most people in Chinatown have never seen it. . . . [W]here is the Chinatown YMCA? Well, in the far back of the basement there is a recreation area consisting of a few pinball machines and a pool table.[78]

In another cover story, *Yellow Seeds* displayed an image of a demolished Chinatown block, with an image of CC&CC superimposed, as if standing alone in the middle of the block. The headline asked, "Is this T.T. Chang's urban renewal plan?"

> The Chinatown "Y" is a tourist attraction, a museum that shows nothing about Chinese-American people today, and a restaurant. Yes, even a restaurant in a place that gets government money in one hand to serve the community and in the other hand money that actually takes business from existing restaurants in the very community it is supposed to serve.[79]

Franklin Park, "T. T.'s Play Toy," was another source of rancor. *Yellow Seeds* accused Chang of taking advantage of the Holy Redeemer situation to insert himself with a proposal to use a "fixed-up" Franklin Park to replace the Holy Redeemer gym.[80]

At times, *Yellow Seeds* even questioned the tactics of its ally PCDC. Yee recalls the relationship as "not mild—it was mixed":

> George [Moy] was very sympathetic to Yellow Seeds; he understood the concept of having a united front against the Redevelopment Authority even though we might not totally agree with each other. We got red-baited all the time. And then there were people who were kind of neutral that basically felt that we were the ones that would be out front and be vocal and active, so they appreciated that, because they themselves didn't want to do that. And then there were people that just thought we were radicals. We were rabble-rousers, you know.[81]

Asking, "Where Are Our Misleaders?" *Yellow Seeds* demanded greater activism and transparency from PCDC:

> People were real angry when they heard that another building was being torn down. Yellow Seeds took a strong stand and blocked demolition at 6:30 Tuesday morning. But where was the CBA and PCDC? It was decided that Chinatown will not let the State tear down the rest of the building unless Chinatown's demands are met. It is to be remembered that the building and all house empty lots are a symbol of our need to struggle for our survival. It is symbolic in the same way when, last fall, Chinatown told the State that no more buildings were to come down until the Plaza over the highway was promised to us. They did not make that promise and they took down another building. Obviously, the State does not serve the people. . . . At the end of the rally there was a march to City Hall to see the Mayor. We waited while some PCDC Board Members met behind closed doors with the

Deputy Mayor. We do not know what went on, but any meeting with the government concerning Chinatown should be open.[82]

Yellow Seeds "helped push Philadelphia Chinatown Development Corporation forward," according to Yee, by criticizing it in the organization's magazine: "We often criticized PCDC and at the same time supported them, because we felt that their stand was not strong enough, and I think we were able to basically put pressure on it. And to take a more militant stance for China-town." Yee also believes it was important for Yellow Seeds to push PCDC to consider larger questions of social justice that informed the Chinatown predicament:

> Because the group that organized around PCDC was mainly Catholic and mainly alumni of HR [Holy Redeemer] . . . when I came, I helped broaden it by saying, "Oh, this is a community center and not just the HR auditorium. And here is a church that's an institution, not just the Catholic Church. Plus, this is taking out a quarter of the housing in Chinatown. You've already lost housing from Independence Mall 4. So this is an issue of democratic rights, because they're not even asking you to be involved in the planning process." So then Yellow Seeds kept saying, "This is a democratic rights issue."[83]

Yee reflects that Yellow Seeds "questioned the basic assumptions" of agencies about land use and planning, traffic counts, and projections. Yee also provided a foil for PCDC in its relationship with the PRA: "I would be adversarial, and then Cecilia [Moy Yep] and George [Moy] would be kind of conciliatory, and then in the end we got kind of where we needed to be."[84]

Yellow Seeds' divergence from PCDC was more than tactical; it was also ideological. Its approach typically opposed government and the larger status quo in general, a stance that sometimes conflicted with PCDC's desire to work with government and existing institutions. In fights against demolitions, Yellow Seeds activists hung banners on bulldozers with the slogan, "Fight the Highway! Fight the State. Fight to Win!" One *Yellow Seeds* issue reporting on the protest declared, "The Government is our enemy." As Yee asserted at a town meeting at the On Leong Association in May 1973: "The government would rather take our tax dollars and spend them by the billions bombing Indochina and perpetrating the war and promoting big business than spending it on community renewal." The term "state" was used in *Yellow Seeds* discourse to characterize various levels of government.[85] In May 1973, for example, the magazine indicted government agencies generally with taking citizens' money in the form of taxes and placing profits over those citizens:

The government agencies have placed the needs of a long established community below the needs of big business and commuter traffic. Both the city's and the state's responses clearly place profit above people, office space above homes and traffic above ecology. The struggle exists between the interests of big business and the democratic rights of the ordinary citizen. If the government is truly representative of the people, the choice is obvious.... The tax dollars from Chinatown are not being used to build up the community. Instead they are being channeled to projects that threaten to destroy the community.... The paper concluded, "Both the city and the state have abandoned the cause of community self-determination for the cause of corporate profit. To rely on them would guarantee defeat."[86]

Focusing on self-determination, community empowerment, and racial justice, Yellow Seeds members also sought to make connections between the Chinatown struggle and the larger struggle of people of color in the United States and globally. With a radical Maoist orientation, Yellow Seeds urged Chinatown youth to fight the state and question authority. In a community that had long eschewed connections to the Chinese communist state, Yellow Seeds pursued its activities with an unabashedly leftist tone. "Same Struggle, Same Fight," one of the group's key slogans, referred to the shared concerns of Asians, African Americans, and Latinos and was grounded in Third-World ideology. *Yellow Seeds* noted links between New York's Chinatown's fight against police brutality and the fight against urban renewal in Philadelphia, reported on the eviction of Japanese American residents in San Francisco and Los Angeles and the war in Vietnam, and in general emphasized the fight for democratic rights against the oppression of all minority and working or Third-World people, borrowing issues and tactics from the Black Panthers or Young Lords.

These shared concerns engendered Yellow Seeds' relationships with other activists in the city, particularly Puerto Rican groups in North Philadelphia. Yee recalls:

The other thing that we did, though, was to reach out to other Third-World communities. So we were in coalition groups with the Puerto Rican Socialist Workers Party, which is the successor to the Young Lords. And then with . . . Black United Front, North Philly, and also the people that put out—let's see, they're called the Revolutionary Union, people that were working in Kensington, white workers in Kensington. And then we had some other ties, not so tightly, with [the] Philadelphia Workers Organizing Project.

But, in every city though, especially between New York and Philadelphia, the Puerto Ricans and the Asians knew each other, because we partied together. . . . [W]e used to have groups that would get together and discuss issues.[87]

As part of a larger genesis of AAM, Yee describes how Yellow Seeds also maintained relationships with other Asian activists, particularly in other Chinatowns in the Northeast:

We had a network, so that we knew people in New York and Boston and then people who were from someplace else, people from wherever, California. Between college and where people grew up, we had a network. Then in 1972, after Nixon went to China, I was lucky enough to be put on a youth delegation that went to China, that's people from all over. . . . Then it was even a stronger network with more people. One of the meeting groups at that time was in New York City, and they were more ideological than the Yellow Seeds was, but they also had a newspaper, and they hooked up with Jesse Jackson's Rainbow Coalition and the Young Lords and the Panthers. And so they followed basically a pattern like the Black Panthers—they had a breakfast program and all that kind of stuff.[88]

Yellow Seeds was part of both a national social movement of Asian American youth focused on broad global social change and a local movement focused on the defense of specific ethnic territory. It was successful in Chinatown because its members were able to reach out to older working residents as well as to second- and third-generation youth, bridging generational and ideological divides to facilitate the community's ability to speak externally with a collective voice, while broadening the range of resistance tactics available to that community.

Yellow Seeds' work with PCDC and the "Save Our Church" group points to the complex ways in which Philadelphia's Chinatown organized against and for urban renewal. Unlike other Asian American communities, where young students allied with elderly workers, Philadelphia's movement drew on the significant power of another second generation (represented by PCDC) who had grown up or raised children in Chinatown. This middle generation—neither student movement nor old Chinatown leadership—was critical to the "Save Chinatown" fight and the subsequent rebuilding of Chinatown.

A "least-destructive" Future

The campaign against the Vine Street Expressway was sophisticated not only in its coalition building across the community but in its strategies as well. The protracted nature of the fight allowed Chinatown to explore multiple fronts of resistance, employ multifaceted "mobilizing structures," and benefit from changing urban-planning and environmental-policy frameworks, particularly regarding community participation and input.[89] Passage of a national Environmental Policy Act (EPA) in 1969 created a legal structure for the assessment of development projects' potential effects on communities, requiring environmental-impact studies (EIS) for federally funded projects. In 1972 or 1973, PCDC crafted a long, pointed letter about the right to have an EIS done in response to a public notice soliciting comments on PennDOT's plans in light of the EPA. PCDC insisted that the state undertake a now legally required EIS for the highway and other redevelopment projects in Chinatown. Initially PennDOT resisted, according to Yee, claiming that this legal requirement did not apply to projects that were already underway. PCDC threatened to sue, and the state caved: "We threatened to sue them—we didn't have the money to do it—but again we heard California had the same situation, [and] they sued and they won. So if we sued, we would win."[90] The EPA also put in place legal guidelines and mandates for the assessment of ongoing projects. In response, PennDOT engaged the engineering consulting firm of Howard, Needles, Tammen, and Bergendoff to conduct an EIS of the Vine Street Expressway. Aiming to address air quality, noise levels, land use, and "socioeconomic and cultural considerations," the environmental impact team held a series of public meetings at CBA.[91] Under environmental consequences and mitigation, the EIS called for the relocation of Holy Redeemer Church and School, a provision that was actively opposed by PCDC.

PCDC, with the help of additional experts, negotiated with the state for a revised expressway plan. Eric Chung, a local Chinese American architect who had studied with Kahn, helped the organization understand and address the issues involved. By 1980, PennDOT abandoned the existing plan for Vine Street, instead proposing two alternative models, including a "scaled-down" version that, among other features, spared Holy Redeemer from demolition or relocation. PCDC hailed this choice as "the most efficient design" and the "least destructive to Chinatown's socio-physical links and environmental quality."[92] That same year, a Vine Street Task Force was created to facilitate work with local communities on the Vine Street design and its construction. PCDC played an active role in this process, representing the community, communicating with CBA and other Chinatown constituents, and attempting to negotiate the most favorable plans for Chinatown. In 1981, an additional EIS was conducted for the new plan that recommended adoption of the reduced-scale Vine Street Expressway and significant community-impact mitigation. In the new EIS, Chinatown was described as a "unique social, cultural and economic resource for the city," a "highly cohesive and self-sufficient community" that had undergone a "major rejuvenation." The EIS acknowledged the investment in and recent expansion of Chinatown in the prior decades: "Only fairly recently have Chinese Americans been unhindered in the purchase of real estate; there has been a significant shift in ownership patterns to reflect this opportunity. This increase in ownership, growth in retail business, and more use of redevelopment programs has brought about major rejuvenation to Chinatown, removing previously dilapidated physical conditions in the area and raising expectations about the community's future."[93] By 1983, the Federal Highway Works Administration accepted the EIS and supported the mitigation plan and reduced-scale project, clearing the way for the completion of the project in 1991.

The outcome was a compromise, but one that preserved Holy Redeemer and the community and afforded PCDC some standing with the city. The organization used that standing to address other issues of concern to the community as the expressway project continued. Noise walls were proposed, featuring graphic elements that would "emphasize the identity of Chinatown," and modifications to the Tenth Street crossing were created to allow for a pedestrian plaza and decorative plantings. Concerns from PCDC included making the plaza safe for children and preventing its use by "derelicts," worries that certainly reflected Chinatown's historical situation. Foo Dog statues at Tenth and Vine were proposed but then abandoned because of a budget shortfall.[94] PCDC protested this change, arguing that the exit off Vine Street was important for Chinatown's visibility, a visibility that undergirded the local neighborhood economy: "Chinatown is a community whose stability is dependent on tourists for the restaurants, gift shops, and related businesses. The business community must have visibility. With the noise walls so high, drivers would pass without ever knowing that Chinatown is here. Therefore, the Foo Dogs are important landmarks . . . [that] also offset the negative features of the noise wall."[95] At this point, the protest by PCDC was less about the survival of the community per se but rather how to use the expressway project to mitigate against a lack of visibility by drawing attention to Chinatown's cultural identity, to troubleshoot negative effects of the project on the community, and to further brand structures on the northern edge of Chinatown to drive business traffic to the neighborhood.

An important outcome of the expressway fight was the emergence of a new structure of leadership in Chinatown, with a different generational and gendered face and focused on a new set of community priorities. The intergenerational coalition that grew from the "Save Chinatown" movement had important implications for organizational life and leadership. Women came into leadership roles for the first time, as did second-generation Chinese Americans. Such groups as Yellow Seeds invested energy in bucking the authority of the established social hierarchy, represented by CBA, while PCDC maintained a balancing act of deference and independence, bridging the two and serving as a representational conduit for interactions with outside agencies and authorities. All parties played important roles in the coalition. PCDC leaders brought strong attachments to and a history in the neighborhood and the city. They had investments in the neighborhood as well as the larger city as a home. The participation of university students and young professionals with backgrounds in urban planning, engineering and architecture brought new skills and knowledge to the "Save Chinatown" fight and enhanced PCDC's abilities to resist and negotiate solutions with the city and state. Their efforts also worked to reframe the struggle for Chinatown as a struggle for ethnic and racial self-determination and justice, not only within the spaces of Chinatown but also within the city and society as a whole.

Chinatown was now visible to politicians and agencies at the state and local levels in a way it had never been before, a force to be reckoned with. It was also a new site of urban redevelopment—community-driven redevelopment—in the form of PCDC. To effectively work in urban renewal, PCDC had to shift its focus from fighting City Hall to working with it. As Moy recalls, "We were too small a community to outright fight the city, state, and federal government. We had to get public relations on our side. So that's why, being part of progress, we're not going to block progress, but give us a chance to live with it."[96] Living with progress was increasingly PCDC's goal, and it was a complex balancing act that involved focus on urban development and close work with PRA and other city agencies, even as it continued its resistance to state and local plans that were deemed detrimental to the community. By the time the expressway was completed in 1991, PCDC had spent twenty years as a community developer in Chinatown, moving beyond protests of city and state actions to a complex working relationship with local agencies to create a new Chinatown landscape, one that embodied a continued insistence on Chinatown as a culturally distinctive, living place.

4

"Be part of progress, not its sacrificial lamb"

Community-Development Strategies,
1970–2000

On September 12, 1971, the Grand Court of Wanamaker's Department Store at Thirteenth and Market was awash in the color and motion of Chinese lion dancers, a kung-fu demonstration, and a "display of ancient Chinese fashions." The occasion for this transformation was the launch of a one-hundred-day celebration commemorating the centennial of Philadelphia's Chinatown. Over the next three months, the Chinatown community hosted a variety of events: a street festival; lectures on Chinese Americans, United States–China relations, Chinese literature, and Chinese philosophy; and a fashion show.[1] On Sunday, October 17, the main day of the celebration, a newly restored Chinese Benevolent Association (CBA) building at 930 Race was ceremonially reopened, followed by a parade, banquets, and entertainment. Also included over the course of the three months were discussion programs on "the Next Century" of Chinatown. These discussions centered on general areas that had long concerned the community, such as cultural, language, educational, and social issues. But they also highlighted some issues specific to that moment in Chinatown's life cycle: health services, the problems of youth, a chronic housing shortage, the need for a nursing home for the aged, and relations with the city.[2]

Given the state of the last concern in 1971, Chinatown had reason to look ahead with anxiety as well as hope. Although a venerable one hundred years old, Chinatown was a community under threat in the early 1970s; demolitions had already taken about 25 percent of its housing, and the community was five years into a prolonged fight against the proposed Vine Street Expressway. Chinatown had grown exponentially in the last decade but was still a modest neighborhood, home to about 549 Chinese Americans, 10 restaurants, 5 shops, and 3 churches. An estimated 25 percent of the population lived below the poverty level.[3] By 2000, after several decades of diversifying immigration from Hong Kong and Southeast Asia (particularly ethnic Chinese from Vietnam), Chinatown's population had grown to 2,924 residents, 2,436 of them Asian American. A total of 67,654 Asians lived in Philadelphia (138,043 in the larger five-county region), among whom Chinatown was an important regional cultural center.[4] Had the area offered more housing options, the number living in Chinatown undoubtedly would have been much higher. The growth was due also in part to the work of Chinatown's organizations and activists to develop and preserve Chinatown in its historic location downtown. This preservation was spatially rooted and culturally distinct, aimed at reclaiming property and asserting ethnic territory based on historical presence.

Around 1971, a new community-development corporation (CDC) was founded to work with city agencies to plan Chinatown's future, at least in terms of redevelopment. But it struggled to determine priorities and learn the processes and politics of urban renewal. By 2000, this new organization, the Philadelphia Chinatown Development Corporation (PCDC), had constructed 215 units of housing, erected the largest traditional Chinese gateway in North America, and successfully fended off numerous threats to the community. Working in complex relationship with city-planning agencies, such as the PRA, the Philadelphia City Planning Commission (PCPC), and various community constituencies, PCDC self-consciously claimed and ethnically marked the landscape of Chinatown for Asian Americans throughout the final decades of the twentieth century. Guided by a comprehensive plan (the "Chadbourne Report"), PCDC worked as a developer to obtain PRA-controlled lots, secure special zoning for Chinatown, and complete a wide range of projects, including various affordable housing and residential-commercial mixed-use structures and an "authentic Chinese" Friendship Gate (this last project made possible by a transnational city trade mission). In doing so, it engaged an emerging repertoire of strategies for ethnic spatial theming, from architecture to streetscaping, which reclaimed territory for Chinatown, stabilized the neighborhood's boundaries, and asserted a sense of place.

Philadelphia's Chinatown's practice of community development was similar to that of other Chinatowns and other Asian enclaves across North America. Many battled redevelopment and rebuilt or expanded with Asian-themed architecture and commercial-/residential-use strategies. Most constructed large gateways or arches to mark their areas as Chinatowns. Chicago's Chinatown—which also had been bisected by expressways—focused on not only creating housing but also expanding the community across barriers on its south side. The Santa Fe Project, undertaken in 1984 by the Chinese American Development Corporation, reclaimed the former Santa Fe Railroad yards for commercial and residential redevelopment as "South Chinatown." Subsequent development in Santa Fe's "South Chinatown" included erecting a traditional Chinese gateway and creating Chinatown Square, a new center of activity for the community. In Canada, the national government played an active role in redevelopment in the 1970s and 1980s, leading to change—often destructive—in that country's Chinatowns. Many Chinatowns disappeared or were greatly reduced in size. Vancouver's Chinatown survived slum clearance and a freeway threat in the 1950s to rebuild its community across an east–west barrier. In Montreal, new construction since the 1980s has focused around a pedestrian mall with arches and improved streetscaping.[5] In Los Angeles's Little Tokyo, anti-eviction organizers transformed into a CDC—the Little Tokyo Service Center Community Development Center—that worked with the city's redevelopment authority to revitalize Little Tokyo as a residential community, building low-income housing. Its efforts resulted in, among other things, a fourteen-year campaign to build a gym and community center, the Budokan, as an anchor for the neighborhood's ethnic identity.[6]

From Protest to Planning

Like those of Little Tokyo, Philadelphia's Chinatown activists moved from protesting to planning early on, often volleying strategically between the two. Even as it continued to wage a fight against the Vine Street Expressway as part of the "Save Chinatown" coalition, PCDC immediately began leveraging its newfound connections to city agencies into formal plans for redeveloping the area. Representatives George Moy and Cecilia Moy Yep discussed possible redevelopment with the PCPC as early as 1966, shortly after they learned of the expressway plan's potential effects on Holy Redeemer Chinese Catholic Church and School (see Figure 4.1). When Damon Childs of the Planning Commission met with the community in March 1966, he reported back that in addition to concerns about the expressway, there was "a group who wanted to institute an urban renewal project to help Chinatown develop residential and commercial areas. . . . The group was sympathetic to the setting up of a committee to submit a proposal to the Redevelopment Authority for the development of these parcels."[7] Minutes of the newly formed committee indicate that members were considering all possible options for saving Chinatown. In 1967, PCDC (as the Philadelphia Chinatown Development Committee of the Chinese Benevolent Association) focused on thinking through how to respond to Chinatown's lack of presence in city planning and development. It considered existing conditions, community needs, current city plans, and possible expansions of the neighborhood and methods for getting there. Reporting back to CBA in 1967, the group offered three alternatives for Chinatown: relocation (to Washington Square West, a now-upscale neighborhood to the south), use of a private developer to create a comprehensive plan and develop Chinatown, or formation of a nonprofit corporation under CBA to develop and improve Chinatown. The third option led to the incorporation of PCDC

Figure 4.1. Cecilia Moy Yep and George Moy in the PCDC offices, 1980s. (Courtesy of the Philadelphia Chinatown Development Corporation.)

as an independent organization in 1969. The corporation was authorized to create a comprehensive plan, raise necessary funds, and engage in contacts with private and public agencies: "We feel the great need to take immediate action, as other Chinatowns throughout the country have done."[8]

The decision to formalize an aspect of the "Save Chinatown" movement as a CDC was a formative one. By forming as a CDC, PCDC's founders committed themselves beyond activism per se to engagement with the urban-planning and economic-development apparatuses of local and federal government. A relatively new concept in the late 1960s, many CDCs emerged, as did PCDC, out of local civil-rights and community-advocacy movements. One hundred CDCs were operating nationally by 1970. Their numbers grew significantly during the 1970s out of growing community resistance to urban renewal, redlining, physical displacement, and other fights for justice in urban neighborhoods. By the end of the 1970s, more than one thousand CDCs were operating across the country, and this number grew exponentially in the 1980s.[9] Although CDCs utilize a variety of methods to address a range of urban issues, most share three characteristics: community control of activities, economic development, and the targeting of a specific geographic area. Inherently place-based and locally focused, the CDC was an entity well designed to assist residents in constructing, strengthening, and maintaining a sense of place.

Formed at a time when federal funding for community development and other social programs began a protracted period of withdrawal, CDCs worked as "corrective capitalism," drawing on partnerships with local governments and for-profit entities to craft responses to urban problems.[10] CDCs emerged at a point in urban history when "devolution meets revolution," when cities pulled back from large-scale investment in redevelopment, particularly at the neighborhood level, and at a time when grassroots movements, particularly for people of color, were trying to reclaim neighborhoods from blight, abandonment, and neglect. Thus even as CDCs were formed from civil-rights struggles, they were early on enmeshed in the politics of city governments. Many city governments supported CDCs, which could handle the nitty-gritty work of neighborhood development while City Hall focused on downtown growth.[11] In this way, CDCs are perhaps one hallmark of the emergence of neoliberal urban-development philosophies at a more global level. As a strategy shaped by neoliberal approaches to urban problems, CDCs are inherently contradicted, sometimes torn between their activist origins and market-driven development realities. However, when organizations can balance the two viewpoints, they become "development technicians with a political orientation and political activists with technical development skills."[12]

PCDC's goal to "be a part of progress, not its sacrificial lamb," according to co-founder Moy, echoes this doubled agenda.[13] "Progress" for PCDC meant primarily answering the chronic and acute need for housing in the neighborhood.[14] To this end, it began planning ways to increase housing, first for the elderly and those displaced by renewal. In an initial study undertaken by PCDC, 60 percent of respondents indicated they would purchase new houses in Chinatown, and housing was also identified as a need for new immigrants and those living in overcrowded conditions. Demolition along East Ninth Street and plans for Independence Mall were identified as primary forces of dislocation. Yet this area was also identified as the best possible for community expansion, and the committee urged that a proposal be developed. Responsibility for redevelopment in PCDC initially lay with the Planning Committee, formed early on to develop and propose plans for redeveloping the neighborhood. Members included Yep, Moy, Yellow Seeds founder Mary Yee, and architect Eric Chung.

In some cases, concerns about the effect of ongoing development projects on Chinatown led to a conflation of their fight against city and state projects (a confrontational and defensive posture) and neighborhood redevelopment (a cooperative posture). In March 1973, Moy wrote to Lynne Abraham, the director of the Philadelphia Redevelopment Authority (PRA), to voice objections to the plan for Market Street East, including a list of community concerns, from the loss of Holy Redeemer to the need for housing and recreational facilities. Moy urged Abraham to help the community, arguing that PRA was an "instrument by which the community can offset its loss" of Holy Redeemer. In her reply, Abraham rejected Moy's assertion that PRA "must help Chinatown offset its loss" with a strict interpretation of agency roles, arguing that responsibility for that property lay with the Pennsylvania Department of Transportation (PennDOT), not with the city. Later, as protests over the expressway escalated in 1973, PCDC was reminded to keep separate the community's concerns about other redevelopment projects and the projects it was pursuing with the agency. Dealing with PRA and PCPC entailed a delicate balancing act between compromise and advocacy, pushing city agencies to negotiate with the neighborhood while accepting necessary compromises and learning to conform to city agencies' priorities. As Moy reflects, "Here's a group you can talk to, who's willing to compromise, make sacrifices, and get something that they want, give something that government wants."[15]

The "Chadbourne Report"

PCDC leadership was tenacious and tireless in their attempts to work with the city to secure funding for redevelopment planning and housing construction. They also benefited from changing policies and best practices in urban planning that increasingly encouraged community involvement in planning. Because the lack of a feasible plan for development continued to dog PCDC's efforts throughout the early 1970s, a major turning point came in 1974, when PCDC at last successfully petitioned PCPC for a planning study of Chinatown. This study, which became known as the "Chadbourne Report" (after the consultant who performed the work, Christopher Chadbourne, of the New York firm Gluck and Chadbourne), provided PCDC with a powerful tool for redeveloping the community, a concrete plan that took the area's special needs into account as well as market realities. It was not only a practical tool for future planning but also a signal of the city's commitment to Chinatown, following its certification as an Urban Renewal Area. Chadbourne acted as an "advocacy planner" and spent months canvassing the neighborhood, interviewing residents and business owners to get a deep knowledge of what the community needed and wanted.[16] In particular, PCDC urged Chadbourne to address issues of housing, according to Yep: "We only had three [priorities]. The comprehensive stated three needs. It needed the rental people being displaced, it needed the property owners being displaced, and it was the elderly that never were taken care of. We demanded that the consultant consider the elderly, because there were a lot of elderly living in those apartments that could not afford their rent."[17] Chadbourne weighed these needs against the realities of real-estate markets and federal-/state-/city-funding mechanisms and codes. He acknowledged that many of the challenges facing Chinatown were the "result of cumulative actions, piecemeal progress, accommodation, and adjustments," the result of agencies, investors, and communities "pursuing their own narrow objectives without necessarily understanding the consequences on other communities, or even, at times, other agencies." The effect of this, he concluded, was "devastating," and the extent of demolition through government action was "staggering."[18]

For the first time, an outside entity acknowledged the investment and improvement that residents and business owners had put into the aging neighborhood. Chadbourne observed:

Rehabilitation in both commercial and residential properties has occurred to some degree during the past few years in Chinatown. Several "new wave" restaurants have opened featuring lavish interiors. Private residences have been rehabilitated and one or two larger buildings, notably 218 Ninth Street, have been refurbished as apartments. ... [T]he costs of material and labor have escalated so that almost all rehabilitation is done on a self-help non-union basis, with the exception of the basic trades such as plumbing and electrical. The Chinese simply extend their 9 to 14 hour work day and become carpenters. The result is a reduction in rehabilitation costs of approximately 50%.[19]

The nature of the housing market in Chinatown, however, precluded widespread rehabilitation of structures, Chadbourne surmised: "However, the absolute maximum of rental money available from Chinese families cannot generate sufficient cash flow to justify institutional rehabilitation loans for any form of extensive rehabilitation."[20]

Guided by PCDC and recognizing the community's acute needs, Chadbourne devoted the largest portion of the report to Chinatown's pressing issue of housing. From the beginning, Chadbourne maintained that the Chinese market and demand for housing was "unique": "Extended family and district associations form the basis of community organization; as the family is the basic Chinese unit of social organization, so are ownership of property and sense of place basic Chinese values." Chadbourne noted that money traditionally went back to China or was used to bring family to the United States. He also noted that Chinese immigrants saved a great deal of their income, and when they did buy, they could often put down 50 percent cash for property.[21] The results of a survey conducted regarding the housing market in Chinatown suggested the importance of four forms of housing: duplexes or triplexes, apartments, mixed-use commercial/residential structures, and elderly congregate housing.[22] Chadbourne advised that relocation should be kept to a minimum and that existing housing clusters should be strengthened, making Spring Street the residential "spine" of the community. A variety of housing types should be offered and directed to the Chinese market in terms of price and type.[23]

A powerful part of Chadbourne's report was its recognition of the unique landscape that characterized Chinatown, particularly the predominance of mixed-use commercial/residential structures. As part of his conclusions, Chadbourne recommended rezoning Chinatown from C4 to RC7, essentially a residential zone that permitted, but did not mandate, commercial activity on the ground floor of buildings. Tenth and Race Streets required special provisions to stimulate retail commercial expansion and permit the legitimate existence of L4 uses, which at this time included the garment trades. An overlay district entitled the "Chinatown Special Zoning District" was proposed that would mandate sign restrictions, require retail or commercial activity at grade, retain residential-scale considerations, encourage preservation of existing stock including usable loft structures, and permit a continuation of the store-below/residences-above pattern of Chinese development. Street uses would relate to active pedestrian activity, and yard requirements would reflect the nature of a mixed-use zone.[24]

Chadbourne also suggested that the first input of money should be made in the core areas of Chinatown: "The core must be strengthened before Chinatown can leapfrog to the west, or north, and construction to the east is impeded by construction of the commuter rail tunnel." This was a message that PCDC took to heart, according to Yep: "At that time there was so much other land available that one of the recommendations of the Chadbourne Report was to strengthen the core of the community. He said, 'Don't go, not right away, stay here and make sure that everything is taken first and then move. But,' he says, 'strengthen the core of the community.' And that stuck with me."[25] The Chadbourne Report played a crucial role in PCDC's ability to come up with concrete feasible plans for redevelopment and effectively answer the requirements of government agencies. It also gave them a roadmap that provided direction for systematic development of the neighborhood for the next fifteen years.

The result of Chadbourne's efforts was the 1975 Chinatown I Urban Renewal Plan, which earmarked $2.4 million for property acquisition, demolition, housing, and site improvements (new sidewalks and pavements) in Chinatown; $1.4 million of this amount would be needed for land acquisition. Monies were to be used to cover the city's and state's administrative costs for the projects. PCDC received no funding but could apply to be a developer. Land acquisition was outlined with conveyance to approved developers.

But creating the plan was only the beginning; it would have to clear City Council as Bill No. 2067. PCDC worked with PRA, which began amassing land parcels in the area. PCDC and Yellow Seeds mobilized the community to attend the City Council hearing on the bill, arguing that "increasing adequate housing in Chinatown itself is the key to saving Chinatown and helping it prosper. We also all know about the possibility of losing Holy Redeemer Church and School. Strengthening and adding to our housing stock in Chinatown can help us demonstrate that we need Holy Redeemer more than ever."[26] Reminding readers that institutional and governmental uses had already taken up huge areas that were part of greater Chinatown, PCDC claimed that "unless the community acts in its own interest, unifies, and controls the development in the area the future of Chinatown looks bleak."[27] The opponents of the measure, according to PCDC, lacked "understanding of the forces and impacts that adversely affect Chinatown" by emphasizing commercial development only, which would "put the area up for grabs. It would encourage speculation and uncontrolled development that would eventually choke out the many segments making up the Chinatown community." When the plan was approved, Moy commented that it was "partial proof that the system can be made to work for the little guy."[28]

"Without housing, there is no community"

With approval for a Chinatown redevelopment plan secured, PCDC moved forward to implement the various components. Highest priority, and most difficult to achieve, was the construction of new housing, particularly for those who had been displaced by historic demolition. When PCDC had difficulty generating feasible proposals for housing, financing was consistently the issue. Two years before the Chadbourne Report, after six years of meeting with the city, PCDC had presented eight plans to PRA and PCPC, but "all had been deemed unfeasible due to rigid technical city codes and regulations."[29] Feasibility, in many cases, meant financial feasibility. As PCDC discovered, developing low- to moderate-income housing in an area of the city with rising real-estate values was a challenging economic problem. PRA head Abraham cited two factors that limited the ability to produce such housing: "the fixed geographic area of the community and the economic feasibility of development, influenced by high land value, dense development and lack of subsidies for the production of housing which meets the income limits of community residents." The latter was a reference to the increasing lack of federal programs for low- to moderate-income homeownership.

From 1975 to 1997, PCDC undertook a range of redevelopment projects, most of which were aimed at providing housing for the community. During the late 1970s and 1980s, as PCDC began its development activities in earnest, federal housing policy underwent a period of flux, ultimately moving toward greater privatization. Historically, policy had focused on subsidizing homeownership in the suburbs and producing public housing for inner-city populations, particularly African Americans, many of whom had been displaced by highway and other renewal projects. In Philadelphia, public-housing efforts had focused primarily on units for African Americans located in an inner ring of blighted neighborhoods. These efforts, however, were not applicable to Chinatown's situation or scale. Under the policies of the Nixon administration, federal money for low-income housing began to shrink, and Section 235 and 236 mortgage subsidies fell under scrutiny and scandal, temporarily suspended in 1971–1972.[30] During an era of budget deficits, funding cuts, and stalled economic growth, federal policy shifted focus away from inner-city housing construction toward the rehabilitation of existing structures and the subsidization of rents through Section 8 housing allowances.[31] Increasingly, federal monies were offered through community block grants and funneled through the hands of local and state agencies. What this meant for organizations like PCDC was that while federal funding would be available for senior housing, few federal funding mechanisms existed for low- to moderate-income home construction and ownership, particularly for new construction in city centers. PCDC would have to rely heavily on local and state agencies for support and leverage public financing with substantial private investment to successfully bring these projects to completion.

PCDC's projects were more modest in scale than those in other China-towns. In part this scale was suggested by the existing landscape (row houses and low-rise commercial buildings), but in other cases it was determined by available financing. Four projects in particular embody the range of PCDC's work in housing, each drawing on a different approach to planning and financing: Mei Wah Yuen (1982), row houses and apartments along Spring Street between Ninth and Eleventh; On Lok House (1984), Section 8 senior housing; Gim San Plaza (1989), a mixed-use housing/retail section along East Ninth Street; and Hing Wah Yuen (1998), a housing development in China-town North. Each of these projects—present in some form in the Chadbourne Report—advanced PCDC's housing agenda, with other important effects for Chinatown's landscape. They worked first to stabilize the core of historic Chi-natown, particularly its residential character, then to secure the southern and eastern boundaries of Chinatown as ethnic territory. Hing Wah Yuen also aimed to expand Chinatown, claiming space north of Vine Street.

Mei Wah Yuen ("Beautiful Chinese Homes") was the first housing project PCDC undertook in 1975, as part of a larger housing proposal that included plans for development of fifty-three Section 8 rental apartments and six com-mercial units at Race Street between Tenth and Eleventh Streets, and elderly housing at Tenth and Spring. Co-developed by the Philadelphia Housing Development Corporation and designed by Venturi Rauch and Scott Brown, the project eschewed high-rise apartments and called for single-family row houses with rental floors. The final result was twenty-five housing units—thirteen row houses and twelve duplex condominiums—ten of which would be sold under the 235-mortgage subsidy program and the rest sold conven-tionally.[32] Mei Wah Yuen was intended as housing for those who had been displaced by urban-renewal projects (including Yep) and constructed on land parcels that were the site of demolitions during an earlier period. The row houses were tucked into what seemed like an alleyway, running south–north from Spring to Winter Streets, between Tenth and Eleventh Streets. The loca-tion also worked to preserve privacy apart from commercial bustle and the tourist gaze, a feature also manifest in Dynasty Court (Wing Wah Yuen), a rental development of fifty-six Section 8 rental apartments and six commercial units at Race Street between Tenth and Eleventh Streets that PCDC completed the following year. After years of planning and negotiation, Mei Wah Yuen was dedicated in April 1982, the result of patient, unflagging persistence on the part of Yep and PCDC. The dedication, attended by Mayor William Green, celebrated the opening as a milestone in the ongoing struggle of the community. James Duffin of the Philadelphia Housing Development Corporation, a co-developer of the project, declared, "The Chinatown community is an example where the people did not give up. . . . [T]hey carried on this battle with the one resource they had in abundance—the knowledge of the moral rightness of their cause. . . . They have given us an example of convinced citizens seeking justice through petition and dialogue." Holy Redeemer students performed at the ceremony, which concluded with a lion dance, firecrackers, and a Chinese banquet at the Lotus Inn.[33]

With single-family housing underway, PCDC turned its attention to a development for seniors. From the beginning of the "Save Chinatown" movement, attention was paid to the necessity of housing for older Chinatown residents, particularly the large number of aging single men who lived in substandard boardinghouses. Throughout 1973–1975, Yellow Seeds emphasized the plight of these men in its magazine, and elderly housing was identified as a critical need in the Chadbourne Report. Thus, elderly housing was a high priority for the organization. In 1978, PCDC organized a subcommittee called the Acting Committee to Organize Residences for the Elderly (ACORE) to study the problem of elderly housing and recommend a strategy. Under the leadership of Yam Tong Hoh, the former pastor of the CCC&C, ACORE met frequently during 1978–1979. The group visited several elderly/senior housing complexes in the area, including the Friends Neighborhood Guild, to study existing models. ACORE considered several options for completing the development: (1) partnering with another nonprofit, (2) partnering with a private developer, or (3) forming the housing entity as a nonprofit. The group studied the U.S. Department of Housing and Urban Development (HUD) guidelines for Section 8 housing, knowing that the elderly residents of Chinatown were limited in what they could pay. Its findings, put forth in a report in November 1978, included recommending that a representative nonprofit corporation be organized and vested with responsibility and authority for the project, so that the "community retains control over the construction and management of the project." A board of managers was quickly assembled. Knowing that getting HUD funding would require $10,000 in seed money, the members of the committee each contributed $1,000 to establish an escrow fund for the project.[34]

HUD was identified early on as the most appropriate entity to underwrite elderly housing, particularly since rent subsidies would be needed. Additionally, the housing plan would have to be approved by the PRA and City Council. PCDC's initial 1979 application to HUD Section 202–208 to build at 910–914 Cherry was denied; a second application, submitted in 1980 for the site of the former Eagle Paper Factory at Tenth and Spring, was approved (see Figure 4.2).[35] The HUD funding provided $2.6 million for a building for the elderly and handicapped, housing fifty-four apartments (forty-eight one-bedrooms and six efficiencies). Also included in the plan were a residents' lounge, a store, and a walled garden at the Spring Street corner.[36] The primary goal of the On Lok House ("House of Peace and Tranquility") development was not only to provide affordable housing for the elderly but also to serve as a gathering place for older Chinatown residents, a community center where they could share meals and cultural programs and access special services, such as translation. The project met a chronic need in the community; when On Lok opened, four hundred people were on a waiting list for fifty-five units, and On Lok still maintains a full waiting list capped at one hundred, suggesting that the demand for senior housing was barely touched with this project.

Both Mei Wah Yuen and On Lok House worked to stabilize the core of historic Chinatown, following Chadbourne's recommendations to map a residential "spine" along Spring Street. A later project addressed the edges of Chinatown, particularly the long-contested territory on the east side of North Ninth Street. PCDC had set its sights on this area for some time; the two blocks on Ninth between Arch and Vine had great significance as the site of demolitions in the late 1960s and early 1970s. East Ninth Street was the home of the "Chinatown Alamo," Yep's house. The blocks had been cleared for exit ramps from the Vine Street Expressway to Market East that ultimately never materialized, and a new commuter rail tunnel was being constructed to run underground to Market East. As the tunnel neared completion in the early 1980s, negotiations began over what PRA would do with these parcels. PCDC declared in 1982 that Chinatown had a "social, economic, and moral claim to the land."[37]

PRA indicated that the three parcels of Independence Mall Urban Renewal Area #4 along East Ninth Street would be offered for open bid. Chinatown developers James Guo and Stephen Pang, with PCDC as a sponsor, created a proposal for a project known as "Chinatown East," a Chinatown "Trade Center and exhibition hall," featuring a residential/commercial/office complex of thirty-two four-story structures facing Ninth Street from Arch to Vine. Guo passed the torch to PCDC, which kept its eyes on Ninth Street. For Yep, the acquisition of this parcel was also personal, a way to reclaim territory that had been seized by the city from Chinatown years before:

> The Redevelopment Authority took that; they took my house; they took my parking and everything else. . . . But when we heard that they were going to take my property and all East Ninth Street, I was very upset. And at that time, Wilson Goode was the mayor, and I called him up and I said, "I have to talk to you, I have to talk to you." So I went down to City Hall. I didn't make an appointment. I went down to City Hall, went to the mayor's office, and I'm sayin', I thought, "Podia-

Figure 4.2. *Top:* On Lok House site before: Eagle Paper Company, Tenth and Spring Streets, late 1970s. (Courtesy of the Philadelphia Chinatown Development Corporation.) *Bottom:* On Lok House, 2009. (Photograph by the author.)

try is not gonna take my property! I'm not gonna give it up for a foot
school!" I was ranting and raving and crying. I was hysterical! Because
it was a borderline of Chinatown. And it meant something to Chinatown. Not me personally, but Chinatown.[38]

Yep was not the only Chinatown denizen who felt strongly about East Ninth
Street. For many years, a building on the northwest corner of Ninth and Race
adjacent to a vacant lot that had been demolished for the commuter rail tunnel
was painted with the declaration, "This is, was, and will be Chinatown." Below
was written, "Our forefathers built the railroad, but this is going TOO FAR!
This land is our land. Give Ninth Street back to us."[39] Earlier protests against
the expressway had used similar language.

PCDC documents outlining plans for the site consistently utilized terms
that highlighted the land as territory, as part of Chinatown distinct from the
city: "It should be noted that this land is historically a part of Chinatown,
although it is listed by the City as 'Independence Mall Urban Renewal Area,
Unit No. 4.'"[40] The slogan stating that Ninth Street "is, was, and will be" Chinatown articulated a sense of ownership beyond legal title per se—a claim based
in historical presence and community investment. It also articulated a strong
sense of territoriality, of Chinatown as a separate entity circumscribed by distinct social and cultural borders. PCDC staff made repeated references to the
eastern "border" or "boundary" of Chinatown and the necessity of securing
and stabilizing it. A June 1986 PCDC newsletter announced, "Gim San Project Is On Its Way!" adding, "PCDC believed that this strip of land was very
important to stabilize the eastern boundary of Chinatown. Chinese families
had previously lived on this land and were displaced due to urban renewal
projects. PCDC's struggle was successful in getting back this land for the Chinatown community."[41]

With both PCDC and the nearby School of Podiatric Medicine (at Eighth
and Race) eager to acquire the land, negotiations with PRA were difficult and
sometimes heated. The PRA "treated us like we were small fry," according
to Yep. In the end, PRA offered the land to PCDC on the condition that the
group act quickly: "So the chairman of the board, Bob Hazan, the Redevelopment Authority board, said, 'OK, we'll give your community two weeks. You
come up with a site plan, potential buyers for the property and bank approval
for a construction loan.'" Yep got to work. She commissioned a rough plan
from architect Sabrina Soong and called a community meeting to gauge who
would be interested in buying homes on East Ninth Street. Then she went
back to PRA:

In two weeks I had this site plan, I had a list of potential buyers—fourteen buyers plus fourteen back-up buyers—and I had gone to the bank,
and I got half a million dollars in down-payment money. . . . I got a

Figure 4.3. Gim San Plaza, 2009, showing a mural by Lily Yeh. (Photograph by the author.)

construction loan from PNC bank. What I did, I went to the Redevelopment Authority and I said, "I got everything you asked me for. Now, give us the land." They had to give us the land. The board members said, "You asked for this, she gave you this, you have to give it to her." So, Podiatry was very upset, but we got the land. . . . We know our community. We know our market. We know where the needs are. . . . I had twenty-eight buyers for fourteen properties.[42]

In April 1985, PCDC was designated as the developer of East Ninth Street from Cherry Street to Race Street, parcel 7 of Independence Mall Urban Renewal Area #4. Gim San ("Gold Mountain") Plaza broke ground in May 1987 after numerous political and logistical challenges (including the need to shore up an entire city block and construct a cantilevered foundation over the city commuter tunnel) and added twenty residential units and fourteen commercial spaces to the Chinatown landscape (see Figure 4.3).

Theming and Reclaiming Space

One central strategy PCDC pursued was that of urban-district theming, an increasingly popular strategy by the 1970s and 1980s. To this end, the group worked to theme and brand Chinatown's landscape to improve neighborhood infrastructure and appearance. In doing so, PCDC drew on a repertoire of spatial practices, including streetscaping and architectural theming, which allowed it to enhance the "Chinatown-ness" of Chinatown. In many ways, PCDC's strategies resembled those that were being pursued in other ethnic neighborhoods in Philadelphia and around the country. Like Chinatown, Latino merchants in the North Fifth Street barrio worked in the 1970s and 1980s to fight area blight by installing streetscape features that created an image of the "*bloque de oro*/Golden Block." Decoratively painted sidewalks and banners, for instance, were installed by the Spanish Merchants Association in the early 1970s. In the 1980s and 1990s, another Latino CDC, the Hispanic Association of Contractors and Engineers (HACE), continued the trend of theming the barrio landscape through business-façade improvements, streetscaping, and the architectural design of various housing projects. Other organizations, such as Norris Square Neighborhood Project, founded in 1973, reclaimed blighted vacant lots with Latino-themed community gardens and murals.[43]

In addition to street-level upgrades, such as trees, pedestrian lights, and new bollards on Spring Street, the Chadbourne plan called specifically for a "unifying element" that could mark curbs and sidewalks. PCDC used the Urban Renewal Area designation to receive monies for streetscape improvements that themed and marked the cultural identity of the neighborhood. Consulting Dover design sourcebooks, PCDC staff chose a Chinese calligraphic symbol, *shou* (meaning "long life"), taken from an early-twentieth-century Chinese embroidery design, as the "identifying element" for the neighborhood. The *shou* symbol was crafted into sidewalk medallions installed along Tenth, Ninth, and Race Street sidewalks. The *shou* symbol was adopted by PCDC as its organizational logo and appears on many PCDC projects as an architectural or decorative element. Many residents have also embraced the symbol, incorporating it into decorative ironwork on doorways, front stoops, and mailboxes.

PCDC also got creative with the large numbers of now-vacant lots left by previous demolition. As the expressway project lay dormant, PCDC petitioned PennDOT in the wake of the group's visit to Governor Milton Shapp for use of that land. With assistance from the Pennsylvania Horticultural Society, a lot on the southeast corner of Tenth and Vine became a community garden in 1974, where residents, many of them seniors, planted Chinese vegetables and herbs. "Our vegetables are living proof," commented the PCDC newsletter, "that the Chinatown community is dynamic in spite of the fact that the community is surrounded on all four sides by urban renewal projects."[44] PCDC leased vacant lots along Vine Street from PennDOT and used them to provide much-needed parking space for Chinatown. The organization also played a proactive role in negotiating the nonrenewal of liquor licenses and working with landlords to remove bars in the area. One bar that was of particular contention was Chick's Bar, located in a building owned by the Gee How Oak Tin Association. When this property was marked for acquisition by PRA, negotiations with owners left the building intact contingent on removal of the bar.[45] All these moves worked to consolidate changes and begin building a cohesive ethnic identity for the neighborhood.

New housing construction was deliberatively Asian themed at all levels of project design: architectural form, spatial configuration and use, and decorative elements. In some cases, projects drew on the existing landscape for inspiration. Mei Wah Yuen was notable architecturally for its abstracted evocation of the surrounding landscape (primarily through curved eaves over entryways and decorative balconies) and its use of the row-house form. The second-floor balconies and railings drew the attention of one architectural critic, Garth Garrett of the Foundation for Architecture, who claimed they were "derived from Georgian Chippendale antecedents" (which were themselves derived from Chinese designs). "Intentionally the complex has few Chinese style gestures," Garrett noted, "keeping the focus on the community's needs."[46] In each case, the developments architecturally mimicked other surrounding structures of Chinatown. While Mei Wah Yuen perpetuated the row-house form common on Spring Street, Dynasty Court, located a block away on Tenth and Race, retained the mixed-use residential-second-floor/commercial-first-floor structure so common to Chinatown's main street.

Replicating the common pattern of traditional Chinatown spatial use, On Lok was conceived as a mixed-use structure, with small-scale retail and community space at street level and six stories for apartments. Original designs by architect Soong featured traditional Chinese design elements—green tile eaves, red pillars, and mosaic ornamentation[47]—but they proved to be cost prohibitive and eventually were discarded. The final scaled-back design relied on a stripe of red and gold enameled bricks running along the top of the first story. The entrance to the center is a round "moon gate" wood and glass doorway surrounded by two red pillars and a thick turquoise cornice that hangs over each street-level window to the senior center, reminiscent of the original tiled eaves. The remaining retail entrances are unadorned. The entrance to the residences, to the left of the center entrance, is protected by an iron fence and gate featuring the *shou* motif. The ornamentation suggests an abstraction of traditional elements, the Chinese influence being most visible in the building's color scheme and doorway design (see Figure 4.2).

There is evidence of discussion and negotiation around the dilemmas surrounding themed space as redevelopment strategy, as exemplified by the approach to Gim San Plaza at Ninth and Race. James Guo and Stephen Pang, with PCDC as a sponsor, had originally created a proposal for a project known as "Chinatown East," a Chinatown "Trade Center and exhibition hall," featuring a residential/commercial/office complex of thirty-two four-story structures facing Ninth Street from Arch to Vine. This complex would feature elevator access, accessory parking in rear, "Chinese design motifs," and a "landscaped promenade" behind the stores, ending in a "traditional Chinese garden" at the Vine Street end. The center would serve as a marketplace for Chinese products. The estimated total project cost was $10.8 million.[48] The project was designed to contribute to "promoting Philadelphia's potential as a major trade port and tourist attraction." Playing to the city's strategic desire to be an international port, the proposal proclaimed: "Both the City and Chinatown are in accord with the belief that increased tourism and international trade will play a major role in the City's future economy. The proposed Chinatown East project could become the initial impetus that propels Philadelphia firmly on course toward being an 'international city.'"[49]

The design of the structure, initially outlined by Soong, was traditionally Chinese. "Sympathetic to the existing scale, density, and land uses in Chinatown," the building would feature "Chinese architectural and graphic motifs," such as "projecting pagoda roofs," latticed balustrades on the upper floors, and a "moon gate and traditional decorative artifacts" for public areas. Traditional colors (red, green, blue, and gold) and materials (ceramic glazed tile, wood, stucco, and brick) would "stimulate the eye in a rich combination of hue and texture." A visually unified development, the project aimed to be a "lively round-the-clock locus of activity with restaurants, shops, offices, and residences. Its architecture and decoration will lend a festive international ambience to this edge of Chinatown and Center City." The southern end of the development would be occupied by a "Chinese Trade Center" hosting international exhibitions and containing wholesale showrooms, offices, and other supportive services. At the northeast corner of Ninth and Arch Streets, the center would be clearly visible from the Ninth Street entranceway of Gallery I. This "distinctive and exotic structure w[ould] herald visitors approaching Chinatown" from the south; it would constitute a "vital and necessary urban design linkage" between Market Street East and Chinatown.

Descriptions of the site clearly located the project within a traditional Chinese design aesthetic to represent a Chinese identity and appeal to an exhibitionary, touristic experience of Chinese difference:

What will it be like to visit Chinatown East? Having arrived at the corner of Ninth and Arch, the visitor may wander into the Trade Center exhibition hall to view Chinese rugs, furniture, antiques and other products on display. Outside again he will find a moon gate beckoning entrance to a landscaped promenade which runs along the back of the structure. In good weather a stroll along this walkway, to be furnished with Chinese inspired street furniture and lighting, brings one by outside cafes and restaurants exuding strange wonderful smells from their doorways; shops playing Oriental music with colorful imported wares displayed in windows and out-of-doors; stores selling more prosaic items but filled with signs in Chinese characters; and Chinatown mothers and grandmothers with young children chatting on benches. Reaching the end of the promenade near Vine Street, one will see a jewel-like park slightly to the east. The park offers a joyful surprise; it is a traditional Chinese landscaped garden with unusual stone forms, miniature pagodas, and even a pond filled with colorfully varied carp. . . . This delightful experience makes an imprint on the mind of the visitor which continually draws him back again for another temporary adventure which challenges his sense and invites him to explore different aspects of another culture transported to America.[50]

This passage highlights the importance of identifiably Chinese or Asian landscape as a marker of the neighborhood's identity and the object of the visitor's gaze, experience, and pleasure. Here the landscape is essentialized ("a culture transported to America") and defined by exotic architectural features and an inaccessible language ("signs in Chinese characters"). This is a description of the district for the outsider, the visitor, the nonresident. But it is not wholly objectified if we consider the description of "Chinatown mothers and grandmothers with young children chatting on benches," which embodies the status of Chinatown residents as the object of the tourist's gaze as it belies historical stereotypes of Chinatown as an exotic male-only milieu, underscoring the presence of families in the area, since historically the absence of women and families in the communities was a mark of Chinese Otherness. Here, Chinatown is female as well as male; it is not only a collection of restaurants but also a community of families, albeit one composed of those living a quaint, intergenerational way of life.

The death of Guo in 1985 spelled the end of that iteration of the Chinatown East project, which eventually became Gim San Plaza. Architecturally and symbolically, Gim San Plaza was a significant contribution to the Chinatown landscape. The building, designed by Richard Martin, of the Martin Organization, preserved the commercial-first-floor/residential-upper-floor structure that distinguished most of Chinatown's use of space. Fourteen commercial units grounded the structure at street level, with apartments on the second and third floors. PCDC had requested that the architect incorporate "Oriental features in the design on the front façade." These features consisted of vestigial red iron balconies on the second-floor windows, round moongate perforations along the upper-story pediments, *shou* emblems embedded along the roof, and ornamented doorways. Red pillars surrounded the front windows of the retail units. The centerpiece of the building's Asian theme was a tiled mural by Chinese American artist Lily Yeh, included to satisfy the city's "1 percent for art" requirement for public buildings. Yeh was chosen from a list of Fine Arts Board–approved artists. Yeh, who emigrated from Taiwan in 1963 to attend the University of Pennsylvania's Graduate School of Fine

Arts, was originally reluctant but decided in the end that she wanted to "do something for the Chinese community." Her instructions were to work with ceramic tiles and traditional Chinese motifs. Yeh's design needed to satisfy both the buyers and the city's Fine Arts Board. Original designs of three-feet-by-three-feet tiles painted with flowers at the center of the iron balcony frame on each second-floor unit were rejected by buyers, who believed that the "design was too bold and abstract to suit their taste" as well an antipathy to decorations on the façade of the building. The final concept, approved by all, was a fifteen-feet-by-twenty-four-feet tiled mural entitled, "The Vision of Paradise," installed on the northern gable of the building along Race Street (see Figure 4.3).

Literally translated as "The Golden Mountains, the *Fu Shang* cosmic tree, and Longevity in a Fairy Land," the mural depicts a large tree inhabited by beautiful red birds. In the foreground are mountains of gold. The name of the building project, Gold Mountain, or Gim San in Cantonese, referenced the "Gold Mountain" that early Chinese immigrants came to seek. For Yeh, the mountain indicated "height, glory, and majesty," and gold signified prosperity, good fortune, and wealth. The gold mountains symbolized the "dream of the community." Although the buyers had asked for traditional Chinese themes, Yeh eschewed what she felt were "visual clichés of dragon *fen huang* (phoenix), pine trees, sweet-looking birds and flowers." She chose instead the motif of *Fu Shang shu*, "the Chinese cosmic tree which roots deeply into the earth and rises up to the sky, symbolizing the deep rootedness in history of the Chinese community that dared to dream of achievement." The tree could just have easily represented the community's insistence on planting roots in this particular soil. Yeh remarked that the mural is "very Oriental in intention and feeling, but contemporary in its technical innovations and in its playful juxtaposition of colors and objects."[51] The mural was placed to "establish a strong presence for the eastern boundary of Chinatown."[52]

The approach to Gim San was typical of the way in which PCDC leaders considered many strategies for preserving the district as a Chinese enclave. More often than not, they began with more elaborately Asian designs, especially for projects located on main streets, such as Ninth, Race, and Tenth, but were usually forced to settle, often for economic reasons, for more abstract motifs. For Yep, it was important to incorporate some aspect of Chinese culture in every project PCDC undertook: "They accuse me of being old-fashioned. I always try to incorporate something [that is a] reflection of the Asian culture. Like even at Mei Wah Yuen, you see the roofs that are pagoda type almost. . . . And on Gim San, I have these longevity signs on each building. So I incorporate something Asian on every building. . . . I think anything we do as a Chinatown community development corporation should reflect the culture of the community. That's important to me. Because if you build something plain, it could be anywhere. But this is Chinatown."[53] According to Yee, "It was kind of just reaffirming the identity of Chinatown through these buildings, through whatever visual elements we had":

> I think all of us felt it would be nice to have some kind of Asian motif somewhere around, and that was back in the seventies—this is before Southeast Asian immigration and all of that. And so our models might have been San Francisco Chinatown or L.A. Chinatown, where they had the phone booths with the Asian roofs and some tile work. San Francisco had streetlights that had Asian motifs and then latticework, ironwork. So those were ideas that we all had at the time, and we didn't think that they were hokey or anything. . . . Some of it was China, like latticework, looking at Dover Publication books [laughs]. . . . We didn't go overboard on it.[54]

This approach ultimately suited the aesthetic of the neighborhood, however, which had always been hybrid in nature, both an internal sanctuary for Chinese and Asian residents and an external marketplace for Asians and non-Asians alike. It also embodied the dualistic nature of PCDC's approach—to challenge the powers that be on behalf of the neighborhood, its survival, and its priorities while playing ball with city, state, and federal agencies to realize concrete projects that developed a blighted neighborhood.

Themed space corresponded to the priorities and investments of the city to the extent that it contributed to the distinctiveness of Chinatown as part of the downtown spectacle. One PCDC project that employed traditional architecture and motifs aimed at an outward constituency was the Friendship Gate, erected in 1984. A formal gate at the entrance of Chinatown was a concept that had first been considered as early as 1968. In 1979, PCDC received a grant from the National Endowment for the Arts to study the concept further. As part of this study, members of the planning committee surveyed gateways in other Chinatowns. A traditional design, drawn from Ming and Qing dynasty aesthetics, was put forth by architect Soong. According to Yep, the gate had its genesis in a plan drawn up by architect Gray Smith, who drew up a map with four gates at every end of the neighborhood. Yep recalls, "We said, 'No, we only want one gate, because the Gallery was built and turned its back on Chinatown.' . . . I mean it wasn't that they could look out and see that Chinatown's here—it was like a barrier. . . . We've got to think of something that you could look at from Market Street and see and draw the people to Chinatown."[55]

The gate became a reality during the Green administration, its origins emerging from negotiation with the city over development priorities for Chinatown. For the city, the position of the neighborhood as a cultural attraction was clearly most important, distinct from PCDC's goals of preserving and fostering spaces for family living. While PCDC sought support for affordable housing projects, city representatives went further down the organization's wish list to embrace the creation of a cultural attraction:

> We went in to talk about housing, and Dick Doran says, "I can't help you with housing, but I like this. I like this gate." We're going in for housing, and he likes the gate! I was a little upset, to tell the truth. But then I came back and I said, "Jimmy [James Guo], Dick Doran likes your gate, but he doesn't like our housing." He said, "We should have a gate. . . . I'm all for a gate. . . . I think it's an answer to draw people into Chinatown."[56]

For PCDC, the gate was a distraction from primary priorities, as Moy comments: "We had all these other fights and struggles going along, [and] you have time to have a gate up? You've got this highway, and you ignore the community that's trying to survive."[57] The city's approach to PCDC's requests and its focus on the gate were typical of the market-driven approaches to urban development that came to characterize the 1980s and beyond, approaches that engendered the commodification of ethnic identity and urban space to create cultural attractions.

The gate was thoroughly embedded in schemes for the new globalized city. Plans for the gate were negotiated through the work of a transnational trade delegation, including Yep and Guo, who traveled to China to craft a port agreement between Philadelphia and Tianjin, China, signed in Tianjin on November 11, 1982. As part of this agreement, the gate was included in the city's budget for 1982–1983, officially commissioned by the Department of Commerce and the Department of Public Property. Work was completed in the winter of 1983–1984. Special building materials and partly assembled sections arrived from China in November 1983. The gate was completed by ten artisans from the Peking Ancient Architectural Construction Corp, a firm responsible for restoring and maintaining Beijing's historical monuments. The completed structure was massive and unmistakable, rising forty feet and weighing eighty-eight tons, the largest structure of its kind in the United States. The gate was dedicated on January 31, 1984.

More than any other PCDC project, the gate came to define Chinatown to outsiders, serving the needs of the destination city. Although tourism was not a main goal of PCDC, Moy admits it was "in a way. We knew that we had to put Chinatown in a positive light." Not coincidentally, that light is one that shines back to the traditional Chinese past. At the same time, the gate, with its immense size and weight, ensures Chinatown's future in this location. Now owned by the city (PCDC transferred ownership when the insurance costs proved untenable), the gate was restored in two phases in 2004 and 2008, a restoration that received a Preservation Achievement Award from the Preservation Alliance of Greater Philadelphia in 2009.[58]

Expanding Territory: Chinatown North

Having successfully articulated and stabilized a core of Chinatown, PCDC turned its sights to the area north of Vine Street, which came to be known as Chinatown North. Here, PCDC faced issues that differed from those raised by previous projects in Chinatown proper. Chinatown North, unlike the historic core, was primarily a postindustrial area, the landscape characterized by shuttered warehouses and factories, weed- and trash-filled vacant lots, abandoned cars, blighted housing, and utility substations (see Figure 4.4). PCDC identified a site for housing at Wood Street between Eighth and Ninth Streets, which would become Hing Wah Yuen. This site posed several challenges, the most daunting being the assembly of parcels of land for redevelopment. The 2.9-acre plot was divided into seventy-eight parcels, controlled by a complicated web of state, local, and federal agencies and even some deceased individuals. PennDOT owned or operated seventeen pieces of land, much of it acquired before the expressway was built. Each agency involved—the city, the state, the Federal Transportation Administration, and the Southeastern Pennsylvania Transportation Authority (SEPTA)—had its own rules for how to sell off property. "It was a nightmare assembling that package," Yep recalls, "because there must have been twenty-five ownerships. And it took us two years, I think, to get that done, and the worst part was that it sits right over the Center City Commuter Rail Tunnel, and you cannot build sixty feet on each side." PennDOT wanted $287,000 for the 13,100-square-foot piece and said state law mandated that the land be sold at "fair market value." An appraiser hired by PCDC and PRA estimated the value of the state's portion of the land at $65,000. Noel Eisenstat, executive director of PRA, commented at the time that the city and state owed Chinatown residents this project: "A commitment was made to them. People should live up to their commitments. This is just government at its worst."[59] Faced with the constraints of the tunnel, PCDC redesigned the project with sixty-foot easements on the exterior of the houses. This area was then earmarked for parking. A modest fee would cover the maintenance of the development. As PCDC wrangled with city and state agencies and redrew its plans, construction costs climbed, bringing the project's final cost to $6.9 million.

The financing of Hing Wah Yuen was typical of the way PCDC worked in many cases, leveraging a combination of city and state funding with private funding and bank loans. For Hing, PCDC received a $200,000 grant from the Pennsylvania Department of Community Affairs; $1.5 million from the City

Figure 4.4. Chinatown North before redevelopment, 1989. (Courtesy of the Philadelphia Chinatown Development Corporation.)

Housing and Community Development, HOME Program; and $175,000 from the Federal Home Loan Bank Affordable Housing Program. Private lenders contributed $5 million, and PNC Bank extended a construction loan for $4.9 million. High demand for housing in Chinatown ensured that units would be occupied; mortgage assistance helped buyers meet the purchase price.[60]

If Gim San and Mei Wah Yuen reclaimed territory for Chinatown, then Hing Wah Yuen claimed new territory and asserted that the future of Chinatown lay north of Vine Street. After 1998, Hing Wah Yuen became an anchor in plans to develop north of Vine. In 1999, PCDC built new offices adjacent to the complex on the northeast corner of Ninth and Vine Streets and completed a comprehensive plan for the growth and development of an area that became known as Chinatown North. That same year, PCDC initiated Bill No. 980895 to rezone forty-four acres of land bounded by Vine to Spring Garden and Eighth to Eleventh Streets for Chinatown expansion. In this legislation, PCDC recognized that "Chinatown is important to the economic vitality and diverse character of Center City in that it serves as a major tourist attraction and as a cultural center for Chinese and Asian Americans."[61] The district was established to "protect the historic, cultural and economic vitality" of Chinatown and "preserve and encourage revitalization" of Chinatown as a "unique cultural nucleus," particularly its unique mixed-use landscape of "residential, small scale commercial and light industrial activities."[62]

The 1999 Comprehensive Urban Design Plan for Chinatown North, completed by the architectural firm Environmental Research Group, focused on defining an area north of Vine Street for residential and mixed-use development, making the area distinct but "identifiable as part of Chinatown." For the purposes of the study, Chinatown North was defined as Eighth and Vine to Ninth and Spring Garden to Thirteenth Street on the west and Spring Garden to Vine. According to the plan, Chinatown North would be developed primarily as a residential area but with supportive mixed uses. It "should be seen as part of Chinatown proper, but not as a commercial competitor to it." The primary goal of the development was to "expand the range of residential choices available," function as a "gateway to Philadelphia from the east," and be an "extension of the Chinatown core but not a replica of it." As designed, the plan drew on the Tenth Street corridor as the primary geographic link between the Chinatown core and the area to the north. Shopping areas would be confined to Tenth, Eleventh, and Callowhill Streets, leaving the remainder of the area for residences, both adaptive reuse of existing structures and new construction. A community center would be built at Tenth and Vine, a 65,000-square-foot building to hold a 3.3-meter swimming pool and basketball court. Tenth Street at Vine would constitute a new "heart" for Chinatown, with the community center to the west and the Holy Redeemer church, school, and playground to the east. Tenth Street would also be the major artery and retail area in Chinatown North.[63]

Incorporating housing for about one thousand, the plan envisioned Chinatown North as "a residential area with allied retail shops and social support facilities to make it a good place to live for the future families of the children at present growing up in Chinatown so that they will be able to remain in the area in adulthood, middle-income families, the elderly, including empty nesters presently living in the suburbs, and recent immigrants from Asia. An area which provides facilities—industrial, residential, recreational, that are not available in the Chinatown area."[64] Because of the undeveloped, blighted nature of the area, safety was also a concern. Chinatown North must be a safe environment, signaled by the provision of low walls around play spaces, grade-separated pedestrian crossings, visible entrances and lobbies, and abundant nighttime lighting. Outdoor areas should, the plan asserted, "come under the natural surveillance of people as part of their everyday activities," and "outdoor spaces should have specific uses and be under the 'control' of people in specific buildings."[65]

In its development work from 1970 to 2000, PCDC systematically targeted land previously claimed by demolition, reclaiming the space for Chinatown. This reclamation did more than just add to Chinatown's geography, however. It rendered in concrete and visible ways a vision of the community that belied its external image as merely a collection of restaurants and other Asian-themed businesses. It strategically embraced and eschewed traditional Orien-

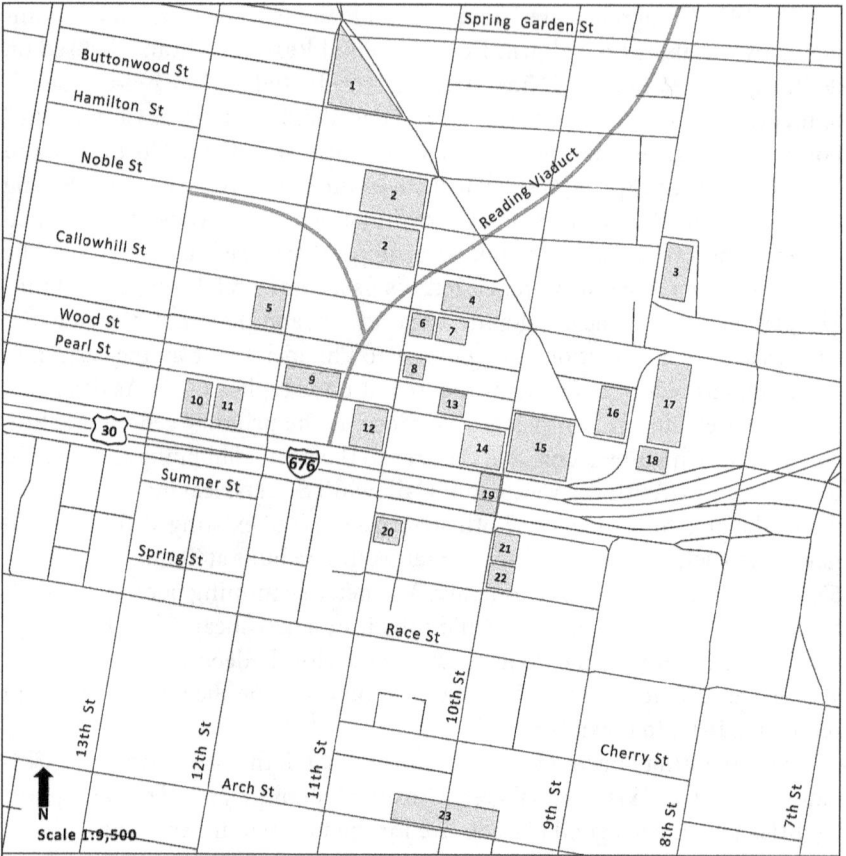

Figure 4.5. Chinatown North landmarks. (Illustration by Amber J. Boll and Damien E. Hesse.)

1. Proposed apartment complex opposed by CNA in 2013
2. PECO substation
3. Trigen substation
4. Folk Arts-Cultural Treasures School/Asian Americans United
5. Wolf Building
6. Trestle Inn
7. Wholesale food distributor
8. Vox Populi Gallery/Khmer Arts Gallery
9. Goldtex apartment
10. Philadelphia Hoyu Chinese American Association
11. Asian Arts Initiative
12. Chinese Christian Church and Center annex
13. Tofu factory
14. Eastern Tower Proposed Site
15. Holy Redeemer Chinese Catholic Church and School
16. Sing Wah Yuen
17. Hing Wah Yuen
18. PCDC offices
19. 10th Street Plaza
20. 6th District Police station
21. History of Chinatown mural
22. Chinese Christian Church and Center
23. Friendship Gate

talism and filled in its landscape with structures that embodied its vision of itself, which reaffirmed the presence of families, honored the elderly, and paid tribute to its merchant past. By 2000, PCDC staff began to create a plan for the new community center at Tenth and Vine and move forward with the realization of its plan for Chinatown North (see Figure 4.5). Little did they know that a new city plan for the area of north of Vine Street would soon threaten the dream of Chinatown North and disrupt their plans. This threat would once again mobilize the community to draw on its past to protect its future.

"A legacy of resistance"

Chinatown North and
Twenty-First-Century Challenges

On June 25, 2009, a crowd gathered outside 718 Market Street in down-town Philadelphia to witness the "Anti-Casino Circus," a protest perfor-mance mounted against a Foxwoods Casino proposed for the northwest corner of Eighth and Market Streets, in the former Strawbridge and Cloth-ier building. Passersby were invited to experience the "Incredible Two-Faced Mayor!" "High-Flying Casino Economics—without a net!" "The Foxwoods Site Shell Game!" and "Daring Feats of Doublespeak!" as well as consume cotton candy, play games of chance, and listen to lively rhetoric from activists. The circus was planned by a citywide coalition of anti-casino organizers— the "No Casino in the Heart of Our City Coalition"—that included Casino Free Philadelphia (formed by Chinatown's Asian Americans United; Liberty Resources, Inc.; Arch Street United Methodist Church; Black Clergy of Phila-delphia; and the Media Mobilizing Project). The coalition had claimed the empty storefront at 718 as a "No Slots Spot" to challenge a City Council vote thirteen days before to approve zoning changes that would pave the way for the casino downtown. While not located directly in Chinatown, the casino site was of great concern to Chinatown residents, not only because of its close proximity to residences but also because of the history of gambling addiction among residents in the community and casino marketing practices that tar-geted that community.

The proposed Foxwoods Casino was, for Chinatown activists, not only a current issue based on concerns about predatory marketing and gambling addiction in the community but also the latest in a long line of urban-develop-ment schemes proposed by the city without considering input from or impact on the Chinatown community. After the threats of the Vine Street Express-way and commuter tunnel, the construction of the new convention center at Twelfth and Arch Streets in the 1980s displaced families and businesses along the western side of Eleventh Street, blocking off any expansion of the neighborhood in that direction. In 1992, plans were announced for a 750-bed federal detention center at Eighth and Callowhill, to protests from the community, who hoped to expand Chinatown north of Vine Street in the coming years. And in 2000, a baseball stadium was proposed for Twelfth and Vine Streets.[1]

In combating plans for a casino two blocks from Chinatown, Chinatown activists joined with other neighborhoods and organizations across the city to push back and fight for their right to urban space on their own terms. When the Pennsylvania Gaming Control Board rejected Foxwoods' license for Center City and urged relocation in South Philadelphia, the anti-casino group claimed a temporary victory.[2] Asian Americans United (AAU), a Chinatown-based group that spearheaded the fight against the casino, has gone on to oppose and organize against casinos around the city. Reflecting on the fight, Debbie Wei, of AAU, mused that the Chinatown community's history of struggle and activism was an important factor in marshaling support for an effective challenge to the casino: "There is a legacy of resistance that has been passed on in the community, so like it or not—or whether people even really realize it—there is a legacy of resistance, and it's kind of cool, because I think the city itself also knows about the legacy of resistance. I think if Chinatown didn't have its track record, that casino would have been built."[3] Wearing T-shirts that proclaimed "No ~~Stadium~~ Casino in Chinatown," the anti-casino protestors from Chinatown drew on a living history and memory of community activism that continues to shape responses to community challenges. In recent fights to save Chinatown, residents have rallied around a sense of the community's history of struggle, its right to remain a living place in the face of new development, gentrification, and other threats. In doing so, they have built on a legacy of resistance and activism while also expanding coalition building, reaching out beyond Chinatown to forge larger relationships with other community-based groups across the city and the region.

"What it means when you say, 'Chinatown'"

The legacy of Chinatown resistance, particularly the radical work of Yellow Seeds, lives on in the history and work of AAU, which was founded in 1985 with the original Yellow Seeds charter. Organized by former Yellow Seeds activist Mary Yee; her husband, Paul Uyehara; educator Debbie Wei; and others, AAU works for social justice for Asians in the Greater Philadelphia area. As part of this mission, AAU has organized for tenants' rights and educational access and against police harassment and racial profiling. Anti-Asian violence has been a special concern, especially for its youth programs, such as the Community Youth Leadership Project. Although AAU's activities were and are located in several neighborhoods around the city, Chinatown became a central meeting place for the organization, in part because it offered physical and cultural safety for young people. AAU located its offices in Chinatown at Eighth and Arch Streets early in its history and again in 2007, at 1023 Callowhill, its current location. The safety provided by Chinatown has been critical during a period, since the 1980s, of ongoing violence and racial profiling against Asian youth in Philadelphia's public schools and neighborhoods.[4]

According to Ellen Somekawa, AAU's director from 1996 to 2014, the choice to locate in Chinatown was a "conscious decision and not an easy one," given that the organization works with Asian Americans all around the city. But Chinatown represented a central location geographically and a protective zone where young people could congregate: "You are trying to figure out, well, where is a place where people from all over the city would feel comfortable coming to? Chinatown fit that bill." AAU leaders were also aware that "Chinatown is still struggling, and why wouldn't we try part to be a part of that community? So it was a coming together of those different aspects, but a big part of it was wanting consciously to connect to Chinatown as well."[5] This reasoning is echoed by AAU board member Helen Gym:

> I think that the decision around Chinatown was largely because it's sort of a landing place; it seemed to supersede boundaries. . . . Chinatown was a place where everybody came and gathered. There were people that would meet here for lots of different reasons. People of all different ethnicities—that there was something about Chinatown feeling very Pan-Asian and Asian American, also its kind of historical role of being a long community, and the feeling that with the onset of urban renewal, that was not a community that people could count on being there forever. That it would have to be a presence that was fragile, and that the investment had to be in a place that had to be—that would be fiercely protective and active. Not just in terms of "we're gonna name it Chinatown" but . . . people will understand what it means when you say, "Chinatown."[6]

For Gym, "what it means when you say Chinatown" is that the community is "fiercely protective and active" about creating not only a place of safety but also a place of history and Asian identity based in resistance to social injustice, a resistance embodied by the community's history of activism.

At a time when most Asian immigrants do not settle initially in Chinatown or, indeed, always in the city, Chinatown serves as a regional center and cultural touchstone for a larger "cultural community," which continues to diversify.[7] Vietnamese (many of them ethnic Chinese), Korean, Burmese, Indonesian, and other Asians (and non-Asians) locate their businesses in Chinatown. Chinese and other Asians live in South Philadelphia, West Philadelphia, the Greater

Northeast, and other suburban areas, with a large percentage in Montgomery County. New immigration has continued to increase the size of this cultural community in the twenty-first century; the 2000 Census reported 17,390 Chinese in Philadelphia (31,663 in the five-county region), and this figure rose to 29,396 in 2010, with 53,133 in the five-county region.[8] In 2011, the *Metro Chinese Weekly* estimated that more than 150,000 Chinese lived in the Greater Philadelphia metropolitan region, most of them outside Chinatown. The larger Asian population has likewise grown exponentially in the past few decades; currently, Asian immigration accounts for 39 percent of Philadelphia's foreign-born population, and Asians constitute 6.3 percent of the city's population.[9] The Greater Northeast in particular has become a "second Chinatown" according to Glenn Hing, who serves many residents of that neighborhood at his law office at Ninth and Race Streets.[10] Concentrated in the neighborhoods of Mayfair and Oxford Circle, these populations also make up a larger percentage of the population served by the Philadelphia Chinatown Development Corporation's (PCDC's) services. The Chinese Christian Church and Center (CCC&C) recently opened up a satellite congregation in the Northeast, and according to center volunteer Kenneth Eng, 40–50 percent of his students also come from that area.[11] The Greater Northeast is also the location of the Greater Philadelphia United Chinese American Chamber of Commerce, an organization started by new immigrants from mainland China. Most of the new immigrants to Philadelphia since the 1990s have been Mandarin-speaking immigrants from Fujian.[12] And Chinatown itself is increasingly pan-Asian in character. Although the largest resident population remains Chinese, other Asians are a visible presence, particularly in businesses. Chinatown is home to Vietnamese, Burmese, Korean, Japanese, and Malaysian businesses (see Table A.2 in the Appendix).

For many Asians, Chinatown serves, as it did a century before, as a familiar cultural territory and a sanctuary against racism and its effects. Chinatown's safety for new immigrants and youth is exemplified in the experience of Xu Lin, who emigrated from Fujian in 2001 at the age of sixteen and now works with youth through AAU. Throughout his years at Furness High School in South Philadelphia, Lin and his schoolmates were subjected to ongoing violence from other students. For Lin and his parents, Chinatown has been a "transitional center place" that offers a zone of physical safety and cultural comfort:

> [My father] will never leave Chinatown, because everything he knows is in Chinatown. Outside of Chinatown, he cannot communicate with others. My parents don't speak English, so that's bad. And also Chinatown is really convenient in terms of grocery shopping or transportation. And safety. For me now, I don't feel completely safe walking in South Philly, but in Chinatown, it's like home. I'm relaxed. It's a different environment. . . . In Chinatown, it's mostly Chinese. I think it's

about 80 percent. If you live here for a while, you get to know people. The restaurants you go to, the stores you go to. People know each other. People see familiar faces. And also, racial tension is real. You can get targeted just because of who you are, what language you speak. So, in Chinatown, there is [less of] a consciousness about myself, but in other places, I need to be aware of where I am, who I'm around, what language I speak.[13]

This safety extends beyond Asian Americans per se, according to Lin:

> Chinatown itself is really small, but many people, including not just Chinese, including other Asian ethnic groups—people find China-town as . . . mostly safe. A sense of community. In other parts of the city, people live with other people, and there's a lot of tension between different ethnic groups. So in this sense, Chinatown is really unique. People can speak here and relax. Even my Mexican friends, my high school friends, they will come to Chinatown to hang out, because this is a place where they can be safe. People won't point at them or push them from behind.[14]

Lin notes that almost all the Chinese students and many other Asian students with whom he works at South Philadelphia High School have a connection to Chinatown: "For Chinese students, this is a place where people hang out. Even for other Asian students, Chinatown is a place to hang out. The Vietnamese students I know, they just come to Chinatown. We can see them after school. It's safe. It's familiar."[15] Lin's comments echo those of the previous generation, when Chinatown was "the safe space" for Chinese and Chinese Americans. They also point to the position Chinatown occupies as not only an ethnic touchstone but also a launching point for new immigrants, who have specific neighborhood needs, such as affordable housing, services, and language access.

No Stadium in Chinatown!

Chinatown's legacy of resistance and its role as the center of a larger cultural community were codified in early 2000 when city plans for a new baseball stadium for the Philadelphia Phillies were announced.[16] Stadiums, like casinos, have become common projects undertaken by struggling cities, which turn to market-based solutions and private developers to attract capital and address urban problems.[17] Stadiums in particular have been popular undertakings based on the promise that their presence will stimulate economic development in the surrounding area, creating entertainment-oriented districts and commodifying urban space for public consumption. In the 1990s, sixty major league facilities were constructed in cities across the country at a cost of $18 billion, with approximately 55 percent of these funds coming from public sources. Since 1980, thirty-four cities in North America have invested in new sports facilities in downtown or near downtown areas, in part to drive (re)development of urban districts.[18]

On April 12, 2000, at the first public hearing in City Hall, Mayor John Street's transition team recommended a downtown ballpark for the Phillies and released a list of potential sites, including one, favored by the mayor, at Twelfth and Vine Streets. The list drew protests from residents in Chinatown and Fairmount, who opposed the plan for a stadium in their neighborhood, as well as Port Richmond and Northern Liberties, whose neighborhoods were passed over by the plan.[19] For Mayor Street, the downtown stadium site showed promise because of its proximity to the Market East transit hub, the convention center, and the city's nightlife. A downtown stadium, the logic went, would create economic and civic spinoffs that could not be gleaned with a South Philadelphia site. The presence of a stadium would create a "sense of event" in the downtown area each game day, according to the *Inquirer*. "There would be a psychic factor," commented Mayor Street. "I don't know when this city will get another $500 million investment opportunity downtown where it could create other amenities."[20]

The announcement of a stadium north of Vine was an unwelcome surprise to Chinatown residents and their advocates. Somekawa and Wei recall hearing about the stadium site on KYW radio. Wei remembers, "I heard it on KYW news radio and I was like, 'What?!' and I listened to it and I went, 'Oh my God!' I went over to the AAU office, and Betty Lui was there, and I said, 'Betty, I need you to help me, because I want to go talk to the guys in CBA [the Chinese Benevolent Association], and I want to know if they know about this, because it's all in English, on English radio, but nobody in Chinatown has heard of this.'"[21] John Chin only learned of the plan when he was caught off guard by a call from a reporter asking about the stadium deal. Like Wei, his reaction was "That is crazy."[22]

Several days later, Chin was invited by the mayor's office to a meeting to discuss the stadium plans. Also in attendance were Cecilia Moy Yep, Debbie Wei, Ellen Somekawa, and others active in the Chinatown community. Attendees have various memories of the encounter with the mayor. Chin remembers an "amicable" and respectful meeting, catered with Chinese food:

> I think the mayor was trying to reach out to us, to explain to us what was being proposed and what they were thinking. . . . [W]e as PCDC really did want to hear out the mayor and see what his thoughts were. We really wanted to hear how he thought the stadium would benefit Chinatown. I don't remember if he had any answers for us at that time, but he wanted to hear us out. My feeling is that he wanted to meet with

us because we asked for a meeting, and he accommodated our request, and I think he wanted to give the message out to the public that he's not here to force a stadium down the throats of Chinatown. But he was willing to hear our concerns. . . . [W]e did walk away with some assurance that there would be communication between the administration and PCDC.[23]

In contrast, Somekawa remembers a hard sell from the mayor on the benefits of the stadium:

This meeting was different associations and PCDC and AAU, and it was Councilman [Frank] DiCicco and then the mayor trying to tell us what a good thing this was going to be for Chinatown. It was basically, "Well, what do you want? Haven't you always wanted a community center? This is your time to get one." I think people were just kind of silent. Like, if any of that talk happened, it was not going be in that room. If anybody wanted to talk to the mayor or DiCicco about a community center, it was not going to happen in that room. Right? I don't think they were hitting a particularly receptive audience, and I think it started out from a feeling of being slighted to start with. Now we're at the table after it's already been announced on the radio was a big part of the feeling.

According to Somekawa, "Pretty quickly our frame was that they are trying to make it sound like, 'This will help your businesses,' which made [us] think, 'You're not even seeing this as a neighborhood, are you? You're seeing it as a series of businesses who gain from this thing.'" This pitch was ineffective, Somekawa reflects, because similar promises had been made more than a decade before regarding the convention center, with no payoff:

The other interesting thing is that people had learned from the experience of the convention center, where that was also the pitch, and then people looked at it and said it wasn't really as promised. Didn't overall help businesses. Doesn't help Chinatown when there is massive influx of people for three days and then they disappear for two years and then they come back. It doesn't help us. It's gonna make us into a gigantic parking lot.[24]

The city's claim that the stadium would boost Chinatown business was not only implausible but also reminiscent of the dominant view of Chinatown as a commercial district rather than a true residential neighborhood.

For Chinatown, the stadium was seen as another instance of the city's historic disregard for the community. After decades of development and growth, the neighborhood remained highly vulnerable, especially outside the historic core. The need to expand north of Vine Street, so critical to planners' sense of the neighborhood's future, seemed betrayed by the stadium proposal. According to Chin, the proposal broke a promise the city had made—that north of Vine would be the target of future Chinatown development: "We were promised that Chinatown North was an area of expansion, so you've pretty much shut that off if the stadium comes here. . . . [I]t was a lot about how Chinatown was promised certain things in exchange for previous development projects happening to us."[25] For Gym and others, it was "a defining battle for Chinatown."[26] PCDC, AAU, and other organizations quickly mobilized to form the Stadium Out of Chinatown Coalition (SOCC) to fight City Hall on Twelfth and Vine as a stadium site. PCDC's rhetoric invariably emphasized the history of city projects' negative effect on Chinatown since the 1960s, as in an editorial penned by Ignatius Wang, PCDC's chairman. After providing a narrative of the community's history with the city and urban development, Wang decried the "surprise to the community" regarding the site recommendation. This plan, Wang continued, would "deny any hope for Chinatown to expand from its current size" and "discounted all the public, community, and private efforts in the last twenty-five years to restore Chinatown as a viable neighborhood." He pointed out that "traffic, noise, trash and congestion" were considerations, but more important was the "thirty years of institutional memory" embodied in the government's policy toward a minority community.[27]

The city's response denied that the proposal targeted Chinatown, or even that it would affect Chinatown, a claim that was based on a conservative delineation of the neighborhood's boundaries. William Hankowsky, president of the Philadelphia Industrial Development Corporation, commented in the *Inquirer*, "In part, we were trying to be respectful of Chinatown's expansion plans, which were, basically, as we best understood them, east of Eleventh Street." Mayor Street echoed this rhetoric, adding the claim of community benefit: "We believe that their concerns about traffic all have to be reasonably and sympathetically handled, but we don't think at this point in time that this proposed stadium at Twelfth and Vine is such an imposition on that community that it shouldn't be done. . . . We, in the end, think it will be a huge benefit to the Chinatown community, particularly the businesses that are there—and we think we can meet their concerns about expansion north of Vine."[28] Chinatown was not convinced. Even given such a strict interpretation of Chinatown North's boundaries, the mayor's plan still would have placed the stadium one block from Holy Redeemer and a proposed community center, and two blocks from Hing Wah Yuen. Associated spaces, such as parking lots, would place the entire complex even closer.

Covering the meeting, the *Inquirer* reported the community's skepticism and concern: "Several leaders who attended the meeting—and who have said they are dead set against a stadium in their neighborhood—said they felt as if the mayor were softening them up in anticipation of an announcement that he wanted to build the new baseball facility at Twelfth and Vine Streets." "It's hard to be invited to a meeting like that and not feel that this is the site," Edward Kung, a board member of both the PCDC and On Lok House, remarked to the *Inquirer.* Jason P. Choi, owner of the Choi Funeral Home on Twelfth Street, south of Vine, concurred: "My sense of it was, he was preparing you for the blow."[29] An unconvinced Wei commented, "It can't be worth the cost."[30] Others were also suspicious. Chin recalls that the "veterans" of the Chinatown struggle, such as Yep, immediately urged action: "Based on their past experience, they realized that this thing was bigger than anything that's ever challenged the community. As much as the expressway was a huge financial project, the stadium would have a larger negative community impact. It was bigger than the federal prison. I believe that these individuals understood this and understood that PCDC alone was not going to be able to fight this off. It was larger than us. It was larger than the Chinatown community. And the only way to have a chance of fighting this off was to build this coalition."[31]

After the initial meeting with Mayor Street and the formation of SOCC, activists began strategizing ways to oppose the action. A May march was planned, although coalition members disagreed on an overall strategy for organizing (see Figure 5.1). The "Stadium Out of Chinatown" fight, like the "Save Chinatown" campaign three decades before, was successful in uniting the Chinatown community across generational lines and other internal divisions, but it also highlighted differences within the Chinatown community over strategies and tactics, differences that embodied internal power, ideology, and leadership politics. While PCDC wanted to target politicians and pursue legal strategies, AAU argued for a grassroots organizing approach that would include less-represented members of the community, particularly new immigrants. Chin remembers the conflict as one between AAU as "process-oriented" and PCDC as "results-oriented":

> So you have one side of the table just trying to get results and stop the stadium, and then AAU is saying, "Let's slow down a little bit. We need individuals to come to consensus and agree [on] how we're going to do it and what we're going to do." One example was our very first public demonstration—we ended up marching from Chinatown to City Hall. So Ellen Somekawa was really, really pushing for community-based protesting. I think she wanted something at the gate. She wanted the youth organizations, the Chinese lion dancing clubs to come out with their drums, and she imagined a community rally building up support around this issue. And then Cecilia [Moy Yep]—these two were the ones that were debating what should be done—she thought, based

Figure 5.1. Anti-stadium protest, 2000. (Courtesy of the Philadelphia Chinatown Development Corporation.)

on her experiences, that our message should be taken to the people in power. Where are the people in power? City Hall.[32]

While supportive of a march to City Hall, AAU's Somekawa suggested that the emphasis should be on broadening community awareness and opposition and that a grassroots campaign would achieve greater impact in the long run. Representatives from the Chinese Benevolent Association (CBA) agreed and proposed a general strike in Chinatown, a suggestion that was initially rebuffed by SOCC organizers. Disagreements over strategy and the manner of including newer immigrants and businesspeople at the grassroots level led to the campaign's split into two different coalitions: SOCC, led by PCDC; and PCCOS (Philadelphia Chinatown Coalition to Oppose the Stadium) led by CBA, with AAU bridging the two groups as member of both.

This split over tactics and strategy mirrors in some ways the differences between a "community-building" community-development corporation (CDC) model and a "transformative model" of grassroots organizing also identified in Boston's Chinatown community during the same period. When that community was threatened by an expansion of Tufts New England Medical Center in 1993 (a takeover of the infamous Parcel C), the Chinatown Neighborhood Council attempted to negotiate with the center and the Boston Redevelopment Authority for a new Chinatown community center. In Philadelphia, no deal was cut or desired by PCDC, who clearly opposed the stadium and joined with other activists to fight it. But PCDC's employment of strategies that spoke to city power brokers, as opposed to grassroots organizing, was similar. In both cases, a broad coalition of Chinatown community members successfully opposed a larger institution's redevelopment plans.[33]

Of particular issue in both communities was inclusion for those who did not speak English, a salient concern for a community that had recently experienced an influx of new immigrants. Some new immigrant leaders and members of CBA, according to Wei, felt "slighted and marginalized in the process and frustrated":

> One of things I really remember was being in this meeting, and there's twenty, twenty-five people in the room—and this meeting is all strategy about fighting the stadium, and it's all conducted in English. And then there is a point in which people say, "Well, we really need to hire a lawyer." . . . And then somebody came over to some of these Chinese immigrant leaders, I think the CBA-type leaders, and started talking to them in Chinese about the need for money, and it just seemed so disrespectful, that you would conduct this whole meeting—everybody's comfortable in English, and the guy gabbing and debating, and then the time comes when we need money, and then *that's* the time you are going to go interpret for somebody. So that was just a sign that things were not quite right. . . . We tried to raise the concern with PCDC, and they said, "Look, they like it when we speak for them." And then we talked to them and then they said, "No, we don't like it."[34]

Ping Leung Cheung, head of CBA, articulated this feeling in an e-mail announcing CBA's withdrawal from SOCC and the formation of the PCCOS coalition. Affirming that "people of Chinatown, regardless of language or immigrant status should have a voice in deliberations regarding the stadium," Cheung wrote that CBA and its member organizations had been excluded from "a higher level of participation" and felt "uncomfortable" in meetings that were held exclusively in English. While attending the Steering Committee meetings, Chueng noted, "We felt disrespected and were made to feel invisible." Of particular issue was a June 5 meeting with Councilman Frank DiCicco, which PCCOS opposed because DiCicco had not taken a "firm and open stand against the stadium." PCDC attended the meeting for SOCC, much to CBA's consternation.[35]

The issue over language inclusion, according to Debbie Wei, was and is a significant one for Chinatown: "How can English be a power broker in a community like Chinatown? It's the language of power, it always has been, it always will be, but, I mean, you can understand it as a language of power but not hold it against others in the community who don't have it. . . . [I]f you see who's in power and how things are or [are] not communicated in the community, English is still the power broker. . . . [I]t's a form of internalized racism."[36] The language issue was also intimately connected for many to the issue of strategy:

> The Chinese-speaking restaurant owners came forward right at the beginning of that announcement and offered to stage a strike—which is unheard of, a work stoppage—in Chinatown to support the opposition of the stadium, and PCDC ignored them. They were all Chinese speaking, and I was like, this is huge! A general strike in Chinatown, this has never happened, but they felt they kept trying to get access to these meetings and to information and nothing was ever translated. So I met with them, and I said, "Well, what do you want to do?"[37]

While CBA businessmen had long ceded control (albeit sometimes reluctantly) to PCDC, this time non-English-speaking immigrants whose businesses would be affected by the stadium sought greater inclusion in strategy discussions.

A dramatic centerpiece of the anti-stadium campaign was a branded march and demonstration to City Hall held in early June 2000, organized by PCCOS and involving members of all the coalitions. At the suggestion of CBA leader Derek Sam, participants wore custom-designed "Stadium Out of Chinatown" T-shirts and carried a collective banner. The *Inquirer* described the scene:

> With a mammoth march that clogged several Center City streets and a major business shutdown, Philadelphia's tight-knit Asian community yesterday delivered an urgent message to City Hall: "This is Chinatown, Stadiums Not Welcome." That was just one of the protest slogans plastered on windows and poles in the heart of Chinatown and carried by throngs of marchers on their way to City Hall in a boisterous procession of bells, cymbals and drums. "We are angry because everyone from the mayor to City Council to the newspapers are telling us we should welcome a project that will destroy our community," declared Debbie Wei, a protest leader, in front of City Hall. "We are here to say: Never again! Never again will you render our community invisible. . . . You will never put a stadium in Chinatown!"[38]

As part of the June 8 demonstration, PCCOS organized Chinatown businesspeople and residents into a general strike. Before the City Hall march, the *Inquirer* reported, about 75 percent of the two hundred businesses in Chinatown were expected to participate in the strike, taping yellow-and-black "Closed" signs to their shop windows or doors. The protesters formed a group—at Holy Redeemer Church and School at Tenth and Vine—to march through Chinatown to City Hall. Police later estimated the size of the crowd at 1,500.[39]

Activists also attended City Council hearings on stadium financing, questioning the cost of the stadium given other urban priorities. A June 21 City Council hearing turned into "an unrelenting, eight-hour tirade against the mayor, the Phillies, the Eagles and their stadium plans," according to the *Philadelphia Daily News*. Challenging the lack of numbers on stadium cost, "Community members—the bulk of the more than 100 speakers who testified—attacked Street on his key agenda issues of neighborhoods and children. One after another, city residents—many from Chinatown and other areas adjacent to the proposed Twelfth and Vine streets Phillies site—accused Street of putting sports ahead of schools, day care centers, community centers and parks."[40] The issue of financing hit home for Chinatown residents, who saw in the stadium deal another indication of the city's lack of interest or investment in their community. One AAU flyer questioned "The City's Priorities": "Our community has no public school, no library, no community or recreation center. City-wide our schools and neighborhoods are in crisis. It's a disgrace to pour a billion dollars into projects to make sports teams and real estate speculators richer."[41]

Despite these and other protests, Mayor Street ultimately chose Twelfth and Vine for the stadium site in June 2000. In the public announcement of his decision, he asserted the economic benefits of stadiums and the role that they played in a new approach to urban development. "Let's not be known as a city without a vision, a city that never considers its possibilities or potential," Street said, declaring that the downtown stadium would be part of a "new era for Philadelphia."[42] Once again, Chinatown was being portrayed as anti-progress, a barrier to a new era in the city's growth:

> Chinatown leaders were incensed at Street's remarks that opponents only wanted "to condemn anything new" and weren't considering the bigger picture of benefits to the city's tax base and image that a new ballpark would bring. "We do have a vision for our community," said Debbie Wei, a leader of Asian Americans United. Chinatown activists said they have long had plans to acquire land north of the Vine Expressway for new housing, a park, and community and recreation centers.[43]

After Street's announcement, SOCC retained attorney Robert Sugarman to initiate a suit against the city under Pennsylvania's right-to-know act in Common Pleas Court on September 1, demanding evidence supporting the site choice: copies of parking and engineering studies, plus feasibility and financial analyses.[44] One goal of the lawsuit was to determine the projected source of stadium funding, as the presence of federal monies would enhance SOCC's case in claiming the stadium choice had a "discriminatory effect."[45]

The combined coalitions employed a variety of strategies in fighting the proposal in addition to mass demonstrations and marches: letter writing and media releases, petitions and pressure on local politicians, legal threats, and broader coalition building. In addition to unifying divergent internal voices, the stadium campaign reached out beyond Chinatown to involve the larger Asian cultural community and other community organizations. Callowhill residents joined PCDC in petitioning against the stadium. Somekawa recalls: "Beyond the marches, which are the most visible sign of the protest, was just the systematic petitioning, trying to get people to different parts of the city to say, 'This doesn't even make sense for us.' I mean, I live in Northeast Philly, and this doesn't even make sense for me. There was also a lot of just hard work on the ground, like a massive citywide petition campaign and other work like that."[46]

Activists articulated these concerns and others in a letter-writing campaign in June 2000, given shape by a series of talking points that emphasized a variety of issues from project costs to the community's quality of life. At issue was the cost of the stadium (a cool $200 million in addition to the costs of other sites under consideration) and the need to spend that city money on schools and recreation areas/parks and services, all assets Chinatown lacked. AAU insisted that, contrary to charges, this was not a "NIMBY" [Not in My Backyard] issue for Chinatown: "For [Chinatown] in particular, which has had 30 years of governmental projects, the issue is not NIMBY. Basically, if you already took my front yard, both side yards, and the driveway, isn't it just a matter of fairness to say we've had our share and you have to go somewhere else this time, especially when it appears that there are several viable sites that may not generate any neighborhood opposition?"[47] Other issues were the support for "corporate welfare" represented by the subsidy of private ventures, the "myths" about the benefits stadiums provided to cities (citing Neil de-Mause's book *Field of Schemes*), and the economic impact of development for city residents versus suburban commuters, a recurring theme in Philadelphia planning.[48] The point about the opportunity cost for this area of the city centered in part on whether the area north of Vine Street was blighted, as it was portrayed by the city. This image troubled those who had worked to begin developing Chinatown North. Describing the area as a "no man's land" also effaced the existing presence of people and businesses that were living and working there: "That area is far from blight. It is home to a diverse group of residences, businesses, multipurpose spaces, etc. The city claims it wants to clean us up, but it feels a lot like it simply wants to clean us out."[49] Others noted that at least four old factory buildings in the area were being redeveloped privately as residences or commercial space.

AAU marshaled the expressive power of its youth programs to support the letter campaign. One Central High School student, Fong Wa Chung, wrote to the *Inquirer*:

> When I first found out that our mayor was going to propose Twelfth and Vine as the site for the new stadium, I said, "Oh, that's not *really* in Chinatown." . . . [T]hen as everything became more publicized, I thought about it. Twelfth and Vine is one block north and two blocks west from where I live in Chinatown. I started to hear about all the absolutely great reasons why the site is perfect and I became outraged. Why? Because the mayor has reduced my community to a bunch of restaurants that should just be grateful for the extra business a new stadium would bring. . . . I live in Chinatown with my family and hundreds of other families. Many people think that the residents of Chinatown are uneducated, don't speak English and happily fry rice all day. Well sorry. I am a student at Central High School, I speak English perfectly and I am not willing to get out of the way. I will not allow this stadium to destroy my home and put our education in the back seat.[50]

Another student emphasized the history of negative city impacts: "Chinatown is fed up to here with the City's empty promises about development benefiting our community! Enough is enough! I have seen the impact of these so-called civic improvements like the Vine Street Expressway and the Convention Center. This is the reality of living with these monstrous intrusions into a residential life."[51] Yet another student raised issues of racism and racial politics:

> Unlike any of the other sites, the choice of Eleventh and Vine Street was made without any prior discussion or even consultation with any leadership in the CT [Chinatown] community. . . . All information about the stadium proposal was disseminated through the mainstream English media, though clearly many, if not most, of the residents of CT get information in Chinese. . . . [T]he process as well as the act of choosing Eleventh and Vine, effectively sealing and choking CT by downtown development projects, raises questions of how Asian Americans are viewed in this city and by this administration.[52]

Negative stereotypes of Chinatown and immigrants, lack of service to the community, and even environmental racism were charges laid at the city's feet.

In retrospect, Somekawa believes that the various approaches within the anti-stadium effort were "complementary" and that the combined efforts effectively rallied the community against the stadium initiative, allowing for a unified external voice and the ability to build a coalition with others across the city. PCCOS's goal, according to Somekawa, was to "figure out how to unify this whole thing" and organize in a way that allowed working people and business owners to participate:

> I think one of the biggest marches that happened on the stadium hap-
> pened with that idea of those banners, unified T-shirts. They are also
> the people that said, "Well, if community people are gonna sit in all-
> day hearings on the stadium, we are gonna feed them." [*Laughs*] So
> they solicited food from Chinatown, and they brought in hundreds of
> boxes of lunch, and they fed the entire gallery. They fed hundreds of
> people. So they would come up with "What does it take to keep this
> movement together? What does it take to move things forward?" And
> so they would come up with these things that we thought were not
> in our normal, just radical repertoire—but ways of doing things that
> really made sense for this community.[53]

Despite internal divisions, largely imperceptible to the outside, Chinatown was effective in raising awareness of the stadium's potential effect on the community and marshaling widespread support for the stadium fight. In November 2000, after sustained resistance from both coalitions, the Philadelphia Phillies, and other Philadelphia lawmakers balking at the $350-million price tag, Mayor Street abandoned Twelfth and Vine Streets as a proposed site for the stadium, relocating the complex to South Philadelphia.[54]

Resistance to the stadium ultimately revolved around two propositions about Chinatown. The first was that Chinatown was a community like any other neighborhood in Philadelphia and deserved respect as a "neighborhood of families":

> On a summer day, when a visitor to [Chinatown] is strolling down
> Tenth Street, do his senses register anything besides the restaurant
> signs and the smell of food? Does he see the children rushing to the
> only playground at Holy Redeemer with their water guns and roller
> blades? Does he hear the teenagers bouncing their basketballs on
> the way to the junior league at the Christian Church? Does he see
> the elderly working in the community garden they redeemed from a
> drug-littered and trash-infested lot? Can he understand that the words
> people are making all around are those of greeting, thanks, sympathy,
> anger, and love?[55]

As the AAU Freedom School Chinatown Site Platform of Action reiterated: "We want acknowledgement of Chinatown as a community."

A second proposition asserted the ways in which Chinatown was not like other neighborhoods, focusing on Chinatown's importance as an Asian center for the region and a historic place of cultural and physical safety for immigrants: "CT [Chinatown] is not just another neighborhood within Philadelphia. For 130 years CT has been a cultural, racial and ethnic home to Chinese immigrants, citizens, and Asian Americans throughout the Delaware Valley. If CT does not exist, there are no other Asian neighborhoods in this region that can begin to approximate its historical, cultural, and social value."[56] As Suette Lo, a Chinese American resident of Ambler, Montgomery County, remarked to the *Inquirer*, "Even though I don't live in that small piece of land, I care. . . . They are destroying opportunity." "We have a lot of people who are not living in Chinatown, commented Kin Lam, assistant pastor of the CCC&C, "but Chinatown is a central activity for them, a place to come back to every week. They feel a sense of attachment, of belonging to this community."[57] Part of the reason to save Chinatown was also its status as a historic neighborhood. When Shen Hao, a fifty-three-year-old dentist from Broomall, was running errands in Center City and heard about the June 8 protest on the radio, he rushed to join the march. "It's a historic area. . . . [O]ur origins start here," Hao commented to the *Inquirer*. "We don't want it to be destroyed."[58] Ultimately, the stadium fight and the support it marshaled affirmed the significance of Chinatown to Chinese Americans and Asians all around the region, highlighting its importance as a center of the larger cultural community and a historic point of origin.

"Chinatown didn't move—Center City moved": Gentrification

Another threat facing the Chinatown community in the last twenty years—one for which it is harder to marshal resistance—is gentrification. As the property values in Center City real estate skyrocketed in the early 2000s, parcels along the margins of the district, like Chinatown, became more attractive to developers. As Debbie Wei observes, "Chinatown didn't move—Center City moved." In the Chinatown core, property values continued to rise. The median house value in Chinatown has risen over the last twenty years, from $69,800 in 1990 to $262,700 in 2010. An examination of the listed sale prices in Philadelphia's property database indicated that nearly one-third of the buildings in Chinatown sold for more than $250,000, and thirty-four properties sold for more than $1 million.[59] Since the early 2000s, new condo developments have been established at a brisk rate, adapting old hotels and factories. The Grandview at Eleventh and Vine is a former textile plant (constructed in 1928) that was converted into a suite hotel in 2000, then subsequently into condominiums by Metro Development Company. The 296 units were quickly sold, averaging from $300,000 up to $400,000 when the building opened, well out of range of most Chinatown residents and workers. Developer David Grasso commented to the *Inquirer* in 2004 that he was "well aware of the ramifications that condominiums could pose for Chinatown" and considered placing some low-cost housing within the Grandview, but "it just didn't make economic sense. . . . It's a valid concern, that they need housing for people who can't afford it," he said. "Our building, it's a business. We had a responsibility to our investors."[60] In 2012, a one-bedroom/one-bath condo sold for $150,000; a two-bedroom/one-bath condo sold for $266,000.[61] Another condo project, Ten Ten, developed in 2003 by Lance Silver, of Silver and Harting Real Estate, repurposed Clarion Suites (formerly the Heywood Brothers Chair Factory, established in 1892) at 1010 Race into condos originally listed between $125,000 and $325,000.[62] Units in the building have since sold for as much as $385,000.[63] A third high-rise condo development, Pearl Condos, was constructed at 111 North Ninth Street. Units in this building have recently sold for $228,000 to $374,000.[64] Many of the purchasers of these properties are Asian; some are Chinese Americans who live in Bucks County or suburban New Jersey, often "empty nesters," who are looking to move to the city to reduce their commute to Chinatown businesses. But they do not resolve the critical housing shortage for new immigrants, for whom rental properties are scarce or financially out of reach.

Chinatown activists express concern that the increasing construction of premium condominiums will raise property values, taxes, and rents so high that the neighborhood's traditional, working-class residents will be forced out. Rising property values, unlike concrete city projects, are more elusive and difficult to organize against. "There isn't even anything to demonstrate against," says Wei. "Where would you march?"[65]Concerns about gentrification extend to and are most active in Chinatown North, the site of Chinatown's future and the only area into which Chinatown can grow in response to community needs (the neighborhood is blocked in other directions by Independence Mall to the east, Gallery East to the south, and the Philadelphia Convention Center to the west).

In Chinatown North, the tensions around past, present, and future are more acute as Chinatown contemplates larger urban changes and forces, both for redevelopment and preservation, and where the blighted landscape presents a different but related set of issues and competing thematic imperatives. Chinatown North sits on a "frontier line" of gentrification, a "no man's land" defined by its blighted postindustrial physical environment, lacking social identity or political presence. Symbolically it has represented the future for Chinatown since the 1980s, and the community has expanded north of Vine by both default and design. After the construction of Hing Wah Yuen in 1998, PCDC relocated its offices to Ninth and Wood Streets. Sing Wah Yuen, a housing project for low- to moderate-income families, across Ninth Street from Hing Wah Yuen, was constructed in 2003, solidifying the energy for formal redevelopment north of Vine Street. Chinatown North also functions as a production and supply area for the Chinatown core, and some Chinatown businesspeople have built businesses in structures zoned for industrial use:

at least two tofu factories are located there as well as other wholesale food distributors and a sign company. Several automotive and tire-service sheds and a building-supply company reinforce a sense of the neighborhood as mixed commercial/industrial. Hidden brothels and sweatshops still dot the landscape, as do vacant lots, many filled with debris. A Philadelphia Electric Company (PECO) substation, at Eleventh and Noble, is an immoveable eyesore. Property ownership in Chinatown North is likewise mixed, with some parcels held by resident Chinese Americans and other individuals and many more by absent landholders and private real-estate developers. Asian American investment has driven piecemeal private development, resulting largely in new construction; at Twelfth and Buttonwood, a block-long complex of three-story townhouses/row houses with ground-floor retail units was recently built by a Chinese American entrepreneur.

Planned expansion of the neighborhood by PCDC focuses on constructing mixed-income housing (a critical need in a neighborhood that still serves as an entry point for new immigrants and a symbolic return for retirees), streetscaping, greening, recreation, and other anti-blight and adaptive reuse initiatives. Ongoing gentrification and rising property values due to speculation pose challenges, as real-estate companies purchase parcels for development, hurting PCDC's ability to buy and hold parcels in "land banks" for later development. "I don't think people realize the consequences," says Lai Har Cheung, whose roots in Chinatown go back three decades. "This neighborhood could end up being a little amusement park."[66] Again, the residential quality of Chinatown is cast as essential to the survival of the neighborhood and its ability to expand northward, yet the area is often seen from without as largely uninhabited.[67]

Sitting on a gentrification frontier line, the planned expansion of Chinatown North is now often in conflict with a parallel movement to redevelop a former warehouse area just northwest of Chinatown known as Callowhill, to others as the "Loft District," or even "Eraserhood," after its role as an inspiration for David Lynch's movie *Eraserhead*. As an emerging neighborhood, Callowhill seeks to capitalize on its adjacency to North Broad Street and the Avenue of the Arts, the Pennsylvania Academy of the Fine Arts, and an existing infrastructure of former factories and warehouses that can be adapted into residential lofts and artists' studios. The area has already seen some development in the form of loft conversions by developers (some of it temporarily stalled during a recent economic downturn). The area was included in the National Register of Historic Places in 2010 and recently named a national historic district (bounded by North Broad Street to the west, Hamilton Street to the north, Pearl Street to the south, and Twelfth Street and the curve of the Reading Railroad Viaduct to the east—a smaller area to preserve historical "integrity"). Powers and Company, a national consulting firm specializing in the preservation and rehabilitation of historic structures, prepared the national historic district nomination at the behest of the owners of the Heid Building at 323 North Thirteenth Street, who wanted to seek tax credits for rehabilitation of the historic building.[68] The financial incentives with historic districting, combined with the prospects of high profits in the earlier phases of gentrification, have contributed to the development of this neighborhood as a "stylish-yet-still-transforming neighborhood" with "edge and verve" defined by artists' studios and galleries, boutiques, and concert venues amid large urban postindustrial structures and the remnants of cobblestone streets, offering up the "kind of hidden cultural gems that intrigue visitors and residents alike" and keep the "creatively inclined blood pumping."[69] In 2012, 50 percent of the parcels in this area were occupied by vacant land or abandoned buildings, but development has accelerated in recent years.[70]

One influential long-time resident who has witnessed dramatic change is artist Sarah McEneaney, who moved there in 1979 to reclaim an old carriage house.[71] McEneaney was one of the founders of the Callowhill Neighbors Association (CNA), an organization created out of residents' resistance to the stadium in 2000. "We didn't have a neighborhood association, and yet a lot of our neighbors got to know each other through the stadium fight, and then we looked around and said, 'Oh there is more of us here than we realized,'" McEneaney recalls. For CNA, the Callowhill area is defined as Vine to Spring Garden and Eighth to Broad: "There is no neighborhood association in this neighborhood, and so because we worked so closely with PCDC and the folks in Chinatown, we wanted to include the whole residential and commercial area."[72]

Chinatown leaders define the area differently and do not necessarily identify with inclusion in the Callowhill district. For them, Callowhill represents a potential threat in the form of gentrification, according to Chin:

> You had the people in the Loft District say, "Hey, you know what, this is an opportunity to move here." So since that time, the real-estate prices have driven up tremendously. . . . [G]entrification is a concern. . . . During the real-estate boom, they converted and built nine hundred new condo units, all market rate. So we were very concerned about the affordability of Chinatown and how to build more. So gentrification. We're trying to work with the city's government agencies to get the few parcels of land that remain under their ownership and provided to us to build more affordable housing—that's another goal of ours.[73]

Gayle Isa, director of the Asian Arts Initiative (AAI), a pan-Asian arts organization that opened new headquarters at Twelfth and Vine in 2008, expresses a similar concern: "I think that people who do describe it as 'the Loft District' tend to think of this as an industrial neighborhood and don't necessarily realize that there have been homes—maybe not in a huge abundance—but homes occupied by some immigrant families and also African Americans and some white folks, but definitely preexisting the development of the luxury condo or apartment complexes."[74]

Callowhill and Chinatown North collided in 2004 when the Delaware Valley Regional Planning Commission (DVRPC) began a planning process for Chinatown North, an area it defined as spanning between Sixth Street, west to Broad Street, and north from Filbert to Spring Garden, a significant expansion of traditional boundaries. Participating in the process were Kise Straw and Kolodner, a noted Philadelphia consulting firm, and a neighborhood task force of more than fifty organizations and individuals, including Councilman DiCicco, PCDC, AAU, the Callowhill Neighborhood Association, and the Philadelphia City Planning Commission (PCPC). According to Barry Seymour, who heads the DVRPC, undertaking planning with a neighborhood like Chinatown presented special challenges "because of the language" and the historic mistrust of government: "A lot of the Chinatown residents, I think, have a long-standing distrust or caution to any sort of public government-viewed process. We tried to let this run through the CDC and not come off as kind of a heavy-handed government plan or anything like that. But there is still a natural resistance. The battle over the baseball stadium was still pretty fresh in everyone's mind there. So what was good is that they were somewhat organized, but they were organized to fight. So there were trust issues that had to be overcome there."[75]

Other challenges related to competing interests in the area. One was the definition of district and neighborhood boundaries in the area. Both Callowhill and Chinatown claimed overlapping territory, according to Seymour: "A lot of redevelopment was happening to the west in Callowhill, the Loft District—a lot of industrial buildings in Callowhill were being converted to artist housing and loft apartments. Chinatown felt that was sort of their neighborhood, but it was already happening, the loft conversions were already happening. It was a little bit of a no man's land."[76] The boundaries of the study were expanded to include Callowhill as well, but the difference in community identity was a mismatch: "Those residents [in the Loft District] generally were not Asian. They didn't so much have an identity to much of Chinatown. It wasn't so much a conflict, but they were already there. They felt like it was their community as well. So Chinatown residents felt that they should have rights, but the market was happening already. . . . [It] wound up being kind of two plans that were joined, although we kept trying to bring them together."[77]

The DVRPC plan outlined several major developments to the Chinatown North/Callowhill area. The first was the need for low- to moderate-income housing. The plan recommended two key initiatives to address this need. The first was to work with the Philadelphia Housing Authority to directly acquire land reserved for affordable housing, protecting the land from speculation, and the second was to expand the number of housing-development partners, including private developers, to work with local organizations to offer subsidized housing, incorporating restrictions to maintain affordability. The plan also suggested developing market-rate housing for an Asian market. It outlined the need to develop design guidelines for new and existing developments to counteract and prevent recent "historically and culturally insensitive façade renovations" and "emphasize Chinatown's neighborhood character."[78] More significantly, the plan outlined "The Big Lid" covering the Vine Street Expressway with green blocks or some other continuous cover, greening, streetscaping, additional Asian-themed gateways at each entrance to Chinatown, and a centrally located "town square"–style park. To expand recreation, the plan also included the transformation of a parking lot at Seventh and Callowhill into a Chinatown playfields/gateway. This feature would also work to strengthen the connection to Franklin Square, another recommendation. Finally, the plan indicated the need to establish a "new major anchor" and "town center" for Chinatown North/Callowhill that would bring focus to future development.

"Share your vision for Chinatown North"

The largest point of contention during the DVRPC planning process was the fate of a historic nineteenth-century viaduct used by the Reading Railroad (and still owned by Reading International Company), a large stone edifice, darkened with age and overgrown with vegetation (much of it native plants), which cuts diagonally across the area in a larger Y pattern. Built in the 1890s, the viaduct is a combination of embankment sections, bridged by steel structures and arched masonry bridges, which runs ten blocks through the Callowhill and Chinatown North neighborhoods, from Vine Street to Fairmount Avenue. Reading Railroad commuter trains used the 4.7-acre, mile-long viaduct to access the Reading Headhouse Terminal at Twelfth and Market Street (currently the Grand Hall of the Pennsylvania Convention Center) until 1984, when the Center City commuter tunnel was opened. Viaduct proponents, led by McEneaney, see the structure as a valuable historical feature of the landscape and wish to preserve and convert it to an elevated green space along the lines of New York City's Highline: "I see it as a boon, a big jewel waiting to be developed and turned into something useful again."[79] To Chinatown developers, it is an unsightly, hulking impediment that casts a long shadow over an already blighted neighborhood. While Callowhill residents seek transformation of the viaduct, PCDC would like to see the edifice demolished to make way for a neat residential grid populated with new mixed-income housing. Others, such as Somekawa, understand the concerns about gentrification but see the potential benefit for youth of having neighborhood green space.

Viaduct-project supporters claim that a restored and transformed viaduct would act as a powerful agent of neighborhood renewal: "As a reclaimed public space, the Reading Viaduct will successfully bring together economically and culturally diverse communities, generate economic development, and provide a catalyst for the redevelopment of this section of North Philadelphia. Similar projects in Paris, France (the *Promenade Planteé*) and in New York City (the Chelsea High Line), they point out, have contributed to the rebirth of surrounding neighborhoods and initiated an economic development boom."[80] The idea has increasingly gained traction throughout the city. Inga Saffron, the architecture critic for the *Inquirer*, was an early supporter. Writing about the NYC High Line in 2009, Saffron concluded that the viaduct could be "a refuge for the old-fashioned flaneur, a place to stroll, people-watch, or just do nothing." This opportunity was "unfortunately," according to Saffron, being opposed by Chinatown:

> Unfortunately, Chinatown leaders have loudly opposed the idea, arguing—like the New York developers—that the viaduct should be torn down to create land for housing. Forget the huge cost of demolishing the viaduct—estimated at $35 million. Losing the noble stone structure would actually strip Philadelphia's Loft District of a potentially valuable amenity and make it a less distinctive place to live. As the High Line shows: Leave it and they will come.[81]

Comments on this story, published on Saffron's blog, repeated a familiar refrain in public opinion—that Chinatown is anti-progress—and revealed a circumscribed geographic conception of Chinatown as well as latent racism, according to Isa. Reflecting on the comments following Saffron's story, she observed that there were "kinds of comments about, 'Why does everyone in Chinatown keep complaining?' 'They depend on tourism. . . . [I]f they don't like it, they should just go back to where they came from.' I know that I can be a little oversensitive, but still I felt like the comments were just barely toeing that line."[82]

Underlying the viaduct controversy are competing historical legacies and visions for the neighborhood's future. For McEneaney, the viaduct represents a sense of connection to the industrial past and her own personal history in the neighborhood, which dates back more than thirty years. McEneaney originally wanted to call the Callowhill neighborhood "Trestletown," after the railroad's presence in the area; she views the tracks with nostalgia:

> When I first moved here in 1979, the trains were still running, and I used to get on at the station at Spring Garden Street to go to visit friends from Germantown. . . . [S]ome trains didn't go, stop there, and you'd have to go to Reading Terminal, and the train would go right

through my neighborhood, and I could look out the train and see my house as I went by, and so I relate to it as when it was still a functioning railroad.[83]

The viaduct also expresses her sensibilities about historic preservation and as an urban pioneer:

To me, it represents history, it represents the past, the railroad history. And then it represents what we—how we treat our past in terms of how you remember and also how we reuse our existing structures. I bought an old building. This was an old carriage house. I wouldn't really be interested in having a new house. I like the idea of reusing our history and reusing old structures. And that's even more important as we've all become more conscious about ecology and being green. This was just a trashy weedy lot, and I slowly turned it into a garden. . . . I mean, I'm definitely someone who likes history and architecture and wants to see things worth preserving [be] preserved.[84]

PCDC's position on the viaduct is based on Chinatown's history of activism and fight for decent housing, healthy living conditions for working families, and an identified place that is Chinatown, according to PCDC Board Member Andy Toy:

There is a lot of protectiveness, I think, involved in Chinatown—for good reason, because of the history. So when we're discussing new opportunities or new things, we are usually very careful where we are going with it to make sure that it is not going to hurt what already exists. In some neighborhoods, you might have a different idea, where people want to just grow and build and things like that. The other thing is making sure that we are taking care of the people that have been hurt by other policies—specifically when the Redevelopment Authority came and took people's houses, the idea was we would replace those, and that's sort of how PCDC got started in the housing development field. . . . Stability of community, protecting the community, is always paramount.[85]

These competing visions for the viaduct are both rooted in the process of historic place making and a desire to preserve or perpetuate the heritage of that place.

Although ostensibly settled in the DVRPC plan's compromise, the viaduct continued to be a lightning rod for tensions over the future of the Callowhill/ Chinatown North. The issue bubbled up at a July 2009 AAI Chinatown In/flux community forum on Chinatown North. "Share your Vision for Chinatown

North." Flyers for the event promised: "Hear what community organizations are planning." Representatives from Callowhill, including McEneaney, sat in the front row of the crowd. When the floor was opened for discussion, they were the first to speak, and at length, about the viaduct and the need to preserve it in its entirety. PCDC Board Member Toy, also sitting in the front row, countered by pointing out that McEneaney's statement seemed to negate the "compromise" that had been reached in the DVRPC planning process.

In 2011, CNA partnered with the Center City District and engaged in planning studies underwritten by local foundations (Samuel S. Fels Fund, William Penn Foundation, and Poor Richard's Charitable Trust) funneled through the district. These studies concluded, among other things, that rehabilitation of the viaduct into a park would be less costly than demolition. The viaduct issue resurfaced again when Councilman DiCicco introduced legislation before the City Council creating and endorsing a Callowhill Reading Viaduct Neighborhood Improvement District (CRVNID). Proposed improvements to the neighborhood included street cleaning and lighting, recreational facilities, preservation of open space, trees and other landscaping, trash receptacles, enhanced safety, and public art, but the viaduct was the centerpiece of the NID proposal.[86] Reaction to the NID from Chinatown was largely negative, emphasizing a lack of dialogue with local residents and with Chinatown: "With no public meeting held, the CRVNID claimed that they have gained support from Chinatown residents and businesses. . . . Their process was not transparent and engaging."[87] This lack of inclusion was perceived as insulting, according to Chin: "But it was really offensive, because these people who are moving into the lofts have no history or connection to the neighborhood. They don't understand that promises that were made to Chinatown. . . . If they wanted to be neighborly, which obviously they didn't, that was a poor way of doing it. They did it with such disrespect."[88] When protests were mounted against the NID, DiCicco redrew boundaries of the district to exclude Chinatown. Opposition to the proposal, which would levy a 7 percent tax on residents to provide for the NID services, continued after City Council approved the measure in September 2011. Local residents and businesspeople organized resistance through letter writing and petitioning, and the revised measure was defeated in February 2012.[89]

That an urban neighborhood would reject an anti-blight redevelopment plan suggests that diverse stakeholders in the Chinatown North/Callowhill area possess very different visions for the neighborhood and that the viaduct reflects larger conflicts of class, culture, aesthetics, and redevelopment priorities. McEneaney and others in the Loft District express discomfort with Chinatown's insistence on perpetuating and expanding an ethnically specific enclave, claiming the future of the neighborhood is and should be multicultural and multiethnic:

I don't see any division between Callowhill and Chinatown North. To me, I see them as being one and of the same. Chinatown North—the way it's described sometimes by the PCDC folks, my understanding is they sort of use Eleventh Street as a cutoff point. And there have been times when I feel like they're trying to say to us, "Well, you can have west of Eleventh," and I don't like that. I don't like the sort of carving it up, because there's Chinese, or there's Asians that live over here, and there's—everybody's all kind of mixed up. There's also a whole lot of Mexican immigrants in this neighborhood these days. So it's very mixed up, and everyone's all over the place, and I don't really want to carve things up into little sections—I'd rather keep it one neighborhood. . . . I mean this complex here [next door] was built by Chinese Americans, but it's [a] totally diverse population who's living here. There's Asians, there's black people, there's white people, there's all different ages, and I think that's great.[90]

Class dynamics also play a part, particularly given that for developers of the Loft District, a future of low- or mixed-income housing is perceived as having a negative effect on their bottom line, according to Chin:

People that bought the lofts and in my conversation with some police officers, right, is that number one: these people that are part of the planning group did not want any association with affordable housing—that affordable housing is low-income people means a certain thing to people with money, and they don't want that. So I started figuring out and putting two and two together. People paid a lot of money to move into these lofts. They moved into a really derelict neighborhood. A lot of homeless guys hang out. . . . [S]ome residents have said so much to the police officers that patrol that area. I put so much money, invested so much, in my loft. I'm not going to live in a blah blah blah crappy neighborhood. They're motivated toward gentrification and protecting their investment.[91]

A more recent conflict in 2013 over zoning for a new construction apartment complex for the 1100 block of Ridge Avenue planned by a Chinese American entrepreneur, who also runs a tofu factory at 1018 Wood Street, replayed these divisions. CNA opposed the complex, raising concerns over issues of "density" and "proposed clientele," terms that indirectly referenced discomfort with what would be mixed, low-income immigrant housing (the housing was geared to "people who want to live and work in the neighborhood"). "I would like to be excited about new construction in the neighborhood," commented McEneaney.[92]

Other concerns center on the emphasis on the viaduct project as an engine of neighborhood development, fearing it will reinforce inequality amid gentrification. Chinatown developers are concerned that discussion of the viaduct does not assume the park will spur development, keeping visible the question of "what's under the park." This concern is shared by AAI's Isa:

> The fear that I've heard and personally share is that if the High Line concept is pursued, ways then people who live in those luxury loft buildings that tower high enough to look down upon the elevated parkway can enjoy it, but that other folks who are poor or working class may end up just living in the shadows. Although I feel like there are ways to—whether it's through zoning or agreements with private developers—to try to adjust and create equitable development so that there could be truly mixed-income housing and low-income housing units that are also able to exist along that.[93]

For PCDC, the issue is not only that "under the park" should be developed but also that it should be developed with specific populations in mind. Preservation of existing historical structures is not a concern. PCDC emphasizes the creation of housing for immigrant families, and the idiosyncratic lots created by the diagonal viaduct path make the area difficult to develop in this regard: "The most critical issue facing Chinatown's most underserved population—an adequate supply of affordable housing—has been neglected and even rendered impossible to deal with."[94] There is every indication, based on past approaches to Chinatown North, that PCDC would proceed through processes of demolition and redevelopment, clearing blighted structures and rebuilding anew. Adaptive reuse has not been its approach in the past.

Housing is also a goal of Callowhill developers, as is adaptive reuse, but not for mixed-income housing, which would not drive increased investment in and profit from the neighborhood. The primary goal of developers in Callowhill is rehabilitation of the postindustrial structures to create a high-end destination neighborhood with a large return on investment. The Post Brothers, developers of the Goldtex apartments at Twelfth and Wood (a reuse of the old Goldtex shoe factory), market their developments on their success in raising local property values and rents for higher profit. "Post has an extremely successful track record of finding and exploiting unmet rental market demand niches, and each of Post's completed projects has achieved a rent level far higher than previously existed in their submarket," they boast on their website.[95] For these developers, neither preservation nor gentrification is a concern. For residents like McEneaney, gentrification is less a concern than preservation, with adaptive reuse of existing structures as a goal, if not social preservation of those currently residing in blighted areas.

If priorities continue to be at odds, attitudes have softened considerably with the passage of time. In 2010, McEneaney emphasized the ability of both visions to coexist: "My main thing about the viaduct is that I don't feel like we are really in conflict with the PCDC folks, 'cause like I said, I fully support more housing and affordable housing, and I just believe there is room to do that and have a great viaduct park."[96] In 2012, Toy also suggested he has changed his mind about the viaduct, with qualifications: "I'm convinced that it could be something good. But again, in order for it to be good on top, it has to be good underneath too. We've said we're okay with it if we can make sure that there are some parcels that are attached to it that we can set aside for some mixed-income housing and make sure the development of Tenth Street continues up with the retail and residential component that's fairly dense. Not just these vacant lots or something."[97]

To date, both the costs of demolition or reuse of the viaduct are prohibitive. Nevertheless, the city is in talks with Reading International Company to take control of the larger section of the viaduct. The Center City District is working with SEPTA, the city transit agency, on a legal agreement to create a park on the shorter western section of the viaduct owned by SEPTA (less than one-fourth of a mile, following a curve from Callowhill Street between Eleventh and Twelfth going west to Thirteenth and Noble Streets). The district commissioned a design study for what could be the first phase of the elevated park in 2012, including such amenities as new trees and plantings, seating, an outdoor classroom, swings, and more.[98] PCPC's new plan for Philadelphia, "Philadelphia 2035," also embraces the viaduct park. In February 2013, PCPC adopted a new strategic plan for Callowhill/Chinatown North: the plan takes advantage of new zoning designations, adopted in 2012, to rezone seventy acres of the area to permit a mix of residential and light industrial uses, reflecting the current direction of neighborhood development. Other improvements in the plan include the creation of new pedestrian- and bike-friendly streets and green park spaces—chiefly, the creation of the viaduct park.[99]

Chinatown North continues to be a work in progress. New investment in the neighborhood comes not only from community developers and entrepreneurs but also from activist, education, and arts organizations seeking creative adaptive reuses for existing industrial and commercial structures in the area. Many are building on Chinatown's "legacy of resistance" to transform community life and pursue development through new methods and perspectives. These organizations, many with a pan-Asian or even pan-immigrant focus, are breathing new life into the area and thinking outside the box of loft-style development, working to transform spaces on the footprint of the once-proposed baseball stadium, and pushing the neighborhood's boundaries west and north.

One transformative reuse of industrial space in Chinatown North has been the creation of a charter school by Asian Americans United (AAU) on the 1000 block of Callowhill Street. The Folk Arts and Cultural Treasures Charter

School (FACTS) is the result of collaboration between AAU and the Philadelphia Folklore Project (PFP) and grew out of AAU's work organizing the Chinatown Parents' Association in the 1990s.[100] AAU's experiences with Chinatown's parents consistently reiterated the need for a public school for Chinatown. AAU and PFP started planning FACTS in 2001 and opened it in 2005, locating it at 1023 Callowhill Street in 2007. The K–8 charter school, which draws on cultural traditions and issues of social justice, is the first publicly funded school in Chinatown. The curriculum is immigrant friendly beyond an Asian focus per se, also incorporating Liberian, Tibetan, and other immigrant folk artists in addition to Mandarin Chinese and Singapore Math programs.

The school is housed in a former factory, a space made available through the generosity of a Chinatown businessman, Mr. Wong, a first-generation immigrant who owns several properties in the area. Described by Wei as a "working-class guy, [who] made his way in little restaurants slowly," Wong was receptive to the idea of a school on the property: "And he said, 'Look, I've gotten a lot of offers on this building to turn it into condos, to turn it into a hotel.' He said, 'Chinatown has all those things already—what we don't have is a school.'" Wong agreed to hold the building while the school secured the necessary permissions and paid to convert the building so that it could function as a school. Wei recalls his act of generosity:

> We made out these stipulations that surely did not make it an attractive venture for a businessman, and he just was adamant. He said a school was a good thing for the community. "I can always make more money, but I don't really need more money," he said. "Chinatown needs a school more than I need money." He said, "I'm holding it, and I'm going to get the loan to make the school." And he did. He always donates money to the school, and he always comes over and walks around with his wife and has this big smile on his face.[101]

For Wei, Wong's involvement in the school "is what community's all about." It also represents an alternative imagining of the postindustrial development priorities for Chinatown North outside market imperatives.

Although FACTS by law serves a broad potential student population, locating the school in Chinatown was important to AAU as a way to contribute to the development of public space and resources in the community it had fought to protect, according to Wei, who served as the school's first principal:

> It was a conscious choice because of the politics of gentrification. There were two reasons: one was the politics, gentrification. We were sitting in the third-base parking lot [of the formerly proposed stadium], because the city said you're not going to do anything with this land anyway, and we kind of did an "in your face" type thing. . . .

But also we wanted to be multiracial, and in particular we wanted to be immigrant friendly, and we needed to be in a neighborhood where immigrants could come and feel like it's okay to be an immigrant in this neighborhood, and Chinatown is one of the few places where that's possible. It was those two things that made us choose Chinatown.[102]

AAU director Somekawa echoes these sentiments:

Well, it was very deliberate in that we knew that [we] had to put this school in Chinatown. . . . That at that time, the level of poverty in the neighborhood as well as just the lack of space, the lack of supports—right, like if you go in different neighborhoods in South Philadelphia, there will be a library there, there will be a school there, there will be a park there, a community center there. You come to Chinatown then, there's none of that there. So we knew that it had to be in Chinatown.[103]

FACTS founders hope that the school can become another important public space for Chinatown, according to Somekawa:

The abhorring lack of public investment in Chinatown was another impetus. Where is the infrastructure, where is any sign that the city recognizes this is a neighborhood that deserves a public space? So all those things came together, the realization that the reforms we were fighting for weren't enough, the need for public space, the notion of expanding impact and having a longer sustained relationship with more people all sort of contributed to this idea that we should start a charter school. . . . We had always wanted this also to be a center of community life. And we're still working towards that, because we're still trying to figure out how to financially support that possibility. . . . [T]his year, we had an adult ESOL class meeting here. . . . We have a Chinese Immigrant Youth Group that meets with AAU here. But ultimately, you'd want a learning center for people of all ages. We just haven't figured out how to create the resources to actually make that program happen[104]

Toward this goal, the school makes its space available to local Chinatown organizations such as the Chinese Opera Society. And in an interesting twist, AAU and FACTS have benefited from a relationship with Reading International, securing permission to generate more green space for Chinatown North in the form of a community garden on vacant land abutting the viaduct behind the school. School supporters welcome the development of the viaduct park, which would sit right outside the rear windows of the school and be another resource for students. But above all, the specific location of the school in Chinatown North was also symbolic of the community's struggle, according to Gym: "We built this school on the outer footprint of what would have been that stadium, and to us it's just a massively different form of vision and definition of progress and development than what was being proffered to Chinatown by other people."[105]

Chinatown North emerged at the turn of the twenty-first century as Chinatown's new battleground and fertile field. Whether building low-income housing or a school on the footprint of the proposed 2000 stadium, the Chinatown community embodies its legacy of struggle and resistance in proactive reclamations of contested territory, insisting that urban renewal in the former industrial area of Chinatown North serve the community's needs. In Chinatown North and the adjacent Callowhill, the often ad hoc, largely private, piecemeal development is symptomatic of a neoliberal approach to urban renewal, which relies heavily on market-driven private investment and can engender geographic and demographic fragmentation as well as gentrification.[106] In Chinatown North, reliance on strictly private development would, many believe, create inaccessibility to those who most need Chinatown to grow: working immigrant families. While private developers have proceeded with enthusiasm in Callowhill, creating a postindustrial destination neighborhood, Chinatown developers have had to labor, often for years, to acquire land parcels and leverage public/private funding sources to develop even modest housing projects. Likewise, they are insistent that development of the viaduct and its surrounds support the needs of "those who want to work and live in the neighborhood"—that is, Chinatown. These competing priorities for urban space and concerns about historic preservation, as well as larger public ambivalence about the growth of an ethnic-specific landscape within that space, drive the Chinatown community to draw on its "legacy of resistance" to ensure a future for Chinatown North.

6

"We are the ones who should be telling the story"

Representing Chinatown

Every Friday night, Joe Lowe and his buddies drive in from the suburbs and gather at Holy Redeemer to play basketball in the gym. Afterward, if the weather is nice, they hang out in the parking lot at the Philadelphia Chinatown Development Corporation (PCDC) offices across the street, drinking beer, grilling burgers, and remembering old times, shooting the breeze like they used to do outside Tuck's (Tuck Hing, the oldest Chinese grocery in Chinatown) back in the day.

When he can, John Chin skips out of the PCDC office and visits sites around the neighborhood that he works to preserve and develop. He often stops at the House of Dragons, Engine Co. 20 of the Philadelphia Fire Department (at 133 North Tenth Street), a favorite childhood haunt:

> The Chinese Christian Church has the summer basketball league, and my son, who is only eight-and-a-half, is in it now, so I'll skip out of work on a Friday and go watch him play basketball, 'cause that was one of the centers of Chinatown. And then I go to the On Lok Senior Service Center and I sit there, once in a while, and watch the activities of the seniors. I don't say anything; I don't do anything; I'll just sit there and watch. And then once in a while I'll see if the guys that I know at the fire station are there, and I'll chat with them, because I grew up across the street from them.

Another favorite destination is the various family associations:

> It brings back the old memories. 'Cause around Chinese New Year's, the Chinese Benevolent Association would host trays of cooked food

for members, just the community members. You'd have to walk up three flights of steps, and they had this great big altar for the ancestors. You go up there, and you light three incense, and you bow three times, and you put the incense in a little pot there to pay respects to the elders. And then afterwards, at twelve midnight, the celebration comes out.

Chin reflects, "Those are the places that if I go there, I find some kind of peace."[1]

As Cecilia Moy Yep stands at the intersection of Tenth and Race Streets, she sees Chinatown's past, present, and future. For her, this neighborhood landscape is filled with personal and communal touchstones, sites of struggle and achievement:

Of course I love Chinatown. This is where I spent my whole life. Well, I said one time, I could stand at the corner of Tenth and Race and look in every direction and see my work. How gratifying is that? How many people have that opportunity? I can look south and see the gate, I can look north and see Chinatown North, and I can see Gim San, and I can see Dynasty Court. How many people can stand in a certain spot and see all their work? It's my lifetime's work, but still, it's so gratifying. . . . I can look at Gim San and say, "That's where people stayed for three days and nights"—there are a lot of pictures of that around. To me, that makes my feeling of belonging even deeper, and I could never give it up.[2]

Yep also tells of her neighbors, all of whom grew up in Chinatown, who can walk around the neighborhood and point to the second-floor apartments where they were born: "And some of the women who were born in Chinatown before there were hospitals, before you went to the hospital, they can point to places where they were born on the second floor. And we talk about that often." She adds, "One of the nice things about Chinatown that people don't realize is there's this continuity—like the kids who went to Holy Redeemer when I went there are living alongside of me. They're my classmates. And we're all eighty years old. That's nice, you know? And still surviving and the fact that we still invite each other to the kids' weddings. . . . [O]ur kids are close. That is so meaningful."[3]

For folks like Yep, Chin, and Lowe, attachment to Chinatown is deeply rooted in experiences of community and identity, embodied in a sense of place focused not just on language and outward symbols of ethnicity but on spaces of memory and lived community relationships, such as family homes, churches and temples, a senior-citizen center, family associations, and a district fire station. This lived neighborhood memoryscape contrasts with the neighborhood as a cultural attraction, primarily identified by tourism, restaurants, and gift shops. Unlike touristic discourse, resident discourse and decision making about the landscape connect the past and future of Chinatown in a lived experience of place and a collective memory of struggle. Whether discussing the history of the neighborhood or reflecting on what makes Chinatown Chinatown, residents' memories locate Chinatown within historical time, verbally mapping the continuities in and transformations of the neighborhood landscape over previous decades and highlighting their own experiences and agency in that landscape. This mapping reveals another side of Chinatown unseen or unnoticed by a casual visitor to the district: a sense of the "small town" where everyone knew one another; memories of play, family, and conflict; and historic sites of demolition, rebuilding, and continued struggle.[4]

These memories and the spaces associated with them present a powerful counternarrative to the often ahistorical image of the neighborhood that is offered within local mainstream and touristic representations of Chinatown, representations that focus on traditional Chinese culture and sites and allow for objectified consumption of the neighborhood. In crafting a neighborhood that serves both the needs of tourism and its community, Chinatown residents, activists, community developers, artists, and businesspeople work within available resources, longtime dilemmas of representation, and symbols of collective identity to improve the local environment, meet acute housing shortages and other needs, and generate income and traffic to the neighborhood. Amid the bread-and-butter challenges of housing, education, and economic development, PCDC and other organizations also work to brand and promote Chinatown through the thematic commercialization of the neighborhood. Other residents, businesses, and community organizations in Chinatown express their vision of Chinatown's identity in new hybrid ways, exploring the nature of the community through creative approaches to community spaces, drawing on the arts and other disciplines to reimagine the neighborhood's past and future. In doing so, they generate creative responses to the neighborhood's challenges, representing a collective identity that is hybrid, strategic, at turns passionately felt and playfully staged, and always conscious of history and the neighborhood's legacy of struggle.

"We can't afford history"

How and on what terms to preserve and present the past is an ongoing question for Chinatown. Many of the buildings in the neighborhood date to the nineteenth century, from 1830s row houses to 1890s commercial buildings, and almost all suffer from decades of deferred maintenance. In addition, structures important to Chinatown's history, such as 913 Race, the Chinese Benevolent Association (CBA) at 930 Race, the former Far East Restaurant at 907–909 Race, and the Chinese Cultural and Community Center (CC&CC) on Tenth Street are all threatened by damage and decay. But historic preservation has not always been a priority for a community that has so many other acute needs. Often, other, more pressing, economic necessities intervene.

In the late 1970s and early 1980s, PCDC considered, then rejected, pursuing historic-district designation as a strategy for neighborhood preservation. In 1977, PCDC had conversations with the Advisory Council on Historic Preservation about ways to preserve Chinatown as a cultural district. Staff completed an application to the National Endowment for the Arts' (NEA's) Livable Cities program that same year to "find a means of preserving Chinatown historically and as a cultural district."[5] For Yep, creating a historical district presented insurmountable challenges to the community: "They told us that it is historical, but we didn't know about it. And we don't go along with it, because it's too—how should I say it—it's too difficult. Chinatown majority is below average, below the poverty level. How do you restore things when you are in poverty level? It just holds back the whole growth of the community, because people don't want to touch it."[6] Ultimately, historic designation was considered and rejected, considering the cost of imposed design and material criteria, as articulated by PCDC in 1985:

> While historical certification of individual buildings may at times be desirable for tax purposes, the certification of the entire Chinatown area as historical will pose a serious threat to future development. Historical certification would mean that before any renovation or new construction could take place in Chinatown, a full hearing before the City's Historic Preservation Board would have to be conducted. In addition to delays in construction, imposed design and material criteria might well make rehabilitation unfeasible.[7]

Yep acknowledges that there were buildings in Chinatown that should have been preserved: "There was one at Ninth and Race that had the stained-glass Chinese restaurant. But they tore it down. All the historical stuff is gone. It's all been renovated. And I thought that was a shame." Mentioning the Far East building at 907 Race Street, Yep observes, "That's the start of Chinatown. . . . Certain things like that I think are good, because that's good for the community to remember and to think about this is where Chinatown starts."[8]

The question of securing Chinatown's unique landscape in the face of redevelopment became more acute in the late 1980s, when the city unveiled plans for a new convention center at Thirteenth and Arch. The proposed center would take the west side of Eleventh Street from Arch to Race and displace Chinese living and working on Eleventh and Twelfth Streets. During the 1988 City Council hearings on the project, Mike Masch, director of Economic Analysis for the City Council, noted in his testimony that speculation by outside (and inside) parties had driven recent property values in Chinatown up threefold, and nearly sixfold within the past ten years.[9] This rise in property values posed a threat to those who would keep Chinatown affordable and safe from real-estate speculation that could threaten the ethnic and family-oriented character of the neighborhood. PCDC had been keeping an uneasy eye on rising property taxes for years, as discussed in this 1985 editorial on rising property values and unfair taxes:

> As development occurs within and outside our community, we are faced with the awful specter of gentrification. Because the land values are increasing around us, our property taxes are skyrocketing. If this continues, the current residents of Chinatown will no longer be able to afford to live here. PCDC has fought for 20 years to keep the City from turning Chinatown into highways and shopping malls. We did not struggle for 20 years only to see Chinatown fade away in the face of such tax increases.[10]

Once again, protecting the residential character of Chinatown was a priority expressed by PCDC in its September 1988 newsletter:

> The most damaging effect is the developmental pressures caused by the Convention Center. Taxes will increase, rent for businesses and residents will skyrocket to a point where our people may not be able to afford to live in the area. . . . If Chinatown is to continue to exist, we must have protection. . . . The core of Chinatown is only four blocks square and there will always be a market for properties. It will control the value of the land which will make the taxes affordable. If the land value increases, because of the proposed five hotels to be located in the area, our taxes will increase to the point where we cannot afford to live here anymore. If this happens, there will no longer be a Chinatown.[11]

The creation of a historic district, then, was seen as an agent of gentrification, or, like city-driven redevelopment, at odds with the residential needs of Chinatown.

Historic districting, now a common strategy of redevelopment in older urban areas, can be problematic for ethnic neighborhoods that continue to serve as an entry point for new immigrants.[12] Such neighborhoods are often characterized by a population in flux and a necessary flexibility of reuse to meet housing and other emerging needs. Historic districting can also fuel gentrification, improving structures and raising property values while pushing out less lucrative enterprises and imposing more rigid aesthetic imperatives that can disadvantage newcomers. Gentrification focuses on preservation of the built environment and physical structures, without attention to "social preservation" of existing populations and their neighborhood culture.[13] Historic branding "fixes" the landscape (referred to as "integrity" in preservation criteria) into an established architectural aesthetic that may or may not resonate with new immigrants arriving from modern China or other cultural origins. The hybridity that characterized the early Chinatown landscape, preserved as history, cannot necessarily accommodate a new hybridity that would result from recent immigrants putting their own stamp on the neighborhood. While the neighborhood would benefit from the tax incentives and other benefits of designation, design and renovation strictures might hamstring struggling entrepreneurs. Likewise, such communities often face challenges, such as poverty, a lack of services, and inadequate housing, and pressures from transnational-translocal investment and development priorities, which historic designation cannot readily address or accommodate.[14]

One answer, PCDC concluded, lay in zoning Chinatown as a special district, which would allow the community to control building sizes (thus eliminating the threat of high rises) and establish the residential features of the landscape into legally binding development guidelines. Working with the Philadelphia City Planning Commission (PCPC), PCDC initiated Bill No. 429 in 1989, establishing a Chinatown Special Zoning District to preserve the community from urban-developmental pressures. This bill created specific regulations tailored to the needs of Chinatown's community that would control the uses and building size of existing and new structures in Chinatown: "The limitations on height are necessary, because the restriction makes the building of high rises financially unfeasible. However, if a high rise building were to benefit the community, the people can have a public hearing and support the builder's request for a variance. In this manner, the people will have input as to what will be built in Chinatown. In this way, we ensure the existence of Chinatown."[15]

Although, as Chin remarked in 2009, "We can't afford history," Chinatown has undertaken preservation and public-history activities in recent years.[16] In 1995, the 125th anniversary of Chinatown, PCDC installed a commemorative plaque at 913 Race Street to mark the site of Lee Fong's laundry and the start of Chinatown. It reads: "In commemoration of our forefathers, this plaque is dedicated to those who came to the *gim san* (Gold Mountain) to seek their fortunes." That same year, a mural was commissioned for the southeast corner of Tenth and Winter Streets that illustrates the history of Chinese Americans in Philadelphia. Designed by artist Arturo Ho, the mural depicts early railroad workers and laundrymen, the Friendship Gate, Holy Redeemer, and the battle against the highway (see Figure 6.1).

After many years of rejection and revision, a more official historic landmark for the neighborhood was finally secured from the Pennsylvania Historic and Museum Commission and installed on October 8, 2010, at 913 Race. With no surviving primary documents to substantiate the specific claim of neighborhood founding at this site, the landmark reads: "Founded in the 1870s by Chinese immigrants, it is the only 'Chinatown' in Pennsylvania.

Figure 6.1. History of Chinatown mural by Arturo Ho at Tenth and Winter Streets, 2010. (Photograph by the author.)

This unique neighborhood includes businesses and residences owned by, and serving, Chinese Americans. Here, Asian cultural traditions are preserved and ethnic identity perpetuated." Marking the presence of the neighborhood first in historical time—since the 1870s—the marker then locates Chinatown in an ahistorical realm of heritage where "traditions are preserved and ethnic identity perpetuated." But when? By whom? And under what circumstances? For members of the community however, the marker represents long-overdue recognition of Chinatown's historic contributions to the region and its historic claim to this area of the city. "This is the story of so many people standing here today," Chin remarked on the occasion, emphasizing continuity with the past: "Today is a story of 1870, it's a story of 1963, it's a story of 2010." "The community character, that's the important aspect of the marker," observed PCDC Board Member Inspector Anthony Wong. "In all of this time, the community has fought back against adversities, and it's survived." "It's like history happening," reflected Yep. "When our forefathers came, they didn't dream we'd be here 140 years later and that Chinatown would grow to what it is today."[17] This sense of historical origin and the struggle to preserve Chinatown at this specific location are central to collective memory and community identity. Other commemorative activities mark the neighborhood landscape, celebrating beloved spaces and individuals in Chinatown history, such as the 2010 renaming of the street sign at Tenth and Spring Streets to "Mitzie Mackenzie Place" in honor of the Chinese Christian Church and Center's (CCC&C's) long-time and much-beloved director. The church's recently refurbished playground is also named in her memory.

Chin admits that he has a "very different perspective of history in Chinatown" a few years later, recognizing its value for promoting the neighborhood. As part of its mission to "protect, preserve, and promote" Chinatown, PCDC undertakes public history activities to identify and preserve other places in the Chinatown landscape. A video project in the summer of 2011 funded by the Preservation Alliance of Greater Philadelphia's Neighborhood Preservation Program allowed for the documentation of lesser-known sites in Chinatown.[18] In its application to the program, PCDC pointed to three specific challenges facing Chinatown: (1) a lack of awareness of its place in Asian American and Philadelphia history, (2) a lack of investment in its built environment, and (3) the public perception of Chinatown that overlooks its residential character. The purpose of the video project was to recognize the historic significance of the Chinatown neighborhood and identify the development of key landmarks and milestones of historical events. Tied into the unveiling of the historical marker and upcoming streetscape improvements, it aimed to raise awareness of Chinatown's history and its ties to neighborhood preservation.[19] The stories collected were the basis for a Tumblr blog, *Chinatown Places*, which encouraged users to ask and answer the questions, "Why is Chinatown worth preserving? What is its place in Philadelphia history, and its future?"[20]

PCDC also encourages the preservation and stabilization of historic structures in Chinatown. In 2012, PCDC received a "Pride of Place" historic preservation grant from the Preservation Alliance of Greater Philadelphia to complete a feasibility study for restoration of 907–909 Race Street, the site of the famous Far East Chinese Restaurant and the current headquarters for the Hoy Sun Ning Yung Benevolent Association, which owns the building (see Figure 6.2). The second floor of the building sports an elaborate cast-iron balcony in an Oriental fashion and is the most recognizable and extensive

Figure 6.2. The 900 block of Race Street showing 907–909 Race and a hybrid mix of twentieth-century architectural façades, 2010. (Photograph by the author.)

architectural remnant of the past, a landmark and visual index of old China-town. The architectural firm of UCI Architects, Inc., completed the study in 2012, and prepared a nomination for the site to the National Register of His-toric Places. The proposed alterations to the first-floor storefronts include new wood projecting signage, new aluminum storefront glazing with painted sign-age, and new stucco façades as well as masonry cleaning and repair, new or repaired windows and doors, and replacement of visible roof and gutters. The iron balcony, because of its historical significance, received the most extensive recommendations for cleaning, repair, and repainting of all metal surfaces, as did the replacement of missing elements and other historically significant elements, such as pendant fixtures and metal signage, along the cornice of 907. Total cost of the restoration, which focuses on the façade only, is estimated at $247,000.[21] The Chinese Cultural and Community Center, T. T. Chang's Chi-natown YMCA at 125 North Tenth Street, entered the Philadelphia Register of Historic Places in 2013. A Mandarin-style relief erected on the façade of an 1830s Federal-style row house in the early 1970s, the structure now suffers from deferred maintenance on both the interior and exterior.[22] Both these buildings were the subject of Historic American Buildings Surveys and are signature sites on the Chinatown landscape.

The proposed restoration of such sites as 907–909 Race Street raises the question of the extent to which Chinatown could or should preserve and present its past in the contemporary landscape. If prior generations relied on self-Orientalism as a key strategy, then to what extent would preservation or reconstruction of these strategies perpetuate stereotypical images of Chinatown and Chinese Americans? If such preservation is initiated by state or local governments, does this constitute a form of "neocolonialism"?[23] Yet without such structures, there is little in Chinatown's landscape to embody its past, to use as a narrative launch for telling the story of settlement, discrimination, Orientalism, and the agency of Chinese immigrants in creating a sense of place. For Chin, the Far East balcony represents an opportunity to tell the story of the community's origins and institutions: "I'm thinking, let's figure out how to preserve that, but let's see if we can tell a story. Use that balcony to tell a story about the place that this used to be, and why it's important to Chinatown." Why the balcony is important extends beyond the distant past to individuals' personal memories of Chinatown, as Chin adds, because the balcony is something seen "since I was a little kid."[24]

Preservation of the ethnic character of the historic core can contribute to larger goals of marketing Chinatown while promoting social preservation, particularly if it preserves and interprets structures that represent the collective memories and experiences of the community as opposed to ethnic character per se, Chin explains:

> I was born here, and I have emotional attachments. This was a wonderful place for me and for many other people before and after me. And Chinatown really has played an important role in the immigration story. It's played a really important role in the history of neighborhoods in the city of Philadelphia. . . . Let's tell people why it's important. Why should the city provide grant support to us? To sustain Chinatown. Why should the state or the federal government, for that matter, do the same thing? Why should the foundations? Well here's why: because we have such a rich history of culture and struggle. I'm starting to realize that we are who we are because of the place we're associated with, because we didn't just arrive at this time. A lot of things happened to get us to this point.[25]

Drawing on local memories, preserving historic structures with all their cultural baggage, and articulating a history of struggle allow Chinatown to create cultural resources for resistance and critique, making connections with the past to stage thoughtful representations in the present.

More practically, historic preservation brings money into Chinatown. Preservation activities are in keeping with current urban-redevelopment agendas focused on community branding and marketing, realized in such opportunities as the National Trust for Historic Preservation's Main Street Program. Main Street's approach is preservation-based, assisting the revitalization of traditional commercial districts through cross-site organization, promotion, design, and economic restructuring. The corridor managers are expected to build public-private partnerships to leverage additional funding and investment in the community. The Main Street Program has been a presence in Philadelphia's urban-renewal movement since 2002, when it was adopted as part of the Philadelphia Local Initiatives Support Corporation (LISC). The LISC worked with the National Trust Main Street Center to bring historic preservation–based economic-development strategies to eight community-development corporations (CDCs) for the development of eight aging commercial corridors. Over three years, the Philadelphia Commercial Corridor Redevelopment Initiative (PCCR) gave more than $1.5 million to improve these distressed districts.[26] Two of these, Chinatown and North Fifth Street (the Latino *barrio*), are ethnically specific communities. Others, like Mount Airy's Germantown Avenue and University City's Baltimore Avenue, are areas of historical significance with more diversified populations. University City was already undergoing renewal and had significant stakeholder resources to draw on, such as the University of Pennsylvania (which has been a primary agent of redevelopment since the 1970s, clearing out entire blocks of the old streetcar suburb to make room for its expansion). The Main Street designation, geared toward commercial revitalization, has allowed PCDC to enhance the visitor-oriented environment of Chinatown but has not assisted its other goals, such as meeting the pent-up need for Chinatown housing or transforming the blighted spaces of Chinatown North. The approach is typical of neoliberal approaches to urban revitalization, offering market-based solutions to urban renewal that, with their reliance on market viability, result in often piecemeal improvements to urban districts.

Main Street activities also further the theming and commodification of the spaces of Chinatown in ways that visitors will comprehend and experience. As part of its Main Street–funded activities, in 2011 PCDC installed long-desired "foo dog" statues and other landscape features at the northern entrance to the historic core over Vine Street to create the Tenth Street Plaza. It produced new streetscape enhancements, such as bronze sidewalk medallions depicting signs of the Chinese zodiac, pedestrian lights in the style of a "Chinese palace lantern," decorative crosswalks, trees, and other cultural elements "designed to promote the ethnic identity of the neighborhood"[27] Local merchants were encouraged to apply for Main Street funding to renovate their storefronts, although only a few pursued the opportunity. A "dollar a day" program was instituted in 2011 to encourage business owners to contribute to a street-cleaning service, improving the trash situation in the neighborhood, although illegal dumping remains a problem. Other promotional activities have included participation in the Food Trust's Night Market, an evening food-cart festival, an event local restaurateurs initially resisted, fearing it would compete with their businesses. In 2012, PCDC launched an annual

Chinatown Flower Market, held in late January in the days preceding Chinese New Year at the newly created Tenth Street Plaza. The New Year's flower market is a tradition in many other Chinatowns and in China, as families purchase fresh flowers, lanterns, and other supplies for the annual celebration. At the Chinatown flower market, vendors sold daffodils, orchids, and chrysanthemums as well as banners, lanterns, fruits, candies, and other treats. The market is, according to Chin, a way to draw on "nostalgic memories and cultural preservation" for residents, a way to make "make Chinatown more like home to immigrants," while also, like the Sunday lion dance parades, a way to attract visitors to the district at a culturally significant time of year.[28] For Chinatown, creating themed space to attract visitors and promote commerce is not a new story; the support of outside foundations and funders for heritage production is. The political and economic impact of themed space in terms of its ability to help Chinatown meet its other needs remains to be seen.

"We have to look like Chinatown"

The ethnic character of Chinatown's landscape, particularly its historic features, is complex in meaning and cannot be reduced to visitor expectations or Orientalism. It is a basis on which to build Chinatown's economic future, through neighborhood branding and promotion. It is a remnant of past objectification and cultural misconceptions. It is also the aesthetic of the Chinese American memoryscape.

Harry Leong takes a pragmatic, matter-of-fact attitude toward the issue of design: "They're going to put Chinese zodiac signs on the street. I mean, that's a Chinese thing, it's a nice design, but we are Chinatown, and we see that as, well, you have businesses and you have visitors coming, so we have to look like Chinatown. . . . [W]e're in a community, so if we're what we, are let's do it."[29] In this way, Chinatown is like other ethnic neighborhoods that convey a sense of cultural difference to visitors, according to Kenneth Eng: "I think some of them are commercialized. I would agree with that, but it never bothered me. I would say, people want to make it Italy, just go to South Philly, Italian market. It's no different."[30] Over time, the Friendship Gate at Tenth and Arch Streets has come to symbolize Chinatown almost exclusively in tourist brochures and websites and is the most photographed landmark in the neighborhood. In Chinatown, then, as in other branded neighborhoods, themed space like the gate or the CC&CC façade can function as a fragment that stands for the whole, excluding disharmonious elements in the name of cultural authenticity or historic "integrity" and becoming a hyperreal truth in and of itself.[31]

Many in the community express a nostalgic fondness for the "Chinesey" aspects of Chinatown as part of their memories and sense of community heritage. For Laurence Tom, the current pastor at CCC&C, its "Chinesey" ceiling is a cherished childhood memory that pulled him to ministry in Philadelphia.[32] The sanctuary at Holy Redeemer is likewise marked by culturally specific touches meaningful to the congregation: Chinese lanterns hang from the ceiling, decorative woodwork is Asian in style and incorporates an abstracted *shou* circle, Asian filigree and Chinese characters decorate the front altar, and a painting portrays a Chinese figure preaching to a variety of worshippers in Asian dress as well as several Christian monks and a nun. Much of the streetscaping in the district and outward landscaping extends this Asian aesthetic, such as PCDC's Chinese lantern–styled streetlights and smaller "foo dog" statues marking the entrance to stores or association buildings. Some structures represent an older generation of Chinatown architecture, such as Imperial Inn's recessed wooden balcony and Joy Tsin Lau's elaborate façade, adorned with carved red pillars and green tiled eaves. Other traditional building façades, such as the Fo Shou Temple on Cherry Street, are the product of new immigration. These traditional Chinatown structures reside side by side with high-rise condos; postmodern Asian bazaars; sleek contemporary sushi, dumpling, and teahouses; adaptively reused warehouses; and stock row and town housing. They express a multivalent, hybrid sensibility that bridges old and new, local and transnational, inside and outside.

Chinatown's landscape is also themed in less obvious and more informal ways through a variety of vernacular practices that are culturally identifiable or unique to this neighborhood. Residents' gardens, both private and public, express Chinese sensibilities through the culturally specific vegetables and flowers grown as well as garden statuary, such as stone pagodas. Some residents have embraced the *shou* symbol for their homes, attaching it to mailboxes or incorporating it into wrought-iron railings and door grates. These touches call to mind the yard shrines and decorated front windows of Italian South Philadelphia as well as the gardens, casitas, murals, and red-tiled housing projects of the Latino *barrio*.[33]

Themed space has been a mode of spatial reclamation and community preservation in the face of ongoing urban renewal, but it also effaces the other elements of the neighborhood that fit less neatly into a historic or even historically timeless image of Chinatown, elements that are critical to the neighborhood's survival as a family-oriented living community. Whether visitors look deeper, residents and other community members understand that the "whole" of Chinatown is more aesthetically and politically complicated. For Chinatown developers, the task is to carefully balance the need to maintain themed space and identifiable cultural distinctiveness with changing community needs and aesthetics. Ethnic urban space must function as not only a themed cultural attraction but also a living community for multiple generations of immigrants old and new. This duality presents a challenge when preservation and development are considered together. To what extent are the two processes compatible or competing? How much thematic or historical coherence and cohesiveness can be expected of a living community that must serve the dynamic and changing needs of new immigrants' everyday lives as well as its larger image making?

For Chin, the historic identity of Chinatown can be retained but transformed through its juxtaposition with a newer aesthetic that communicates Asian-ness without reinforcing historic stereotypes:

> The identity of Chinatown—well, the stereotype is red and gold with pagoda eaves and that exotic image of Chinatown. Right. But if you go to Asia now, you don't see that.... So what's the new design and trends for Asian culture and Asian communities? We have the Streetscape Project—we're not doing the bright red for our street lamps, but we're doing a muted, traditional kind of red that's almost brownish-red that you see in a lot of artwork during a certain time period. We're moving more towards classic Chinese that's less about color and more about texture, feel, and design.

Chin makes a distinction between the outside attribution of "Chinesey" aesthetics and a self-embrace of these aesthetics to communicate heritage: "Some people are more sensitive to the message that this sends, the ongoing stereotypes, and then there are people who are less sensitive to that. But again, I always believe that it comes down to, well, we are the ones who should be telling the story. If we tell the story, then we should feel safe that anybody that comes and visits should walk away with the right feel and history and the attitude and sense of this community."[34]

For second- and third-generation artists, organizations, and businesspeople, the Chinatown landscape is a hybrid multivalent environment ripe for self-exploration of Chinese/Asian American ethnicity and history through creative approaches to community spaces and businesses, drawing on the arts and other disciplines to reimagine the neighborhood's future. Displaced from its space at 1315 Cherry in 2007 as a result of expansion of the Pennsylvania Convention Center, the Asian Arts Initiative (AAI) reclaimed commercial space at 1219 Vine to develop a multi-tenant arts facility incorporating its offices and gallery as well as artists' studios, program space, and a black box–style theater. AAI hopes the space, which has already attracted a dance company and other arts groups, will foster "arts-based civic dialogue and connections across people's histories and aspirations." A December 2012 Chinatown North Arts Crawl partnered with art gallery Vox Populi (319 North Eleventh Street) and other galleries on the outskirts of Chinatown for an evening exploring what local press called a "rising artistic hotbed." With community participation and a focus that includes arts and Chinatown community partners, these programs have the potential to bridge some of the underlying tensions in the Chinatown North/Callowhill neighborhood.[35]

Gayle Isa, executive director of AAI, is aware of these bridging opportunities as well as the complicated effects of the arts and economic development on the class dynamics of a changing neighborhood:

> Well, I actually also feel very conflicted. Because I think that, as I'm sure you know, that the arts are definitely something that right now we need to argue would promote economic development, but at the same time oftentimes who benefits is not the working-class community that still wants or needs housing in Chinatown. And the fact that artists moving into a neighborhood is often, what is it, that canary in the tunnel? Like a sign that gentrification is about to explode. And so I literally feel torn, feeling like there is a way that our presence will benefit the businesses that are in the Chinatown core. I think that it will benefit in terms of making the Vine Street Expressway a more lively pedestrian corridor, civic corridor. And then I actually have fears about how we are part of a gallery district or an artist district that could perhaps unintentionally displace the possibilities of other working-class people to remain or to be in this neighborhood.[36]

To this end, many of AAI's projects emphasize partnerships or identification with Chinatown and incorporate Chinatown community members' voices and memories through oral histories.

The organization's presence on Vine has effectively shifted Chinatown neighborhood boundaries farther west, and it sponsors programmatic opportunities to reflect on and reimagine the spaces of Chinatown North, including a revitalization project on Pearl Street (which runs parallel to Vine behind AAI's building to Tenth Street), part of the initiative's "Social Practice Lab," which will reimagine an underused alley to create "prototype amenities," pop-up events and an exhibition exploring both Pearl Street and the Reading Viaduct as neighborhood icons. Both AAI and PCDC demonstrate, in their visions of and plans for the neighborhood, what has been called "gentrification consciousness," the complicated politics of ethnic community institutions whose identification with place and history of activism make them critical of gentrification, even as their roles as neighborhood stabilizers and renewal agents may engender and benefit from gentrification. In the case of AAI, its success in creating an arts destination in Chinatown North, while potentially feeding the ongoing gentrification of the area (particularly in Callowhill, which is already being developed into an artsy destination area), is offset by the cultural content of many artists' work and ongoing community input into its programming. PCDC's history of activism and commitment to mixed-income housing in Chinatown North manifests this consciousness amid its marketing and promotion of the neighborhood as a cultural tourist destination.[37]

This consciousness also encompasses awareness of and sensitivity to Chinatown's history of Asian stereotyping and commodification. AAI's reimagining of Chinatown spaces was first explored in 2006 through "Chinatown In/flux," the initiative's biennial series of neighborhood-based site-specific art installations, which began exploring the past and heritage of Chinatown, framed within ideas of change and the future. The title "In/flux" referred "to the growth of the physical boundaries of the neighborhood, as well as Chinatown's constant flow of new immigrants and changing ethnic demographics" and suggested "shifting perspectives of the viewer and the viewed . . . joining expertise from the established arts field with local community participation," according to an AAI account of the project. In its first year "Chinatown In/flux" generated site-specific installations created by seven artists at more than a dozen diverse locations throughout Chinatown—from restaurants and storefronts to community centers and outdoor plazas—engaging residents and visitors alike to shift their perceptions of art and definitions of community.[38]

The artists in the subsequent "Chinatown In/flux: Future Landscapes" were selected through an intensive planning process, beginning with an open call in 2007 that generated nearly 40 applications, which were then vetted by a curatorial advisory committee. The selected artists attended a retreat with Chinatown neighborhood representatives to learn about community hopes and concerns and worked over the course of months to "establish relationships with community partners, conduct outreach workshops, and catalyze conversations about the neighborhood's development."[39] In 2009, the "In/flux" projects crossed the "historic barrier of the Vine Street Expressway" to "help the community to stake claim to Chinatown North."[40] These artworks invited participants to envision a future for Chinatown north of Vine with an understanding of the historic symbolism of the highway. Works included Rebecca Hackemann's "Visionary Sightseeing Binoculars," at the Tenth Street Plaza and Twelfth and Vine Streets overpass, which showed historical images and drawings created by artists, students, and community members to encourage alternate visions of the Vine Street Expressway and how it could "look as an asset instead of a barrier for Chinatown's growth." Kikuchi + Liu's "Chinatown Orange" painted the parking lot at 1001 Vine Street, site of the proposed future Eastern Tower, using the Sherwin-Williams brand paint color named "Chinatown Orange." Jonathan and Kimberly Stemler reenvisioned the contested Reading Viaduct at Carlton Street between Eleventh and Twelfth Streets through a project entitled "the little red string." The Stemlers hung a series of lanterns underneath the viaduct to "light the way for the community's expansion in Chinatown North." The lanterns were inscribed with personal stories from community members "describing their connection with the night sky in their respective homelands and traditions."[41] All these works in some way commented reflexively on the nature of Chinatown's development and the spatial elements of Asian heritage.

Figure 6.3. Abakus storefront, 2009, showing front window with sneakers and Peking ducks. (Photograph by the author.)

A new generation of Asian American artists and entrepreneurs has continued to express a more playful and irony-laced sense of heritage. An example of this play was found in the spaces of Abakus, an urban sneaker and clothing shop located in a former takeout restaurant at 227 North Tenth Street from 2008 to 2013 (see Figure 6.3). In Abakus, the building's history was preserved and represented in a whimsical fashion that embraced Asian kitsch within an urban-design sensibility. Abakus owners Ky Cao and Jackson Fu paid tribute to the building's past through the playful use of restaurant spatial and aesthetic components, such as the use of bulletproof Plexiglas (used in many Chinese takeout windows) for display cases. Peking ducks hung in the front window with sneakers. Illuminated menu signs in the style of a takeout restaurant outlined the various clothing offerings. The bones of a Chinese restaurant kitchen were recreated in the rear space, including fryers and woks that displayed shoelaces, hats, and other accessories. Also located in the back of the store was the changing room, constructed as a meat refrigerator, closed by a large stainless steel door and painted inside with the image of a whole butchered pig hanging from the ceiling. The owners also drew on the remnants of the building's former décor, installing never-used Chinese ceiling tiles (found in storage in the upper stories of the building) in the new shop, according to Cao.[42]

Abakus's hip-hop presence in Chinatown connected to another aspect of the neighborhood's history and tradition: basketball. Fu and Cao both volunteer with the Philadelphia Suns, a youth sports and service organization founded in 1972 by a handful of younger Chinatown basketball players from Holy Redeemer and the CCC&C, including Brendan Lee and Glenn Hing.[43] Leong, of the CCC&C, has been director of the Suns since 1989. Under Leong's leadership, the Suns draw more than 150 Chinese and other Asian American youth from around the area to play competitive basketball and volleyball, engage in community service, and preserve the art of the lion dance, performing each Chinese New Year. Both the gym at Holy Redeemer and an outside court at the CCC&C playground are used, depending on the weather. The older generation of players, like Lee and Lowe, remain involved with the organization, which, according to Lee, "keeps kids off the streets" and reinforces Chinese cultural heritage: "A lot of being a Sun is making sure you are doing the right thing. You don't mess up, you come, and if you want to play basketball, you gotta do the lion dance; you want to come play volleyball, you gotta do the lion dance. You want to do this, you gotta come out and do a community project with us. Everything is part of a lesson and values and getting something, earning something, as opposed to expecting something." The Suns' lion dance holds a special attraction for many in the community, since it is performed by the "kids from Chinatown."[44]

Abakus's connection to the history of the built environment and several generations of participation in the Suns embodies the hybrid aesthetic sensibilities and social interconnectedness of the Chinatown community. For members of the Chinatown community, ultimately the themed landscape—ironic or otherwise—is not what makes Chinatown Chinatown. The Asian elements signal a shared sense of cultural identity and are familiar, but for most, what makes Chinatown is "the people." For Hing, Chinatown is "a reflection of the people, a reflection of the churches, the community groups."[45] For those who have spent their lives working in and for the community, like Debbie Wei, it is "all about the people":

> For me, I think it's memory of the relationships. To me, and I feel like sometimes it might be losing its character, but I can walk down a street in Chinatown and always run into someone I know, and you always have to stop and talk. I find that I look for that. If I'm walking around Chinatown, I always have one eye out for people I know, because I don't want to insult people by ignoring them. There is something special about having that kind of space in this place and time, and I think it's a human impulse. I think people are meant to have communities like that. . . . I have so many memories that are based in that space that if Chinatown disappears, then my memories are gone. It's sort of like

your childhood home. . . . [I]t's like this space and your community and the people you hate most in the world are there and the people that you love the most in the world are there.[46]

The neighborhood represents a sense of origin, of locatedness. "Chinatown has always been my root," comments Eng:

It's a good testament for the memories we have in Chinatown; the people will come back for the sake of Chinatown. . . . [S]ome people, I think there are a few people [who] were like, "Okay, well, I got out of the neighborhood dump." You know what? There are dumps, right. There are dumps that you want to get away from, but there are dumps you look back [at] and say, "Hey, it wasn't such a bad dump."[47]

"Being immigrants, we're not very choosy," he reflects. This sense of origin and home is largely embodied by the relationships with family and friends, claims Hing:

What makes Chinatown Chinatown? For me, I guess you'd have to look at it from the perspective that Chinatown is home to me. It's the place where I grew up, it's the place where I feel safe, it's the place where my kids initially grew up, it's the place where my family is, it's the place where my business is. I mean, it's the package deal. If I didn't grow up in Chinatown, I would think of Chinatown differently. I would think of Chinatown more as a collection of businesses, an Asian collaborative of businesses and services and people, a social hub, outside looking in. But having been part of that social hub, I think I look at it a lot differently, and I think that the fact that I have so much affiliation and connection with Chinatown [means] I'm much more protective of it. I see things that I don't like, I've been involved in one fashion or another and every fight down here, from when I climbed up on the mountain, the rubble, to fighting stadiums, fighting the stadiums down here, fighting the casinos down here. I've been in it, and I give back.[48]

People with personal associations with Chinatown recognize Chinatown as a construct of memory, as another imagined geography of a different sort. Hing reflects, "Having moved out of Chinatown, having moved outside of Chinatown, it's not Chinatown, physical Chinatown, it's the cerebral kind of town," by which he means the conceptual, affective construction of Chinatown within his personal memories and relationships, his memoryscape.[49]

"Beyond the restaurants": Tourism

This "cerebral" Chinatown of memory contrasts with the Chinatown that serves commerce and tourism. Tourism has been a part of the Chinatown scene and economy since the late nineteenth century. Chinatown residents and business people are sanguine or at least practical about tourism, recognizing the important role that it plays in their local microeconomy. Jackie Wong, who worked in a restaurant in the 1970s, claims that tourism "didn't shape the neighborhood at all," at least in terms of the experience of workers in the restaurants, because "I think that Chinese people still think they are outsider. American comes in, they still think that they are different races. So if you get a whole tour, they [the Chinese restaurant workers] still seeing that is regular America. They didn't see they don't make much difference to them. Just a group of regular Americans come to eat. I didn't see that they bother them."[50] Expecting to be treated as essentially different, Wong's colleagues in the restaurant simply accepted and ignored visitors outside of serving them. Today, Harry Leong sees tourism "as helping our businesses in the community, too, from the gate renovation to the landscape improvements":

> Those types of things are in consideration of not only the residents and businesses in this community or even the people that travel into the community but also for the visitors that come. . . . We're multifaceted, and since we have residents, we have businesses, and we have visitors. So that's kind of been accepted as far as what our nature of our community is. I mean, we are a tourist area; we do have a number of groups coming in. I can say every month we have a number of groups that come and just knock on the door: "Hey, we're in the area, tell us a little bit."[51]

For PCDC founder Yep, tourism is essential to the local economy, but it does not go far enough; she is often frustrated by the representation of the community in Philadelphia tourism campaigns, which she sees as inadequate:

> I don't know that the city has made us a destination, unfortunately. Because they just look on us, they don't think people are living here. They think that we're just a row of restaurants, basically. And they don't know on top of every restaurant, there are like two or three families. It's just amazing how we do survive, because the competition is so incredible. We have, what, fifty restaurants all serving the same kind of food, the same prices, [you know] what I'm saying? And yet we survive. If it wasn't for the tourists, we would not survive, because some restaurants now serve the Chinese people, but for the most part it's the Caucasians that frequent the restaurants.[52]

Yep's frustration seems somewhat justified; in 2009, when PCDC participated in the Welcome America! festivities (an annual citywide festival held around the Fourth of July), Chinatown mounted a neighborhood block party but was not included on the festival event map in the official brochure, effacing the community's participation in the larger festival. On the Greater Philadelphia Tourism and Marketing Corporation (GPTMC) *visitphilly.com* website, Chinatown is not explicitly listed as a destination. Most of the Asian restaurants listed are outside Chinatown, and a search for Chinatown attractions lists only AAI and the "Wok'N Walk" tour offered by Chef Joseph Poon. Likewise, the link to "Explore Philadelphia Neighborhoods" now focuses on neighborhoods in proximity to Center City, and neither Chinatown nor the *Centro d'Oro* is included. Callowhill, however, is included, represented by railroad tracks that visually reference the Reading Viaduct.[53]

Community members' ambivalence about tourism is shaped by memories of past objectification and the historic dependence of the neighborhood economy on the generation of exotic spectacle. Mary Yee remembers tourist buses coming through Boston's Chinatown in the 1960s and the protests against them, "dating our community and looking at it as exotic and all that stuff." The experience of touristic objectification is disturbing and contributes to the marginalization of the community, its sense of separateness from Philadelphia. Wei describes the reaction of her son to being part of a Chinatown tour:

> He said, "They look at us like we are in a zoo and they don't—these tourist buses come by and they look at us, and I'm just trying to live my life as a kid." It was just heartbreaking to me, 'cause I thought, he was like eight, and just for him to have that sensibility and that feeling, and thinking, like what other kid has to put up with that? Like, "Ooo, look at the little Chinese boy. . . ." What other kid has to put up with that as part of, like, their childhood norm?[54]

Wei's remarks underscore the objectification and distance that touristic representation relies on to create "experience," an experience by definition outside that of tourists' everyday lives. Seeking immersion in the daily, ordinary, authentic life of another culture or place, tourists' needs focus on diversion and entertainment on the one hand and extraordinary but "real" experiences on the other. Implicit in this is also the idea of a tourist gaze, which structures the meaning of another place or culture as a mirror for the self, distancing from that other's subjectivity.[55]

Such distancing, for Wei, is one factor that enables the continued vulnerability of Chinatown:

> I know there is just a certain degree of the economy in the community that is tourist-based, but I believe that—the vast majority, I truly

believe, is not. I also feel like these fights against the destruction of
Chinatown will continue to happen as long as you don't view this as
a community, and it's not you. People are shocked when I say it's a
residential community: "I didn't know that people lived there." . . .
Like a lot of people believe that, they don't believe that people actually
live there. . . . I don't know what they think, almost like an amusement
park, Epcot Center. That at the end of the day, you go home. No, this
is home.[56]

Effacing the residential nature of the neighborhood effaces its existence as a
home, erasing the ways in which it is like other neighborhoods. It emphasizes
Chinatown's difference as "not you," as opposed to a fully realized community
identity in its own right and on its own terms.

The contrast between the Chinatown of tourist consumption and that of
residents' memories was thrown into relief in 2006 when AAI worked with
PCDC and the GPTMC to create a tour of the area. This tour was part of
a larger Neighborhood Tourism Network (NTN), a citywide neighborhood
tourism effort created by GPTMC in 2003 to showcase the culture and heritage of the "city of neighborhoods." According to GPTMC, tour participants
would "experience the culture, heritage and diversity of Philadelphia's neighborhoods by sampling authentic foods and participating in lively cultural performances or events. Experienced guides provide in-depth information on the
historical and social trends that have shaped each neighborhood."[57] As Patricia Washington, the network's initiator put it, "You can tour the world by just
touring your own city."[58] NTN represented a common trend in contemporary
urban tourism toward "niche tourism," or the segmentation of tourist markets and spaces into more specialized markets, often tied to ethnic or cultural
branding, part of a larger move by many cities toward "place marketing" as
an engine of urban development. In the case of NTN, tours were aimed specifically at a subset of tourist identified as "urban explorers," or local/regional
residents seeking a deeper knowledge of Philadelphia.[59]

Some of the tours offered through NTN focused on ethnic neighborhoods,
such as the Latino *barrio*, or "Golden Block," at North Fifth Street and Lehigh
Avenue ("Latin Soul, Latin Flavor"). Other tours explored historic neighborhoods outside Center City, such as Germantown ("Taking a Stand for Freedom"). In the case of Chinatown, the tour "Voices of Chinatown" centered on
traditional cultural heritage, promising an experience oriented toward visitor pleasure and relaxation: "Get caught up in the excitement of a lion dance,
taste dim sum specialties and learn about the curative power of herbs during
a visit to a traditional Chinese pharmacy in Chinatown."[60] In 2006, GPTMC
invited tour participants to "immerse [themselves] in Asian American culture
during this insider's tour of Chinatown. Explore some of the neighborhood's
distinctive dining options along Race Street, as well as hidden treasures like

Figure 6.4.
Photographing the
lion dance, 2010. The
tourist gaze is alive and
well in contemporary
Chinatown. (Photograph
by the author.)

the 'underground market' and beautiful Buddhist Temple."[61] In both cases, the language used to promote the tours foregrounded aspects of the neighborhood that lent themselves to a tourist gaze, a gaze that sees and consumes identifiably "Asian" objects (see Figure 6.4). For Washington, "Chinatown was a natural" for the network.[62] Chinatown was a "natural," not only because PCDC (GPTMC's community partner) had promotion of the neighborhood as one of its mission goals but also because Chinatowns have been tourist attractions since the 1880s. Tourists who seek out Chinatown today do so within a historic legacy of objectification and mystification rooted in the tales of early-twentieth-century thrill seekers who consumed legends of Chinatown vice and venality.[63] Promising an "insider's" view of Chinatown's "hidden treasures," GPTMC perpetuated this discourse of Chinatown mystery.

One challenge of designing and implementing the neighborhood tours, according to Washington, was creating what was needed for a successful touristic experience when working with organizations and sites that previously have not been involved in tourism: "One challenge that you have dealing with sites that are in the neighborhood is that you don't have professionals that understand conservation, visitor readiness. How do you develop the interpretive plan for a site? They are coming from a different mind-set. It may be from a family point of view; it may be from the community, the neighborhood, the development point of view, and it's not the museum, curatorial, or even tourism point of view." For Washington, the "tourism point of view" is embodied by the idea of visitor readiness:

> There is a sense of when you walk up to a place, it says, "Welcome!" or "You've arrived!" And this is a special place, either because there's pretty planters outside, there's like, I don't know, a flag or a banner, signage. And there is a sense, this is a special place, come in and explore. There is an invitation that the message is that's translated when you get right on the sidewalk that you are being invited into a place that's very special, that you have arrived. But often at the neighborhood level, it's not like that. It's sort of a hidden treasure. You have to kind of dig and be in the know to know that it's there. And you have to know sort of the people to get in and get inside at all.[64]

Visitor readiness in the neighborhood tours meant a balancing act between "immersive" experience, neighborhood voices, and necessary control by the agency:

> For the neighborhood tours that we did, we decided to completely control the experience. And we wanted it to be immersive, we wanted there to be first-voice interpretation, and that meant getting members of the community involved in telling the history of their community and talking about the culture of their community. We wanted it to be welcoming, so it was, like, members of the community inviting you in for this special conversation and social sharing of culture and history and place. And I think we accomplished that.[65]

Washington articulates the dialectic tourist sites must incorporate, between a sense of novelty and distance on the one hand and familiarity and tourists' safety and comfort on the other. Such a dialectic normally codifies the ways in which a place is different and offers newness while also providing cues that contain that difference within visitors' established expectations, particularly non-Asian visitors.[66]

During the planning phase, GPTMC worked with PCDC and AAI to generate a focus and narrative for the Chinatown tour. This process required an ongoing negotiation of how the neighborhood would be represented, as a site of cultural consumption versus one of struggle and community agency. Isa reflects that there was always a "cordial agreement but then this underlying tension" between the groups developing the tour. While GPTMC wanted to focus on traditional cultural attractions, such as cooking and tai-chi demonstrations, a fortune-cookie factory, and the large Friendship Gate that sits at Tenth and Arch Streets, AAI and PCDC wanted to draw on memories of struggle and activism to focus the tour narrative around sites that represented that struggle, including Holy Redeemer Church, the Vine Street Expressway noise wall, and a mural illustrating the history of Chinatown in the tour route. By insisting on the inclusion of these sites in the tour, community members highlighted the history of struggle in the landscape and the active strategic agency of the community in creating that landscape. As Isa recalls: "We definitely focused around the story of activism in the neighborhood, which really wasn't what GPTMC was interested in promoting, I mean, they weren't against it, but they kept—it just didn't turn out [to be] like the greatest alignment in terms of them saying, 'Do you think that you can get lion dancers to show up at a particular site, like at Holy Redeemer?' for instance and so that when you get to that point on the tour, then people can have some form of entertainment, and 'Can you take them into an herb shop, can you take them in to taste at a fortune-cookie factory?'" GPTMC's interest, according to Isa, was more in "what they call culture and then also what I would call entertainment, which makes sense, if you're a tourist."[67] According to PCDC's Chin, there was "a lot of back and forth" during the process: "We wanted to tell our story of an ethnic neighborhood; their approach was, okay, tourism marketing dollars, how do we get tourists to go to the neighborhoods? So our story didn't necessarily present an attractive venue for tourists. . . . It was hard to figure out what worked and how it worked. And at one point, they got cruise ships to buy these tours, but I don't think the cruise-ship people wanted to hear about the struggles, the urban struggles."[68]

Nevertheless, this theme of struggle was a central idea Chinatown folks believed should shape the tour. Chin says that sites that told this story often fell outside the consumable Chinatown:

> It was basically identifying key stakeholders and important struggles in the community. The Vine Street Expressway, the 125th anniversary mural artwork on the wall, education about the family associations, and we sort of shied away from the gate, although we walked by it. We took them to a grocery store, but we emphasized the cultural aspect of healing, so we took them to an herbal store. We wanted to introduce them to history and what is the real culture rather than the flashy typical tour of the gate and something else.[69]

AAI and PCDC insisted on this part of the story and the representation of the community as not just restaurants but homes for families, according to Washington:

> But with Chinatown, they were interested in people knowing the neighborhood beyond just the restaurants, and they were very adamant about that, so . . . we had to go back and forth, because they wanted the tour to be about the community's advocacy and their fight

against encroachment from the stadium development, from the convention center development, and how they really worked as the leaders of the community to preserve that community. And they wanted
to see the community as a place for families, and I think it really did
open up people's eyes. So we really didn't do a lot of food in Chinatown. We went to the church there and met with one of the long-term
activists.[70]

Chin contrasts their approach with another tourist offering in Chinatown,
Chef Poon's "Wok'N Walk Tour," which is largely a food-oriented version
of the GPTMC offering: "So Joe Poon does a great job of his wacky cooking
tour, right? So he can do what he does best, but we wanted to do the education
piece."[71]

The negotiations between GPTMC and AAI/PCDC over the portrayal
of Chinatown and its story are indicative of the underlying tensions that
often accompany the representation of ethnic communities in public culture.
Whether offering public tours or other events, Chinatown's cultural workers
face the dilemmas of spectacle, the way in which tourism practice shifts the
cultural frame from self-representation (and self-identification) to objectification and commodification. In tourism, place (and the people who make the
place) becomes transformed into an object to be consumed by visitors.[72] Ethnic
difference has a long history of such objectification, made more salient in an
age of commodified ethnicity and of heritage, in which "things are made economically viable as representations of themselves."[73] When immigrant and
ethnic cultures are offered as consumer spectacle, they are reduced to things
that can be commodified, such as things that can be eaten (food), purchased
(decorative objects, souvenirs), and experienced (music, performance). In the
case of the neighborhood tours offered by GPTMC, such titles as "Latino Soul,
Latino Flavor" reinforced a sense of the ethnic neighborhood as a zone of
consumption. These commodities are delivered through a frame of "staged
authenticity" that fosters a sense of discovery and intimacy.[74]

But such representations and performances also exact a "price of "performance," placing the ethnic "object on a pedestal while tethering it to a
post" of difference that perpetuates a sense of distance from the larger society
and its economy.[75] This distancing is compounded by the discourse of heritage practice, which represents the Chinatown community and its culture as
"traditional" (residing in a distant or timeless temporal place), obscuring the
dynamic living ways in which folk culture responds to the concerns and con-
texts of a community in the present.[76] In Chinatown, a focus on culture alone
effaces the historically conditioned nature of the neighborhood landscape,
the way in which it emerged from Orientalist expectations as well as immigrant cultural needs, and the way in which its current vibrancy is the product
of ongoing struggle and development by the community for more than five

decades. By focusing on cultural heritage, particularly traditional culture, as in the Chinatown tour, tourism locates communities out of historical time, suggesting a timelessness of tradition, a freezing of time. Germantown has history; Chinatown has heritage. If heritage is indeed "a new mode of cultural production in the present that has recourse to the past," then we must ask: what past, and for what present?[77]

In crafting the "Voices of Chinatown" tour, Chinatown community members inserted themselves back in historical time, insisting on a story that highlighted the contingent and contested nature of the neighborhood's cultural landscape and the way in which it was a product of history. In doing so, they asserted their own values and resisted in part the disciplining forces of tourism imperatives. They also presented a sense of self that would be recognizable to visitors as "ethnic"—as Chinese, as Asian, or as Chinatown—even as that representation might feed preconceived ideas about the neighborhood or potentially collapse into an essentialized vision of Chinese-ness. In this way, they strategically deployed the "risk of essence" to preserve and present some authentic sense of self, albeit one grounded in a historically conditioned sense of place.[78]

That sense of self is heightened in the context of larger Asian communities that are growing and expanding Chinatown's role as a regional cultural center. Mary Yee points to the increase in local Asian populations that feeds a new demand for Chinatown businesses:

> Certainly it's [tourism] part of the economy, there's no doubt about that, not the tourist buses per se, but the fact you have outsiders coming in to eat and to, say, patronize certain shops and all that stuff. So, I don't think that the Chinatowns could ever have really survived without that. . . . Chinatowns from the fifties and sixties weren't big enough in terms of their own native population to support a local economy. Now there are so many Asians here, like you have a barber shop, you have a hardware store—I mean, you can make a go of it. Before, those weren't even options.[79]

This change, according to Yee, has shifted the neighborhood's microeconomy away from reliance on business enterprises that cater strictly to non-Asian visitors and allowed for the diversification of enterprises that serve Asian consumers from around the region: "Now I think you have more of a critical mass where you have Chinese restaurants basically, or Asian restaurants basically, patronized by Asians—you don't need any outsiders to come in to make it a go."[80] For Yee, there is also a qualitative difference between the tourism of big buses and the way in which outsiders can sincerely experience cultural difference and interaction: "I'm kind of distinguishing tourism of the buses, which is a different kind of thing. . . . [I]f people really try to, say, teach in a multicultural way, then there are really opportunities in different ethnic communities to broaden people's perspectives to educate people, and so it's not really tourism, but it's basically bringing outsiders in and having them participate in the local economy."[81]

This kind of experience is also of interest to Philadelphia's Asians as a way to learn about or celebrate ethnic identity, especially across the generations. As former resident Kenneth Eng points out, the various festivals, events, and representations of Chinatown are a way to introduce his suburban-raised, second-generation children to Chinese tradition: "I think it's good to appreciate a culture, and my children come down, and they appreciate the culture. The Moon Festival in September, Moon Cake Festival, my kids enjoyed it. They would never experience it; I couldn't organize it for them, so in some ways, I'm not against it, unless it gets overboard and becomes fake." For Eng, if a cultural representation "rings true," it does not matter whether "it is a little commercialized." He draws on these occasions to engage his kids in a dialogue about cultural difference and identity: "I say it to my children—you take the best from here, and you take the best from there."[82]

One community event that has resisted objectification and commodification to serve that intergenerational function is the Mid-Autumn Festival, celebrated every year in the early fall. The event is a traditional Chinese harvest festival that falls around the time of the autumnal equinox, a time when families gather to carry lanterns, eat mooncakes, and watch the moon, traditionally considered a symbol of harmony. In Philadelphia, the Mid-Autumn Festival in its current incarnation was born of the cultural displacement of immigrant youth and one Chinese American's reconnection to Chinese tradition as a student. The idea first developed in Debbie Wei's years abroad in Hong Kong, where she witnessed the customs of the festival firsthand. After her children were born, she began sharing the festival with them. What began as a family celebration expanded through Wei's work with recent immigrant youth:

So these kids—I will never forget this—we were down by the river, and we went for a picnic, and we're sitting around, it was August, and I said, "Mid-Autumn Festival is coming up. What do you guys do for Mid-Autumn Festival?" Because we always do a little thing. And they were like, "Well, we don't do anything," and one kid started talking about how his parents—these were all Fujianese kids—and that his parents left him in China with his grandfather and they came to the U.S. and were working and then when he was old enough, like six or seven, they sent for him so he could go to school here, and how he hasn't seen his grandfather since, and that he missed his grandfather a lot, his grandfather raised him, and that his parents were never around, they were always working, and then he said, "Oh, my grandfather probably gets really lonely."[83]

As the young people talked, the idea for the event quickly became an intergenerational community celebration:

> It kind of segued into the elderly in Chinatown and how lonely they must be and how sad it is that this festival comes and goes and nobody knows what it is and nobody knows anything about it. I said, "Well, why don't we make a festival?" and they were like, "Can we do that?" "Well, let's try it," I said. "We can make a festival, and we can invite all the senior citizens to come and watch the moon with us. And even though we are not their grandchildren, we can pretend to be their grandchildren, and we can make it something special for the seniors."[84]

The first Mid-Autumn Festival was held at Holy Redeemer in 1996, "because it was protected, we couldn't be on a street, we didn't have a permit." Asian Americans United (AAU) rented a little stage and decorated the churchyard with lanterns. AAU youth presented a "homegrown" play based on Chinese folktales: "It was just this sweet little thing that all, this group of kids, these seven kids, and me and Ming, Alex Wong, and this Chinese exchange teacher that was living with us helped with. And so we mounted this Autumn Festival, we made flyers, and that first year what we said was it's potluck, bring food to share with everybody, bring a blanket, we'll sit under the moon, the children will entertain you."[85] Planning for twenty to thirty people, the group did outreach to seniors at On Lok House. Four hundred people showed up for the first night, and Wei was "blown away": "And so that was when we realized, oh my God, this has struck a chord, this kind of sense of longing. So none of the kids knew what the hell they were doing out there, but the seniors and the immigrant parents, they were hungry for it, they were like, 'Oh, finally there is a place for us to gather under the moon, the way you are supposed to, on this day and this festival.'"[86]

The goals of the Mid-Autumn Festival, articulated in 1996, are to "promote Chinatown community unity through cultural reclamation; to promote pride in Chinese culture and community; to engage various sectors of the community in support for a community-wide celebration; and to promote intergenerational cooperation." According to AAU, the sponsor of the festival, the event is "an expression of community pride and collective responsibility" in which participants "gather to reclaim old traditions and establish new ones, and in so doing, assert their right to exist as a community."[87] Ellen Somekawa expands on this idea:

> When we create a street festival, we strengthen connections among people, honor the knowledge of the elders in our communities, activate people, and value our own cultures. This is fundamental to social justice work because if people don't care deeply about their neighbors,

their fellow workers, or themselves, what will motivate them to stand up for each other? And if people are not up for caring about themselves or their neighbors, what happens when it comes time to stand up for those who are defined as "other"?[88]

For AAU, the festival can act to raise the consciousness of the Chinatown community about the "fundamental human right to culture." This right resides in a sense of history and belonging-to-place, roots, sense of community, and memories, protected by the "fight for the time and space to celebrate." For some participants, such as volunteer Ally Vuong, the festival is symbol of Chinatown's triumph through struggle: "We've been struggling as a community fighting against the development of highways, baseball stadiums, and casinos that only harm and constrain us. Mid-Autumn Festival is our time to celebrate our triumphs and be proud that we're an awesome community together."[89]

According to Wei, the festival has "morphed into this huge thing—like, it's just got its own life." The event lasts an entire day and evening and features cultural performances, carnival games, arts activities, a lion dance, and a lantern parade. The festival culminates in a new tradition created by AAU, a mooncake-eating contest. The festival is run with high school volunteers and has become a "rite of passage" for them. Success comes with other pressures, though. Wei muses: "I think AAU is trying to keep the spirit of it intact so we don't do commercialism—like, a lot of the street festivals you go to, it's just vendor after vendor after vendor, and ours, the only vending is sort of like drinks and little snacks and stuff, but it's all mostly free."[90] She recognizes that the pull toward larger marketing and commercialization is always there in a neighborhood like Chinatown: "There is always the tension when new members come on the committee and it's like, 'We have to market this for tourism.' And it's not intended for that."[91] Although the festival is now held at Tenth and Arch at the Friendship Gate and draws "thousands" of attendees each year, AAU is committed to keeping the event "homegrown" and tied to community "well-being," not a spectacle for outsiders (see Figure 6.5).

If Chinatown represents something larger beyond individual memory or tourist diversion, it is in the collective community memory of its struggle for survival and growth. For Gayle Isa, "it's the history of struggle and resilience. I can get all teary about this, but I think it's so important that despite all the internal community conflicts, that there's a way that the neighborhood has found, has been forced to have, the ability to work together and to be resilient and to survive."[92] Helen Gym echoes this "fierce history of self-preservation," adding that it brings with it a specific "political consciousness" that goes beyond the physical and cultural landscape and embodies a fluid, strategic ethnic identity and cultural content:

Figure 6.5. An intergenerational crowd at the Mid-Autumn Festival, 2009. (Courtesy of Asian Americans United. Photograph by Bret Flaherty.)

PCDC and other organizations have taken a look at physical boundaries and the physical defining and definition of Chinatown . . . its very physical landscape, and then I think that what AAU has tried to bring to the table is a very strong consciousness of what's within those boundaries and what does it mean to have a Chinatown. Is it really just a set of boundaries, and really anything can exist within it, and that it could be anything from exotified kinds of perceptions of what Chinatown is, or is it going to be a very self-determined, articulate notion of an evolving Chinatown, something that represents new immigrants that are coming into the city as well as a rising Asian American consciousness . . . a very politicized, active, engaged—civically engaged—and politically and socially responsible Chinatown.[93]

For Mary Yee, Chinatown's significance lies in not only the community's identification with a history of struggle but also its "contested location in Center City":

It's important as an example of a community of color that still is in Center City and is there because it struggled to stay there by trying to assert and reinforce its identity in the various ways we talked about—culturally, physically, spiritually, politically. . . . It's also an act of resistance against this hegemonic racist society that we live in. For all the talk about multiculturalism and so forth, at the bottom of this, we still have a lot of very deep issues around racism to deal with. And so I think it's important for ethnic communities to exist, as a way to also preserve heritage and identity in that also to give strength to the people that live there.[94]

This preservation is unique, according to Yee: "When you look at communities where they're kind of fragile, if not falling apart, DC and Seattle, where Chinatowns have not been able to kind of hold up. Philadelphia surprisingly does not have a huge [immigrant population] compared to other cities—it is on the tail end of cities that are able to both attract and also retain immigrants. So to me, it's also even more amazing."[95] Philadelphia's Chinatown, with its history of struggle, remains a living space for the exploration and sharing of Asian American culture as well as a symbol of this community's survivance, a complex community genealogy embodied by landscape.

Epilogue
"Is, was, and will be Chinatown"

I t is a Saturday afternoon in June 2014, my last research visit to Chinatown, five years after the first. I am walking up Tenth Street from Arch. I watch a middle-aged Asian woman stop to snap a picture of the Friendship Gate. Not all the tourists are non-Asian, I think to myself. Three twenty-something African American women holding shopping bags gather at the base of the Gate, looking around, trying to decide what to do next. A woman with long blonde hair examines a display of jewelry in a store window. A middle-aged white woman points out the Chinese characters painted on a shop window—a dentist's office—to her son, a young boy of about five or six.

It is the weekend, so many Asian families have come in from outlying areas to shop, dine, and attend various events. The sidewalks are packed with people who cluster around the boxes of produce set out on the sidewalk outside various groceries, offering durian, lychee, small golden mangoes. It is difficult to get through the crowds. An older Chinese man is blocking the sidewalk, enthusiastically taking a picture with his cell phone of two white blond-haired twins as their delighted parents stand behind the stroller, bemused at the attention.

At various points along Tenth Street, vendors, many of them older women, are selling jade jewelry trinkets and plant seedlings, starter plants for Chinese gardens, such as "longevity fruit," Chinese eggplant, peppers, and more. They smile and point to the jade items, beckoning me to buy. A man lowers a large net into a box-shaped tank on the back of a flatbed truck and lifts a netful of flopping fish, lowering them down into a plastic freight container that sits on a scale. Two men weigh the fish and swiftly carry the container into a small market, while gathered children laugh in delight. An intergenerational group of Asian American women hovers outside one bubble tea place, discussing whether to enter. Inside another tea shop and bakery, several extended families enjoy dim sum, ice cream, and Chinese-language movies on two wall-mounted televisions.

As I walk up Tenth Street toward Vine, I pass new streetscaping features: red streetlights in the style of Chinese lanterns and crosswalks painted in an Asian-style parquet pattern. Abakus, the sneaker store located in a former takeout restaurant, is shuttered. Across Tenth and Winter, I pass a large foo dog statue and a figure of the Fujianese hero Zexu Lin beside a large pergola structure. A mix of older men (black and white) occupies the benches underneath, some dozing, others sitting up, holding shopping bags. These landscape features were not here when I started the project five years ago, I recall. Across the intersection, I see people entering and leaving the entrance to the Holy Redeemer compound, where a Philadelphia Chinatown Development Corporation (PCDC) Expo is happening. Featured on the program: homeowner information sessions and a special workshop on gambling addiction.

Toward the end of the afternoon, I see Asian families and older men and women carrying orange plastic bags of produce and other groceries back up Tenth Street to Chinatown North, where I assume they have parked their cars. A young man, shirtless in burgundy gym shorts, is sitting outside a shuttered restaurant begging for money. A group of teenage boys carry large pieces of lumber toward the corner of Tenth and Winter. I hear a sound system being tested over on Spring Street. The Chinese Christian Church and Center (CCC&C) is hosting its annual carnival in a few hours. There will be home-made games of chance, music, and probably a watermelon-eating contest.

Walking along these streets after five years of study, I see a place that has changed but that is also marked by stability and familiarity. Chinatown clearly continues to be a place for Asian Americans to live and work, and it remains an important center for Chinese and other Asian Americans. Local and regional immigrants from New Jersey and Pennsylvania use Chinatown as a base, traveling in on the weekends to shop, dine, attend events, and, on Sundays, go to church, just as folks did in the past. Family banquets and other significant gatherings are held here. This afternoon, there are many young people on the street—children with their parents and grandparents, teenagers on their own—all busy, all engaged with their surroundings. This place is vibrant and living.

Yet I am also aware that this vibrancy is tenuous and that this place is, as it has always been, vulnerable. A study on Chinatowns issued in 2013 by the Asian American Legal Defense and Education Fund (AALDEF), "Chinatown Then and Now," reported that three East Coast Chinatowns—in Boston, New York, and Philadelphia—are increasingly under threat, largely due to gentrification. The report cited some discouraging statistics from the perspective of "living community." From 2000 to 2010, the share of the Asian population in all three Chinatowns decreased, and the foreign-born population now represents less than half of all residents in all three Chinatowns. In Philadelphia's Chinatown, the foreign-born population decreased from 42 to 33 percent between 2007 and 2011. Likewise, family households are also on the decline: the neighborhood saw a decrease in the share of family households from 61 to 46 percent between 1990 and 2010, a significant change. Populations of youth under seventeen years old and elderly over sixty-five years old have also declined. Decreases in family households and the foreign born signal a potential shift away from the kind of community that has characterized Philadelphia's Chinatown to date. Boston's and Philadelphia's Chinatowns are also less Asian; their white populations doubled between 2000 and 2010, even as the white populations decreased in those cities overall.[1] Philadelphia's Chinatown has the highest rate of homeownership among all three China-towns at 30 percent, rising by 10 percent from 2000 to 2010, although it is not clear who owns these units; some or many may be luxury condomini-ums. In the past few decades, median house values and rents in Philadelphia's Chinatown have illustrated the increased value of land downtown—and the neighborhood's ongoing gentrification. While the statistics for Philadelphia are undoubtedly shaped by the defined geographic area, which includes the Callowhill neighborhood, the numbers give anyone interested in the future of Chinatown pause.

Amid the decline in these representative populations, there are some signs of continuity. Since at least the 1990s, some leaders of community associations have purchased a modest number of multi-unit buildings in Chinatown as a way to preserve affordable housing, often for new immigrants from their same regions. PCDC recently undertook a program aimed at alleviating the tax burdens of Chinatown homeowners after tax reassessments raised their rates, allowing them to retain their homes. Approximately 74 percent of the busi-nesses located in Philadelphia's Chinatown are small or local businesses; there are no Starbucks or Benetton shops yet as there are in some other Chinatowns. Food and restaurant-supply manufacturers remain in the area, employing immigrants and serving other local businesses. "Retaining these land uses in these neighborhoods," the report declared, "is vital to the restaurant and grocery sectors, and thus to the larger Chinatown economy and labor market, even as warehousing and manufacturing are often targets of increased nui-sance complaints in gentrifying areas."[2] Of the forty-seven restaurants with sales prices listed since the 1980s, with most sales beginning in the 1990s, 34 percent sold for a nominal fee of $20 or less, suggesting the buildings' transfer between family members. A core group of Chinatown restaurants clearly remain family-owned businesses. Of the restaurants, 85 percent served Asian cuisine, the majority (62 percent) being Chinese cuisine. Meanwhile, 11 percent served Vietnamese cuisine, 5 percent served Malaysian cuisine, and the remaining Asian cuisine restaurants served Japanese, Thai, Burmese, and other Asian food. Many of the non-Asian restaurants, at just about 15 percent of the total, were located on the edges of the neighborhood. According to the report, "The significant number of Asian restaurants indicates Chinatown's strength in continuing to serve a local and regional Asian immigrant population."[3]

The continuing diversification of Asian restaurants demonstrates that Chinatown is increasingly pan-Asian in character, a trend that reflects the broader immigrant population. According to the 2010 Census, the bulk of Chinatown residents are still Chinese, although the area is now also 4.4 percent Asian Indian, 4 percent Korean, 2 percent Vietnamese, 1 percent Filipino, and 1 percent Japanese. There are also smaller numbers of Indonesian, Malaysian, Cambodian, Pakistani, and Burmese residents (see Table A.2 in the Appendix).[4] Such organizations as the Asian Arts Initiative (AAI) and Asian Americans United (AAU) express this pan-Asian identity and cultural sensibility, working with broader constituencies across the city and region. In addition, Chinatown's workforce extends beyond those of Asian origin; many restaurant workers, for example, now hail from Mexico or Central America, and Spanish is as common in Chinatown's kitchens as Cantonese once was.[5]

Recent growth in the Chinese economy shifted push/pull factors for Chinese immigration, and the most recent waves of immigration from Fujian are also diverse by class. While earlier waves were poor, often undocumented, more recently some immigrants are wealthier entrepreneurs who come to open or invest in businesses. New immigrants bring new identities and new capital. They also may have less attachment to or identification with Chinatown and its history. Long-time Chinatown developers worry that new immigrants are less likely to participate in marketing, cleanup, or other business-corridor improvements or to make long-term investments in Chinatown. New immigrants have stronger transnational ties; their interests lie in trade missions, educational exchanges, import/export, international expos, and tourism/hospitality. The Greater Philadelphia United Chinese American Chamber of Commerce, for example, which was founded in the 1990s by Chinese students and immigrants, focuses on partnerships with mainland China to bridge U.S. and Chinese businesses. The chamber's mailing address is located in the Mayfair area of the Greater Northeast (a site of recent Chinese immigrant settlement), not in Chinatown, and its primary focus seems to be the promotion of a China Trade Center, aimed at hosting an international trade exposition in Philadelphia.[6]

New immigrant entrepreneurs are making a significant impact on Chinatown, however. As PCDC's Sarah Yeung points out, many new immigrants were entrepreneurs in China during the recent boom; they have capital, or access to it; and they are savvy about marketing and advertising.[7] In addition, Chinatown is a draw for increasing numbers of Chinese students from local universities. Many younger and second-generation immigrants are opening businesses in Chinatown, some of which cater to this population. In addition to the sneaker store Abakus (sadly, closed in 2013), there are numerous bubble tea shops, all owned and operated by younger Asian Americans, as well as hip bars and nightclubs.[8] These businesses reflect a new Asian aesthetic, eschewing the imagery of classic Chinatown in favor of sleek modern interiors that suggest a contemporary China, or ironic gestures to an Oriental past. Jack Chen, the Fujian-born owner of Sakura Mandarin, a contemporary-style soup dumpling house, asserts that new immigrants from Fujian have opened close to 50 percent of the restaurants in Chinatown and purchased up to 40 percent of the properties in the past 10 years.[9] Other informal estimates suggest even higher rates of new immigrant business in Chinatown. These new immigrants and young entrepreneurs are infusing Philadelphia's Chinatown with a dynamism that belies the death knell repeatedly sounded about the district; their stories deserve further exploration and study.

Aesthetically and practically, Chinatown's developers are responding to this transnational sensibility. A critical part of PCDC's imagination for the area's future, for example, revolves around the construction of a new community center on the northwest corner of Tenth and Vine Streets that will speak to the multiple needs of Chinatown constituencies.[10] A community center for Chinatown is a long-held dream; in the early 1970s, activists pointed out a lack of recreational spaces, and Gim San Plaza was originally conceived as a community center. Tenth and Vine is a significant corner, symbolic of the community's past and present: across Tenth Street from Holy Redeemer, long a vacant lot turned parking lot after Vine Street Expressway–related demolition forty years before. As PCDC's John Chin notes: "We picked a prominent location where it would strengthen the community, and at the time we started talking about it, we had just started crossing over Vine Street. Vine Street has been kind of this dividing line because of the expressway that severed the north and the south. So, the thought was the community center being north of Vine Street would become eventually more central, so it would encourage development to the north."[11]

The planned community center, known as "Eastern Tower," will be housed in a modern glass high rise with no traditional "Chinesey" Chinatown characteristics. According to Andy Toy, who is directing the effort for PCDC, the design is meant to be generally "Asian" and resemble a series of sliding screens. The building's architect, Tejoon Jung, envisions the façade of the building as consisting of interlocking glass boxes that evoke a Chinese puzzle box. The sections are roughly the size of the four-story buildings typically found in the surrounding neighborhood. These modern puzzle-box sections are accented with wood eaves, suggesting the slatted underside of Chinese courtyard houses, a solution to the problem of conveying "Chinese character without resorting to stereotypical motifs, such as pagoda tiers or dragons" (see Figure 7.1).[12] For Chin, the aesthetics of the new center are deliberately non-traditional, designed to make the tower a "statement building" signaling the

Figure 7.1. "Eastern Tower," the proposed Chinatown community center at Tenth and Vine Streets. The Tenth Street Plaza is shown in front. (Courtesy of the Philadelphia Chinatown Development Corporation.)

vibrancy of the Chinatown community and resonating with contemporary Asian architecture:

> This development's sending a message that we're secure in the vision of Chinatown North. And because of the tens of thousands of cars that come by here on Vine Street, this is actually a statement building that sets this as Chinatown. . . . [W]hat it means for us is that Chinatown North is our opportunity to decide how the community should look and feel. . . . And it also sends a message to those people that are looking to continue to move up the economic ladder, thinking, "Now I've been living in this apartment, where's my opportunity to stay in Chinatown?" Well, here's one opportunity, and there'll be more just like it. So this also says that first, second, and third generation can live in Chinatown if they choose to.[13]

Eastern Tower will be the site of a multiuse community center hosting a variety of functions, including an adult day care facility, children's day care facility, and afterschool activities. Volleyball and leadership activities will be offered in the afternoon. The Philadelphia Suns will use the space for basketball practice, and the gymnasium will also be rented to a local sports league.

Toy envisions the center as a "one-stop shop" for community needs, including attorney and immigration assistance and health services. Retail components will include a pharmacy, gift shop, and other outlets, including a Dunkin' Donuts, owned by a local Chinese entrepreneur who owns more than thirty franchises in the area. Eastern Tower's multiple functions mirror the traditional spatial pattern of historic Chinatown, according to Chin: "Because Chinatown is basically [a] kind of mixed-use community, a mixed-income community, we think that that's a great model to follow. So the mixed use is definitely the only way that we should do that."[14] Toy echoes the sentiment that mixed use is central to the center's conception: "Having that mix of uses in there will actually make it a much more vibrant, 24/7 kind of space." Toy also stresses the intergenerational aspect: "What's really exciting is the idea of having the idea of the old elders, seniors, and young people using it at the same time and having some intergenerational activities and the kind of cool stuff that we can do."[15]

The tower's residential component is conceived as mixed income, with 22 percent of the units affordable to people who earn 80 percent of the median income without a low-income housing-tax credit. The creation of new lower-income rental properties is key to PCDC's vision for the structure, seeking to meet a chronic need. It "will allow some people that are living in really crowded, overcrowded, or substandard conditions to move from the main part of Chinatown as well, opening up more units for other people. . . . [T]here's going to be some demand for this."[16] Working to keep Eastern Tower in sync with community needs, PCDC is partnering with a private developer with a community-development background: "It's not like trying to convince some for-profit developer that we should be doing this because it's the right thing, even if it doesn't make financial sense."[17] The project, which will cost $71 million, is being financed through a variety of public and private sources. PCDC received Community Development Block Grant funding ($50,000) from the city and applied to the Pennsylvania Office of Budget for stimulus/economic-development funds in 2012. The project qualifies for a special type of "new market" tax credits, which are allocated by the U.S. Treasury for certain low-income communities.[18] Citibank is committing $42 million in tax-credit funding. Another $10 million will come from a series of smaller grants from PCDC itself, the Commerce Department, and a $5-million Redevelopment Assistance Capital Program grant from the state.

One component of financing is new for PCDC and embraces the globalized position of Chinatown—a significant portion of support, $33 million, is targeted to come from overseas investors, specifically from China as well as India, Bangladesh, and other countries: "I think because of where we are in the United States, we really do need to leverage the connections and the networks of the Chinatown and Asian communities. It's an advantage that we have, and the city doesn't really take advantage of it," Toy comments.[19] To access these investors, PCDC has partnered with Global City Regional Center, an entity created in 2011, one of 440 such centers across the nation approved by U.S. Citizenship and Immigration Services (USCIS), to access the federal EB-5 Green Card for permanent residence by investing at least $500,000 in a new commercial enterprise in the United States.[20] The design and financing for the proposed Eastern Tower embodies the nature of contemporary Chinatown, rooted in the past by its historically significant location yet gesturing toward the present and the future in its design and financing.

The city, for its part, seems to have a new consideration for Chinatown's presence in planning efforts, and the new center will be linked to a larger landscape planned for downtown. A 2012 plan for Market East created by the Philadelphia City Planning Commission (PCPC) clearly includes Chinatown and outlines development of Tenth Street as a corridor spanning Chinatown to the north and Jefferson Hospital to the south, including the planned Eastern Tower in its swath. A pedestrian bridge at the Gallery is designed to mimic an Asian gateway, speaking to the traditional gate to the north and integrating Chinatown. This integration answers a long-articulated complaint that Market East/Gallery "turned its back" on Chinatown long ago. Chinatown, it seems, is here to stay.

But on what terms? Chinatown has been in a perpetual state of renewal since the 1960s, even since the 1920s. Its progress has been modest by larger urban standards, or even the standards of other larger Chinatowns. Housing, so key to the neighborhood's survival, remains a chronic need. Its lower-income immigrant residents make it an unattractive investment for most private developers. Much housing remains substandard and in very short supply. PCDC's housing projects are small in scale and volume, and some question how truly affordable that housing has been.[21] A majority of Chinatown's population still lives below the poverty line and is underemployed.[22] Gentrification continues to push at Chinatown's edges, available redevelopment strategies privilege the commercial aspects of the neighborhood, and some public voices question the need for an ethnic-specific area downtown, suggesting that Chinatown let itself go the way of other ethnic successions.

Other ethnic districts in Philadelphia suggest trajectories Chinatown could take. North Philadelphia's *barrio*, while not subject to the same land and development pressures as Chinatown, has pursued similar renewal activities since the 1960s. Struggle has been a defining feature of this neighborhood, as residents have organized to fight blight, neglect, poverty, and stigmatization (portions of this neighborhood were known as "the Badlands" in the

1980s and 1990s). Community-development corporations (CDCs), such as the Hispanic Association of Contractors and Engineers (HACE), have collaborated with service and arts organizations and businesses to reclaim a neglected postindustrial area of the city and construct affordable housing, create a Latino-themed commercial corridor, and build cultural attractions for a thriving arts and culture scene that can attract middle-class Latinos back to the neighborhood. Ethnic spatial theming played a central role in this effort. Taller Puertorriqueño, a Latino arts organization, is currently fundraising to build a new modern cultural center; recent streetscaping efforts have enhanced the Caribbean look and feel of the area. This neighborhood has evolved over the last half century from a Puerto Rican enclave into a larger pan-Latino district serving a geographically dispersed population from the Caribbean, South and Central America, and Mexico. As Latino immigration and migration continues apace (Latinos are the largest and fastest growing population in the city), this area will undoubtedly grow. Could Chinatown do the same as a pan-Asian destination? Commercially, this path seems likely, although without affordable housing, Chinatown cannot remain a destination for new immigrants.

Another trajectory concerns a historic nineteenth-century/early-twentieth-century enclave in the later stages of ethnic succession. In South Philadelphia, along South Ninth Street, the "Italian Market" is now a multiethnic area where Latino and Southeast Asian enterprises thrive amid vestiges of a historic Italian American district. The market abuts a concentration of Vietnamese and Cambodian retail and wholesale businesses, including numerous restaurants, that emerged during the 1980s and 1990s. Latino immigrants, particularly Mexican, have flocked to the area in the last two decades. Recent immigrants continue to be attracted to this area due to its affordable housing options (many new Chinese immigrants also live in South Philadelphia). Farther south, the area surrounding East Passyunk Avenue, once almost exclusively Italian American, is an eclectic commercial landscape of traditional red-gravy restaurants, cheesesteak joints, and old family businesses mixed with gastropubs, a gourmet gelateria, trendy boutiques, Mexican cafés, and organic beauty salons. The East Passyunk Avenue Business Improvement District, which has been working to revitalize and promote this area since 2002, sponsors ongoing promotions, festivals, and other events to draw visitors to the area for food and culture, a now-standard strategy of business-driven community development.[23] Old ethnic groups with new immigrants and young professionals make for a dynamic mix in a neighborhood that is rapidly gentrifying.

Chinatown likely has a future as a symbolic center for Asians in the region, embracing a transnational identity to survive as an emblem of globalized Philadelphia, as a destination for ethnic entrepreneurs, and even as a robust commercial and cultural center. But the living space that makes this

Chinatown so special and unique may require continued struggle. If redevelopment focuses only on what can be sold, whether land or culture, and perceives neighborhood value in this way, then important aspects of urban experience, identity, and social justice are ignored. The irony of ethnic renewal in Philadelphia's Chinatown is that urban ethnic community development is supported by market-driven approaches to urban renewal, but often only within the specific parameters of commodified ethnicity, parameters that neglect a fuller articulation of the community's spatial identity, needs, and values. Chinatown's small size enables the continuation of a strong tradition of activism and community defense that continue to preserve aspects of place that constitute lived space, living community. These aspects—churches, homes, gardens, playgrounds, family businesses—are the most vulnerable to erasure, especially within a neoliberal environment that privileges market-driven development, tourism, and other aspects of place that can be commodified and consumed. It remains to be seen whether ethnic renewal results in a better quality of life for the working poor, whether tourism dollars are leveraged into better and more affordable housing, and whether redevelopment can proceed without collapsing into gentrification.

As the rumors of Chinatown's demise circulate once again, it can turn to its past to reimagine and fight for its future. One crucial factor will be the attitudes of younger Asian Americans, particularly those with personal connections to the neighborhood. For Melody Wong, who ran PCDC's Main Street Program in 2009 and now works for AAI, Chinatown "is a place of the past" for second-generation Chinese: "Second generation, you don't live in Chinatown anymore, because your parents have worked their ass off to get out of a one-bedroom apartment for four. And that's the truth of it. This is where people stay, where old people stay. So they could be closer to their friends and speak Chinese, they have limited mobility and can go down and play *mahjongg* and go for their dim sum or whatever. Unfortunately, that's how we are. . . . There has been a reluctance of people [in] my age group or maybe the one before my generation to come back and give back to the community."[24] Debbie Wei notes that her children's generation "doesn't need Chinatown anymore; they don't have to go to Chinatown" when friendships are multiethnic and there is access to diverse cultures.[25] But Xu Lin's experience of violence and harassment as a newcomer suggests that Chinatown as a "safe space" is still salient for a generation of new Asian immigrants. The hundreds of young people who volunteer each year to create the Mid-Autumn Festival, the participants in AAU's Youth Community Leadership program, the basketball and volleyball players of the Philadelphia Suns from all over the city, are all forming their own place attachments to Chinatown, creating new memoryscapes for a new generation. They may organize to preserve this "cultural homespace" when the next threat manifests itself.

The history of Philadelphia's Chinatown suggests that for communities of color in American cities, redevelopment and struggle are integral to each other in an ongoing quest for spatial justice. Chinatown, like other Asian enclaves in cities across the United States, was the product of discrimination and segregation. Providing a haven for immigrants, these districts, aging and blighted by the postwar period, were stigmatized as slums, disregarded in urban planning, and subject to displacement. Philadelphia's Chinatown residents and advocates—long-time second- and third-generation Chinese Americans, youthful Asian American Movement (AAM) activists, and traditional association leaders—joined forces to defend the neighborhood's sanctity when a major renewal project, the Vine Street Expressway, threatened the heart and soul of a living neighborhood. Through a commitment to systematic urban planning, creative and geographically strategic redevelopment, new immigration, continued activism, and, at times sheer determination, the community reclaimed space, celebrated place, and continued to defend its interests within a larger urban-renewal agenda. It continues its activism, marshaling support and building alliances across the city and the region to fight projects that do not support their vision of living community, most recently in response to proposed casinos. Today, Philadelphia's Chinatown lives the complex legacies of this historic struggle and its representational dilemmas, strategically deploying its identity as ethnic space to meet community needs, mitigate gentrification, and retain a sense of place that embodies the collective and individual memories of several generations of Chinese Americans and other Asians. In this way, Chinatown continues to serve as the spatial embodiment of home for Asian Americans around the Philadelphia region, a place of historic struggle and origin. As the community and the city move forward, Chinatown will continue to consciously, contestedly, and creatively renew itself.

Appendix
Chinatown Populations

Calculating the population of Chinatown for the period of this study proved to be a difficult and sometimes confusing task for this quantitatively challenged folklorist-historian. For more than a century of data, the categories through which the U.S. Census documented the population of Chinatown and Philadelphia Asians varied considerably. Prior to 1950, Census workers notated the specific ethnicity of residents, including their place of birth. Because these full Census documents have been released, it is possible to gather data at the block level. For the years 1880–1940, therefore, I took manual counts of the Chinese population over a specific area identified to be Chinatown. For these purposes, the area of Chinatown was defined from Eighth Street to Eleventh and Vine to Race. In the case of 1940, Census numbers differ considerably from a contemporary community estimate, and it is assumed that numbers of Chinese in the neighborhood and city were consistently undercounted for a variety of reasons. For the larger Philadelphia area, population numbers were generated by completing a race/nationality keyword search using the online U.S. Census site search engine.

After 1940, block-by-block information is not yet available, so for the post-1940 period, I relied more heavily on online search functions and Census Bureau summary reports. Unfortunately, racial and ethnic categories once again changed, and reports from the 1950 Census did not include racial characteristics for Asians, except as part of "nonwhite others," reporting on only white and black populations. Therefore, the number in Table A.1 includes the population of "nonwhite others" for Census tract 10A, which encompassed Seventh Street to Fifteenth Street and Vine to Arch and was used for comparative purposes for 1950 and 1970. It is assumed that some nonwhite others were not Chinese or Asian and that additional Chinese lived in Census tracts 14B and 13B above Vine Street on either side of Tenth Street during this period, based on oral histories. These numbers were negligible, though, for the nonwhite-other category. The Census began reporting racial categories again for Asians in 1960 and national origin for Asians in 1980, at which point much more accurate counts could be made. In addition, the 1980 Census recorded populations for the Philadelphia Metropolitan Statistical Area beyond the city of Philadelphia, available for 1980 for the first time. However, since I had nothing to compare this to, I con-

TABLE A.1. CHINESE AND ASIAN POPULATIONS, 1870–2010

Year	Group	Chinatown	Philadelphia	Five-county region
1870	Chinese	—	13	—
1880	Chinese	12	79	82
1900	Chinese	235	1,177	—
1910	Chinese	190	1,148	—
1920	Chinese	144	1,087	—
1930	Chinese	167	1,681	—
1940	Chinese	164	725	—
1950[b]	Chinese	—	—	—
	Nonwhite "Other races"	355	2927	
1960	Chinese	—	1,810	2,287
1970	Chinese	549	2,784	—
1980[d]	Chinese	703	4,987	7,964
	Vietnamese	24	2,038	3,798
	Asian	732	17,764	34,781
1990[d]	Chinese	1,018	11,691	18,314
	Vietnamese	41	5,701	9,045
	Asian	1,107	43,522	82,035
2000[d]	Chinese	1,289	17,390	31,663
	Taiwanese	3	393	1,023
	Vietnamese	23	11,608	18,005
	Asian[a]	1,421	67,654	138,043
2010[c]	Chinese	2,026	29,396	53,133
	Taiwanese	13	639	1,647
	Vietnamese	51	14,431	23,806
	Asian	2,466	93,526	21,2638

Source: U.S. Federal Census, 1880–2010; U.S. Census of Population, 1970; Census of Population, Supplementary Report, Race of the Population by County: 1970; U.S. Census of Population 1950–2010, Prepared in Social Explorer, http://www.socialexplorer.com/tables/C1980/R10848611; http://www.socialexplorer.com/tables/C1990/R10848606; http://www.socialexplorer.com/tables/C2000/R10759276; and http://www.socialexplorer.com/tables/C2010/R10759301 (accessed June 26, 2014, and November 30, 2014).
a Refers to "Asian alone."
b Chinatown figures calculated from Census tract 10A.
c Chinatown figures calculated from Census tracts 2 and 376.
d Chinatown figures calculated from Census tracts 2, 126, and 127.

tinued to rely on the five-county area as a regional frame, including Philadelphia, Bucks, Delaware, Chester, and Montgomery Counties. These counts, therefore, do not include counties in southern New Jersey that may be considered part of the greater Philadelphia region. For 1980–2000, I utilized the digital resource Social Explorer to compile information for Census tract 2 to represent the historic core of Chinatown, and for two tracts (126 and 127) north of Vine on each side of Tenth Street to represent Chinatown North. For 2010, I looked at tract 2 for the core and tract 367 for Chinatown North/Callowhill.

To gain a better sense of recent demographic changes within Chinatown, particularly related to pan-Asian patterns and gentrification in the last twenty years, for Table A.2, I once again utilized Social Explorer, which allowed me to search via county and

TABLE A.2. CHINATOWN POPULATIONS, 2000–2010

Race	2010	Census tract 2	Census tract 367	%	2000	Census tract 2	Census tract 126	Census tract 127	%
Total population:	5,923	2937	2,542		2,924	1,362	835	727	
White alone	2,586	711	1,875	31.1%	561	162	355	44	19.2%
Black/African American	704	295	409	22.6%	818	74	309	435	28.0%
Hispanic/Latino	260	79	181	4.8%	197	58	94	45	6.9%
Asian alone	1,960	1,856	104	41.6%	1,421	1,085	127	209	48.6%

Asian groups	2010	Census tract 2	Census tract 367	%	2000	Census tract 2	Census tract 126	Census tract 127	%
Total Asian, with one Asian category only:	2,436	1,833	603		1,415	1079	127	209	
Asian Indian	107	77	30	4.4%	37	21	16	0	2.6%
Bangladeshi	1	1	0	0.0%	0	0	0	0	0%
Bhutanese	0	0	0	0.0%	n/a	n/a	n/a	n/a	n/a
Burmese	4	4	0	0.2%	n/a	n/a	n/a	n/a	n/a
Cambodian	19	5	14	0.8%	13	1	0	12	0.9%
Chinese (excl. Taiwanese)	2,026	1,578	448	83.2%	1,289	1,012	84	193	91.1%
Filipino	26	16	10	1.1%	10	3	7	0	0.7%
Hmong	0	0	0	0.0%	0	0	0	0	0%
Indonesian	17	12	5	0.7%	7	7	0	0	0.5%
Japanese	25	9	16	1.0%	8	4	4	0	0.6%
Korean	97	62	35	4.0%	11	4	7	0	0.8%
Laotian	7	0	7	0.3%	3	0	1	2	0.2%
Malaysian	15	14	1	0.6%	1	1	0		0.1%
Nepalese	0	0	0	0.0%	n/a	n/a	n/a	n/a	n/a
Pakistani	13	6	7	0.5%	2	0	2	0	0.1%
Sri Lankan	0	0	0	0.0%	0	0	0	0	0%
Taiwanese	13	8	5	0.5%	3	3	0	0	0.2%
Thai	3	0	3	0.1%	0	0	0	0	0%
Vietnamese	51	31	20	2.1%	23	18	5	0	1.6%
Other Asian, specified	0	0	0	0.0%	3	3	0	0	0.2%
Other Asian, not specified	12	10	2	0.5%	5	2	1	2	0.4%

Source: U.S. Census Bureau, 2000 and 2010 Census of Population and Housing. Prepared by Social Explorer, http://www.social explorer.com/tables/C2000/R10759276 and http://www.socialexplorer.com/tables/C2010/R10759301 (accessed June 26, 2014).
Note: Census Tracts: 2 and 376 for 2010; 2, 126, and 127 for 2000. Includes Callowhill area.

Census tract. In these cases, a comparison of the tracts over a twenty-year period revealed a decline in the Asian, Latino, and African American populations of Chinatown and Chinatown North, with a concomitant rise of whites from 19.2 percent to 31.1 percent, doubtless due to gentrification and the development of the Callowhill area. This comparison also revealed a slight rise in Asian Indian, Vietnamese, Filipino, Malaysian, Japanese, and Korean residents (with a slight decline in Chinese from 91.1 to 83.2 percent), pointing to the emergence of a pan-Asian base within Chinatown that resonates with changes in the business and arts/cultural sectors of the community.

In gathering data from multiple sources, some discrepancies certainly arose. For example, counts I generated using Census summaries and online searches yielded results that were slightly different from those generated by Social Explorer in some but not all cases. However, when the numbers differed slightly, they were generally "in the same ballpark," retaining the same scale and relationship to previous numbers. To achieve some consistency for two separate periods, I used Social Explorer for the post-1960 era. In this way, all pre-1960 numbers were generated using the same method, and all post-1960 numbers were generated using the same method. The numbers, then, are consistent within these two sets. Read across the sets, they must, of course, be viewed as approximate but roughly equivalent.

Recently, the category of "Asian" has also included numbers for those who are of more than one race, complicating exact counts. For the sake of simplicity, I did not include numbers outside "Asian alone," although these are and will be increasingly significant. In addition to all these issues, one must assume that the U.S. Census continues to undercount this population, particularly in Chinatown, where cultural and linguistic barriers present themselves as they do in many other immigrant and minority communities. Likewise, the Census does not record the number of Asians working in Chinatown while living in the suburbs (and thus part of the larger cultural community), or others, such as Latinos, working in Chinatown and living elsewhere, important factors when considering the ethnic character and cultural significance of Chinatown.

Notes

AAI   Asian Arts Initiative
AALDEF   Asian American Legal Defense and Education Fund
AAU   Asian Americans United
CCC&C   Chinese Christian Church and Center
DVRPC   Delaware Valley Regional Planning Commission
GPTMC   Greater Philadelphia Tourism and Marketing Corporation
HSP   Historical Society of Pennsylvania
NARA   National Archives and Records Administration, Mid Atlantic Branch
PCA   Philadelphia City Archives
PCDC   Philadelphia Chinatown Development Corporation
PCPC   Philadelphia City Planning Commission
PRA   Redevelopment Authority of Philadelphia
TUUA   Temple University Urban Archives

Preface

1. *Juk sing*, or *jook sing*, is a term derived from Cantonese slang that literally means "bamboo" or "hollow rod." The term is considered a derogatory term for American-born Chinese ("ABCs"), implying that the second and third generations have lost touch with their Chinese language and culture and are thus "hollow." Another analogy suggests that as water will not flow through bamboo, so too are these second and third generations imperfect conveyers of Chinese heritage.

Introduction

1. John Andrew Gallery, *The Planning of Center City Philadelphia* (Philadelphia: Center for Architecture, 2007), 35–39; Gregory L. Heller, "Salesman of Ideas: The Life Experiences That Shaped Edmund Bacon," in *Imagining Philadelphia: Edmund Bacon and the Future of the City*, ed. Scott Gabriel Knowles (Philadelphia: University of Pennsylvania Press, 2009),

29–31; and Christopher Klemek, *The Transatlantic Collapse of Urban Renewal: Postwar Urbanism from New York to Berlin* (Chicago: University of Chicago Press, 2011).

2. Chinese quarters or Chinatowns exist around the globe—throughout Southeast Asia, Europe, and Latin America—and map the movement of Chinese peoples' larger historical labor and trade flows. For overviews of Chinese diaspora and immigration to North America during the nineteenth century, see Iris Chang, *The Chinese in America: A Narrative History* (New York: Penguin Books, 2004); Roger Daniels, *Coming to America: A History of Immigration and Ethnicity in American Life* (New York: Harper Perennial, 2002); Dušanka Miščevic and Peter Kwong, *Chinese Americans: The Immigrant Experience* (Southport, CT: Hugh Lauter Levin Associates, 2000); Benson Tong, *The Chinese Americans* (Boulder: University Press of Colorado, 2003); Sucheng Chan, *Asian Americans: An Interpretive History* (Boston: Twayne, 1991); Peter Kwong and Dušanka Miščevič, *Chinese America: The Untold Story of America's Oldest New Community* (New York: New Press, 2005); and Shih-Shan Henry Tsai, *The Chinese Experience in America* (Bloomington: Indiana University Press, 1986). For the experience of Chinese in mining, see Liping Zhu, *A Chinaman's Chance: The Chinese on the Rocky Mountain Mining Frontier* (Niwot: University Press of Colorado, 1997).

3. On the great driving out and Chinese expulsion from the West and Asian exclusion, see Jean Pfaelzer, *Driven Out: The Forgotten War against Chinese Americans* (Berkeley: University of California Press, 2008); and Andrew Gyory, *Closing the Gate: Race, Politics, and the Chinese Exclusion Act* (Chapel Hill: University of North Carolina Press, 1998).

4. The increased concentration of Chinese in Chinatowns during this period is noted by, among others, Charlotte Brooks, *Alien Neighbors, Foreign Friends: Asian Americans, Housing, and the Transformation of Urban California* (Chicago: University of Chicago Press, 2009). Many other East Coast and midwestern Chinatowns had their beginnings during this period, such as St. Louis (1869), Chicago (1870), and Boston (1875).

5. Erika Lee, *At America's Gates: Chinese Immigration during the Exclusion Era, 1882–1943* (Chapel Hill: University of North Carolina Press, 2007); Estelle Lau, *Paper Families: Identity, Immigration Administration, and Chinese Exclusion* (Durham, NC: Duke University Press, 2006); and Lucy E. Salyer, *Laws Harsh as Tigers: Chinese Immigrants and the Shaping of Modern Immigration Law* (Chapel Hill: University of North Carolina Press, 1995). Nonmerchants had to prove they had at least $500 in personal property to travel to China and return to the United States.

6. On racial attitudes toward the "unassimilable" Chinese, see Gyory, *Closing the Gate*; and Najia Aarim-Heriot, *Chinese Immigrants, African Americans, and Racial Anxiety in the United States, 1848–82* (Urbana: University of Illinois Press, 2003). Naturalization for Chinese immigrants was made possible by the passage of the Magnuson Act in 1943. On the process of racially Othered European immigrants' "becoming white," see David Roediger, *The Wages of Whiteness* (New York: Verso, 2007); Noel Ignatiev, *How the Irish Became White* (London: Routledge, 1995); Matthew Frye Jacobson, *Whiteness of a Different Color* (Cambridge, MA: Harvard University Press, 1999); and Nell Irvin Painter, *The History of White People* (New York: Norton, 2011).

7. On immigration to Philadelphia as the workshop of the world, see Sam Bass Warner, *The Private City: Philadelphia in Three Periods of Its Growth* (Philadelphia: University of Pennsylvania Press, 1968); Russell F. Weigley, *Philadelphia: A 300-Year History* (New York: Norton, 1982); and Caroline Golab, *Immigrant Destinations* (Philadelphia: Temple University Press, 1977).

8. On the segregated experience of pre–World War II Chinatowns, see Nayan Shah, *Contagious Divides: Epidemics and Race in San Francisco's Chinatown* (Berkeley: University of California Press, 2001); Bernard P. Wong, *Chinatown, Economic Adaptation and Ethnic*

Identity of the Chinese (New York: Holt, Rinehart, and Winston, 1982); Xinyang Wang, *Surviving the City: The Chinese Immigrant Experience in New York City, 1890–1970* (Lanham, MD: Rowman and Littlefield, 2001); Victor Nee, *Longtime Californ': A Documentary Study of an American Chinatown* (New York: Pantheon Books, 1973); Huping Ling, *Chinese St. Louis: From Enclave to Cultural Community* (Philadelphia: Temple University Press, 2004); and Huping Ling, *Chinese Chicago: Race, Transnational Migration, and Community since 1870* (Stanford, CA: Stanford University Press, 2012).

9. On industrial growth and spatial/neighborhood transformation, see John Henry Hepp, *The Middle Class City: Transforming Space and Time in Philadelphia, 1876–1926* (Philadelphia: University of Pennsylvania Press, 2003); Warner, *The Private City*; and Weigley, *Philadelphia: A 300-Year History*. On immigration, neighborhood segregation, and racial ethnic patterns in Philadelphia, see Allen F. Davis and Mark H. Heller, eds., *The Peoples of Philadelphia: A History of Ethnic Groups and Lower-Class Life, 1790–1940* (1973; repr. Philadelphia: University of Pennsylvania Press, 1998); Golab, *Immigrant Destinations*; Murray Friedman, *Jewish Life in Philadelphia, 1830–1930* (Philadelphia: ISHI Publications, 1983); Rakhmiel Peltz, *From Immigrant to Ethnic Culture: American Yiddish in South Philadelphia* (Stanford, CA: Stanford University Press, 1998); Stefano Luconi, *From Paesani to White Ethnics: The Italian Experience in Philadelphia* (Albany: State University of New York Press, 2001); Richard N. Juliani, *Building Little Italy: Philadelphia's Italians before Mass Migration* (University Park: Pennsylvania State University Press, 1998); and Roger Lane, *William Dorsey's Philadelphia and Our Own: On the Past and Future of the Black City in America* (New York: Oxford University Press, 1991).

10. On Chinatown as a racialized product of the Western imaginary through landscape, see Kay J. Anderson, "The Idea of Chinatown: The Power of Place and Institutional Practice in the Making of a Racial Category," *Annals of the Association of American Geographers* 77, no. 4 (1987): 580–598; and Kay J. Anderson, *Vancouver's Chinatown: Racial Discourse in Canada, 1875–1980* (Montreal: McGill-Queen's University Press, 1991).

11. Orientalism is a style of thought based on ontological and epistemological distinctions made between "the Orient" and (most of the time) "the Occident." See Edward Said, *Orientalism* (New York: Vintage, 1979); Edward Said, "Orientalism Reconsidered," *Cultural Critique* 1 (Autumn 1985): 89–107; and Robert G. Lee, *Orientals: Asian Americans in Popular Culture* (Philadelphia: Temple University Press, 1999).

12. On Harlem as a cultural destination in the 1920s, see David Levering Lewis, *When Harlem Was in Vogue* (New York: Oxford University Press, 1989). The connection between Chinatown and Harlem has also been made by Brooks, *Alien Neighbors, Foreign Friends*.

13. The term "gilded ghetto" is used to describe San Francisco's Chinatown from the period 1945–2000 in Judy Yung, with the Chinese Historical Society of America, *San Francisco's Chinatown* (Charleston, SC: Arcadia Publishing, 2006).

14. For a discussion of Chinatown as an important launching point for Chinese American incorporation, see Min Zhou, *Chinatown: The Socioeconomic Potential of an Urban Enclave* (Philadelphia: Temple University Press, 1995). Ethnic enclaves have been widely studied, particularly in sociology. Enclaves function as important entry points for immigrants, offering employment and economic opportunity. See Mark Abrahamson, *Urban Enclaves: Identity and Place in America*, 2nd ed. (New York: Worth Publishers, 2005); John R. Logan, Wenquan Zhang, and Richard D. Alba, "Immigrant Enclaves and Ethnic Communities in New York and Los Angeles," *American Sociological Review* 67, no. 2 (April 2002): 299–322; and Alejandro Portes and Leif Jensen, "Disproving the Enclave Hypothesis: Reply," *American Sociological Review* 57, no. 3 (1992): 418–420. Recently enclaves have garnered attention as critics claim they impede or slow incorporation. See Jimy M. Sanders and Victor Nee, "Problems in Resolving the Enclave Economy Debate," *American Sociological*

Review 57, no. 3 (1992): 415–418; Jimy M. Sanders and Victor Nee, "Limits of Ethnic Solidarity in the Enclave Economy," *American Sociological Review* 52, no. 6 (1987): 745–773; Per-Anders Edin, Peter Fredriksson, and Olof Aslund, "Ethnic Enclaves and the Economic Success of Immigrants," *Quarterly Journal of Economics* 118, no. 1 (2003): 329–357; Natasha T. Duncan and Brigitte S. Waldorf, "Becoming a U.S. Citizen: The Role of Immigrant Enclaves," *Cityscape* 11, no. 3 (2009): 5–28; Stephanie Bohon, *Latinos in Ethnic Enclaves: Immigrant Workers and the Competition for Jobs* (New York: Garland, 2001); George Pierre Castile and Gilbert Kushner, eds., *Persistent Peoples: Ethnic Enclaves in Perspective* (Tucson: University of Arizona Press, 1982); and Charles F. Keyes, ed., "The Dialectics of Ethnic Change," in *Ethnic Change* (Seattle: University of Washington Press, 1981), 3–30.

15. Harry Margulis, "Asian Villages, Downtown Sanctuaries, Immigrant Reception Areas, and Festival Marketplaces," *Journal of Architectural Education* 45, no. 3 (1992): 150–160.

16. Lena Sze, "Opportunity, Conflict, and Communities in Transition: Historical and Contemporary Chinese Immigration to Philadelphia," in *Global Philadelphia: Immigrant Communities Old and New*, ed. Ayumi Takenaka and Mary Johnson Osirim (Philadelphia: Temple University Press, 2010), 96–120. On the diversification of Chinatowns with subsequent postwar immigration waves, see Hsiang-Shui Chen, *Chinatown No More* (Ithaca, NY: Cornell University Press, 1992); and Peter Kwong, *The New Chinatown* (New York: Hill and Wang, 1996).

17. The phenomenon of "satellite Chinatowns" is explored by Jan Lin, *Reconstructing Chinatown: Ethnic Enclave, Global Change* (Minneapolis: University of Minnesota Press, 1998). On Monterey Park, see Wei Li, "Building Ethnoburbia: The Emergence and Manifestation of the Chinese Ethnoburb in Los Angeles' San Gabriel Valley," *Journal of Asian American Studies* 2, no. 1 (1999): 1–28; Wei Li, "Ethnoburb versus Chinatown: Two Types of Urban Ethnic Communities in Los Angeles," *Cybergeo* 10 (1997): 1–12; and Timothy Fong, *The First Suburban Chinatown: The Remaking of Monterey Park, California* (Philadelphia: Temple University Press, 1994). The move of Asian immigrants in Brooklyn and Queens is documented by Kenneth J. Guest, "From Mott Street to East Broadway: Fuzhounese Immigrants and the Revitalization of New York's Chinatown," *Journal of Chinese Overseas* 7 (2011): 24–44; Christopher J. Smith, "Asian New York: The Geography and Politics of Diversity," *International Migration Review* 29, no. 1 (1995): 59–84; Logan, Alba, and Zhang, "Immigrant Enclaves and Ethnic Communities in New York and Los Angeles"; Xiaolan Bao, "Sweatshops in Sunset Park: A Variation of the Late 20th Century Chinese Garment Shops in New York City," *International Labor and Working-Class History* 61 (Spring 2002): 69–90; and Min Zhou and John R. Logan, "In and Out of Chinatown: Residential Mobility and Segregation of New York City's Chinese," *Social Forces* 70, no. 2 (1991): 387–407.

18. Bernard P. Wong, "Chinatowns around the World," in *Chinatowns around the World: Gilded Ghetto, Ethnopolis, and Cultural Diaspora*, ed. Bernard P. Wong and Tan Chee-Beng (Boston: Brill, 2013), 1–18; Kenneth J. Guest, "From Mott Street to East Broadway: Fuzhounese Immigrants and the Revitalization of New York's Chinatown," in Wong and Tan, *Chinatowns around the World*, 34–54; Huping Ling, "The New Trends in American Chinatowns: The Case of the Chinese in Chicago," in Wong and Tan, *Chinatowns around the World*, 55–94; Michel S. LaGuerre, *The Global Ethnopolis: Chinatown, Japantown, and Manilatown in American Society* (Basingstoke, UK: Macmillan Press, 2000); and Lin, *Reconstructing Chinatown*.

19. The term "ethnoburb" was coined by Wei Li in work on Monterey Park outside Los Angeles. The ethnoburb is a suburban ethnic cluster of residential areas and business districts in which one ethnic minority group has a significant concentration but does not

necessarily compose a majority. The ethnoburb joins features of the urban enclave and the suburb, often part of communities that lack a specific ethnic identity. Increasingly, ethnoburbs are important new "ports of entry" for immigrants. See Li, "Building Ethnoburbia," 1–28; and Li, "Ethnoburb versus Chinatown," 1–12. Li introduces "ethno-spectrum" in "Beyond Chinatown, Beyond Enclave: Reconceptualizing Contemporary Chinese Settlements in the United States," *GeoJournal* 64 (2005): 31–40.

20. Ruth Mayer, "Introduction: A 'Bit of Orient Set Down in the Heart of a Western Metropolis': The Chinatown in the United States and Europe," in *Chinatowns in a Transnational World: Myths and Realities of an Urban Phenomenon*, ed. Vanessa Künnemann and Ruth Mayer (London: Routledge: 2011), 1–25; Wong and Tan, *Chinatowns around the World*. The idea of "survivance" which draws on notions of survival and endurance as well as struggle, is borrowed from the Native American studies context; see Gerald Vizenor, *Manifest Manners: Narratives on Postindian Survivance* (Lincoln: University of Nebraska Press, 1999); and Sonya Atalay, "No Sense of the Struggle: Creating a Context for Survivance at the National Museum of the American Indian," in *The National Museum of the American Indian: Critical Conversations*, ed. Amy Lonetree and Amanda J. Cobb (Lincoln: University of Nebraska Press, 2008), 267–289.

21. Susan Nakoaka, "Cultivating a Cultural Home Space: The Case of Little Tokyo's Budokan of Los Angeles Project," *aapi nexus* 10, no. 2 (2012): 23–36. On memory as a grounds for claims to space, see Dolores Hayden, *The Power of Place: Urban Landscapes as Public History* (Cambridge, MA: MIT Press, 1997).

22. On constructivist ideas of ethnicity, the seminal work is by Fredrik Barth, *Ethnic Groups and Boundaries: The Social Organization of Culture Difference* (1969; repr. Boston: Little, Brown, 1991). According to Barth, ethnicity is the creation and maintenance of a boundary, "not the cultural stuff it encloses." See also Joane Nagel, "Constructing Ethnicity: Creating and Recreating Ethnic Identity and Culture," *Social Problems* 41, no. 1 (February 1994): 152–176. Norma Alarcon has suggested in lieu of difference "identity in difference," a kind of "tactical subjectivity" that also resonates with interactional, constructivist ideas of ethnicity; see "Conjugating Subjects in the Age of Multiculturalism," in *Mapping Multiculturalism*, ed. Avery Gordon and Christopher Newfield (Minneapolis: University of Minnesota Press, 1996), 127–148.

23. "Ethnoscape" is a term coined by Arjun Appadurai to describe neighborhood landscapes within globalized cities as a dimension of global cultural flows; an ethnoscape is a "landscape of persons who constitute the shifting world in which we live: tourists, immigrants, refugees, exiles, guest workers and other moving groups." Like other landscapes, ethnoscapes are "perspectival constructs" that are "inflected by the situatedness of different sorts of actors." Arjun Appadurai, *Modernity at Large: Cultural Dimensions of Globalization* (Minneapolis: University of Minnesota Press, 1996), 33–48. In the case of Chinatowns, the transnational nature of landscape and spatial use predates the contemporary period of globalization.

24. Jan Lin, *The Power of Urban Ethnic Places: Cultural Heritage and Community Life* (London: Routledge, 2011), 31.

25. Stephen Shaw, Susan Bagwell, and Joanna Karmowska, "Ethnoscape as Spectacle: Reimaging Multicultural Districts as New Destinations for Leisure and Tourism Consumption," *Urban Studies* 41, no. 10 (2004): 1983.

26. On the material manifestation of language, see Jennifer Leeman and Gabriella Modan, "Selling the City: Language, Ethnicity and Commodified Space," in *Linguistic Landscape in the City* (Bristol, UK: Multilingual Matters, 2010), 182; and Jennifer Leeman and Gabriella Modan, "Commodified Language in Chinatown: A Contextualized Approach to Linguistic Landscape," *Journal of Sociolinguistics* 13, no. 3 (2009): 332–362.

27. David Chuenyuan Lai, "The Visual Character of Chinatowns," *Places* 7, no. 1 (1990): 29–31. On the rebuilding and transformation of Chinatown after the 1906 earthquake, see Brooks, *Alien Neighbors, Foreign Friends*; and Erica Pan, *The Impact of the 1906 Earthquake on San Francisco's Chinatown* (New York: P. Lang, 1995). Mayer notes the global reach of this visual paradigm in Chinatowns across the world; Mayer, "Introduction," 1–25.

28. On ethnic neighborhood as urban territory, see Dolores Hayden, "Using Ethnic History to Understand Urban Landscapes," *Places* 7, no. 1 (1990): 11–17. On the creation of ethnic-specific places and territories in urban environments, see James Rojas, "The Enacted Environment: Examining the Streets and Yards of East Los Angeles," in *Everyday America: Cultural Landscape Studies after J.B. Jackson*, ed. Chris Wilson and Paul Groth (Berkeley: University of California Press, 2003), 275–292; Joseph Sciorra and Martha Cooper, "'I Feel Like I'm in My Country': Puerto Rican Casitas in New York City," *TDR* 34, no. 4 (1990): 156–168; Luis Aponte-Parés, "Casitas Place and Culture: Appropriating Place in Puerto Rican Barrios," *Places* 11, no. 1 (1997): 52–61; Arlene Dávila, *Barrio Dreams: Puerto Ricans, Latinos, and the Neoliberal City* (Berkeley: University of California Press, 2004); Jerome Krase, "The Spatial Semiotics of Little Italies and Italian Americans," in *Industry, Technology, Labor and the Italian American Communities*, ed. Mario Aste, Jerome Krase, Louise Napolitano-Carman, et al. (New York: American Italian Historical Association, 1997), 98–127; Ray Hutchinson and Jerome Krase, eds., *Ethnic Landscapes in an Urban World* (Oxford: Elsevier, 2007); Jerome Krase, "Visualizing Ethnic Vernacular Landscapes," in *Race and Ethnicity in New York City*, ed. Jerome Krase and Ray Hutchinson (Oxford: Elsevier, 2004), 1–24; and Elizabeth Chacko and Ivan Cheung, "The Formation of a Contemporary Ethnic Enclave: The Case of 'Little Ethiopia' in Los Angeles," in *Race, Ethnicity, and Place in a Changing America*, ed. John W. Frazier and Eugene Tettey-Fio (Albany: State University of New York Press [Global Academic Publishing], 2006), 131–134.

29. Setha Low writes extensively on the components of place making and of "place attachment," the affective relationship between people and landscape often rooted in experience, creating place as a "meaningful location." See Irwin Altman and Setha Low, eds., *Place Attachment* (New York: Plenum Publishing, 1992). The intimate experience of a neighborhood or environment, imbued with memory and sentiment, is a fundamental component of place, according to Yi-Fu Tuan; see *Space and Place: The Perspective of Experience* (Minneapolis: University of Minnesota Press, 1977), 161–178.

30. David Glassberg, *Sense of History: The Place of the Past in American Life* (Amherst: University of Massachusetts Press, 2001); and Kathleen Gerson, C. Anne Steuve, and Claude S. Fischer, "Attachments to Place," in *Networks and Places: Social Relations in the Urban Setting*, ed. Claude S. Fischer, Robert Max Jackson, Anne Steuve, et al. (New York: Free Press, 1977), 139–161. "History is the essence of the idea of place," manifest in landscape, which inherently expresses a point of view or perspective, according to Henry Glassie, *Passing the Time in Ballymenone* (Philadelphia: University of Pennsylvania Press, 1982), 664. On other cultural constructions of place and time, see Steven Feld and Keith H. Basso, eds., *Senses of Place* (Santa Fe, NM: School of American Research Press, 1996); and John Brinckerhoff Jackson, *A Sense of Place, a Sense of Time* (New Haven, CT: Yale University Press, 1994). On the embodiment of family and community memory in Chinatown commercial spaces, see Sojin Kim, "Curiously Familiar: Art and Curio Stores in Los Angeles' Chinatown," *Western Folklore* 58, no. 2 (1999): 131–147.

31. Debbie Wei, comment at "Chinatown Past and Present," Historical Society of Pennsylvania (HSP), November 8, 2012.

32. The term "memoryscape" emerges from the work of Toby Butler in mapping and preserving the memories of place in London. Other iterations of the term include "global

memoryscape," an addition to Appadurai's "-scapes" of globalization, as a landscape in which "memories and memory practices move, come into contact, and are contested by and contest other forms of remembrance"; Kendall R. Phillips and G. Mitchell Reyes, eds., *Global Memoryscapes: Contesting Remembrance in a Transnational Age* (Tuscaloosa: University of Alabama Press, 2011), 13–14.

33. Henri Lefebvre, *The Production of Space* (1984; repr. London: Blackwell, 1994); and Setha Low, *On the Plaza: The Politics of Public Space and Culture* (Austin: University of Texas Press, 2000). On the erasure of African American memoryscapes in Savannah during the period of urban renewal, see W. Fitzhugh Brundage, *The Southern Past: A Clash of Race and Memory* (Cambridge, MA: Belknap Press of Harvard University Press, 2005). The classic study of the negative effects of urban renewal on community memory is Herbert Gans, *The Urban Villagers* (New York: Free Press, 1982). On the reconstruction and commemoration of urban ethnic memoryscapes through public history, see Hayden, *The Power of Place*.

34. Deborah G. Martin, "'Place-Framing' as Place-Making: Constituting a Neighborhood for Organizing and Activism," *Annals of the Association of American Geographers* 93, no. 3 (2003): 730–750.

35. The emphasis on the black/white binary has been pointed out by Clement Lai, "The Racial Triangulation of Space: The Case of Urban Renewal in San Francisco's Fillmore District," *Annals of the Association of American Geographers* 102, no. 1 (2012): 153–154; and David Diaz, *Barrio Urbanism: Chicanos, Planning, and American Cities* (New York: Routledge, 2005).

36. Asian American activism, particularly during the period of the student movement, focused on improving conditions within urban neighborhoods and combating state-driven processes negatively affecting Asian residents, particularly eviction issues. See Estella Habal, *San Francisco's International Hotel: Mobilizing the Filipino American Community in the Anti-eviction Movement* (Philadelphia: Temple University Press, 2007); Michael Liu and Kim Geron, "Changing Neighborhood: Ethnic Enclaves and the Struggle for Social Justice," *Social Justice* 35, no. 2 (2008): 18–35; and Michael Liu and Kim Geron, "Against the Tide: Mobilization and Community Planning in Asian Ethnic Enclaves," in *Urban Spaces: Planning and Struggles for Land and Community*, ed. James Jennings and Julia Sheron Jordan-Zachery (Lanham, MD: Lexington Books, 2010), 39–53. See Chapter 3 for a discussion of some of these campaigns.

37. Thomas Sugrue, *The Origins of the Urban Crisis: Race and Inequality in Postwar Detroit* (Princeton: Princeton University Press, 1998). On slum clearance and public housing in Philadelphia and other cities, see John F. Bauman, *Public Housing, Race, and Renewal: Urban Planning in Philadelphia, 1950–1970* (Philadelphia: Temple University Press, 1987); Robert B. Fairbanks, *The War on Slums in the Southwest: Public Housing and Slum Clearance in Texas, Arizona, and New Mexico* (Philadelphia: Temple University Press, 2014); June Manning Thomas, *Redevelopment and Race: Planning a Finer City in Postwar Detroit* (Baltimore: Johns Hopkins University Press, 1997); and Arnold R. Hirsch, *Making the Second Ghetto: Race and Housing in Chicago, 1940–1960* (Chicago: University of Chicago Press, 2004).

38. Roger D. Simon and Brian Alnutt, "Philadelphia, 1982–2007: Toward the Postindustrial City," *Pennsylvania Magazine of History and Biography*, 131, no. 4 (2007): 395–444; Doug Hassebroek, "Philadelphia's Post-War Moment," *Perspecta* 30 (1999): 84–91; and Carolyn Adams, David Bartelt, David Elesh, et al., *Philadelphia: Neighborhoods, Division, and Conflict in a Postindustrial City* (Philadelphia: Temple University Press, 1991). On Latino/black migration into changing neighborhoods and Puerto Ricans as "displaced

labor migrants," see Carmen Whalen, *From Puerto Rico to Philadelphia: Puerto Rican Workers and Postwar Economies* (Philadelphia: Temple University Press, 2001).

39. On neighborhood and community resistance to demolition and urban renewal in other cities, see Gregory Crowley, *The Politics of Place: Contentious Urban Redevelopment in Pittsburgh* (Pittsburgh: University of Pittsburgh Press, 2005); Christopher Mele, *Selling the Lower East Side: Culture, Real Estate, and Resistance in New York City* (Minneapolis: University of Minnesota Press, 2000); Anthony Flint, *Wrestling with Moses* (New York: Random House, 2009); Samuel Zipp, *Manhattan Projects: The Rise and Fall of Urban Renewal in Cold War New York* (Oxford: Oxford University Press, 2010); Peter Medoff, *Streets of Hope: The Fall and Rise of an Urban Neighborhood* (Cambridge, MA: South End Press, 1999); Chester W. Hartman, *Yerba Buena: Land Grab and Community Resistance in San Francisco* (San Francisco: Glide Publications, 1974); and Mandi Isaacs Jackson, *Model City Blues: Urban Space and Organized Resistance in New Haven* (Philadelphia: Temple University Press, 2008).

40. In Philadelphia, resistance to urban renewal was also manifest in Society Hill against I-95 and in the Queen Village/South Street area against a proposed Crosstown Expressway; see Klemek, *The Transatlantic Collapse of Urban Renewal*. On opposition to gentrification in Queen Village, see P. A. Levy and R. A. Cybriwsky, "The Hidden Dimensions of Culture and Class: Philadelphia," in *Back to the City: Issues in Neighborhood Revitalization*, ed. S. B. Laska and Daphne Spain (New York: Pergamon, 1980), 138–155.

41. Andrew Feffer, "Show Down in Center City: Staging Redevelopment and Citizenship in Bicentennial Philadelphia," *Journal of Urban History* 30, no. 6 (2004): 792. The "symbolic economy" of the city is discussed by Sharon Zukin, *The Culture of Cities* (Cambridge: Blackwell, 1995); and David Harvey, "From Space to Place and Back Again: Reflections on the Condition of Postmodernity," in *Mapping the Futures: Local Cultures, Global Change*, ed. Jon Bird, Barry Curtis, Tim Putnam, et al. (London: Routledge, 1993): 4–25.

42. On Chinatowns as markers of globalized cities, see Künnemann and Mayer, *Chinatowns in a Transnational World*, particularly Rosemary Sales with Panos Hatziprokopiou, Alessio D'Angelo, and Xia Lin, "London's Chinatown and the Changing Shape of the Chinese Diaspora," 198–216; and Flemming Christiansen, "Chinatowns in Transition: Between Ethnic Enclave and Global Emblem," 217–232. Jerome Hodos notes the importance of international migration to the creation of the global city and has attributed Philadelphia's Chinatown's political clout to its role in supporting the city's aspirations in this regard; Hodos, *Second Cities: Globalization and Local Politics in Manchester and Philadelphia* (Philadelphia: Temple University Press, 2011), 73–98. As Ching Lin Pang points out, however, Chinatowns, at least in Europe, function differently in the urban symbolic economy and develop along divergent trajectories, depending on the embeddedness of ethnic entrepreneurs within a diasporic community of immigrants, the strength of community institutions, and the degree of government intervention, often through architectural redevelopment, in the local ethnic economy, among other factors. See Pang, "Gateways to the Urban Economy: Chinatowns in Antwerp and Brussels," in *Selling Ethnic Neighborhoods: The Rise of Neighborhoods as Places of Leisure and Consumption*, ed. Volkan Aytar and Jan Rath (New York: Routledge, 2012), 52–67.

43. "Place-making" promotes urban renewal through creative arts and culture activities that animate and revitalize urban spaces, often through temporary projects, such as pop-up parks and other microevents or attractions. Placemaking is governed by eleven principles, including the need for community input; an emphasis on collaborative partnerships, particularly between public and private entities; a focus on enhancing local assets; and an incremental approach that starts small and builds over time; see "Eleven Principles

for Creating Great Community Spaces," http://www.pps.org/reference/11steps/ (accessed December 4, 2014). Placemaking has most recently been promoted by the Project for Public Spaces, a New York–based "nonprofit planning, design, and educational organization dedicated to helping people create and sustain public spaces that build stronger communities" (see http://www.pps.org/about/; accessed December 4, 2014). The National Endowment for the Arts has made "creative placemaking" a grantmaking priority, which it defines as "public, private, not-for-profit, and community sectors partner[ing] to strategically shape the physical and social character of a neighborhood, town, tribe, city, or region around arts and cultural activities" (see http://arts.gov/NEARTS/2012v3-arts-and-culture-core/defining-creative-placemaking; accessed December 4, 2014). The concept is explored further in Ann Markusen and Anne Gadwa, "Creative Placemaking," National Endowment for the Arts White Paper, Executive Summary, http://arts.gov/sites/default/files/Creative Placemaking-Paper.pdf (accessed December 4, 2014). In 2013 and 2014, the NEA funded Philadelphia-area placemaking projects under the initiative "Our Town" (see http://arts.gov/national/our-town; accessed December 4, 2014) and "ArtPlace" (see http://www.artplaceamerica.org/; accessed December 4, 2014). The Asian Arts Initiative, partnering with the Center for Architecture, received an NEA Art Place grant in 2014 for $644,855 for the project "Pearl Street + Design Philadelphia PopUp Place," a collaboration with artist Walter Hood to mount a series of weekly microevents along a block of Pearl Street behind the AAI building, as part of its Chinatown North Social Practice Lab; see http://www.artplaceamerica.org/grants/pearl-street-designphiladelphia-popup-place/ (accessed December 4, 2014).

44. On placemaking versus placekeeping (a term coined by Jenny Lee, executive director of Allied Media Projects, a Detroit-based community media network), see Roberto Bedoya, "Spatial Justice, Rasquachification, Race, and the City," http://creativetimereports.org/2014/09/15/spatial-justice-rasquachification-race-and-the-city/ (accessed September 24, 2104). Bedoya advocates a practice of placemaking "not as a development strategy but as a series of actions that build spatial justice, healthy communities, and sites of imaginations," in Bedoya, "Placemaking and the Politics of Belonging and Dis-belonging," *GIA Reader* 24, no. 1 (2013), http://www.giarts.org/article/placemaking-and-politics-belonging-and-dis-belonging (accessed November 30, 2014). "Spatial justice" is the "fair and equitable distribution in space of socially valued resources and the opportunities to use them," according to Edward W. Soja, "The City and Social Justice," *justice spatiale*/spatial justice, no. 1 (September 2009), http://www.jssj.org (accessed November 30, 2014). Soja further explores the theory of spatial justice, including Lefebvre's complementary "right to the city" and "right to difference," in *Seeking Spatial Justice* (Minneapolis: University of Minnesota Press, 2010), 99. The idea of spatial justice acknowledges the spatial components of inequality in processes of urbanization and the distributional inequalities that emerge, often as the net effect of "normalized" urban development processes; see David Harvey, *Social Justice and the City* (Athens: University of Georgia Press, 2009); and David Harvey, "The Right to the City," *New Left Review* 53 (2008): 23–40.

45. By "neoliberalism," I refer to the move, since the 1970s, away from Fordist/Keynesian approaches to governance and economy toward the privatization of public services, deregulation, competition, and the commodification of urban space. In the context of cities, which have increasingly become centers of neoliberal discourse and strategies, urban-development approaches emphasize the necessity of private capital and market solutions, engendering "interlocality competition" through place commodification and marketing and cultural entrepreneurialism. This approach could be said to characterize the work of many CDCs, PCDC included, if only by necessity, as well as various heritage and cultural tourism ventures. Neil Brenner and Nik Theodore, "Cities and the Geographies

of 'Actually Existing Neoliberalism,'" *Antipode* 34, no. 3 (2002): 349–379; Johana Londoño and Arlene Dávila, "Introduction to Special Volume," *Identities: Global Studies in Culture and Power* 17, no. 5 (2010): 455–457; Lena Sze, "Chinatown Then and Neoliberal Now: Gentrification Consciousness and the Ethnic-Specific Museum," *Identities: Global Studies in Culture and Power* 17, no. 5 (2010): 510–529; Neil Brenner and Nik Theodore, *Spaces of Neoliberalism: Urban Restructuring in North America and Western Europe* (Oxford: Blackwell, 2002); Christopher Mele, "Casinos, Prisons, Incinerators and Other Fragments of Neoliberal Urban Development," *Social Science History* 35, no. 3 (2011): 423–452; and Dávila, *Barrio Dreams*.

46. This risk and its effects have been most studied in regard to Latino communities and urban design; see Johana Londoño, "Latino Design in an Age of Neoliberal Multiculturalism: Contemporary Changes in Latin/o American Urban Cultural Representation," *Identities: Global Studies in Culture and Power* 17, no. 5 (2010): 487–509; Arlene Dávila, "Empowered Culture? New York City's Empowerment Zone and the Selling of El Barrio," *Annals of the American Academy of Political and Social Science* 594 (2004): 49–64; Dávila, *Barrio Dreams*; and Frederick Wherry, *The Philadelphia Barrio* (Chicago: University of Chicago Press, 2011). Londoño notes the confluence of multiculturalism and neoliberalism and the "ways multicultural reform in design practice deploys an identity politics that curtails struggles for justice and, in the case of Latino New Urbanism, elides the racial and economic inequality and working-class practices by which the aesthetics and spatiality of the Latino urban environment materialize."

47. Huping Ling, "Reconceptualizing Chinese American Community in St. Louis: From Chinatown to Cultural Community," *Journal of American Ethnic History* 24, no. 2 (2005): 65–101; and Ling, *Chinese St. Louis*. On Chinatown as a "crucial element" in the construction of a Chinese diaspora, see Sales, Hatsiprokopiou, D'Angelo, and Lin, "London's Chinatown and the Changing Shape of the Chinese Diaspora," in *Chinatowns in a Transnational World*, 198–216.

Chapter 1

Acknowledgment: Portions of this text were previously published as "From Bachelor Enclave to Urban Village: The Evolution of Early Chinatown," *Pennsylvania Legacies* 12, no. 2 (November 2012): 12–17.

1. *North American*, November 9, 1876.

2. Thomas Scharf and Thompson Westcott, *History of Philadelphia, 1609–1884* (Philadelphia: L. H. Everts, 1884); and Chi-Chen Loh, "Americans of Chinese Ancestry in Philadelphia," Ph.D. diss., University of Pennsylvania, 1944.

3. On the great driving out and Chinese expulsion from the West and Asian exclusion, see Jean Pfaelzer, *Driven Out: The Forgotten War against Chinese Americans* (Berkeley: University of California Press, 2008); and Andrew Gyory, *Closing the Gate: Race, Politics, and the Chinese Exclusion Act* (Chapel Hill: University of North Carolina Press, 1998).

4. *Tenth Census of the United States*, 1880, Philadelphia Ward 10.

5. Stewart Culin, *China in America: A Study in the Social Life of the Chinese in the Eastern Cities of the United States* (Philadelphia, 1887). On Beaver Falls strikebreakers, see Edward Rhoads, "Asian Pioneers in the Eastern United States: Chinese Cutlery Workers in Beaver Falls, Pennsylvania, in the 1870s," *Journal of Asian American Studies* 2, no. 2 (1999): 119–155; and Edward Rhoads, "'White Labor' vs. 'Coolie Labor': The 'Chinese Question' in Pennsylvania in the 1870s," *Journal of American Ethnic History* 21, no. 2 (Winter 2002): 3–33. The account of Captain John Hervey is mentioned in John Kuo Wei Tchen, "Here

the Struggles Truly Are Local: Philadelphia's Feisty Chinatown," in *Chinatown Lives: Oral Histories from Philadelphia's Chinatown*, ed. Lena Sze (Philadelphia: Asian Arts Initiative and New City Community Press, 2004), 11. The movement of Chinese from the Pacific Coast to Philadelphia was noted by San Francisco's *Evening Bulletin* in an article called, "Chinese in Philadelphia," June 25, 1884.

6. *Tenth Census of the United States*, 1880, Philadelphia; *Twelfth Census of the United States*, 1900, Philadelphia, Chinatown specifics for Ward 10. See Table A.2 in the Appendix.

7. Stewart Culin, "Social Organization of the Chinese in America," *American Anthropologist*, October 1891, 348. This account is at odds with the 1880 Census, which lists no Chinese on the 900 block of Race. According to the 1880 Census, 913 Race was occupied by a German American family named Perpente, a household that included husband, wife, daughter, boarder, and one servant. This block in 1880 was inhabited by single families, most with servants and one or two boarders, all of them of German or Irish American ethnicity. In the surrounding area, Hang Lee and Hong Kee ran a laundry nearby at 836 Arch Street. Quong Kee ran another with four boarders/laundryworkers at 159 North Ninth Street, according to the listing. All were young Chinese men in their early twenties. North Ninth and Tenth Streets were primarily boardinghouses. It was not unheard of during the 1880s for Chinese laundrymen to be listed at addresses where residents of other ethnicities were also listed. Perhaps the laundry was part of a ground-floor retail space that the Perpentes lived above, although this is unlikely. It is unclear how the two accounts can be reconciled, however, and more research is needed. By 1900, 913 Race was clearly part of a mostly Chinese block, home to Yet Ling, grocer, and Kee Lee, restaurant proprietor, as well as at least six other Chinese men who worked as grocers, waiters, or cooks. *Twelfth Census of the United States*, 1900, Philadelphia Ward 10. The loss of the 1890 Census sadly prevents any understanding of how this block changed between 1880 and 1900. Also cited in Grace S. H. Chao Auyung, "Structural and Processual Change in Philadelphia's Chinatown and Among Suburban Chinese," Ph.D. diss., Temple University, 1978, 3–5.

8. By the 1850s, Eighth Street, particularly from Arch to Walnut Streets (as well as adjoining Ninth and Tenth Streets), emerged as a major center for dress goods, hosiery and trimming stores, and millinery and dressmaking shops. George Foster noted the development of this district in 1850 in "Philadelphia in Slices," *Pennsylvania Magazine of History and Biography* 93, no. 1 (1969): 29.

9. *Tenth Census of the United States*, 1880, Philadelphia.

10. On immigration to Philadelphia as the workshop of the world, see Sam Bass Warner, *The Private City: Philadelphia in Three Periods of Its Growth* (Philadelphia: University of Pennsylvania Press, 1968); Russell F. Weigley, *Philadelphia: A 300-Year History* (New York: Norton, 1982); and Caroline Golab, *Immigrant Destinations* (Philadelphia: Temple University Press, 1977). On the patterns of immigrant labor, see Caroline Golab, "The Immigrant and the City: Poles, Italians and Jews in Philadelphia, 1870–1920," in *The Peoples of Philadelphia: A History of Ethnic Groups and Lower-Class Life, 1790–1940*, ed. Allen F. Davis and Mark H. Heller (1973; repr. Philadelphia: University of Pennsylvania Press, 1998), 203–230. Among immigrant groups to Philadelphia, only Jews and Arabs were more likely to engage in nonmanufacturing during this period, often working as hucksters, peddlers, and shopkeepers.

11. *Tenth Census of the United States*, 1880, Philadelphia Ward 10. Boardinghouses for Irish and native-born dressmakers, tailors, cutters, and seamstresses dominated the 1000 block of Race and Eleventh Street; *Twelfth Census of the United States*, 1900, Philadelphia Ward 10. In 1900, Ninth Street also was home to an Italian barber and his brothers. North of Vine Street, a small Jewish enclave formed around Nobel and Callowhill Streets.

12. Ninth Street was a good example of this immigrant diversity: French, Italian, Chinese, and Irish all lived next to one another. The 900 block of Winter was likewise diverse: a Swedish dressmaker, a German waitress, a Mexican electrician, a German painter, and a family of Ukrainian bakers (who also housed a Ukrainian fireman) made their homes there in 1900. *Fourteenth Census of the United States*, 1920, Philadelphia Ward 10. By 1910, Greek boardinghouses were established on Providence Court; *Thirteenth Census of the United States*, 1910, Philadelphia Ward 10. North Tenth was home to boardinghouses for Russians and Lithuanians and a boardinghouse kept by a Spanish-Mexican couple housing Mexican laborers. The 1000 block of Winter Street consisted of single homes for Lithuanian families headed by a cook, a teacher, a mechanic, and a laborer. In the *Fourteenth Census of the United States*, 1920, several boardinghouses for Albanian, Lithuanian, Russian, and Slovak laborers were located at 1012, 1010, and 1008 Race. These interethnic spatial proximities and relationships were not uncommon in working-class neighborhoods of this period; see John Kuo Wei Tchen, *New York before Chinatown: Orientalism and the Shaping of American Culture, 1776–1882* (Baltimore: Johns Hopkins University Press, 1999), 74–95; and Ivan Light, *Ethnic Enterprise in America: Business and Welfare among Chinese, Japanese, and Blacks* (Berkeley: University of California Press, 1972), 85–86.

13. 1875 Hopkins Philadelphia Atlas; 1858–1860 Philadelphia Atlas, Hexamer and Locher.

14. Mark Haller, "Recurring Themes," in Davis and Heller, *The Peoples of Philadelphia*, 283.

15. 1895 Bromley Philadelphia Atlas.

16. Mark Haller, "Recurring Themes," 283–284.

17. Joseph Eng interview, by Jianshe Wang, June 19, 1997, Balch Institute Chinatown Oral History Project, HSP Balch Collection.

18. Nayan Shah, *Contagious Divides: Epidemics and Race in San Francisco's Chinatown* (Berkeley: University of California Press, 2001).

19. Christopher Lee Yip, "Association, Residence, and Shop: An Appropriation of Commercial Blocks in North American Chinatowns," in *Gender, Class, and Shelter: Perspectives in Vernacular Architecture V*, ed. Elizabeth C. Cromley and Carter L. Hudgins (Knoxville: University of Tennessee Press, 1995), 109–117; Christopher Lee Yip, "A Chinatown of Gold Mountain: The Chinese in Locke, California," in *Images of an American Land: Vernacular Architecture in the Western United States*, ed. Thomas Carter (Albuquerque: University of New Mexico Press, 1997), 53–172; and Christopher Lee Yip, "California Chinatowns: Built Environments Expressing the Hybridized Culture of Chinese Americans," in *Hybrid Urbanism: On the Identity Discourse and the Built Environment*, ed. Nezar AlSayyad (Westport, CT: Praeger, 2001), 67–82. On the interior arrangement of Chinese laundries, see Paul C. P. Siu, *The Chinese Laundryman: A Study in Social Isolation*, ed. John Kuo Wei Tchen (New York: New York University Press, 1987), 58–63, which describes a familiar pattern of working/sleeping space.

20. Culin, *China in America*.

21. Wone Wing, DM, case 1999C, M1144 Case files of Chinese immigrants, 1900–1923, District 4 INS, Reel 30, National Archives and Records Administration, Mid Atlantic Branch (NARA).

22. Ibid.

23. 916C. Moy Sam, DL, Case files of Chinese immigrants, 1900–1923, District 4 INS, Reel 12, NARA.

24. Hong Fook Company, 1008 Race, imported Chinese merchandise and Japanese fancy goods and sold art and fancy goods to "every big department store in Philadelphia." John M. Stoner, a merchant at 1115 Front Street, bought goods from Quon Yick Co. and

resold them, selling groceries to the firm in turn. 1975C. Tom Sum Wah, DM, M1144 Case files of Chinese immigrants, 1900–1923, District 4 INS, Reel 27, NARA. Frank Stanley, a salesman at 429 Market Street, sold ducking and flannel to Young Gaw. 1990C. Young Gaw, DM, M1144 Case files of Chinese immigrants, 1900–1923, District 4 INS, Reel 30, NARA. In 1913, San Fat rented 914 Race from Lit Brothers. Others had relationships with other businessmen in the immediate area, revealed in immigration-case testimonies. Immigrating Chinese were required by law to provide two non-Chinese, white witnesses to testify on their behalf. In many cases, the whites Chinese knew were those with whom they had commercial relationships, illustrating these networks. In 1909, for example, Lee Num Yet, member of Sang Fat and Company, 914 Race Street, called on the butcher at Twelfth and Arch Streets and the owner of a hardware store at 18 North Eleventh Street to testify on his behalf. 1295C. Lee Jon, minor son, M1144 Case files of Chinese immigrants, 1900–1923, District 4 INS, Reel 48, NARA. Dong Gook, from Kwon Wo Lung Company, 934 Race, asked neighbors Frank Du Bois, bookkeeper at 147 North Tenth Street, and Davis Forman, cigar manufacturer, Tenth and Race, to vouch for him when he applied to return to China in 1913. Tobacconist J. A. Mayer at 905 Race Street frequently testified for his best customers in the neighborhood. 1991C. Dong Gook, DM, M1144 Case files of Chinese immigrants, 1900–1923, District 4 INS, Reel 27, NARA. This pattern of interethnic interaction and economic interdependence has been noted by Shirley J. Yee, "Dependency and Opportunity: Socioeconomic Relations between Chinese and Non-Chinese in New York City, 1870–1943," *Journal of Urban History* 33 (2007): 254–276; Tchen, *New York before Chinatown*, 74–95; and Light, *Ethnic Enterprise in America*, 85–86.

25. Wong Lin, RM, 402C, M1144 Case files of Chinese immigrants, 1900–1923, District 4 INS, Reel 5, NARA. The partners of Tuck Wah occupied 906 Race Street, managed by a collection of Youngs: Young Chung, Young Ling, Young Sam, Young Wah, Young Bing, and Young Fook. In this four-story building, the ground floor was the storefront, the second floor was a storage room in the back, the front room was rented to the Young Company "for a club room," and the third floor was occupied by partner Young Wah and his family. The fourth floor was used by members of the store "as a sleeping room," and the attic was "rented to Chinese as a Sunday meeting room." Wing Hung Lung and Company, dealer in "teas, chinese silks, stone carvings, bric-a-brac and groceries," run by the Mark family at 933 Race, rented its third and fourth floors in 1907 to the Hip Sing Tong and the Louie Company, respectively. The second floor was "sublet to Chinese for club room purposes." Mark Wing, DM 800C, M1144 Case files of Chinese immigrants, 1900–1923, District 4 INS, Reel 10, NARA; 1327C. Mark Chin Foo, minor son of Mark Du[e], merchant at 933 Race Street Wing Hing Lung Company; "at the present time stock of said store is confined to teas, Chinese silks, stone carvings, bric-a-brac and groceries."

26. Lim Quen, DL, 883C. M1144 Case files of Chinese immigrants, 1900–1923, District 4 INS, Reel 12, NARA.

27. To legally be in the United States and travel back and forth to China, persons had to be merchants and/or possess $1,000 in personal wealth. Like laundries, shares in partnerships frequently changed hands, and some businesses dissolved and relocated with new names as a matter of routine.

28. *Thirteenth Census of the United States*, 1910, Philadelphia, Ward 10. In 1910: 907 Race Street, eighteen men; 909 Race Street, fifteen men; 911 Race Street, fourteen men; 915 Race Street, sixteen men; 917 Race Street, fourteen men; 919 Race Street, eighteen men; 931 Race Street, thirteen men.

29. *Thirteenth Census of the United States*, 1910, Philadelphia, Ward 1. Paul C. Siu, *The Chinese Laundryman: A Study of Social Isolation* (New York: New York University Press, 1987), 92–96. On *jinshanzhuang*, or "Gold Mountain Firms," that sold Chinese goods

wholesale and retail to Chinese living abroad, see Madeline Y. Hsu, *Dreaming of Gold, Dreaming of Home: Transnationalism and Migration between the United States and South China, 1882–1943* (Stanford, CA: Stanford University Press, 2000), 36–40. These firms were often run by kinsmen or people from the same village and thus also had connections to the *huiguan* family or regional benevolent associations. There were approximately 290 operating in North America in 1930.

30. Exclusion encouraged circumvention of the law through the creation of "paper sons," which would also account for the structure of living arrangements along extended family lines, fictive or otherwise; see Erika Lee, *At America's Gates: Chinese Immigration during the Exclusion Era, 1882–1943* (Chapel Hill: University of North Carolina Press, 2007). Details on 925 Race Street appear in *Thirteenth Census of the United States*, 1910, Philadelphia Ward 10. This pattern was repeated at other addresses on Race. In 1910, 909 Race was home to fourteen persons, all with the surname of Jung or Lee, and all of them Chinese goods merchants. Foong Yook Chun, forty-eight, lived at 915 Race with his partners (and perhaps brothers or cousins), Foong Way Hing, forty-six, and Foong Kooy, thirty-two. Kooy's son, Bo, seventeen, was born in California and also a member of the household; all were listed as "merchants." Mock Gee Poo, sixty-nine and retired; with Mock Quong Hook, thirty-eight; Mock Hung Chong, forty-seven; and Mock Yew, thirty-six, were all partners in a merchant business at 931 Race and had immigrated between 1891 and 1895 (with the exception of Hung Chong, who was born in Arizona). Mock Yee, eighteen; Mock Guin, nineteen; and Mock Guk, ten, all with no occupation, had come in 1910, presumably to join an older male relative. At 907, most residents had the surname Leung, ranged in age from forty-five to fifty-five, held a variety of occupations, and arrived between 1885 and 1891. Likewise, 929 Race was home to six Jungs, all single, ages thirty-five to sixty.

31. Mark Sing, Lee Sing, DL, 788C. Reel 10. Other cases: Go Yet, laundryman, lived at 836 Race Street after selling his Jenkintown laundry; Go Yet, DL, 763C, Reel 10; 783C: Eng Sing sold his laundry at 1711 North Thirteenth Street to his cousin in 1912 and lived for more than a year at 923 Race Street while he applied for a return certificate; Eng Sing, DL, 1957C, Reel 30. 929C: Mark Sun testimony in Mark Jim Shing, DM, Reel 12.

32. Culin, *China in America*, cited in David Te-Chao Cheng, *Acculturation of the Chinese in the United States: A Philadelphia Study* (Foochow, China: Fukien Christian University Press, 1948), 121.

33. Culin, *China in America*. Also cited in Cheng, *Acculturation of the Chinese in the United States*, 124–125.

34. Culin, *China in America*. Also cited in Cheng, *Acculturation of the Chinese*, 119. Hip Sing, reported to be organized for the "purpose of blackmail" and the payment of protection money from business owners, was frequently associated with assorted vice trades, including drug dealing, gambling, and prostitution. Tongs provided authority and structure, and Chinatown's leaders or unofficial "mayors" were drawn from their leadership ranks, such as Lee Toy (who was associated with an illegal immigrant-smuggling ring from San Francisco) in the early 1900s and Wong Wah Ding in the 1940s.

35. Siu, *The Chinese Laundryman*, 145.

36. Ibid., 227–249; Stewart Culin, "Chinese Games with Dice" (Philadelphia: 1889). George Moy, interview by the author, 2010.

37. Ruth Louie, quoted in *Philadelphia Inquirer*, June 14, 2000. Louie's grandfather was Jung Sing-lee, a merchant who came to Philadelphia at the turn of the century. By 1908, he had written back for his sons, Jung Kay (later called Henry) and Jung Gong, to join him. Sing-lee returned to China, but his sons brought their wives and children to Philadelphia around 1915.

38. David Chuenyan Lai, "The Visual Character of Chinatowns," *Places* 7, no. 1 (1990): 29–31.

39. "National Chinese cemetery at Old Street Mary's Farm, Wynnewood, 110 Acres, Only One Owned by Chinese in US," *Atchison Daily Globe*, August 22, 1897.

40. "Jung Jo Is Buried after Big Parade," *Evening Bulletin*, November 13, 1910.

41. *Evening Bulletin*, April 1921.

42. On the bicultural nature of Chinese American funerals, see Linda Sun Crowder, "The Chinese Mortuary Tradition in San Francisco's Chinatown," in *Chinese American Death Rituals: Respecting the Ancestors*, ed. Sue Fawn Chung and Priscilla Wegars (Lanham, MD: AltaMira Press, 2005), 201–204.

43. "Chinese Mark Anniversary," *Philadelphia Evening Bulletin*, n.d. (ca. 1921).

44. *Evening Ledger*, February 12, 1915. Carrie Tirado Bramen, "The Urban Picturesque and the Spectacle of Americanization," *American Quarterly* 52, no. 3 (2000): 444–477.

45. *Evening Public Ledger*, February 2, 1916.

46. Chinese American Union of Philadelphia, *First Annual Report of the Board of Managers*, 1886, 8. Poole, an Episcopal minister and missionary to China, was a young man "of slender build" with a "thin and pale" face "still showing the effects of the trials" he suffered in China. He was actively involved in evangelical efforts in both countries and a tireless advocate for Chinese Christians; *New York Times*, April 6, 1894. Poole lived in Bridesburg, a German neighborhood in Northeast Philadelphia. In 1906, he was targeted among others for assassination by one of the tongs. He also lobbied Secretary of State John Hay on behalf of Chinese merchants who had been targeted by the police; *Minneapolis Journal*, July 8, 1906.

47. A kindergarten was established in 1901 "exclusively for the benefit of the tiny residents of Race Street" and by 1906 had moved into permanent quarters at 918 Race Street, incorporating a YMCA. *Kindergarten Review* 12, no. 1 (September 1901): 59–60. About fifteen Chinese pupils attended, as did the "children of American mothers and Chinese fathers"; *Evening Bulletin*, November 1906. Among the early nuclear families settling in Philadelphia's Chinatown at the turn of the century, interracial marriages were common. The 1900 Census listed two such marriages and others around the city.

48. Another mission jointly run by Baptists and Methodists was located at 1002 Race Street in the early twentieth century, and a Chinese Methodist church was founded at 222 North Tenth Street. This mission, later incorporated into an ecumenical Protestant concern, became the Chinese Christian Center in 1941. Saint Andrew's Church established the first Chinese Sunday School in Chinatown in 1872. Chinese American Union of Philadelphia, *First Annual Report of the Board of Managers*, 1886, HSP; and Cheng, *Acculturation of the Chinese*, 190. Cheng, along with other analysts, attributes the Chinese interest in churches to the much-sought-after opportunity to learn English language.

49. Chinese American Union of Philadelphia, *First Annual Report of the Board of Managers*, 1886, 10–11.

50. Ibid.

51. Ibid.

52. Chinese American Union of Philadelphia, *Fifth and Sixth Annual Reports of the Board of Managers*, 1891.

53. *North American*, March 6, 1882.

54. Cited in Auyang, "Structural and Processual Change in Philadelphia's Chinatown and among Suburban Chinese."

55. "Philadelphia Chinese," *Evening Bulletin* [San Francisco], August 10, 1887.

56. Ibid.

57. "They Cleaned House," *North American*, August 10, 1887.

58. "Philadelphia's Chinatown," *Evening Bulletin* [San Francisco], August 23, 1887.

59. "Philadelphia Chinese," *Evening Bulletin* [San Francisco], August 12, 1887.

60. Ibid.

61. "Chinese Have Rights: Policemen Who Exceeded Their Province Reproved by Court," *North American*, July 6, 1887.

62. Him Mark Lai, *Chinese American Transnational Politics* (Urbana: University of Illinois Press, 2010), 10.

63. Tong wars, attributed to gang activity, ancient blood feuds, or "keen economic competition," reached a zenith in the 1920s and were said to end by 1933. At any rate, tong activities drew attention, mostly negative, to Chinatown from the outside media and police, even as they fed a glamorized image of Chinatown as a site of danger. Philadelphia's "tong wars" of the 1900s were covered in various newspapers; see, for example, "Chinese Tongs Declare War," *Washington Herald*, October 19, 1907; "Two Killed in Tong War," *New York Times*, July 8, 1907; "Two Killed in Philadelphia," *New York Times*, April 11, 1910; "Sordid Chinatown, Wallowing in Vice, Known Here No More," *Evening Ledger*, August 3, 1915.

64. "Chinese Shops Closed," *Evening Times*, August 15, 1898.

65. "Chinatown Is 'Wide Open'" *North American*, July 19, 1899.

66. Orientalism reifies the relationship of power between the East and West by "constructing Occident and Orient as cultural polarities defined by real or imagined distance." Edward Said, cited in Robert G. Lee, *Orientals: Asian Americans in Popular Culture* (Philadelphia: Temple University Press, 1999), 27–28.

67. Nathan Dunn, *"Ten Thousand Chinese Things": A Descriptive Catalogue of the Chinese Collection in Philadelphia* (Philadelphia: Nathan Dunn, 1839), 3; Robert G. Lee, *Orientals*, 29; Aaron Caplan, "Nathan Dunn's Chinese Museum" (Social Science Research Network, August 15, 2011), http://papers.ssrn.com/sol3/papers.cfm?abstract_id=2038655 (accessed November 20, 2014) ; E. C. Wines, *A Peep at China in Mr. Dunn's Chinese Collection* (Philadelphia: Printed for Nathan Dunn, 1839); Benjamin Silliman, *Mr. Dunn's Chinese Collection in Philadelphia* (Philadelphia: Brown, Bicking, and Guilbert, 1841); John Haddad, "The Romantic Collector in China: Nathan Dunn's Ten Thousand Chinese Things," *Journal of American Culture* 21, no. 1 (1998): 7–26; and Steven Conn, "Where Is the East? Asian Objects in American Museums, from Nathan Dunn to Charles Freer," *Winterthur Portfolio* 35, nos. 2/3 (2000): 157–173.

68. Casper Souder Jr., *History of Chestnut Street*, cited in Cheng, *Acculturation of the Chinese in the United States*, 66.

69. A similar pattern manifested in Peter's Chinese Museum in New York, 1849, is noted by Tchen, *New York before Chinatown*, 113–123. Peter's also exhibited at Philadelphia and Boston and the exhibition of Barnum's "Chinese Family." Chestnut Street was at this time also home to the National Theatre, Welch's Circus, and numerous "fancy goods" stores. Images of Chinese, comical Chinese acrobats, and lovely exotic Chinese maidens, often appeared on trade cards used to market sewing notions and dry goods, patent medicines, and other goods. By the 1880s, washable celluloid collars and cuffs drew on anti-Chinese sentiment. See the discussion of Chinese stereotyping in market-driven visual culture in Tchen, *New York before Chinatown*, 129–130. In 1835, nineteen-year-old Afong Moy, billed as "A Chinese Lady," sat for public viewing at Washington Hall on South Third Street, her mere foreignness a sufficient attraction to warrant 50 cents admission. Before coming to Philadelphia, she drew huge crowds in New York, where she amazed people by speaking in Chinese and eating with chopsticks.

70. Centennial Exhibition Digital Collection, *Free Library of Philadelphia*, http://www.freelibrary.org/cencol.

71. Bruno Gilberti, *Designing the Centennial: A History of the 1876 International Exhibition in Philadelphia* (Lexington: University Press of Kentucky, 2002), 175–179.

72. These displays form part of an "exhibitionary complex" characterized by Tony Bennett, "The Exhibitionary Complex," *new formations* 4 (Spring 1988): 73–102; and Paul A. Tenkotte, "Kaleidoscopes of the World: International Exhibitions and the Concept of Culture-Place, 1851–1915," *American Studies* 28, no. 1 (1987): 5–29. On catalogs and exhibitions as a form of power/knowledge and control over things Chinese, see Tchen, *New York before Chinatown*, 115–117. Spectacle both addresses and distances the viewing subject, as Susan Stewart observes. Spectacle also moves in a singular direction: "In contrast to the reciprocal gaze of carnival and festival, the spectacle assumes that the object is blinded; only the audience sees"; Susan Stewart, *On Longing: Narratives of the Miniature, the Gigantic, the Souvenir, the Collection* (Durham, NC: Duke University Press, 1993), 108.

73. Trade cards for Wanamaker's children's department, for example, featured fanciful Chinese boys in carnivalesque situations. Exotic images of China and Japan also illustrated cards advertising thread, fancy goods, or millinery. Wanamaker trade cards, author's collection.

74. On Chinatowns and tourism, see Raymond Rast, "The Cultural Politics of Tourism in San Francisco's Chinatown, 1882–1917," *Pacific Historical Review* 76, no. 1 (2007): 29–60; Ivan Light, "From Vice District to Tourist Attraction: The Moral Career of American Chinatowns, 1880–1940," *Pacific Historical Review* 43, no. 3 (1974): 367–394; Ivan Light and Charles Choy Wong, "Protest or Work: Dilemmas of the Tourist Industry in American Chinatowns," *American Journal of Sociology* 80, no. 6 (1975): 1342–1368; Marlene Pitkow, "A Temple for Tourists in New York's Chinatown," *Journal of American Culture* 10, no. 2 (1987): 107–114; and Charlotte Brooks, *Alien Neighbors, Foreign Friends: Asian Americans, Housing, and the Transformation of Urban California* (Chicago: University of Chicago Press, 2009). On the rebuilding of Chinatown after the earthquake, see Bonnie Tsui, *American Chinatown: A Story of Five Neighborhoods* (New York: Free Press, 2010).

75. As of 1912, 909 Race was the home of Chong Wah Co., a business that sold Chinese groceries. The store occupied the first floor, basement, and back room. The immigration inspector described Chong Wah Co. as of the "oldest and most substantial stores" in Chinatown, "with ample stock and prosperous appearance." Both Chong Wah and Kung Wo sublet their second floors to the Far East Restaurant, which occupied both spaces, for $25 a month; see M1144 Case Files of Chinese Immigrants, 1910–1923. For District 4 in the INS, see National Archives Microfilm Publication Reel 27 Case 1810c, National Archives, Mid Atlantic Branch. The Far East was the most represented of Chinatown buildings in the early twentieth century. It was the subject of a watercolor by Frank Hamilton Taylor at this time as well as numerous photographs and postcards from 1910 to 1952, when it ceased operations. Taylor print, HSP.

76. "Two Chinese Banquets," *New York Times*, June 11, 1888.

77. Greg Umbach and Dan Wishnoff,. "Strategic Self-Orientalism: Urban Planning Policies and the Shaping of New York City's Chinatown, 1950–2005," *Journal of Planning History* 7, no. 3 (2008): 214–238. Kay Anderson notes this tendency in *Vancouver's Chinatown: Racial Discourse in Canada, 1875–1980* (Montreal: McGill-Queen's University Press, 1991).

78. *Philadelphia Record*, June 2, 1936.

79. "Chinatown Modernizes Past Glory: Exotic Splendors Live Again as Race and Ninth Sts. Area Woos Fame of Gay 90s," *Philadelphia Record*, June 2, 1936. Charlotte Brooks outlines a similar move by San Francisco's Chinatown merchants to self-Orien-

talize for the 1939 World's Fair and make their storefronts "All Chinese"; Brooks, *Alien Neighbors, Foreign Friends*, 102.

80. The situation of endangerment was a familiar one to many turn-of-the-century Chinatowns. In 1899 and 1906, New York City plans for widening Pell Street and creating a park, respectively, threatened Chinatown, which Comptroller Herman Metz called an "ulcer which should be eradicated at any cost . . . a blot and disgrace on our civilization." In 1906, New York City planners were calling for the eradication of Chinatown to make way for a park that would be an extension of the Mulberry Bend Park, "a little breathing space and monument to good taste and good sense." The plan also had the endorsement of Jacob Riis, who declared, "Wipe out the Chinatown slum. I shall be glad to see you do it." "Comptroller Metz Comes Out in Favor of the Park in Chinatown," *The World*, March 12, 1906. Focused on the tong wars and presence of crime and gambling as well as overcrowding and other conditions in the tenements that violated building codes, the plan was seen as a way to boost land values in that area of the city; *New York Daily Tribune*, March 19, 1899; and *The World*, March 7, 1906.

81. Domenic Vitiello, "Machine Building and City Building: The Planning and Politics of Urban and Industrial Restructuring in Philadelphia, 1891–1928," *Journal of Urban History* 34, no. 3 (2008): 399–434. Vancouver's Chinatown considered relocation in 1911; Anderson, *Vancouver's Chinatown*, 89.

82. Vitiello, "Machine Building"; Russell Weigley, Nicholas B. Wainwright, Edwin Wolf II, et al., *Philadelphia: A 300-Year History* (New York: Norton, 1982).

83. "City's Chinatown Soon Only Memory," *Philadelphia Evening Bulletin*, May 23, 1923.

84. "Dwindling Race Street Chinatown Doomed by Opening of Bridge," *Philadelphia Evening Bulletin*, July 13, 1926.

85. "Chinatown Soon Just a Memory," *Philadelphia Evening Bulletin*, June 17, 1928.

86. Ibid.

87. "Philadelphia's Chinatown Playing Its Swan Song," *Philadelphia Evening Bulletin*, May 5, 1929. Census records suggest that the population of Chinatown was, in fact, decreasing during the first two decades of the twentieth century and changing in character. In 1900, 249 Chinese lived in Chinatown; in 1910, that number declined to 190, and in 1920 to 144. Even as the population declined, it evolved as more merchants and families became part of the community: families numbered five in 1910, nine in 1920, and seventeen in 1930. Merchants and restaurant workers also became more numerous after 1900, as the commercial basis of Chinatown diversified. *Twelfth Census of the United States*, 1900, Philadelphia, Ward 10; *Thirteenth Census of the United States*, 1910, Philadelphia, Ward 10; and *Fourteenth Census of the United States*, 1920, Philadelphia Ward 10. For the purposes of demographic comparison, addresses within the historic core of Chinatown—Race, Ninth, Tenth, Spring, and Winter Streets—were examined, and "families" were counted as married couples or couples with children. Nevertheless, there was some basis to sound the death knell by the 1930s in that during the Great Depression—which also coincided with the beginning of the decline of the hand-laundry industry—some men went back to China or sent their children back to China. The population of Chinatown fell to 167. William Chin, John Chin's father, was born in New York City in 1929 but was sent back to China during the Depression, as were Joseph Eng and Dun Mark, who were born in Philadelphia in 1920 and 1924, respectively. Mark's grandfather was an herbalist and one of the first settlers of Philadelphia's Chinatown. When he was five, his family went back to China in response to the declining U.S. economy. John Chin, interview by the author, 2009; Dun Mark, interview by the author, 2009.

88. "Phila. Chinatown Soon to Be a Thing of the Past," *Philadelphia Evening Bulletin*, February 20, 1934.

89. Cheng, *Acculturation of the Chinese*, 83.

Chapter 2

1. Brendan Lee, interview by the author, July 15, 2010.

2. Ibid.

3. Ibid.

4. Setha Low has written extensively on the components of place making and of "place attachment," the affective relationship between people and landscape often rooted in experience, creating place as a "meaningful location." See Irvin Altman and Setha Low, eds., *Place Attachment* (New York: Plenum Publishing, 1992).

5. The Jewish neighborhoods of Northern Liberties, Strawberry Mansion, and South Fourth Street in Southwark, for example, experienced an almost total turnover of population. The exception to this trend was Little Italy of South Philadelphia. Grounded in the Ninth Street Market and less tied to manufacturing, it retained a distinct ethnic identity even when many Italians relocated to South Jersey and other surburban areas, and later, when new ethnic populations (Southeast Asian, Latino) also located there, resulting in a multiethnic residential/commercial area. In the case of North and West Philadelphia, however, white ethnic flight was the norm.

6. On postwar neighborhood restructuring, see Carolyn Adams, David Bartelt, David Elesh, et al., *Philadelphia: Neighborhoods, Division, and Conflict in a Postindustrial City* (Philadelphia: Temple University Press, 1991), 75–87.

7. On Latino/black migration into changing neighborhoods and Puerto Ricans as "displaced labor migrants," see Carmen Whalen, *From Puerto Rico to Philadelphia: Puerto Rican Workers and Postwar Economies* (Philadelphia: Temple University Press, 2001). On violence against blacks, see James Wolfinger, *Philadelphia Divided: Race and Politics in the City of Brotherly Love* (Chapel Hill: University of North Carolina Press, 2007). On the environmental factors shaping African American protest in North Philadelphia, including the 1964 riots, see Matthew Countryman, *Up South: Civil Rights and Black Power in Philadelphia* (Philadelphia: University of Pennsylvania Press, 2005).

8. David Te-Chao Cheng, *Acculturation of the Chinese in the United States: A Philadelphia Study* (Foochow, China: Fukien Christian University Press, 1948), 72.

9. In the 1940 Census, the addresses of 207, 212, 218, 225, 230, 232, 235, 250, and 254 North Ninth Street were clearly flophouses—all listed with large numbers of residents, all men between ages forty and seventy. 809 and 827 Race were also occupied by large numbers of single male residents. *Sixteenth Census of the United States*, 1940, Philadelphia Ward 10, ED 51–162, 51–164.

10. Cheng, *Acculturation of the Chinese*, 72–73.

11. "Joseph Eng," in *Chinatown Lives: Oral Histories from Philadelphia's Chinatown*, ed. Lena Sze (Philadelphia: Asian Arts Initiative and New City Community Press, 2004), 28.

12. George Moy, interview by the author, July 10, 2010.

13. "Wai Lum Chin," in Sze, *Chinatown Lives*, 22.

14. Debbie Wei, interview by the author, July 16, 2010.

15. Harry Leong, interview by the author, June 17, 2010.

16. Rod Townley, "Chinatown Fights for Its Life," *Today*, August 18, 1974.

17. Lee, interview.

18. Leong, interview.

19. John Chin, interview by the author, July 15, 2009.

20. Glenn Hing, interview by the author, July 1, 2010.

21. Lee, interview.

22. Moy, interview.

23. Kenneth Eng, interview by the author, July 10, 2010.

24. Wei, interview.

25. This is a common theme in U.S. Chinatown communities; see K. Scott Wong, *Americans First: Chinese Americans and the Second World War* (Cambridge, MA: Harvard University Press, 2005).

26. Joseph Eng, interview by Jianshe Wang, June 19, 1997, Balch Institute Chinatown Oral History Project, HSP Balch Collection. On China relief efforts in Chinatown, see "Parade in Chinatown to Raise Money for War Sufferers," *Philadelphia Record*, October 10, 1937; *Philadelphia Record*, July 25, 1937; and *Philadelphia Record*, July 30, 1942.

27. "Mitzie Mackenzie," in Sze, *Chinatown Lives*, 48. On Chinese Americans during World War II, see Wong, *Americans First*; Xiaojian Zhao, *Remaking Chinese America: Immigration, Family and Community, 1940–1965* (New Brunswick: Rutgers University Press, 2002); Jingyi Song, *Shaping and Reshaping Chinese American Identity: New York's Chinese during the Depression and World War II* (Lanham, MD: Lexington Books, 2010); and Peter Kwong, *Chinatown, N.Y. Labor and Politics, 1930–1950* (New York: New Press, 2001).

28. Recounted in Wong, *Americans First*, 66–67.

29. Joseph Eng, interview.

30. Eng's mother was one of perhaps a dozen Chinese women in the city during his childhood. At the age of two, Eng was sent back to China for thirteen years, a common practice at the time, before returning to Philadelphia. His father owned a laundry at 825 Locust Street and eventually located his family to Camden, where they lived behind the laundry.

31. On postwar opportunities and barriers, see Wong, *Americans First*, 207–208. A 1948 feature on Chinatown in *Philadelphia Magazine* noted that despite newfound success outside the traditional occupations, many young Chinese Americans still encountered "prejudice and suspicion against yellow skin and Oriental appearance"; see "Romance Town," *Philadelphia Magazine*, April 1948.

32. Joseph Eng, interview.

33. Dun Mark, interview by the author, July 28, 2009.

34. On changes in U.S. immigration law affecting Chinese during this period, see Roger Daniels, *Asian America: Chinese and Japanese in the United States since 1850* (Seattle: University of Washington Press, 1988); Sucheng Chan, *Asian Americans: An Interpretive History* (Boston: Twayne Publishers, 1991); and Aristide Zolberg, *A Nation by Design; A Nation of Immigrants* (Cambridge, MA: Harvard University Press, 2008). In 1952, the McCarran Walters Act extended to all Asians, introduced a system of preferences based on skill sets and family reunification, and eliminated laws preventing Asians from becoming naturalized American citizens.

35. *U.S. Census of Population, General Social and Economic Characteristics*, 1980, Social Explorer, http://www.socialexplorer.com/tables/C1980/R10848611 (accessed June 27, 2014).

36. *Sixteenth Census of the United States*, 1940, Philadelphia Ward 10, ED 51–162, 51–164. Comparisons made with *Fifteenth Census of the United States*, 1930, Philadelphia Ward 10.

37. Mark, interview; Moy, interview.

38. Mark, interview.

39. Ibid.

40. "Smart Cookie Spurs Fortunes," *Philadelphia Inquirer*, November 21, 1955.

41. "Wai Man Ip," in Sze, *Chinatown Lives*, 34.

42. Ibid.

43. On class divides, intra-Chinese labor exploitation, and the "woes of foreign capital" in New York's Chinatown in the 1970s and 1980s, see Peter Kwong, *The New Chinatown* (New York: Hill and Wang, 1996).

44. On reforming impulses of 1930s and 1940s Chinatown leadership, see Nayan Shah, *Contagious Divides: Epidemics and Race in San Francisco's Chinatown* (Berkeley: University of California Press, 2001), 225–250.

45. Hing, interview.

46. Mark, interview.

47. "Romance Town," *Philadelphia Magazine*, 1948, in Holy Redeemer Chinese Catholic Church, Scrapbooks, MSS 30, HSP.

48. Joseph Lowe, interview by the author, July 7, 2010.

49. Lee, interview.

50. Basketball as an important neighborhood activity in Chinatowns is also discussed in Katherine Yep, *Outside the Paint: When Basketball Ruled the Chinese Playground* (Philadelphia: Temple University Press, 2009). On the 1949 tournament, see Holy Redeemer Chinese Catholic Church, Scrapbooks, MSS 30, HSP.

51. Chinese Christian Church and Center (CCC&C) website, http://www.cccnc.org/church/index-Frameset.htm.

52. "Mitzie Mackenzie," in Sze, *Chinatown Lives*, 48.

53. World Wide Communion Service, October 3, 1954, CCC&C Archives.

54. Boxes of these registrations are in the basement repository at CCC&C Archives. Mackenzie's efforts were also documented by the *Bulletin* in 1966; see "Chinese Depend on Miss MacKenzie and Her Card File for Birthdates," *Sunday Bulletin*, January 20, 1966.

55. Report to the Marks, April 23, 1951, CCC&C Archives [113527].

56. Ibid.

57. Part of the purchase price for the playground ($500) was given by Quaker William Warder Cadbury, "a beloved friend of the Chinese people," who had been a doctor and medical school dean in Canton. After returning to Philly, Cadbury and his wife became interested in the CCC&C of Philadelphia, "the nearest 'China' that could be reached." "In Memoriam," 1959, Yam Tong Hoh papers, Box 11, Folder 2, congregational notices and activities, 1954–1959 HSP.

58. "The work of the Chinese Church in view of new building," ca. 1950–1951, CCC&C Archives.

59. Hoh papers, Box 11, Folder 3, 1960–1967 congregational notices and activities, playground rules, 1960, HSP.

60. Hoh papers, Box 11, Folder 3, 1960–1967 congregational notices and activities, September 14, 1965; congregational notice from Maribelle Mackenzie, HSP; congregational letter from John W. McKelvey and Luther Lee, n.d. [prob. 1959], Hoh papers, Box 11, Folder 2, congregational notices and activities, 1954–1959 HSP.

61. Leong, interview.

62. Kenneth Eng, interview.

63. CCC&C notes, n.d. CCC&C Archives.

64. Kenneth Eng, interview.

65. This double glass door form was also replicated in the new satellite church at Eleventh and Vine, constructed in 2008.

66. "Romance Town," *Philadelphia Magazine*, April 1948. On second-generation Chinese American identity before and after World War II, see Chen, *Asian Americans*.

67. This shift is noted more broadly by Zhao, *Remaking Chinese America*, 102.

68. CC&CC newsletters, passim. PCDC Archives. Kenneth Eng remembers participating in the Dragon Club as a boy (Kenneth Eng, interview).

69. Morley Cassidy, "Chinatown Melting Pot," *Philadelphia Inquirer*, December 22, 1958.

70. T. T. Chang to Edmund Bacon, September 25, 1968. Philadelphia City Planning Commission (PCPC), Box 71 A-2969 Redevelopment—Chinatown—1963–1972, Philadelphia City Archives (PCA).

71. "Chinatown YMCA Project History," March 196[3?]. PCPC, Box 71 A-2969 Redevelopment—Chinatown—1963–1972 PLANS, PCA.

72. Townley, "Chinatown Fights for Its Life."

73. "YMCA Director Seeks Chinatown with Stronger Flavor of the East," *Philadelphia Evening Bulletin*, July 12, 1966.

74. "Chinatown to Toss Open the Gates," *Philadelphia Daily News*, June 11, 1965.

75. "Chinatown YMCA Project History," March 196[3?]. PCPC, Box 71 A-2969 Redevelopment—Chinatown—1963–1972 PLANS, PCA.

76. Chiou-Ling Yeh notes a similar effacement of Chinese American life through the presentation of "authentic" Chinese cultural representations aimed at educating about Chinese culture in the Chinese New Year celebrations in Cold War–era San Francisco's Chinatown; see Yeh, *Making an American Festival: Chinese New Year in San Francisco's Chinatown* (Berkeley: University of California Press, 2008).

Chapter 3

1. Joseph Lowe, interview by the author, July 7, 2010.

2. Images of youth and children had been used in past attempts to advocate on behalf of Chinatowns, particularly in San Francisco; see Wendy Rouse Jorae, *The Children of Chinatown: Growing Up Chinese American in San Francisco, 1850–1920* (Chapel Hill: University of North Carolina Press, 2009). Children were often featured in the Philadelphia press in the 1940s, particularly in news stories, underscoring China's positive image as a U.S. ally.

3. The Model Cities Program was a signature program of Johnson's Great Society and the War on Poverty, enacted through the Demonstration Cities and Metropolitan Development Act of 1966. The program was intended to reform and expand urban renewal through a more holistic approach to urban poverty, incorporating urban rebuilding and rehabilitation, comprehensive urban planning, social services delivery, and citizen participation. Largely considered a failure, the program was discontinued in 1974. Citizen participation proved to be a point of contention in Philadelphia, as African American community activists unsuccessfully jockeyed with the city for control of Model Cities planning processes; see Matthew Countryman, *Up South: Civil Rights and Black Power in Philadelphia* (Philadelphia: University of Pennsylvania Press, 2006), 300–307. For a contemporary view of the Philadelphia Model Cities Program, see Erasmus Kloman, "Citizen Participation in the Philadelphia Model Cities Program: Retrospect and Prospect," *Public Administration Review* 32 (1972): 402–408.

4. Jon Teaford, *The Rough Road to Renaissance* (Baltimore: Johns Hopkins University Press, 1990). The Eastwick project faced significant resistance from existing residents, who were largely displaced; see Guian McKee, "Liberal Ends through Illiberal Means: Race, Urban Renewal, and Community in the Eastwick Section of Philadelphia, 1949–1990," *Journal of Urban History* 27, no. 5 (2001): 547–583.

5. Christopher Klemek, *The Transatlantic Collapse of Urban Renewal: Postwar Urbanism from New York to Berlin* (Chicago: University of Chicago Press, 2011), 94; Neil Smith, *The New Urban Frontier: Gentrification and the Revanchist City* (London: Routledge, 1996), 138; and Teaford, *The Rough Road to Renaissance*.

6. Neil Smith discusses in detail the coordinated work of the Greater Philadelphia Movement, through the OPDC, local professional and elite occupier developers, financial institutions, and other corporate investors (such as Alcoa) in the creation of the Society Hill Towers and the rehabilitation of Society Hill in general in *The New Urban Frontier*, 119–139.

7. On selective demolition and conservatism of such Philadelphia planners as Edmund Bacon, see Gregory L. Heller, "Salesman of Ideas: The Life Experiences That Shaped Edmund Bacon," *Imagining Philadelphia: Edmund Bacon and the Future of the City*, ed. Scott Gabriel Knowles (Philadelphia: University of Pennsylvania Press, 2009), 26, 29. On dilemmas of downtown versus neighborhoods, see Gregory Heller and Guian McKee, "A Utopian, a Utopianist, or Whatever the Heck It Is: Edmund Bacon and the Complexity of the City," in Knowles, *Imagining Philadelphia*, 52–77; John F. Bauman, "Visions of a Postwar City: A Perspective on Urban Planning in Philadelphia and the Nation, 1942–1945," in *Introduction to Planning History in the United States*, ed. Donald A. Krueckeberg (New Brunswick, NJ: Center for Urban Policy Research, Rutgers University, 1983), 170–189; John F. Bauman, *Public Housing, Race, and Renewal: Urban Planning in Philadelphia, 1920–1974* (Philadelphia: Temple University Press, 1987); and Joel Schwartz, *The New York Approach: Robert Moses, Urban Liberals, and Redevelopment of the Inner City* (Columbus: Ohio State University Press, 1993).

8. For a discussion of Rafsky as an urban entrepreneur, see June Manning Thomas, *Redevelopment and Race: Planning a Finer City in Postwar Detroit* (Baltimore: Johns Hopkins University Press, 1997); and Heller, "Salesman of Ideas," 34–47. On CURA, see Heller and McKee, "A Utopian," 61–66.

9. The phrase "mythical future" is from Mandi Isaacs Jackson, *Model City Blues: Urban Space and Organized Resistance in New Haven* (Philadelphia: Temple University Press, 2008), 5.

10. Andrew Feffer, "Show Down in Center City: Staging Redevelopment and Citizenship in Bicentennial Philadelphia," *Journal of Urban History* 30, no. 6 (2004): 791–825. On symbolic economy, see Sharon Zukin, *The Culture of Cities* (Cambridge, UK: Blackwell, 1995). This consensus would, by the 1970s, increasingly characterize postindustrial urban development in Philadelphia and elsewhere. On this shift in urban planning, see Tom Angotti, *New York for Sale: Community Planning Confronts Global Real Estate* (Cambridge, MA: MIT Press, 2008).

11. Paul Levy, *Queen Village—The Eclipse of Community: A Case Study of Gentrification and Displacement in a South Philadelphia Neighborhood* (Philadelphia: Institute for the Study of Civic Values, 1978), 22–71.

12. On urban redevelopment, displacement, and the vulnerability of Chinatowns and other Asian American communities during this period as well as campaigns resisting, see Michael Liu and Kim Geron, "Changing Neighborhood: Ethnic Enclaves and the Struggle for Social Justice," *Social Justice* 35, no. 2 (2008): 18–35; Michael Liu and Kim Geron, "Against the Tide: Mobilization and Community Planning in Asian Ethnic Enclaves," in *Urban Spaces: Planning and Struggles for Land and Community*, ed. James Jennings and Julia Sheron Jordan-Zachery (Lanham, MD: Lexington Books, 2010), 39–53; Kay J. Anderson, *Vancouver's Chinatown: Racial Discourse in Canada, 1875–1980* (Montreal: McGill-Queen's University Press, 1991); Chuen-yan D. Lai, *Chinatowns: Towns within Cities in Canada* (Vancouver: University of British Columbia Press, 1988); Huping Ling, *Chinese Chicago: Race, Transnational Migration, and Community since 1870* (Stanford, CA: Stan-

ford University Press, 2012); and Daryl Joji Maeda, *Rethinking the Asian American Movement* (London: Routledge, 2012), 53–80. St. Louis's Chinatown also underwent a "second removal" after the On Leong Association building was relocated; see Huping Ling, *Chinese St. Louis: From Enclave to Cultural Community* (Philadelphia: Temple University Press, 2004). The fight for inclusive hiring practices for Confucius Plaza and other redevelopment projects in New York's Chinatown is recounted by Maeda, *Rethinking the Asian American Movement*; and Jan Lin, *Reconstructing Chinatown: Ethnic Enclave, Global Change* (Minneapolis: University of Minnesota Press, 1998), 134. On Vancouver, see Anderson, *Vancouver's Chinatown*, 186–210. On Seattle's Chinatown/International District, see Doug Chin, *Seattle's International District: The Making of a Pan-Asian American Community* (Seattle: University of Washington Press, 2001).

13. "Crowding in Residential Areas of Philadelphia, 1950." Housing Association of Delaware Valley, Temple University Urban Archives (TUUA). Reprinted in Bauman, *Public Housing*, 88.

14. Stephen Metreaux, "Waiting for the Wrecking Ball: Skid Row in Postindustrial Philadelphia," *Journal of Urban History* 25, no. 5 (1999): 696.

15. R. Damon Childs, to Edmund Bacon, July 30, 1963, PCPC, Box 71 A-2969 Redevelopment—Chinatown—1963–1972 PLANS, PCA.

16. Smith, *The New Urban Frontier*, 138.

17. This concern was expressed in a "Report of the Special Committee of the Citizens' Council on City Planning on the Approach to the Delaware River Bridge," August 17, 1944. Box 6A-2906 Vine Street Expressway, 1945–1959. PCPC, PCA.

18. Heller and McKee, "A Utopian," 74; John Andrew Gallery, *The Planning of Center City Philadelphia* (Philadelphia: Center for Architecture, 2007), 59; Heller, "Salesman of Ideas," in Knowles, *Imagining Philadelphia*, 47; and Klemek, *The Transatlantic Collapse of Urban Renewal*. On the impact of interstate highways and urban expressways on urban neighborhoods during this period, see Raymond A. Mohl, "Planned Destruction: The Interstates and Central City Housing," in *From Tenements to the Taylor Homes: In Search of an Urban Housing Policy in Twentieth-Century America*, ed. John F. Bauman (University Park: Pennsylvania State University Press, 2000), 226–245; and Mark H. Rose, *Interstate: Express Highway Politics, 1939–1989* (Knoxville: University of Tennessee Press, 1990).

19. *Center City Philadelphia*, November 1963.

20. R. H. Uhlig to Graham Finney, August 5, 1963. PCPC, Box 71 A-2969 Redevelopment—Chinatown—1963–1972 PLANS, PCA.

21. R. H. Uhlig to Graham Finney, August 7, 1963. PCPC, Box 71 A-2969 Redevelopment—Chinatown—1963–1972 PLANS, PCA.

22. R. H. Uhlig to Graham Finney, August 8, 1963. PCPC, Box 71 A-2969 Redevelopment—Chinatown—1963–1972 PLANS, PCA; "Social Facilities between Ninth and Eleventh Streets, Cherry and Vine Streets," PCPC, Box 71 A-2969 Redevelopment—Chinatown—1963–1972 PLANS, PCA.

23. Cecilia Moy Yep, interview by the author, June 16, 2010.

24. Ibid.

25. T. T. Chang to Robert Epp, December 6, 1963. PCPC, Box 71 A-2969 Redevelopment—Chinatown—1963–1972, PCA.

26. Howard Kusterman to John O'Shea, January 22, 1964. PCPC, Box 71 A-2969 Redevelopment—Chinatown—1963–1972, PCA. Kusterman was the general secretary of the YMCA in Philadelphia, and O'Shea was the development coordinator for the city.

27. T. T. Chang to Edmund Bacon, December 5, 1963; Edmund Bacon to T. T. Chang,

December 12, 1963; T. T. Chang to Edmund Bacon, December 15, 1963. PCPC, Box 71 A-2969 Redevelopment—Chinatown—1963–1972, PCA.

28. T. T. Chang to Edmund Bacon, September 19, 1968. PCPC, Box 71 A-2969 Redevelopment—Chinatown—1963–1972, PCA.

29. T. T. Chang to Edmund Bacon, September 19, 1968; Edmund Bacon to Damon Childs, n.d. PCPC, Box 71 A-2969 Redevelopment—Chinatown—1963–1972, PCA.

30. Mary Yee, interview by the author, July 12, 2010.

31. George Moy, interview by the author, July 10, 2010.

32. "Many Forced to Move Out of Enclave," *Evening Bulletin*, November 16, 1969.

33. Moy, interview. June Thomas also notes this lack of recognition by redevelopment plans of local residents' improvements to and investments in their neighborhoods in Detroit; 118.

34. Cecilia Moy Yep, interview by Jianshe Wang, June 16, 1997, Balch Institute Chinatown Oral History Project, HSP Balch Collection.

35. Ibid.

36. Moy, interview.

37. Yep, interview by the author.

38. Ibid.

39. Yep, interview by Wang.

40. Ibid.

41. Yep, interview by the author.

42. Ibid.

43. Ibid.

44. Moy, interview.

45. Ibid.

46. Ibid.

47. Ibid.

48. Yep, interview by the author.

49. *Yellow Seeds* 1, no. 5 (1973); *Yellow Seeds* 1, no. 6 (1973).

50. Yep, interview by the author.

51. *Yellow Seeds* 1, no. 6 (1973).

52. Harry Leong, interview by the author, June 17, 2010.

53. Glenn Hing, interview by the author, July 1, 2010.

54. Mary Yee, interview by Jianshe Wang, July 19, 1997, Balch Institute Chinatown Oral History Project, HSP Balch Collection.

55. Townley, "Chinatown Fights for Its Life."

56. "Help Save Chinatown" petition, PCDC Archives.

57. April 22, 1973, "Help Save Chinatown" flyer, PCDC Archives.

58. October 15, 1974, "Chinatown '74 Town Meeting" flyer, PCDC Archives.

59. "Speak Out" flyer, December 4, 1979, PCDC flyers, PCDC Archives.

60. "Statement of the Chinatown Community," October 1973, PCDC newsletters, PCDC Archives.

61. "Help Save Chinatown" flyer, December 5, 1973, PCDC newsletters, PCDC archive; PCDC flyer, n.d. [describes 1975 actions], PCDC flyers, PCDC Archives.

62. "Save Chinatown! What Does This Mean?" *Yellow Seeds* 1, no. 6 (1973): 4.

63. *Yellow Seeds* 1, no. 6 (1973): 2.

64. "One More Piece of Chinatown Torn Down!" *Yellow Seeds* 2, no. 6 (1975): 3.

65. Yee, interview by Wang.

66. Yee, interview by the author.

67. Ibid.

68. Ibid.

69. These kinds of programs were similar to those offered by other organizations associated with the Asian American Movement in other Chinatowns; see Maeda, *Rethinking the Asian American Movement.* Celebrating the October 1 anniversary of the creation of the PRC would have been problematic for most of Holy Redeemer's congregation, who, as Cantonese and Taiwanese immigrants, were supporters of the Republic of China and the Kuomintang. That Yellow Seeds could do so is a testament to the way in which Holy Redeemer served as a larger community gathering space as well as the way in which Yellow Seeds successfully negotiated relationships with older immigrant generations.

70. Chia-ling Kuo, *Social and Political Change in New York's Chinatown: The Role of Voluntary Associations* (New York: Praeger, 1977), 62–63. The move into Chinatowns (and Japantowns and Manilatowns) was common in cities where Asian American students were active, such as San Francisco and Los Angeles.

71. This rhetoric of civil rights and racial self-determination is in contrast to the language employed in Vancouver's Chinatown's battle against a proposed highway project in the same period. While Philadelphia's activists assumed Chinatown's cultural worth and demanded inclusion on democratic principles, Vancouver's activists emphasized the Chinese-ness of Chinatown and its value as a tourist attraction, arguing that the freeway would destroy the neighborhood's "heritage and character." See Anderson, *Vancouver's Chinatown,* 205–210.

72. This kind of intergenerational activism was characteristic of many Asian communities during this period. See Michael Liu, Kim Geron, and Tracy A. M. Lai, *The Snake Dance of Asian American Activism: Community, Vision, and Power* (Lanham, MD: Lexington Books, 2008); William Wei, *The Asian American Movement* (Philadelphia: Temple University Press, 1993); and Maeda, *Rethinking the Asian American Movement.* Specific struggles in support of elderly Asian residents are detailed in Estella Habal, *San Francisco's International Hotel: Mobilizing the Filipino American Community in the Anti-Eviction Movement* (Philadelphia: Temple University Press, 2007); and Chin, *Seattle's International District.* Maeda discusses Yellow Seeds specifically in the context of urban Asian radical activism in the 1960s and 1970s; Maeda, *Rethinking the Asian American Movement,* 77–80.

73. *Yellow Seeds* 1, no. 1 (1972).

74. "A Place to Live," *Yellow Seeds* 1, no. 3 (1972): 4.

75. "This Is Where Mr. Lao Lives," *Yellow Seeds* 1, no. 1 (1972).

76. "A Place to Live," 4.

77. *Yellow Seeds* 2, no. 4 (1975); *Yellow Seeds* 2, no. 3 (1974).

78. *Yellow Seeds* 2, no. 4 (1975): 1.

79. Ibid., 2.

80. *Yellow Seeds* 2, no. 5 (1975); *Yellow Seeds* 2 no. 3 (1974); *Yellow Seeds* 2 no. 4 (1975).

81. Yee, interview by the author.

82. *Yellow Seeds* 2, no. 6 (1975).

83. Yee, interview by Wang.

84. Yee, interview by the author.

85. *Yellow Seeds* 2, no. 5 (1975).

86. *Yellow Seeds* 1, no. 5 (1973): 2.

87. Yee, interview by the author. On the work of Puerto Rican activists in Philadelphia, see Carmen Whalen, *From Puerto Rico to Philadelphia: Puerto Rican Workers and Postwar Economics* (Philadelphia: Temple University Press, 2001), 231–237.

88. Yee, interview by the author. Yee is likely referring to I Wor Kuen, which published the newspaper *Getting Together.*

89. "Mobilizing structures," from social movement theory, refers to the resources a community may draw on when challenging dominant authority and mounting protests or collective actions. These resources include media, community meeting spaces, and community social entities, such as voluntary associations, families, workplaces, and, of course, money. All these resources work to help sustain protest and convert discrete actions into a more sustained movement for change. See Gregory Crowley, *The Politics of Place: Contentious Urban Redevelopment in Pittsburgh* (Pittsburgh: University of Pittsburgh Press, 2005), 22; Doug McAdam, John D. McCarthy, and Mayer N. Zald, eds., "Opportunities, Mobilizing Structures, and Framing Processes: Toward a Synthetic, Comparative Perspective on Social Movements," in *Comparative Perspectives on Social Movements* (Cambridge: Cambridge University Press, 1996), 1–22.

90. Moy, interview.

91. Meeting announcement, October 24, 1973, PCDC Archives.

92. "Vine Street Plan Is Correct Choice," *Philadelphia Inquirer,* July 22, 1981.

93. Federal Highway Administration and Commonwealth of Pennsylvania Department of Transportation, *Vine Street Transportation Improvements Proposed for Philadelphia, Pennsylvania: Final Environmental Impact Statement, Volume I,* 1983.

94. Foo dogs are traditional Chinese statues dating from the Han dynasty that depict guardian lions. They are usually erected at the entrance to palaces, offices, businesses, and homes of wealthy people as a protective force. Usually displayed in coupled pairs, the male and female lions also embody the forces of *yin* and *yang*. In Philadelphia's Chinatown, the foo dogs are situated along Vine and Tenth Streets, functioning as a gateway to the historic Chinatown core and, perhaps, protecting Chinatown North from further encroachment.

95. Correspondence and town meeting notes, PCDC Archives; "Memo from Vine Street Expressway Project," March 14, 1985, PCDC Archives; "Vine Street Expressway," PCDC News, November 1986, PCDC newsletters, PCDC Archives.

96. Moy, interview.

Chapter 4

1. *Philadelphia Inquirer,* September 13, 1971.

2. Centennial Celebration program and "Next Century Discussion," Yam Tong Hoh papers, Box 29 Centennial Committee, HSP.

3. "Table A-1. Selected Characteristics of Persons and Families by Residence in Census Tracts with a Poverty Rate of 20 Percent or More, 1970," *1970 Census, Supplementary Report, Low-Income Neighborhoods in Large Cities: Philadelphia.* Chinatown fell in "Neighborhood 02." The 1970 Census counted 2,874 Chinese in Philadelphia, and 7,052 in Pennsylvania.

4. U.S. Census Bureau; 2000 Census of Population and Housing. Prepared by Social Explorer, http://www.socialexplorer.com/tables/C2000/R10759276 (accessed June 26, 2014).

5. Chuen-yan D. Lai, *Chinatowns: Towns within Cities in Canada* (Vancouver: University of British Columbia Press, 1988); Huping Ling, *Chinese Chicago: Race, Transnational Migration, and Community since 1870* (Stanford, CA: Stanford University Press, 2012); and Kay J. Anderson, *Vancouver's Chinatown: Racial Discourse in Canada, 1875–1980* (Montreal: McGill-Queen's University Press, 1991).

6. Michael Liu and Kim Geron, "Against the Tide: Mobilization and Community Planning in Asian Ethnic Enclaves, Contentious Sites between Capital and Community," in *Urban Spaces: Planning and Struggles for Land and Community,* ed. James Jennings and Julia Sheron Jordan-Zachery (Lanham, MD: Lexington Books, 2010), 46–49; and Susan

Nakaoka, "Cultivating a Cultural Home Space: The Case of Little Tokyo's Budokan of Los Angeles," *aapi nexus* 10, no. 2 (2012): 23–36. Little Tokyo and New York City are discussed in Karen M. Tani, "The House That 'Equality' Built: The Asian American Movement and the Legacy of Community Action," in *The War on Poverty: A New Grassroots History, 1964–1980*, ed. Annelise Orleck and Lisa Gayle Hazirjian (Athens: University of Georgia Press, 2011), 411–436.

7. Damon Childs to Edmund Bacon, March 29, 1966. PCPC, Box 71 A-2969 Redevelopment—Chinatown—1963–1972, PCA.

8. Chinatown Report 1967, Chinese Benevolent Association, Philadelphia Chinatown Development Committee, HSP.

9. Neal Peirce and Carol Steinbach, *Corrective Capitalism: The Rise of America's Community Development Corporations* (New York: Ford Foundation, 1987); and William Simon, *The Community Economic Development Movement: Law, Business, and the New Social Policy* (Durham, NC: Duke University Press, 2001). On the history of CDCs, see W. D. Keating, "The Emergence of Community Development Corporations," *Shelterforce* 8 (February/March/April 1989): 8–14.

10. For example, in 1979, the Carter administration allocated $2.6 billion for community development; by1985, the Reagan administration had dropped that number to $1.6 billion, and in 1987 to $1.1 billion; see Peirce and Steinbach, *Corrective Capitalism*, 57. The phrase "corrective capitalism" is also from Peirce and Steinbach, *Corrective Capitalism*.

11. Tom Angotti, *New York for Sale: Community Planning Confronts Global Real Estate* (Cambridge, MA: MIT Press, 2008), 101–104.

12. On the contradictions of CDCs, see Randy Stoecker, "The CDC Model of Urban Redevelopment: A Critique and an Alternative," *Journal of Urban Affairs* 19, no. 1 (1997): 1–22.

13. George Moy, interview by Jianshe Wang, June 11, 1997, Balch Institute Chinatown Oral History Project, HSP Balch Collection.

14. Housing was frequently a priority for Chinatown developers in other cities as well. In Chicago, for instance, early development addressed housing shortages through the creation of elderly housing units; see Ling, *Chinese Chicago*, 217–218. Housing shortages also plagued other minority communities in postwar and late-twentieth-century periods. On housing shortages for African Americans in Philadelphia in the 1970s, see Andrew Feffer, "Show Down in Center City: Staging Redevelopment and Citizenship in Bicentennial Philadelphia," *Journal of Urban History* 30, no. 6 (2004): 791–825.

15. George Moy, interview by the author, July 20, 2010.

16. "Advocacy planner" is a concept first put forth by urban planner Paul Davidoff in the 1960s. Advocacy planners were informed by the practices of community activism, using planning to address issues of race and class oppression in the urban environment. Advocacy planners worked with community stakeholders to involve them directly in the planning activities. The concept of "advocacy planner" is discussed in Christopher Klemek, *The Transatlantic Collapse of Urban Renewal: Postwar Urbanism from New York to Berlin* (Chicago: University of Chicago Press, 2011), 207–216; and Angotti, *New York for Sale*, 14–16.

17. Cecilia Moy Yep, interview by the author, June 16, 2010.

18. Gluck and Chadbourne Associates, *Report on Philadelphia's Chinatown Area*, (Philadelphia: Philadelphia Chinatown Development Corporation, 1975), 14.

19. Ibid, 88–89.

20. Ibid.

21. Ibid., 87.

22. Ibid., 97.

23. Ibid., 98.

24. Ibid., 32–33.

25. Yep, interview.

26. PCDC News, December 1975, PCDC newsletters, PCDC Archives.

27. PCDC News, December 1975, PCDC newsletters, PCDC Archives.

28. *Philadelphia Daily News*, June 19, 1975.

29. PCDC newsletter, December 1972.

30. On the discriminatory aspects of housing aid in terms of race and suburbanization, see John Bauman, ed., "Jimmy Carter, Patricia Roberts Harris, and Housing Policy in an Age of Limits," in *From Tenements to the Taylor Homes: In Search of an Urban Housing Policy in Twentieth-Century America* (University Park: Pennsylvania State University Press, 2000), 246–264; Robert Biles, "Public Housing and the Postwar Urban Renaissance, 1949–1973," in Bauman, *From Tenements to the Taylor Homes*, 143–162; and Thomas W. Hanchett, "The Other 'Subsidized Housing': Federal Aid to Suburbanization, 1940s–1960s," in Bauman, *From Tenements to the Taylor Homes*, 163–179. For an overview of housing policy, see R. Allen Hays, *The Federal Government and Urban Housing: Ideology and Change in Public Policy* (Albany: State University of New York Press, 1995). On public housing in Philadelphia, see John F. Bauman, *Public Housing, Race, and Renewal: Urban Planning in Philadelphia, 1920–1974* (Philadelphia: Temple University Press, 1987).

31. Bauman, *From Tenements to the Taylor Homes*; Alex F. Schwartz, *Housing Policy in the United States* (New York: Routledge, 2010), 139–141. In 1977, 5 percent of Section 8 allowances were given for elderly housing; by 1979, that number had climbed to 74 percent and would increase more in subsequent years; see Hays, *The Federal Government and Urban Housing*, 158.

32. The term "235 mortgage subsidies" refers to Section 235 of the Housing Act of 1968, which was designed to assist lower-income homebuyers through mortgage subsidy payments paid directly to the lender by HUD. Attacked in the mid-1970s for abuse and largely unused subsequently, the Section 235 program insurance authority was legally terminated effective October 1, 1989, as a result of legislation contained in the Housing and Community Development Act of 1987.

33. PCDC newsletter, March/April 1981.

34. Hoh papers, Box 31–32, On Lok House, HSP.

35. PCDC News, October 1980, PCDC Archives.

36. "Two Rent-Aided Projects Are Endorsed in Phila," *Philadelphia Inquirer*, September 3, 1981.

37. PCDC newsletter, September 1982.

38. Yep, interview.

39. Folder: Chinatown Notices, "Table of Contents," untitled document; image of this in *Philadelphia Inquirer*, August 24, 1983.

40. PCDC News Release, November 15, 1982, PCDC files newsletters and publications, PCDC Archives.

41. "Gim San Project Is on Its Way!" PCDC newsletter, June 1986.

42. Yep, interview.

43. Kathryn Wilson, "Building El Barrio: Latinos Transform Post-War Philadelphia," *Pennsylvania Legacies* 3, no. 2 (2003): 17–21.

44. "Table of Contents," untitled/undated document c. 1979, Chinatown notices folder, PCDC Archives.

45. Letter from Cecilia Moy Yep to Augustine Salvitti, January 11, 1978; letter from Michael Arno to John Chen, April 24, 1978; letter from Cecilia Moy Yep to Gee How Oak Tin Family Association, April 27, 1978; letter from Michael Arno to John Chen, June 13,

1978; letter from Michael Arno to John Chen, June 16, 1978. All PCDC Archives, Gee How Oak Tin folder.

46. Garth Garrett, "Chinatown: Model Community Stares Down Adversity," Foundation for Architecture, Gim San Plaza files, PCDC Archives.

47. Sabrina Soong (1934–2006) immigrated from Shanghai in 1965 to study architecture at the University of Florida, later moving to Philadelphia in 1973. She worked for architectural firms in Bala Cynwyd, Elkins Park, and Center City before founding her own company in 1982 at 914 Winter Street in Chinatown. She is best known as the architect of the Friendship Gate. She served on the boards of PCDC and On Lok House and frequently consulted for PCDC.

48. PCDC News Release, November 15, 1982, PCDC files newsletters and publications. James Guo and Stephen Pang, both first-generation immigrants from Hong Kong and Canton, respectively, were prominent entrepreneurs in Chinatown at the time. Pang, owner of the Trocadero Theater at Tenth and Arch and other properties in Chinatown, had been criticized by Yellow Seeds for being a negligent landlord and for interfering with the "Save Chinatown" movement's protests against the Ninth Street Ramps in 1973.

49. Narrative Description of Project [Chinatown East], 1982, PCDC Archives.

50. Ibid.

51. Memo from Lily Yeh to the Fine Arts Committee of the Philadelphia Redevelopment Authority (PRA), May 3, 1987, Gim San folder, PCDC Archives.

52. PCDC News, April 1987. Sadly, Yeh's mural was destroyed in 2014 when it collapsed and large pieces of the tile fell from the façade of the building: "3-Story Building Mural Falls onto Chinatown Street," *Philadelphia Inquirer*, April 2, 2014.

53. Yep, interview.

54. Mary Yee, interview by the author, July 12, 2010.

55. Yep, interview.

56. Moy, interview by the author.

57. Ibid.

58. The Preservation Alliance's annual Preservation Achievement Awards are given to "honor projects involving the preservation or protection of historic resources including the restoration, rehabilitation or adaptive reuse of historic properties, sympathetic new construction or additions to historic properties or education, documentation and advocacy work on behalf of historic preservation"; see http://pahistoricpreservation.com/preservation-achievement-awards/ (accessed November 24, 2014).

59. Suzanne Sataline, "A Constricted Chinatown Yearns North for Years," *Philadelphia Inquirer*, December 17, 1995.

60. The Federal Home Loan Banks' Affordable Housing Program (AHP) is one of the largest private sources of grant funds for affordable housing in the United States, funded with 10 percent of the Federal Home Loan Banks' net income each year. The AHP allows for funds to be used in combination with other programs and funding sources, such as the low-income housing tax credit. These projects serve a wide range of neighborhood needs: many are designed for seniors, people with disabilities, homeless families, first-time homeowners, and others with limited resources. See http://www.fhlbanks.com/programs_affordhousing.htm (accessed August 28, 2012).

61. "Goode Moves to Protect Chinatown," PCDC newsletter, May 1989, PCDC Archives.

62. PCDC newsletter, June 1989.

63. 1989 Comprehensive Urban Design Plan for Chinatown North, Environmental Research Group, 20, PCDC Archives.

64. Ibid., 5.

65. Ibid., 16–17.

Chapter 5

1. "Prison's a Tough Sell; 250 Chinatown Residents Protest Plans for Federal Jail," *Philadelphia Daily News*, March 26, 1993. The prison was eventually relocated to Seventh and Arch.

2. Jennifer Lin, "Chinatown Vows to Fight," *Philadelphia Inquirer*, September 11, 2008; Chuck Darrow, "Final Coffin Nail for Foxwoods Project?" *Philadelphia Daily News*, April 8, 2010; "Philadelphia Chinatown Saved from Casino," APA For Progress, August 30, 2009, http://www.apapforprogress.org/philadelphia-chinatown-saved-casino (accessed June 29, 2014); "Philadelphia Chinatown Stops Adjacent Foxwoods Casino," Azine, September 10, 2009, http://www.apimovement.com/casinos/philadelphia-china town-stops-adjacent-foxwoods-casino (accessed June 29, 2014); Joann Loviglio, "Phila-delphia's Chinatown Seeks to Keep Out Casino," *USA Today*, September 13, 2008; John E. Balzarini, "Casino Development and the Right to the City: Conflict and Community Place-Making in Philadelphia," Ph.D. diss., Temple University, 2013; and "History of Casino-Free Philly," Casino-Free Philadelphia, http://www.casinofreephilly.org/about/ history (accessed June 29, 2014). In 2013, new plans were announced for another casino location on the southwest corner of Eighth and Market, which were also subject to protest from Chinatown and others; see Jennifer Lin, "Many from Chinatown Protest 2d Philly Casino," *Philadelphia Inquirer*, May 11, 2013.

3. Deborah Wei, interview by the author, July 16, 2010.

4. The efforts of Asian Americans United (AAU) to combat anti-Asian violence and racial profiling in Southwest Philadelphia are recounted in Scott Kurashige, "Pan-Ethnic-ity and Community Organizing: Asian American United's Campaign against Anti-Asian Violence," *Journal of Asian American Studies* 3, no. 2 (2000): 163–190. On December 3, 2009, at South Philadelphia High School, twenty-six Asian immigrant students were assaulted by classmates, the majority of them African American. Thirteen of those attacked required hospitalization; see "Asian Students under Assault: Seeking Refuge from School Violence," *Philadelphia Weekly*, September 1, 2009; and Helen I. Hwang, "Philadelphia Story: Voices of Asian American Bullying Victims," *Hyphen Magazine*, posted December 10, 2011, on http://newamericamedia.org/2011/12/philadelphia-story-voices-of-asian-american-bullying-victims.php (accessed November 19, 2012). For AAU's statements on the South Philly High situation, see "Statement from Asian Students Association of Phila-delphia (ASAP) on the Justice Department Consent Decree on South Philadelphia High School," AAU, December 15, 2010, http://aaunited.org/campaigns/sphs/sphs-statements/ (accessed November 19, 2012); "Asian Students Describe Violence at South Philadelphia High," philly.com, December 10, 2009, http://mobile.philly.com/news/?wss=/inquirer/ world_us&id=78944382&viewAll=y#more (accessed November 19, 2012); and "Heal-ing the Wounds of South Phila. High," *Philadelphia Inquirer*, April 3, 2011, http://www .philly.com/philly/news/special_packages/inquirer/school-violence/20110402_sv2011_7 .html?c=r (accessed November 19, 2012). On anti-Asian violence nationally, see "Stunning 'Dirty Secret' about Racism in U.S.: Some View Chinese, Vietnamese, Koreans 'Unworthy of Respect,'" WND, June 12, 2012, http://www.wnd.com/2012/06/stunning-dirty-secret-about-racism-in-america/ (accessed November 19, 2012).

5. Ellen Somekawa, interview by the author, June 19, 2012.

6. Helen Gym, interview by the author, June 27, 2012.

7. New immigrants are more likely to originate from other regions of China, most recently the Fujian province. Unlike earlier immigrants who spoke Cantonese, these new immigrants speak Mandarin and represent different regional cultures. The linguistic diversity of Chinatown presents challenges to organizations that seek to serve the community and to attempts to organize the community when threats emerge.

"Cultural community" is a term used by Huping Ling to describe changes in St. Louis's Chinese population as it became a geographically dispersed community; see Huping Ling, *Chinese St. Louis: From Enclave to Cultural Community* (Philadelphia: Temple University Press, 2004); and Huping Ling, "Reconceptualizing Chinese American Community in Street Louis: From Chinatown to Cultural Community," *Journal of American Ethnic History* 24, no. 2 (2005): 65–101. On the twentieth-century emergence of Chinese and Asian enclaves in suburbs and exburbs, see Wei Li, "Building Ethnoburbia: The Emergence and Manifestation of the Chinese Ethnoburb in Los Angeles' San Gabriel Valley," *Journal of Asian American Studies* 2, no. 1 (1999): 1–28; Wei Li, "Beyond Chinatown, beyond Enclave: Reconceptualizing Contemporary Chinese Settlements in the United States," *GeoJournal* 64 (2005): 31–40; Min Zhou and John Logan, "In and Out of Chinatown: Residential Mobility and Segregation of New York City's Chinese," *Social Forces* 70, no. 2 (1991): 387–407; and Grace S. H. Chao Auyang, "Structural and Processual Change in Philadelphia's Chinatown and among Suburban Chinese," Ph.D. diss., Temple University, 1978.

8. Recent Immigration to Philadelphia: Regional Change in a Re-emerging Gateway, Brookings Institution, 2008. The 2010 Census reported 96,405 Asians in Philadelphia County, 6.3 percent of the city population; 6.4 percent lived in Montgomery County; http://2010.census.gov/2010census/popmap/ipmtext.php?fl=42:4260000:4250632 (accessed November 20, 2012).

9. "Chinese American Demographics," Améredia, http://www.ameredia.com/resources/demographics/chinese.html (accessed September 4, 2011).

10. Glenn Hing, interview by the author, July 1, 2010.

11. Kenneth Eng, interview by the author, July 10, 2010.

12. On Fujianese in Philadelphia's Chinatown, see Lena Sze, "Opportunity, Conflict, and Communities in Transition: Historical and Contemporary Chinese Immigration to Philadelphia," in *Global Philadelphia: Immigrant Communities Old and New*, ed. Ayumi Takenaka and Mary Johnson Osirim (Philadelphia: Temple University Press, 2010), 96–120; and Craig LaBan, "The New Chinatown, Delectably Diverse," *Philadelphia Inquirer*, January 13, 2014. On recent waves of Fujianese immigration in New York, including links to Philadelphia, see Kenneth J. Guest, *God in Chinatown: Religion and Survival in New York's Evolving Immigrant Community* (New York: New York University Press, 2003); Kenneth J. Guest, "From Mott Street to East Broadway: Fuzhounese Immigrants and the Revitalization of New York's Chinatown," in *Chinatowns around the World: Gilded Ghetto, Ethnopolis, and Cultural Diaspora*, ed. Bernard P. Wong and Tan Chee-Beng (Leiden: Brill, 2013), 34–54; "Fujian, U.S.A.: A Special Report; Within Chinatown, a Slice of Another China," *New York Times*, July 22, 2001; Fan Chen, "Fujianese Immigrants Fuel Growth, Changes," *Voices of New York*, June 25, 2013, http://www.voicesofny.org/2013/fuzhou-immigrants-fuel-growth-changes-in-chinese-community (accessed June 30, 2014); and Irene Jay Liu, "Chinese Immigrants Chase Opportunity in America," NPR, November 19, 2007, http://www.npr.org/templates/story/story.php?storyId=16356755 (accessed June 30, 2014).

13. Xu Lin, interview by the author, June 26, 2012.

14. Ibid.

15. Ibid.

16. Jian Guan, "Ethnic Consciousness Arises on Facing Spatial Threats to Philadelphia's Chinatown," in *Urban Ethnic Encounters: The Spatial Consequences*, ed. Aygen

Erdentung and Freek Colombjin (New York: Routledge, 2002), 126–141. The struggle over the stadium in some ways mirrors the fight against institutional expansion into Boston's Chinatown, as recounted by Andrew Leong, "The Struggle over Parcel C: How Boston's Chinatown Won a Victory in the Fight against Institutional Expansion and Environmental Racism," *Amerasia Journal* 21, no. 3 (1995): 99–119.

17. Christopher Mele, "Casinos, Prisons, Incinerators and Other Fragments of Neoliberal Urban Development," *Social Science History* 35, no. 3 (2011): 423–452.

18. Ibid. On stadiums, see Timothy Chapin, "Sports Facilities as Urban Redevelopment Catalysts," *Journal of the American Planning Association* 70, no. 2 (2004): 193–209. Robert Baade has examined the impact of stadium projects on urban redevelopment in "Professional Sports as Catalysts for Metropolitan Economic Development," *Journal of Urban Affairs* 18, no. 1 (1996): 1–17 and in "Stadiums, Professional Sports, and Economic Development: Assessing the Reality," *Heartland Policy Study* 61 (March 28, 1994): 1–39. According to Baade, most of these experiments were failures, the exceptions being Denver and San Diego, where stadium constructions went hand in hand with planning to integrate into and feed surrounding districts. For a late-1990s critique of stadiums and urban development, see Joanna Cagan and Neil deMause, *Field of Schemes: How the Great Stadium Swindle Turns Public Money into Private Profit* (Washington, D.C.: Common Cause Press, 2002).

19. *Philadelphia Inquirer*, April 22, 2000.

20. "Aim for the Fence with Much at Stake on a Ballpark, It's Time for Philadelphians to Show Some Vision," *Philadelphia Inquirer*, April 29, 2000.

21. Wei, interview.

22. John Chin, interview by the author, June 27, 2012.

23. Ibid.

24. Somekawa, interview.

25. Chin, interview, June 27, 2012.

26. Gym, interview.

27. Letter from Ignatius Wang to *Chestnut Hill Local*, May 16, 2000, Stadium binder, AAU Archives.

28. *Philadelphia Inquirer*, June 9, 2000.

29. *Philadelphia Inquirer*, May 3, 2000.

30. Ibid.

31. Chin, interview, June 27, 2012.

32. Ibid.

33. The differences between the two models are discussed by Lydia Lowe and Doug Brugge, "Grassroots Organizing in Boston Chinatown: A Comparison with CDC-Style Organizing," in *Acting Civically: From Urban Neighborhoods to Higher Education*, ed. Susan A. Ostrander and Kent E. Portney (Medford, MA: Tufts University Press, 2007), 44–71. On the struggle with Tufts, see Leong, "The Struggle over Parcel C."

34. Wei, interview.

35. E-mail, "Letter to all SOCC members," from Ping Leung Cheung, June 22, 2000, Stadium binder, AAU Archives.

36. Ibid.

37. Ibid.

38. *Philadelphia Inquirer*, June 9, 2000.

39. *Philadelphia Inquirer*, June 6, 2000.

40. *Philadelphia Daily News*, June 21, 2000.

41. "Save Chinatown; Stop the Stadium" flyer, Stadium binder, AAU Archives.

42. *Philadelphia Inquirer*, June 27, 2000.

43. Ibid.

44. *Philadelphia Inquirer*, September 15, 2000.

45. *Philadelphia Inquirer*, July 13, 2000.

46. Somekawa, interview.

47. "Topics to Write About," Letter Campaign, Stadium binder, AAU Archives.

48. Ibid.

49. Ibid.

50. Letter from Fong Wa Chung to the *Philadelphia Inquirer*, Stadium binder, AAU Archives.

51. Stadium binder, AAU Archives.

52. "Topics to Write About," Letter Campaign, Stadium binder, AAU Archives.

53. Somekawa, interview.

54. "Philadelphia Chinatown Wins Stadium Fight," *Asian Week*, November 24–30, 2000, http://www.asianweek.com/2000_11_24/news1_nophillieschinatown.html (accessed July 8, 2013).

55. "Topics to Write About," Letter Campaign, Stadium binder, AAU Archives.

56. Ibid.

57. "A Battle Cry beyond Chinatown for Many, the Plan for a Ballpark at Twelfth and Vine Hits Close to Home—Wherever That May Be," *Philadelphia Inquirer*, June 8, 2000.

58. "In Chinatown, 1,500 Protest Stadium Plans; Marchers Clogged Streets and Closed Businesses to Oppose Mayor Street's Plan for a Ballpark at Twelfth and Vine," *Philadelphia Inquirer*, June 9, 2000.

59. Asian American Legal Defense and Education Fund (AALDEF), "Chinatown Then and Now" (AALDEF, 2013), 39.

60. Jeff Gammage, "Chinatown Is Choking," *Philadelphia Inquirer*, February 15, 2004; "Crowded in Chinatown," originally published in *Philadelphia Life* magazine, September 2007, available at http://www.mookieland.org/chinatown.html (accessed July 30, 2012).

61. From an online survey of recent real-estate transactions dated July 30, 2012.

62. Gammage, "Chinatown Is Choking"; and "Crowded in Chinatown."

63. Gammage, "Chinatown Is Choking."

64. "Pearl Condos," Center City Team, http://www.centercityteam.com/philadelphia-condos/pearl-condos (accessed July 30, 2012).

65. Wei, interview.

66. Lai Har Cheung, interview by author, June 26, 2012.

67. As Neil Smith points out, the frontier language of gentrification presumes that areas of disinvestment are defined as physical not social environments and are thus ripe for settlement by "urban pioneers." Such language effaces and subsequently erases the presence of people who live and work in such areas but do not possess sufficient resources to drive capital to their communities; see Neil Smith, *The New Urban Frontier: Gentrification and the Revanchist City* (London: Routledge, 1996).

68. "Gritty Callowhill Is Recognized as National Historic District," PlanPhilly, July 26, 2010, http://planphilly.com/articles/2010/07/26/gritty-callowhill-recognized-national-historic-district (accessed July 20, 2012).

69. Visitphilly.com (accessed July 18, 2013).

70. Michael Alan Goldberg, "There Goes the Eraserhood: Why Local Artists Are Hoping to Preserve the Callowhill District's Gritty Past," *Philadelphia Weekly*, July 11, 2012; and Delaware Valley Regional Planning Commission (DVRPC), *Chinatown Neighborhood Plan, Including Callowhill Neighborhood* (Philadelphia: DVRPC, 2004), 2.8–2.14.

71. Sarah McEneaney, interview by the author, March 10, 2010.

72. Ibid.

73. John Chin, interview by the author, July 15, 2009.

74. Gayle Isa, interview by the author, July 24, 2009.

75. Barry Seymour, interview by the author, July 1, 2009.

76. Ibid.

77. Ibid.

78. DVRPC, *Chinatown Neighborhood Plan*, 2004.

79. McEneaney, interview.

80. Reading Viaduct Project, http://readingviaduct.org (accessed July 30, 2012).

81. Inga Saffron, "Reinventing a Railroad: New York's Abandoned High Line Is Being Transformed into an Elevated Park That Offers a New Way to Experience the City," *Philadelphia Inquirer*, July 17, 2009.

82. Isa, interview.

83. McEneaney, interview.

84. Ibid.

85. Andrew Toy, interview by the author, June 8, 2010.

86. CRVNID, http://www.crvnid.org, (accessed July 15, 2011). The mailing address for the organization is Sarah McEneaney's.

87. PCDC newsletter, June 2011, PCDC Archives.

88. Chin, interview, June 27, 2012.

89. "City Council Amends Callowhill Viaduct NID Creation in Contentious Meeting," *Philadelphia Metro*, September 20, 2011; and "Democracy 101: Callowhill NID Foes Went up against Powerful Forces . . . and Won," *Philadelphia Daily News*, February 6, 2012.

90. McEneaney, interview.

91. Chin, interview, June 27, 2012.

92. "Callowhill Residents Consider a 12-Unit Ridge Ave. Apartment Complex," *PlanPhilly*, July 9, 2013, http://planphilly.com/articles/2013/07/08/callowhill-residents-consider-a-12-unit-apartment-complex-on-ridge-ave (accessed July 18, 2013).

93. Isa, interview.

94. PCDC newsletter, June 2011, PCDC Archives.

95. Post Brothers Apartments, http://www.postrents.com/about-us/our-history.html (accessed June 6, 2014).

96. McEneaney, interview.

97. Andrew Toy, interview by the author, June 26, 2012.

98. James Zale, "Behold the First Official Renderings of the Proposed Reading Viaduct Elevated Park, Philadelphia's Planned Park in the Sky," *uwishunu*, April 2, 2012, http://www.uwishunu.com/2012/04/behold-the-first-official-renderings-of-the-proposed-reading-viaduct-elevated-park-philadelphias-planned-park-in-the-sky (accessed July 29, 2012).

99. "Callowhill-Chinatown North Strategic Plan," City of Philadelphia, http://www.phila.gov/CityPlanning/plans/Pages/CallowhillPlan.aspx (accessed July 18, 2013); "City Planning Commission Adopts Strategic Plan for Callowhill and Chinatown North," City of Philadelphia News and Alerts, February 25, 2013, http://cityofphiladelphia.wordpress.com/2013/02/25/city-planning-commission-adopts-strategic-plan-for-callowhill-and-chinatown-north (accessed July 18, 2013); and "PCPC Adopts Callowhill/Chinatown North Plan for Mixed Use, Green Space," *PlanPhilly*, February 19, 2013, http://planphilly.com/articles/2013/02/19/pcpc-adopts-callowhill-chinatown-north-plan-for-mixed-use-green-space (accessed July 18, 2013). Reading International began removing rails from the viaduct structure in 2012.

100. During this period, AAU organized the Chinatown Parents' Association to lobby the Philadelphia School District for bus service for their children to McCall Elementary School at 325 South Seventh Street. The effort met with success, but the next year AAU

had to fight to keep the service from being revoked. This need to repeatedly fight similar battles led AAU to conclude that a school for Chinatown was the only real solution.

101. Wei, interview.

102. Ibid.

103. Somekawa, interview.

104. Ibid.

105. Gym, interview.

106. Urban fragmentation as a product of neoliberal development is noted by Jason Hackworth, *The Neoliberal City: Governance, Ideology, and Development in American Urbanism* (Ithaca, NY: Cornell University Press, 2007); Neil Brenner and Nik Theodore, "Cities and the Geographies of 'Actually Existing Neoliberalism,'" *Antipode* 34, no. 3 (2002): 349–379; and Mele, "Casinos, Prisons."

Chapter 6

1. John Chin, interview by the author, July 15, 2009.

2. Cecilia Moy Yep, interview by the author, June 16, 2010.

3. Ibid.

4. See Chapter 2 for a discussion of these spaces within residents' memoryscapes.

5. PCDC Quarterly Report, 1977. According to Miwon Kwon's *One Place after Another: Site-Specific Art and Locational Identity* (Cambridge, MA: MIT Press, 2002), "The Livable Cities Program initiated by the NEA in 1977 as part of its architecture program . . . explicitly sought to find 'creativity and imagination—to get it from the artist and apply it to the problems of the built environment' so as to 'give promise of economic and social benefit to the community.'" See also Louis G. Redstone, with Ruth R. Redstone, *Public Art: New Directions* (New York: McGraw-Hill, 1981), vi.

6. Yep, interview.

7. "Chinatown Development Threatened," PCDC newsletter, August 1985.

8. Yep, interview.

9. "There May No Longer Be a Chinatown . . . What Can Chinatown Do?" PCDC newsletter, September 1988.

10. PCDC newsletter, August 1985.

11. "There May No Longer Be a Chinatown . . . What Can Chinatown Do?" PCDC newsletter, September 1988.

12. On historic districting as a strategy of community development, see Andrew Hurley, *Beyond Preservation: Using Public History to Revitalize Inner Cities* (Philadelphia: Temple University Press, 2010). Hurley, citing David Hamer, points out that in urban areas, historic districting can be at odds with the "defining features of urban history: change and diversity"; Hurley, *Beyond Preservation*, 23; David Hamer, *History in Urban Places* (Columbus: Ohio State University, 1998).

13. On "social preservation" and the different motivations of urban gentrifiers, see Japonica Brown-Saracino, *A Neighborhood That Never Changes: Gentrification, Social Preservation, and the Search for Authenticity* (Chicago: University of Chicago Press, 2009).

14. The conflict between new immigrant priorities and preservation in Vancouver's Chinatown is discussed in Katharyne Mitchell, "Global Diasporas and Traditional Towns: Chinese Transnational Migration and the Redevelopment of Vancouver's Chinatown," *Traditional Dwellings and Settlements* 11, no. 2 (2000): 7–18.

15. "There May No Longer Be a Chinatown . . . What Can Chinatown Do?" PCDC newsletter, September 1988. Jan Lin has also noted the use of zoning as a strategy for protecting neighborhood character in New York's Chinatown; see Jan Lin, *Reconstructing*

Chinatown: Ethnic Enclave, Global Change (Minneapolis: University of Minnesota Press, 1998), 149–152.

16. Chin, interview, July 15, 2009.

17. Jeff Gammage, "Marker in Honor of Chinatown's 140th Year," *Philadelphia Inquirer*, October 9, 2010.

18. The Neighborhood Preservation Program was launched in 2005 with support from the William Penn Foundation. The focus of the effort is to "develop new relationships, or to strengthen existing collaborations with Philadelphia's neighborhoods, by providing expanded services to community organizations, and increased outreach to Philadelphia's historic neighborhoods. The effort includes education, training, information, ongoing technical assistance, printed and electronic information, and tools for neighborhood preservation." Preservation Alliance for Greater Philadelphia, "Historic Preservation Resource Guide for Philadelphia Community Organizations," http://www.preservationalliance.com/files/Historic-Preservation-Resource-Guide.pdf (accessed November 30, 2014).

19. PCDC proposal to the Preservation Alliance of Greater Philadelphia's Neighborhood Preservation Program, 2009.

20. *Chinatown Places*, http://chinatownplaces.tumblr.com (accessed June 23, 2010). Oral histories were also collected by Asian Arts Initiative (AAI) in 2002 on the Web as "Beyond Borders: Oral Histories from Philadelphia's Chinatown" and subsequently published in the book *Chinatown Lives*. See Asian Arts Initiative, http://www.asianartsinitiative.org/programs/chinatown.php and http://asianartsinitiative.org/oralhistory (accessed June 23, 2010).

21. "Feasibility Study, 907–909 Race Street Façade, Philadelphia, PA 19107, October 22, 2012, volume I," prepared for the PCDC by UCI Architects, Inc., Fon Wang, AIA, LEED AP BD+C, and Ruth Embry in association with Wu and Associates, Inc. Courtesy of Fon Wang. Restoration of the balcony only is estimated at $139,000.

22. "New Additions to the Philadelphia Register," *Preservation Matters*, Fall 2013, 5, http://www.preservationalliance.com/wp-content/uploads/2014/09/PreservationMatters_Fall2013.pdf (accessed November 25, 2014).

23. In Vancouver's Chinatown, Mitchell notes that heritage zoning by the city government to protect historic Chinatown is at odds with new immigrant development and is criticized as a form of "neocolonialism"; see Mitchell, "Global Diasporas and Traditional Towns," 7–18.

24. John Chin, interview by the author, June 27, 2012.

25. Ibid.

26. The Philadelphia CDCs collectively raised more than $19 million in investments over three years. See Andrea L. Dono, "Entrepreneurship, Diversity, and Cheese Steaks," *Main Street Story of the Week*, December 2007–January 2008, 246, http://www.preservationnation.org/main-street/main-street-news/2007/12/entrepreneurship-diversity.html#.UdxGTOegW1k (accessed July 7, 2013).

27. "Project Updates," PCDC, 2011, http://chinatown-pcdc.org/pcdc-news/project-updates (accessed April 23, 2012); and "Beautification Project," PCDC, 2011, http://chinatown-pcdc.org/pcdc-news/beautification-project (accessed April 23, 2012).

28. "Planting the Seeds in Chinatown for a Future of Flower Markets," *Philadelphia Inquirer*, January 5, 2012.

29. Harry Leong, interview by the author, June 17, 2010.

30. Kenneth Eng, interview by the author, July 10, 2010.

31. Scott A. Lukas, ed., *The Themed Space: Locating Culture, Nation, and Self* (Lanham, MD: Lexington Books, 2007); David Hamer, *History in Urban Places: The Historic Districts of the United States* (Columbus: Ohio State University Press, 1998); and Frederic

Jameson, *Postmodernism, or, the Cultural Logic of Late Capitalism* (Durham, NC: Duke University Press, 1990).

32. Laurence Tom, interview by the author, June 14, 2010.

33. Dorothy Noyes, *The Uses of Tradition: Arts of Italian Americans in Philadelphia* (Philadelphia: Philadelphia Folklore Project and Samuel S. Fleisher Art Memorial, 1989); and Kathryn Wilson, "Building El Barrio: Latinos Transform Post-War Philadelphia," *Pennsylvania Legacies* 3, no. 2 (2003): 17–21.

34. Chin, interview, July 15, 2009.

35. On the Pearl Street project, see Bradley Maule, "A Cultured Pearl for Chinatown North," Hidden City Philadelphia, April 22, 2013, http://hiddencityphila.org/2013/04/a-cultured-pearl-to-identify-chinatown-north (accessed July 13, 2013); and "Pew Grantees," The Pew Center for Arts and Heritage, http://www.pcah.us/exhibitions/grants-awarded/exhibitions-2013-grantee-asian-arts-initiative (accessed July 13, 2013). On the arts crawl, see Erica Minutella, "The Chinatown North Arts Crawl, This Friday, December 14, Tours the Emerging Arts Community," *uwishunu*, December 12, 2012, http://www.uwishunu.com/2012/12/the-chinatown-north-arts-crawl-this-friday-december-14-tours-the-emerging-arts-community (accessed July 13, 2013).

36. Isa, interview.

37. Lena Sze, "Chinatown Then and Neoliberal Now: Gentrification Consciousness and the Ethnic-Specific Museum," *Identities: Global Studies in Culture and Power* 17, no. 5 (2010): 510–529.

38. "Chinatown In/flux: Future Landscapes," Chinatown In/flux, http://www.chinatowninflux.org/about-temp.html (accessed November 22, 2012).

39. Ibid.

40. Ibid.

41. Text from Chinatown In/flux Chinatown Map, http://www.chinatowninflux.org/index2.html (accessed November 21, 2012).

42. Ky Cao, personal communication with the author, July 2010.

43. Brendan Lee, interview by the author, July 15, 2010; and Glenn Hing, interview by the author, July 1, 2010. Abakus featured Suns activities on its website, and the owners rented their space from Harry Leong, who owns the building next to the CCC&C. On the Philadelphia Suns, see http://phillysuns.org (accessed August 19, 2013).

44. Lee, interview.

45. Hing, interview.

46. Deborah Wei, interview by the author, July 16, 2010. One question I asked everyone I interviewed for this project was, "What makes Chinatown Chinatown?" In almost every case, the respondent said, "The people."

47. Eng, interview.

48. Hing, interview.

49. Ibid.

50. Jacqueline Wong, interview by the author, June 23, 2010.

51. Leong, interview.

52. Yep, interview.

53. "Callowhill is a neighborhood with some of city's best live music venues, a steady-growing restaurant identity and a fascinating cluster of independent artists." Little Italy is represented by "Bella Vista." *Visitphilly.com*, http://www.visitphilly.com/philadelphia-neighborhoods/callowhill/ (accessed August 16, 2013).

54. Wei, interview.

55. Dean MacCannell, *The Tourist: A New Theory of the Leisure Class* (New York: Schocken Books, 1976).

56. Wei, interview.

57. Greater Philadelphia Tourism and Marketing Corporation (GPTMC) press release, May 30, 2003. The "Latin Soul, Latin Flavor" tour of the Latino barrio, also part of this series, is discussed by Frederick Wherry in *The Philadelphia Barrio* (Chicago: University of Chicago Press, 2010), 22–39.

58. Patricia Washington, interview by the author, July 24, 2009.

59. On niche tourism and branding, see Kevin Fox Graham, "Ethnic Heritage Tourism in New Orleans," in *Tourism, Ethnic Diversity and the City*, ed. Jan Rath (London: Routledge, 2007), 130–133; Kevin Meethan, *Tourism in Global Society: Place, Culture, Consumption* (New York: Palgrave, 2001); and Harvey Molotch, "Place in Product," *International Journal of Urban and Regional Research* 26, no. 4 (2002): 665–688. On place marketing as an outcome of neoliberal approaches to urban development, see Neil Brenner and Nik Theodore, "Cities and the Geographies of 'Actually Existing Neoliberalism,'" *Antipode* 34, no. 3 (2002): 349–379.

60. GPTMC press release, May 30, 2003.

61. Neighborhood Tourism Network brochure, GPTMC, 2006.

62. Washington, interview.

63. Ivan Light, "From Vice District to Tourist Attraction: The Moral Career of American Chinatowns, 1880–1940," *Pacific Historical Review* 43, no. 3 (1974): 367–394; Ivan Light and Charles Choy Wong, "Protest or Work: Dilemmas of the Tourist Industry in American Chinatowns," *American Journal of Sociology* 80, no. 6 (1975): 1342–1368; and Barbara Berglund, "Chinatown's Tourist Terrain: Representation and Racialization in Nineteenth-Century San Francisco," *American Studies* 46, no. 2 (2005): 5–36.

64. Washington, interview.

65. Ibid.

66. Hugh Bartling, "Immigrants, Tourists, and the Metropolitan Landscape," in *Tourism, Ethnic Diversity and the City*, ed. Jan Rath (London: Routledge, 2007), 110. Like Wherry, Arlene Dávila notes the role cultural- and development-funding eligibilities and criteria play in privileging institutionalized cultural industries; see Arlene Dávila, *Barrio Dreams: Puerto Ricans, Latinos, and the Neoliberal City* (Berkeley: University of California Press, 2004), 105.

67. Gayle Isa, interview by the author, July 24, 2009.

68. Chin, interview, July 15, 2009. A similar tension between the priorities of heritage marketing and community histories of struggle in East Harlem is described in Dávila, *Barrio Dreams*, 61–65, 95–98. As Dávila notes, East Harlem does not lack cultural resources or a willingness to market its culture—it lacks the resources to promote its values and the history of its struggles. See also Johannes Novy, "Urban Ethnic Tourism in New York's Neighbourhoods: Then and Now," in *Selling Ethnic Neighborhoods: The Rise of Neighborhoods as Places of Leisure and Consumption*, ed. Volkan Aytar and Jan Rath (New York: Routledge, 2012), 16–33.

69. Chin, interview, July 15, 2009.

70. Washington, interview.

71. Chin, interview, July 15, 2009. Poon, who immigrated from Hong Kong in the 1970s, rose to fame through his pioneering Asian fusion cuisine and his dynamic, quirky personality. Despite his national reputation, Poon still locates his operations in Chinatown at the site of his former restaurant at 1010 Cherry Street and offers cooking classes and tours of the area. Poon's website invites visitors to "join us for an insider's tour of this vibrant community and learn about the history, culture and food of Philadelphia's Chinatown. Your tour will include a walking tour of Philadelphia's Chinatown community including stops at a fortune cookie factory, a Chinese herbal medicine shop, a Chinese

place of worship, a Chinese bakery, an Asian grocery store, a fish market and more. Every tour ends with a full lunch or dinner." See "Wok'N Walk Tour of Chinatown," Chef Joseph Poon, http://www.josephpoon.com/wokn-walk-tour-of-chinatown (accessed August 20, 2012).

72. Dennis R. Judd and Susan S. Fainstein, *The Tourist City* (New Haven, CT: Yale University Press, 1999), 14.

73. Barbara Kirschenblatt-Gimblett, *Destination Culture: Tourism, Museums and Heritage* (Berkeley: University of California Press, 1998): "Key to heritage productions is their virtuality whether in the presence of the absence of actualities," 149, 166. On commodified ethnicity, see Marilyn Halter, *Shopping for Identity: The Marketing of Ethnicity* (New York: Schocken Books, 2000); and Arlene M. Dávila, *Latinos, Inc.: The Marketing and Making of a People* (Berkeley: University of California Press, 2001).

74. On the consumer-oriented sensual language used to promote the "Latino Soul, Latino Flavor" tour, see Wherry, *The Philadelphia Barrio*. On "staged authenticity," see Jan Lin, *The Power of Urban Ethnic Places: Cultural Heritage and Community Life* (New York: Routledge, 2011), 257. As Wherry points out, unscripted performances of authenticity are important for scripted performances/narratives to stand; see Wherry, *The Philadelphia Barrio*, 6–7.

75. Wherry, *The Philadelphia Barrio*, 36–37.

76. Time plays an important role in the construction of cultural Otherness. Anthropology, for example, historically represented other cultures of study through a temporal lens of "allochronism," resulting in a "denial of coevalness"; see Johannes Fabian, *Time and the Other: How Anthropology Makes Its Object* (New York: Columbia University Press, 2002). This pattern of freezing time and its effects on the public representation of Chinatown of culture has been noted by Chiou-Ling Yeh in her account of San Francisco's Chinese New Year celebrations, *Making an American Festival: Chinese New Year in San Francisco's Chinatown* (Berkeley: University of California Press, 2008), 156–167.

77. The phrase is Kirschenblatt-Gimblett's. According to her, heritage is the "transvaluation of the obsolete, the mistaken, the outmoded, the dead and the defunct" and created primarily through a "process of exhibition"; see Kirschenblatt-Gimblett, *Destination Culture*, 149. Dávila and Wherry also point out, in the context of Latino *barrio* tourism, that heritage tourism always presupposes the creation of difference.

78. On the "risk of essence," see Diana Fuss, *Essentially Speaking: Feminism, Nature, and Difference* (London: Routledge, 1989), xi–xii, 18–21. Fuss contrasts essentialism—understood as "a belief in the real, true essence of things, the invariable and fixed properties which define the 'whatness' of a given entity"—with a "complex system of cultural, social, psychical, and historical differences," while suggesting the potential benefits of the "risk of essence." Strategic essentialism is a term originally coined by Gayatri Chakravorty Spivak and widely used in postcolonial and feminist thought. It refers to the ways in which subaltern groups or marginalized groups coalesce around a sense of essence to advance larger politically or socially empowering goals and intervene in established representations, see Spivak, "Subaltern Studies: Deconstructing Historiography," in *In Other Worlds: Essays in Cultural Politics* (New York: Metheun, 1987), 205–207. Dávila has described a similar tension in the tourism efforts in El Barrio in East Harlem, where attempts to promote El Barrio as a Latino cultural area are an important response to the ongoing gentrification and de-ethnicization of the area. In this case, the risk of essence constitutes cultural assertion rather than simply marketable ethnicity.

79. Mary Yee, interview by the author, July 12, 2010.

80. Ibid.

81. Ibid. Yee's comments echo Lin's conclusions about the potential for cultural tourism, after Robert Putnam, to act as bridging activities that build social capital between insiders and nonethnics; see Lin, *The Power of Urban Ethnic Places*, 55.

82. Eng, interview.

83. Wei, interview.

84. Ibid.

85. Ibid.

86. Ibid.

87. AAU website, http://aaunited.org/culture/maf (accessed September 26, 2012).

88. Philadelphia Folklore Project, "Under Autumn Moon: Reclaiming Time and Space in Chinatown," http://www.folkloreproject.org/programs/exhibits/maf/index.php (accessed September 26, 2012).

89. Philadelphia Folklore Project, "Under Autumn Moon."

90. Wei, interview.

91. Ibid.

92. Isa, interview.

93. Helen Gym, interview by the author, June 27, 2012.

94. Yee, interview.

95. Ibid.

Epilogue

1. AALDEF, "Chinatown Then and Now: Gentrification in Boston, New York, and Philadelphia" (Philadelphia: AALDEF, 2013), 2–4.

2. Ibid., 35.

3. Ibid., 34.

4. U.S. Census Bureau; 2010 Census of Population and Housing. Prepared by Social Explorer (accessed June 26, 2014).

5. "The 'Amigos' in Chinese Businesses," *Metro Chinese Weekly*, May 2, 2014.

6. Lena Sze, "Opportunity, Conflict, and Communities in Transition: Historical and Contemporary Chinese Immigration to Philadelphia," in *Global Philadelphia: Immigrant Communities Old and New*, ed. Ayumi Takenaka and Mary Johnson Osirim (Philadelphia: Temple University Press, 2010), 110. China Trade Center, http://www.ctcp.org/Asia_America_Group/Asia_America_Group2.htm (accessed June 2, 2014).

7. Sarah Yeung, personal communication with author, 2014.

8. Press coverage has focused on the "speakeasy" Hop Sing Laundromat: "Behind the Scenes with Chinatown's Long-Anticipated Hop Sing Laundromat," *Philadelphia Weekly*, June 20, 2012. On the recent proliferation of bubble tea shops in Chinatown, see Jeff Gammage, "Battle Heats Up among Chinatown Bubble Tea Shops," *Philadelphia Inquirer*, September 4, 2013.

9. Craig LaBan, "The New Chinatown, Delectably Diverse," *Philadelphia Inquirer*, January 13, 2014.

10. Eastern Tower has been widely reported in the local press; see Inga Saffron, "Changing Skyline: Planned Tower May Be a Game-Changer for Philadelphia's Chinatown," *Philadelphia Inquirer*, October 13, 2012; "How New Eastern Tower Community Center Can Be a Modern Symbol of Immigration in Philly," Flying Kite, July 17, 2012, http://www.flyingkitemedia.com/devnews/easterntowerchinatown0717.aspx (accessed March 21, 2013); and "Chinatown to Grow Up," *Philadelphia Business Journal*, November 11, 2011.

11. John Chin, interview by the author, July 15, 2009.

12. Saffron, "Changing Skyline."

13. Chin, interview.

14. Ibid.

15. Andrew Toy, interview by the author, June 26, 2012.

16. Ibid. Housing units will initially be "all rental" for seven years (a condition of PCDC's financing), at which point units may be offered for purchase as condominiums.

17. Ibid.

18. The New Markets Tax Credit (NMTC) Program was established by Congress in 2000 to spur new or increased investments into operating businesses and real-estate projects located in low-income communities. The NMTC Program attracts investment capital to low-income communities by permitting individual and corporate investors to receive a tax credit against their federal income tax returns in exchange for making equity investments in specialized financial institutions called Community Development Entities (CDEs). The credit totals 39 percent of the original investment amount and is claimed over a period of seven years (5 percent for each of the first three years, and 6 percent for each of the remaining four years). The investment in the CDE cannot be redeemed before the end of the seven-year period. See Community Development Financial Institutions Fund, http://cdfifund.gov/what_we_do/programs_id.asp?programID=5 (accessed March 23, 2013).

19. Toy, interview.

20. Julie Shaw, "Foreign Investors Sought for Planned Chinatown North Tower," *Philadelphia Inquirer*, February 21, 2014; and Jennifer Lin, "Towering Ambitions for Chinatown," *Philadelphia Inquirer*, February 6, 2012. EB5 is an immigration provision that makes permanent residency available to individuals who invest $500,000 and create at least ten jobs.

21. PCDC housing, with the exception of On Lok House and Dynasty Court, has focused on for-purchase units sold at market rate, which are largely out of reach of most Chinatown residents.

22. The 1990 Census data indicated that 61.5 percent of Asian households in Chinatown were living below the poverty line, while households of all races in Chinatown and Philadelphia were at 49.0 percent and 20.3 percent below-poverty rates, respectively. Christina Shat, "Health Needs Assessment Executive Summary," PCDC, http://chinatown-pcdc.org/our-community/health-needs-assessment (accessed November 21, 2012). At the time of this study, 21 percent of Asian residents were unemployed in Chinatown, while 58 percent were underemployed.

23. "Has the Italian Market Outgrown Its Name?" *Philadelphia Inquirer*, April 25, 2013; Helen Ubinas, "Time to Rename the Italian Market," *Philadelphia Daily News*, April 3, 2013; Melissa Mandell, "Ninth Street Market," philaplace, http://www.philaplace.org/story/126 (accessed July 2, 2014); Jonathan B. Justice, "Moving On: The East Passyunk Avenue Business Improvement District," *Drexel Law Review* 3, no. 1 (2010): 226.

24. Melody Wong, interview by the author, July 22, 2010.

25. Debbie Wei, personal communication, June 18, 2014.

Index

Kathryn E. Wilson is Associate Professor of History at Georgia State University.

www.ingramcontent.com/pod-product-compliance
Lightning Source LLC
Chambersburg PA
CBHW020342270326
41926CB00007B/285